Edited by

# Peter Knobler

and

# Greg Mitchell

---

CONTRIBUTORS INCLUDE:

P. J. O'Rourke, Richard Price, William Burroughs,

John Lennon, Tim O'Brien, Gilda Radner,

Joseph Heller, Martin Mull, Harry Shearer,

Abbie Hoffman, Tony Kornheiser, Susan Braudy,

Robert Ward, Mark Jacobson, David Black,

Paul Krassner, Al Kooper, Jon Carroll

A FIRESIDE BOOK
Published by Simon & Schuster
New York   London   Toronto   Sydney   Tokyo   Singapore

# VERY SEVENTIES

*A Cultural History of the 1970s,*

*from the Pages of*

## CRAWDADDY

FIRESIDE
Rockefeller Center
1230 Avenue of the Americas
New York, New York 10020

FIRESIDE and colophon are registered trademarks
of Simon & Schuster Inc.

Designed by Hyun Joo Kim

Manufactured in the United States of America

1 3 5 7 9 10 8 6 4 2

Library of Congress Cataloging-in-Publication Data
Very seventies: a cultural history of the 1970s from the pages of Crawdaddy/
edited by Peter Knobler and Greg Mitchell; contributors include P. J.
O'Rourke . . . [et al.].
p.   cm.
"A Fireside book."
1. Popular culture—United States.   2. United States—Social life and customs—
1971–   3. Arts, America.   4. Arts, Modern—20th century—United States.
I. Knobler, Peter.   II. Mitchell, Greg.   III. O'Rourke, P. J.   IV. Crawdaddy.
E169.04.V48   1995                                                        94-44455
973.924—dc20                                                                  CIP

ISBN 0-02-022005-7

FOR DANIEL, ANDY, AND JENNIFER

*from their Crawdaddies.*

# Permissions

# Contents

# Introduction

*by Peter Knobler and Greg Mitchell*

Watergate. Disco. Patty Hearst. The Sex Pistols. "Love to Love You Baby." Marilyn Chambers. Anita Bryant. *Apocalypse Now.* Jonestown. Three Mile Island. Monty Python. Archie Bunker. Andy Kaufman. *Star Wars.* Ziggy Stardust. est. Quaaludes. Carlos Castaneda. Reverend Moon. Led Zeppelin. *Dirty Harry.* Gary Gilmore. Attica. *Animal House.* The Fonz. The Ramones. Mary Hartman. Mary Hartman.

What a strange decade. Between the apocalyptic cataclysms of the '60s and the retrenched reaction of the '80s, the '70s stand as the time that time forgot. What happened? What was important? Was anything actually accomplished besides the booming transition from yippie to yuppie? Or with everyone looking out for number one, was it a decade to be judged by accumulation?

Some decades can be summarized in a phrase, an outlook, an attitude. Tom Wolfe called it the "Me Decade," but the '70s were too scattered to pin down. It has become fashionable to ridicule the entire era as a flighty, frivolous retreat, lacking both style and substance. When many people hear "the '70s" they think of leisure suits, platform shoes, "Disco Inferno," Lance Loud, *Shaft,* "You're Having My Baby," jiggle TV shows, Olivia Newton-John, *Starsky and Hutch,* shirt collars out to your shoulders, mile-wide Afros and Superfly hats, glitter rock, Earth Shoes, *Love, American Style,* Barry Manilow. You know: fluff. And they're right.

But there was more to it than that.

There was great music by '60s holdovers and new artists alike; groundbreaking movies from brilliant young directors; sex that wouldn't kill you; humor-with-bite from a fresh generation of comics; and political movements that made a difference. Any decade that produces Robin Williams, *Taxi Driver,* Bob Marley, Jodie Foster, *Born to Run,* Richard Pryor, *Chinatown,* and Bonnie Raitt, while bringing the Vietnam war to a close and running Richard Nixon out of office, can't be half bad.

That's easy for us to say. We had the best jobs in the world. As editors of *Crawdaddy* from 1971 to 1979 we got to participate in, or at least comment on, everything good and bad that was "going down." We hadn't even reached our mid-twenties when we started. Running a national magazine at that tender age—this itself was very '70s.

The decade started late. The '70s couldn't begin until the '60s had been killed off, and that didn't happen for a while. The Beatles broke up, and Janis Joplin and Jimi Hendrix self-destructed—all in 1970. (Jim Morrison and Duane Allman died a few months later.) When government soldiers shot student protesters at Kent State in May 1970 and all that stuck was a rock and roll song, the idealistic force that defined the '60s had pretty well been defeated. Political activism couldn't keep pace with the government's undercover maneuvers to dissolve it.

The '70s were filled with fits and starts. One-hit wonders abounded. (Peter Frampton came alive, but not for long.) Who were the presidents? A crook and a pair of short-termers. Nixon fell apart in such spectacular fashion that he had to be restrained from taking the presidency down with him. Gerald Ford followed, the dimmest bulb in the White House chandelier. His most notable act was to pardon Nixon of all crimes, known and unknown. His most lasting legacy: Chevy Chase.

Jimmy Carter, campaigning as a populist, barely outran Ford and for a while it seemed that anything might happen. The president quoted Dylan in his speeches. Young Carter advisers were close to the Allman Brothers and there were rumors of pot use in the White House. (At the time this was considered a cultural leap.) Carter had confessed that he "committed adultery in my heart many times." His brother drank to excess. His sister, a faith healer, introduced *Hustler* editor Larry Flynt to Jesus. We're talking '70s here!

Ultimately, however, when the times didn't change, the scurrying for cover could be heard all down the line. When people peeked out again there was a new set of rules: Get What You Can.

The country needed a leader who could perform, and it wasn't until 1980 that a performer finally gained the White House. When Ronald Reagan took hold of the country it was Bob Hope and Frank Sinatra time again. There was no contest between a reigning atmosphere and the coldly conservative one he carried into office; there *was* no reigning atmosphere, only every "me" in the decade looking to hold on to what they'd got and get some more.

The dominant figures in America of the 1970s, however, were not its political leaders but its cultural ones. These people *did* things. They expressed themselves expansively in forms that were themselves expanding, such as computers and video. And they were young. The "Youth Culture" of the '60s grew into the mainstream culture of the '70s as rock and roll took over FM radio, young Turks took over the movies, and cable television started taking over the world.

There was nothing new about Twentysomethings becoming celebrities. The difference was that now filmmakers like George Lucas and Steven Spielberg, and record company execs like David Geffen, wielded *power*. And in the post-Watergate era, young people who had once marched in the streets got elected to high office (Bill Clinton won his first race for governor in 1978) or founded public interest groups. Sports stars became humanized and spoke out on national issues. The national sense of humor tilted as Steve Martin and *Saturday Night Live* went wild and crazy.

Think the '70s were complete nonsense and that everyone was dazed and confused? Consider the following:

The Pentagon Papers. *Exile on Main Street.* The Thrilla in Manila. *What's Going On.* Joni Mitchell. *The Godfather.* Al Green. *Nashville.* Catfish Hunter. *The Harder They Come.* The women's movement. Gay Liberation. The American Indian movement. The antinuclear movement. *Blood on the Tracks.* Lily Tomlin. Steely Dan. Stevie Wonder. *Last Tango in Paris.* Bill Walton. *I, Claudius.* Willie Nelson. Emmylou Harris. *Dog Soldiers. Roe v. Wade. Annie Hall.* Talking Heads. *Gravity's Rainbow.* Frank Serpico. Karen Silkwood. "What's So Funny About Peace, Love and Understanding?" Sadat and Begin. *Rust Never Sleeps.*

One might ask: But where did all that lead? We got Reagan and Bush, and today we still have to deal with a lot of mediocre music, insipid movies, and 57 Channels With Nothing On. But there were more than a few artistic masterpieces and political victories along the way, and the *Crawdaddy* generation is calling its own tune now, from late-night TV right into the White House. And Van Morrison is *still* "The Man."


CRAWDADDY WAS THERE FOR IT ALL, BETWEEN WOODSTOCK AND MTV, from the decline of Elvis Presley to the birth of Elvis Costello.

*Very Seventies* derives its material from the pages of *Crawdaddy,* the first magazine of, by, and for the baby boom generation. *Crawdaddy* was the first magazine to take rock and roll seriously. By its nature, it was a running commentary on the times.

*Crawdaddy* began in February 1966 at Swarthmore College as a ten-page mimeographed collection of record reviews written and stapled together by Paul Williams. He named it after London's Crawdaddy Club, where the Yardbirds and the Rolling Stones got their start. The first issue featured a review of the new Simon & Garfunkel album, *The Sounds of Silence.*

At *Crawdaddy!*—Williams insisted on the exclamation point—rock and roll was art, not commerce. The timing was right; with *Revolver,* "Good Vibrations," and *Highway 61 Revisited* rock and roll had reached a turning point.

At first the magazine had no competitors. The only other publications that wrote about rock were teen rags, song sheets, and the trades. Mainstream publications like *Time, Newsweek,* and *Esquire* rarely covered rock and roll. If young people didn't take it seriously, why should they?

Several of Williams's articles, and reviews by other *Crawdaddy!* pioneers, became classics. Williams moved to Manhattan, but by 1969 *Crawdaddy!* was in financial trouble. *Rolling Stone* and other youth-culture magazines (often staffed by former *Crawdaddy!* contributors) had arrived on the scene. Williams departed, feeling he had lost his "sense of wonder" about rock and roll.

*Crawdaddy* went through several owners, editors, and formats, and lost its exclamation point. Then we arrived, in 1971, determined to revitalize the magazine and reestablish its enthusiasm.

We were no strangers to this field, nor to each other. P.K. had freelanced for the original *Crawdaddy!* and G.M. had written for *Rolling Stone.* We had met, appropriately enough, in 1970, the very beginning of the decade, as editors of *Zygote* magazine in New York City. (You had to be there.) We weren't particularly close—Protestant from Niagara Falls meets Greenwich Village Jew—until we discovered that we were both San Francisco Giants fans and worshiped Willie Mays. Then we started tossing old Dylan lines at each other like a call-and-response chorus ("Geeeez I can't find my kneeees." "Ohhhh, I didn't knowwww that!"). Turns out we had been at some of the same political demonstrations, too.

With P.K. as editor and G.M. as senior editor, along with an able corps of editors, writers, and art directors, we transformed *Crawdaddy* from a hippie-style, ineptly distributed, biweekly tabloid to a professional, national, monthly magazine. We worked in the same room on lower Fifth Avenue, nearly shoulder-to-shoulder, sharing a turntable and literally thousands of record albums, for the rest of the '70s. What's more, we formed a solid left side of the *Crawdaddy* infield (P.K. at shortstop, G.M. at third) in Central Park softball leagues for the entire decade.

Gradually we repositioned *Crawdaddy* as a general-interest, generational magazine, with rock and roll still at its core. This was the generation that was going to stop the war, change the world, and do it all to a soundtrack of rock and roll. We figured we'd pick the cuts.

It was a great time to be professionally young. Baby boomers were slowly becoming consumers, and the magazines they trusted were considered tastemakers by both readers and the entertainment industry. On a good day at *Crawdaddy* you could spend the morning writing an editorial calling for Nixon's head, interview Jane Fonda that afternoon, go to an evening screening of the new Altman film, and then catch a double bill of the Wailers and Bruce Springsteen at Max's Kansas City (this actually happened). It was a tough life, but somehow we survived.

WHAT WAS THE *CRAWDADDY* PHILOSOPHY? WHAT MADE IT DIFFERENT? It's hard to answer this without sounding pompous; we'd rather have you read this book and decide yourself. But here goes.

For one thing, we felt *Crawdaddy* had the hippest taste in rock and roll, perhaps because we generally ignored commercial imperatives (at our peril). We wrote the first article ever about Bruce Springsteen in 1973—and then gave it ten pages in the magazine despite the fact that no one had ever heard of him. Two thousand words on an unknown poet-rocker named Patti Smith? Sure. Put Dr. John on the cover? No problem.

*Crawdaddy*'s political viewpoint was patently radical at a time when most "alternative" magazines were pulling their punches or simply disappearing. We further bucked the trends by sticking with an in-depth approach to reporting, just as *People* was bringing sound-bite journalism to the page. Should we spend thirteen thousand words exploring the mysterious death of cult figure Gram Parsons, and fifteen thousand words investigating the Miss USA pageant? "Go wild," we'd say. (We said it all the time.)

None of this made commercial sense. It didn't help sell ads or copies. We were exquisitely hip, bottom-line foolish. So be it.

But why did we do it? First and foremost, *Crawdaddy* appreciated passion. Our heroes, the artists and athletes and political hell-raisers we supported, all cared deeply about what they were doing, and made others feel the same way. No going through the motions; if you wanted *Crawdaddy*'s attention you had to put out. That's what first attracted us to Springsteen and Scorsese.

Also, if there was one lesson to be learned from the '60s it was that authority in all forms was not to be trusted. U.S. senators, film directors, lead singers—none were to be taken at face value. When we spoke with them we wanted the goods, whether it was Tom Waits or Tom Hayden. We generally assumed the worst about those in positions of power, and they rarely failed to meet expectations. We didn't need a congressional investigation to *know* that Nixon and Kissinger had brought down Allende in Chile.

Politically, we did not like what we saw of the 1970s so *Crawdaddy* attempted to keep the ideals of the '60s alive as long as possible. (Which may be one reason the FBI bugged the home of our chief political writers.) When push came to shove, we endorsed McGovern for president in '72 and Carter in '76, but not before reminding our readers that the most important political work had to be done outside the corridors of power.

Finally, we had a skewed sense of humor. It showed up throughout the magazine, from regular columns by William Burroughs, Paul Krassner, and the Firesign Theater to oddball photo captions. *Crawdaddy* staffers had a true appreciation for the ironic twist, the diseased bon mot. This volume presents some of our more offbeat journalistic experiments: putting William Burroughs together with Jimmy Page, Martin Mull with Woody Allen, Richard Price with Ronnie Spector, Al Kooper with Steve Martin, Kilgore Trout with Kurt Vonnegut Jr., Harry Shearer with Charo.

Every month G. M. compiled several pages of bizarre, true-life news items in The Crawdoodah Gazette, perhaps the most popular section of the magazine. We enlisted Abbie Hoffman—the country's best-known fugitive—as our Travel Editor, which tells you something of what *Crawdaddy* was about. Whatever else he may have been, Abbie was an idealist, a fine writer, and a very funny guy—and he never asked us to pay his travel expenses.

Number two in its field, and working with a limited budget, *Crawdaddy* not only had to try harder, it had to take chances. Sometimes we fell on our face, but often our editors discovered and touted promising newcomers. Call it good taste, call it recklessness, *Crawdaddy* often went against the commercial tide. We'd give an unknown Bonnie Raitt far more space than a superstar like Linda Ronstadt. We ran one of P. J. O'Rourke's earliest magazine pieces (before he turned "political"). When our man, David Black, went to Chappaquiddick he tried to duplicate Ted Kennedy's midnight swim—and nearly got swept out to sea.

We made our share of mistakes, of course. Why *did* we put J. D. Salinger on the cover? We couldn't find him either.

One of *Crawdaddy*'s more prescient decisions was to investigate Vice President Ford's background weeks before Nixon was forced to resign. Appalled by what we found, we put a photo of Ford on the cover, dressed in a parka and ski cap, with the half-serious cover line: "IMPEACH GERALD FORD! This Man Deserves To Be President? On a Cold Day in August." This issue was on the newsstand the day Ford (suddenly) took office—August 9, 1974.

As the decade went on, our audience began to change. People were dropping *in,* and the counterculture was entering the mainstream. We had to find a way to change without compromising everything. We tried to mix progressive politics with cutting-edge cultural coverage, but *Crawdaddy* might have survived longer if we had put Elton John on the cover even *once* (clearly a defensible move) or accepted one of the U.S. Army recruiting ads that were always being dangled in front of us. Younger readers were into Foghat and Black Sabbath. No way we could deal with that. *Crawdaddy* never saw 1980.

*VERY SEVENTIES* GATHERS SOME OF *CRAWDADDY*'S BEST ARTICLES AND best writers. We were all young then, and many of the people who wrote for *Crawdaddy* have reached notable heights. Several stories were selected primarily for what they reveal about a celebrity-in-the-making or the times themselves.

The articles have been placed under six broad subject headings, and organized chronologically within each chapter. You can get a certain sense of the decade by reading the pieces in order. For instance, under Film and TV, we start with the emergence of Jack Nicholson and end with the arrival of John Belushi; Woody Allen, George Lucas, and Clint Eastwood are among those who come in between. You can scan *Very Seventies* piece by piece to take a quick dip in the decade or read it straight through for a full immersion.

Summing up the '70s at the end of the decade, *New West* magazine said, "It was the worst of times, it was the worst of times." *Time* was certain that no one would ever "look back on the 1970s as the good old days." They got it wrong. There was a lot of hot stuff going on and *Crawdaddy,* cutting against the grain, had a very Seventies take on it. Read on and find out. As an article in *The New York Times* recently put it: "The 1970s are back in style."

You don't think so? Well, excuuuse me!

PART II

*'60s into '70s*

# Sly Stoned

*by Peter Knobler*

*June 1971*

*Sly Stone was not only a funk pioneer during the late '60s but also a flaming trailblazer in terms of personal disintegration. Apparently the recent deaths of Janis Joplin and Jimi Hendrix had little effect on him. This article, for its time, offered an unusually frank depiction of a growing phenomenon. Those who followed in Sly's footsteps often made drug abuse a career choice. Sadly, he hasn't made exceptional music since.*

Sly's hotel room was locked and double-locked. The door opened but the chain stayed on when my tentative yet steady knock was answered.

"Who's there?" The question was a growl between two unrevealing walls. I answered, was acknowledged and permitted inside.

The room was stuffy and underlit. As in any major hotel it had the feeling of permanent transience—large empty spaces between furniture and chairs, lots of walking room. It was anything but comfortable.

Six heavies stopped their conversation.

"What's happening?" Sly spoke from a dark grey corner, huddled all arms and legs beside an unlit table lamp. He was a vision in red this evening, red wool knit cap covering a lot of hair and almost obscuring a bloodshot eye. He was incredibly stoned.

"Nothing much," I answered. "How're you doing?"

"Fine." He stared as if daring me to contradict him. "Just fine."

And having said that crossed his arms and stared at me some more. The implication was I didn't believe him. The six large men in the room were immaculately silent.

"Ask me some questions." Sly broke the silence again by daring. The tone was cold, not so much unwilling to talk as unwilling not to be listened to, a grudge match between Sly and whoever he chose to believe you were.


AT ONE TIME SLY COULD MOVE MOUNTAINS. HIS MUSIC CAPTURED ecstasy and gave it willingly to everyone willing to take it. It demanded ACTION, movement, LIFE. "You don't have to die before you live." It had to have begun spontaneously; it seems impossible to calculate such incredible joy.

"I dig people," Sly said from his dark corner. "You can quote me on that. I dig the shit out of people." He smiled a smile that was just a little too broad—his "charming" smile—then collapsed again into a red leather jumble of tassels and fringe. There was a silence.

Dave Kapralik, Sly's manager at the time, pranced into the room and all eyes trained on him for the moment. He asked Sly a few details, like a teacher drumming tables into a third-grader, and Sly mumbled monosyllables trying to ignore him. None of the heavies—one by each of the doors and in each corner but Sly's—said a word. Kapralik gave up and split. I started to ask a question but Sly interrupted.

"I want to be natural, man." He spoke in a drugged slur, now sprawled long–legged half off the couch. He paused for a moment. "Do you want me to be natural? Because I want to be natural." It was again almost a dare—as if he knew I didn't want what he had to give, knew it so well he'd decided not to give it even if I wanted it. That kind of foggy belligerence.

"Sly, man, I want you to be natural." I answered his rhetorical question because he expected it to be answered.

He paused again—"Oh yeah?"—not believing a word of it. "Because I can be as straight as shit, man. I can get myself together . . ." he sat up, pulled his collar cleanly around his neck—tidied up . . . "and be as straight as you could ever want me to be." He put on a mock English accent for the occasion. "But . . ." he slid back down into his corner, "I'd rather be natural." He watched me. "You don't *mind*, do you?"

I tried to mumble something pleasant, but one of the men at the door started to leave and Sly caught him.

"Don't leave me, man." The door was already unlocked and

open—the chain had grated in the lock and turned Sly's head around as fast as his dulled reflexes would allow.

"I'm just going out for a little walk. I'll be right back." The man was big, and black, and spoke with a trace of a smile on his large face.

Sly squinted as the light hit him, then fell back into a sprawl as the man closed the door and walked on down the hall. He looked around, remembered I was there, looked down and saw his red vest. "You wanna see my vest, man?" It was hardly a question.

"Sure."

He began to stand up, didn't make it, tried again and managed to rise halfway before he got hung up. For just a moment he was suspended in an angular squat between standing and sitting. Then he righted himself and smiled a reorienting smile.

"A chick gave me this," he said as he pulled the weighty vest over his shoulders. It hung on him in layers, tassels and fringe and beads and all. "A chick came by and gave me this at three o'clock in the morning." He smiled his first real smile.

"Three o'clock?" I smiled back.

"Three o'clock," he said. "Can you dig it?" We both laughed. He stopped abruptly, looked at me intently and sat back down, without a word. He kept staring, as if I'd tricked him or he had blown something and wanted to make sure he wouldn't get burned.

Another heavy went to the door.

"Don't leave me, man." Sly was adamant this time and the bigger man backed down. He walked heavily past Sly and sat back down in a chair.

"I'm sorry, man." Sly waited a moment before talking, sensing hostility in a silence that he felt he had to break. "But just don't go away like that."

AT NEW YORK'S MADISON SQUARE GARDEN A YEAR OR SO AGO SLY still had his magic. The evening had dragged on with Fleetwood Mac and Grand Funk offering volume if little substance to the full house. Sly came on late, but not too late, and the wait was worth it. It took him all of two songs to have the crowd on its feet. Nobody sits through a Sly concert—it's almost a physical impossibility.

The crowd rushed the stage. People poured down from the rafters like a mudslide, drawn to Sly *and to each other*. There was dancing continuously. The ushers, more used to older, belligerent hockey fans, couldn't cope with the movement of the Possessed.

Sly was in great form, singing brilliantly, playing keyboards with the only authority recognized all night. "Stand!" he sang. "In the end you'll still be you. One that's done all the things he sets out to do."

"Stand!" It was an invitation to move and let go and be possessed by whatever possesses you. And do it with someone. Sly's music invited you to grab a friend.


"LET'S GET OUT OF HERE." SLY ROSE QUICKLY. OR TRIED TO. WHEN HE did get up he fumbled with the door. "I'm going to my room. C'mon." A henchman solved the lock and Sly marched into the corridor. I followed, and was followed at a slight distance by a short, compact guy called "Buddha."

The corridor went on forever. Sly jingled as he walked, tassels and beads sounding like loose change. He was obviously feeling the rush after sitting for so long, jogging all elbows and knees down the hall, a stone soul leprechaun. He jumped and clicked his heels together, landing with a clump and running to do it again. It was less joyous release than bravado, or maybe just a physical impulse, but he kept on running. He passed an open door revealing about twenty conservatively suited, crew-cut men obviously doing a convention celebration.

He got winded a few doors down, stopped, and was standing hands on hips like a recuperating miler when he thought he heard a sound. He stopped dead in his tracks. I watched astounded as Sly began what seemed almost a frightened search. Like a cat chasing his tail, Sly, still out of breath, turned one way and then the other to find whatever he thought was after him. It was only a moment, but Sly's fear slowed him. He walked the rest of the way to his room. I followed, and the Buddha followed me.

At his door, Sly pounded a special Sly beat—some sort of signal, no doubt. A code. The drums. Nobody answered. He tried again. As he waited for response, two busboys fiddled with a serving cart further down the hall. His chin rose and he stormed after them. It took him almost five steps to realize what he was doing, and he turned back to the door. But the fear—it was more than simple caution; his eyes were wider now and alerted by necessity—the fear was just below the surface. Who did he think was after him? Why the guards? Why all the precautions?

A woman finally opened the door. Bleary-eyed and obviously roused from bed, she hugged Sly as he went in. After a moment we were let in too.

The TV was on, flipping vertically, the color all askew. An electric organ stood obtrusively in the center of the room, plugged into the wall and poised for action. A small amp was at its side. Buddha took a chair by the corner and I sat on the couch. Sly paced restlessly.

"Hey," he said, "I'll be right back," and disappeared into the bedroom of the two-room suite. He came back immediately. "I really will. I'll be back in a few minutes. I mean it."

He was in the other room five minutes when someone knocked at the front door. I opened it and was faced with a monster. In every espionage flick there's a Heavy. Broad-shouldered in a well-tailored suit, a slight bulge under the left breast pocket, the guy at the door was a bodyguard incarnate. His features were symmetrical, distinct, each obedient to the whole. There was the scent of defense to him, so he wasn't a cop. Buddha saw him and motioned to the door Sly had entered.

A minute later there was the clatter of glass as a couple of bottles hit the bathroom tile floor.

Sly came back in twenty minutes. The television was still flipping and he watched it for a moment. "That's weird," he noticed, but didn't try to fix it.

"Okay, man, what's happening? What's going on?" He cocked his head slightly to the left as he looked down to where I was sitting. I was about to begin when the symmetrical man came back and began whispering to Buddha.

"Hey, man. We're doing something here." He glared at the intruder, then turned back to me. "Yeah, what were you saying?"

I began again, and again Sly turned to the guard, this time with anger in his voice. "Hey, man, I told you to be quiet. I got this thing going on."

We began to talk, casually. Planned or obviously probing questions would be deadly. "How come these guys are always around?" I motioned toward the guard and Buddha.

"Well, man, they don't have to be around." It was a hedge. He looked at them and they watched him in return. "They're my friends, my buddies. Isn't that right, Sam?" The muscleman nodded, his jacket off now and shoulder holster showing. "They're working with me.

"I am like I am, you know? Well, they are like they are. The Buddha has to be the Buddha, you know, because he *is* the Buddha." The reference was to the short man's actual personality, not a cosmic parallel. Sly creates his own references, and the only way to really communicate with him is to know from in front what he means. If he senses you know what he means the first time he'll try some more. He speaks in a system only he can fully understand, but allows glimpses if you're willing or able to use his symbols.

"And Sam is Sam." He looked over to the man. "He's gotta be Sam, because that's who he is. He's Sam . . . My friend, right, Sam?" He was making up, in his own way.

"Right, Sly."

"No, really." Sly sensed the dishonesty and, still through his own fog, wanted it not to be there. "Right?"

"Right, Sly." Sam raised his voice protesting—not wanting to be disbelieved, or lose his job. "Right!"

"So you see, everybody is what he has to be, because that's what he is. Now I want to do what I do, and let people get behind it and do what they want to do."

This concern with his fellow man didn't square too well with his history of gargantuan lateness and occasional no-shows. In Chicago last summer, for instance, people were shot and killed by police when a crowd gathered for a Sly concert got impatient after a few hours' wait.

"I was there," Sly protested. "I was there on time, but by the time I got there the riot was already going on. I wanted to go on but the cops wouldn't let us in. The equipment was there, and I was gonna play. Honestly, that's what happened."

Sly seemed to believe it. "I feel bad about what happened to those kids. What I'm gonna do," he said straight-faced, "is get some of those kids and some Chicago police and put them together into a choir and take them on the Johnny Carson show."

I thought that was the farthest-out idea I'd ever heard, and we laughed together for the first time.

For other latenesses, though, he didn't have any excuse. "You want to know why I'm late sometimes? I oversleep. That's all, I just oversleep and nobody can wake me up. I mean, when I wake up I'm . . ." he growled and looked startled-mean. "I'm liable to do anything. But that's over with. Now I've got me some guys who can wake me up."

SLY DOESN'T HAVE CONTROL ANYMORE. NOT RIGHT NOW, ANYWAY. IT'S more than a sound sleep he falls into, it's drugged, and even when he's awake it must be hard directing him toward the stage. On those days, when he's wrecked and out of control and *has to play,* there must be a personal horror he faces that can only be intimated by the agony of late arrivals and short sets.

Sly knows how good he can be, how good he was. He also knows—if he prefers not to concentrate on it it's understandable—

the extent to which he's fallen. Not showing up is not thinking about it. Oversleeping—for whatever reason, no reason to be cute about it—is simply the easiest solution to the problem of living in fear. Short gigs were probably just bad gigs cut off out of psychic horror.

Sly says, "I'm me, man. I'm Sly." He is, only when he can be.

# Lennon Imagines

*by John Lennon*
*December 1971*

*John and Yoko moved to New York about the time* Crawdaddy *was revived in the early '70s, and it didn't take long to strike up a special relationship with Lennon.* Crawdaddy *conducted a (then rare) joint interview with John and Yoko in 1971, published some of Lennon's political song lyrics before they appeared on albums, and ran this self-review of* Imagine. *Paul McCartney had just ripped him on* Ram, *and Lennon responded with "How Do You Sleep?," which he describes here as "an angry letter." Then he congratulates Paul on becoming a father (again).*

### 1. Imagine
Is a song conceived in my head without melody. The 1st verse came to me very quickly in the form of a childlike street-chant *da da da da dadee dee da dee da ee a eeeh.* The piano intro I've had hanging around in my head for a few years—the chords and melody followed naturally from this. The middle eight was "conceived" to finish off the song. I think it works as a song. Of course, there is always room for improvement—otherwise I wouldn't make any more. The 3rd verse came to me in an 8-seater plane. It's a song for children.

### 2. Crippled Inside
Arrived in bed with nary a thought to whether it was "done before," "witty," or such like bullshit. "One thing you can't hide is when you're

crippled inside" came complete with melody. The rest I just filled in. The middle eight melody is from some old traditional song I heard a few years ago. It fits well. We did it in one take—it shows—it swings.

### 3. Jealous Guy

The melody came from an idea I had a few years ago (India). I never did anything with it but always liked the melody. The words were silly, anyway. I sang it to Yoko, Phil [Spector], and a few people and they always winced. I decided to change it—and with Yoko's help I did. I don't believe these tight-skinned people who are "never jealous"!

### 4. It's So Hard

I like to sing blues-rock or whatever it is, the words were written with *the sound* in mind rather than meaning. Although both are useful. I also like playing guitar. This was the first finished record I made at Ascot Studios in our home, we didn't have any limiters at the time, etc.—but it sounded alright to me! King Curtis (who was killed a week later, R.I.P.) and the Flux Fiddlers were overdubbed at Record Plant New York. Everyone calls them "eastern"—they're just violins playing guitar parts!

### 5. Soldier

Started off in the "Working Class Hero" days, finished virtually in the studio. It has a peculiar rhythm and Jim Keltner and the rest of them do a fantastic job keeping up. Another 1st take! (Obviously.) The words are lost or wrong sometimes and I also sing it in many keys at once. But it still has a nice feel—it depends on what mood I'm in, liking it or not. Yoko sticks up for it! (Each song takes on a personality when it is finished and we get possessive!)

### 6. Truth

Another "oldie" (India again) with words finished recently. I was wondering what truth I was after in India. George does a sharp solo with his steel finger (he's not too proud of it—but I like it). I like the overall sound on this track tho' I'm not sure if I'd go out and buy it.

### 7. Oh My Love

A joy to write and a joy to sing and record! Written with Yoko—based on her original lyric—we finished it very quickly one late night together. The beginning of the melody was started last year. Writing songs is like writing books—you store little melodies/words/ideas in your mind library and fish them out when you need them.

### 8. How Do You Sleep

I know you'll all be wondering about this one! It's been around since late '69 in a similar form to this—but not quite (i.e., more abstract). I'd always envisioned that heavy kind of beat for it and wanted to record it, whatever the lyric turned out to be. Then I heard Paul's messages in *Ram*—yes there are dear reader! Too many people going *where?* Missed our lucky *what?* What was *our* 1st mistake? "Can't be wrong" huh! I mean Yoko, me, and *other friends* can't *all be hearing things*. So to have some fun, I must thank Allen Klein publicly for the line, "just another day." A real poet! Some people don't see the funny side of it at all. Too bad. What am I supposed to do, make you laugh? It's what you might call an "angry letter," sung—get it? George Harrison's best guitar solo to date on this cut—as good as anything I've heard from anyone—anywhere. I'm singing sharp again—but me rhythm guitar makes up for it. A good "live" session from all the band. I don't think about Paul this way every moment of my life, in case you're wondering.

### 9. How

Is George's favorite song, I'm proud to say. Wish I'd sung it better but it's a nice tune, it was hard doing the breaks. Mellow.

### 10. Oh Yoko

Is an easy come easy go song—like whistling down the lane to meet your lover. She's mine and I'm always singing/thinking/being about her—it came naturally, we did one take and enjoyed it. Phil and me croaked on the backing "chorus" later. I always do the wrong songs first—so when it's time to sing softly I've wrecked my throat rocking!! I'll never learn—"Twist and Shout" was recorded at the end of a 12-hour session. Jesus, what torture (old man's reminiscences). That's all folks, if you like it, listen to it, if you don't, shutup.


P.S. Congratulations to Paul and Linda from the both of us.

# Hanoi Jane

*by Peter Knobler*
*November 1972*

*The Jane Fonda we knew and loved—and the one she now attempts to white-wash. Our headline was, "Why Does Jane Fonda Infuriate America?" We asked her if she was a Communist. She gave it serious consideration.*

What is it about Jane Fonda that so infuriates America? Is it her turning away from wealth, the symbolic ingratitude of spitting out the silver spoon, that occasions such derision? Is she "too pretty to be so serious," the old Woman's-Place-Is-in-the-Home syndrome, hanging heavy on a woman whose home has always been a sound stage? What is it about Jane Fonda that brings both the House Internal Security Committee and the *National Lampoon* down around her head?

She's an easy target, that's for sure. She is learning to use her access to the media for ends she chooses—learning manipulation of the manipulators, as it were—and while she is finding the most efficient methods of spreading the word she is also stumbling over such snags as the media's penchant for easy cynicism, the public's demand for professionalism, and her own identifiable guilt. She's turning over liberal rocks and finding caches of conservative pack rats.

But perhaps *because* she lives in a glass house, she's throwing stones.

Fonda has brought her suspect publicity to one radical cause after another. (*Life* magazine's headline for their cover story on her

was "Nag, nag, nag.") Her activities brought lots of exposure but little understanding of the issues she was raising. A good organizer
needs a healthy combination of both to succeed.

Rounding out the charges against her was a Lack of a Sense of
Humor. This Dick Cavett necessity, the ability to pun on the word
*atrocity*, was perhaps most damaging and then most perplexing.
Roger Vadim is supposed to have called her "Jane of Arc," to which
(he says) she didn't even crack a smile. Of course this is a man
whose wife has left him, but anyone who can't take a joke isn't a real
person. Another game down in the loss column.

But she didn't quit. She retrenched, as she learned from mistakes.
The "You can't laugh while people are being bombed" approach
didn't work; if they can't relate to you they won't listen at all. She had
first to find out whom she could move, then how best to do it.

"For a while out of, I guess, middle-class guilt that a lot of people
go through," she explained, sitting informally in a hotel conference
room, "anybody that asked me to help, I thought it was my duty,
right?" She smiled an amused, high-focused smile as if playing to
the large crowd that this time wasn't there. She's a consummate actress (winning one Oscar in spite of her politics and losing another
because of them) and I found myself testing her sincerity.

"And I discovered," she was saying, benign smile and all, "that I'm
not an Indian, and I'm not black, and I'm not poor. I'm what I am.
I'm a performer."

How did her transformation take place?

"Well," she began, "I'm thirty-four and a half, and when I was
thirty-two I discovered that I had wasted thirty-two years of my life.
And the reason that I started to even question what I had done with
my life was because of the war.

"I was living in France and the French knew where the war was
coming from because they were there before we were. And I remember people saying to me, 'There are atrocities being committed there. You're committing war crimes.' And I really resisted it.
And I started . . ." she rubbed her hands together absently, "that
was around the time of the Bertrand Russell war crimes tribunal,
and a lot of books were beginning to come out, besides the fact
that there was a very powerful peace movement growing in this
country and you couldn't avoid it. And so I started reading. And I
started to listen and, I don't know," she shrugged at the inevitability,
"once that happens it opens a floodgate. Then you have to question everything.

"There are some people," she continued, "who questioned from
the very beginning, and I am really jealous. If I am jealous of any-

thing," she admitted, "I'm jealous of eighteen-year-olds who don't take anybody's word for it and find out for themselves.

"But I went through thirty-two years of my life playing a role that other people laid on me, thinking that security has to come through a man, thinking it was my own problem I was in a social problem. And when you find out that you wasted—despite the fact that I'm upper middle class, white, privileged, famous, and all the rest of it—" here was the moment of recognition and betrayal, all in one, "when you find out that it's down the drain . . . and there's no way to rationalize that, you get angry.

"I don't see myself as being somewhere helping other people," she pressed on. "I feel that I am part of a struggle. I know that it's my struggle. I know there are tens of thousands of people like me, no matter what class they come from, because they're women and have to go through a certain kind of thing, feel a certain way about themselves because they're women. Our lives have been totally determined by men and I see that as directly connected with the war. I see that as directly connected with racism. I don't see them as separate issues.

"It's really hard, you know. All of us change and I've become kind of glib about it. It's going to be very hard for me to undo all the easy answers I've been giving you and going back and really finding the subtleties."

FONDA'S ENTIRE RELATIONSHIP TO HERSELF AS A STAR AS WELL AS organizer is ambivalent. She'd prefer to talk issues publicly, having access to information that you don't find regularly in *The New York Times*. "Everything I do," she said, "for better or worse, is public. Maybe it shouldn't be that way but for the time being it is."

She must digest questions before answering. Innuendo, the Rona Barrett school of journalism, is so easy and so very disruptive to serious political speaking that it too must be guarded against. Intent, as well as content, must be weighed and dealt with accordingly. Jane often seems to find herself caught between caution and annoyance. On one side is paranoia, the other far-reaching misrepresentation.

"How does it feel to be the most misunderstood woman in America?" some fool once asked. Fonda, sensing a headline, laughed incredulously and said, "I don't know whether that's really an apt description. I think all women are misunderstood," and continued from there. There was a certain delight you could feel from her; she'd turned a challenge into a forum with grace and undeniable goodwill.

With this election being billed as the "clearest choice of the century," what were her plans for the campaign?

"My plans are to talk about the war," she stated. "Putting the war as the primary issue, not a particular candidate. I think our responsibility is to get Nixon out of office; he is the all-time war criminal. He is lying to the American people; he is tearing asunder the fabric of American society." It was one of the few stock phrases she indulged in, but having made the point continually I suppose she decided a paraphrase was a waste of energy.

"I'm not campaigning for any candidate," she said finally. "I will vote for McGovern and I will tell people as much as I can, try to transmit what the soldiers have told us about the war.

"I think people should know how we're being lied to, how the war has been escalated, how Nixon and his administration is relying on the institutionalized racism in this country, banking on the fact that Americans won't mind if by dropping three thousand tons of bombs each day we're 'changing the color of the corpses.' That's a quote from Ellsworth Bunker, our ambassador in Saigon," she noted vehemently.

"In the beginning of the war in Vietnam, it was relatively easy for people to see—bombs were dropping, people were being killed, soldiers were being killed, *American* soldiers were being killed, there were five hundred thousand of our men there. The peace movement in this country and the soldiers who were fighting the war made it impossible for this or any other administration to ever wage a war like that again. We wouldn't put up with it, so they've found new ways of doing it. It's what Nixon calls a 'low American profile.'

"You don't wage it anymore with American soldiers," she insisted. "You wage what is virtually an automated war . . . so removed from the actual battlefield that it's hard for soldiers to identify with what they're doing, a push-button war and a ground war being fought by the people in that country.

"Ninety percent of the population of Vietnam are peasants and the United States' bombing and defoliation have destroyed one-half of the arable land. It has bulldozed their villages, forcing the people out of the countryside into the cities, creating a proletariat in Vietnam. The only place they can get work at this point is in the army. It is the only job you can get if you're a man. If you're a woman, the only way you can survive is to sell yourself into prostitution.

"They don't have any reason to fight their own men, their own people, to save Nixon's face. It's just that they haven't got very much choice now."

Doesn't she ever let the madness get her down? Doesn't she get tired?

"Everybody gets tired," she admitted. "Articles get written that say, you know, this is the kind of pants she wore—when you're talking about genocide . . . and you get a little tired after a while." She almost indulged in a sigh.

"But we should take a lesson from the Vietnamese people," she said, rejuvenated. "You know, there may be short-term defeats but history is on our side, and there are too many people changing— the soldiers who went over and are coming back vets and joining organizations like Vietnam Veterans Against the War and in the most imaginative ways are displaying their disgust. I don't know," she said seriously, "I think it should fill us with optimism."

"The fact that the Vietnamese are *winning*," she emphasized. "You know, no matter what some of the papers in this country say, the fact is that they are winning." It was a confident avowal. "Practically the entire Mekong Delta is liberated. Vast areas of the central highlands in the northern part of South Vietnam are liberated zones."

She looked for a way to bring the point home. "I just know that there are an infinite number of ways to organize ourselves," she said, "develop a sense of struggle, voice our protests. The vote is, of course, one way. I don't think it's the end.

"I don't think we should vote under some misguided conception that McGovern is anything but what he is: a good corporation head who will wage wars with a heavy heart. He may run the business a little differently than Nixon, but nobody is going to get in that office and change things fundamentally. What we have to do is stop the bombs that are assaulting the Vietnamese people and then start figuring out why we got there in the first place and decide what kind of country we want. Just for ourselves, you know. What do we want in America? And nobody's going to do that except us."


THE NEXT TIME I SAW JANE FONDA SHE'D JUST RETURNED FROM NORTH Vietnam with documentation of American bombing of the dikes that hold that country's economy and life together. It was a big-time press conference: all the television networks sent film crews; radio wires led like a spider's web to the speaker's stand.

Where she had been relaxed before she was high-strung now. Her face was tight, her eyes firmly set in that On Camera distance she once learned and must now concentrate to undo. She was not among friends and she knew it.

She had (wo)manned an antiaircraft gun in North Vietnam, had spoken over Radio Hanoi revealing what American pilots were really bombing and why they should stop. Many Americans called for her indictment for treason. It must have been upsetting to leave the camaraderie of active revolutionary struggle, the daily life of North Vietnam, and return full blast to the American furnace.

The room was a madhouse. A couple of minutes into her prepared speech the cameramen had to change film. She waited patiently as cases clapped open and shut and beefy soundmen watched their needles. After more delay she continued. Questions flew like beanballs, a network ego stitched in each.

"Were these pilots brainwashed, Miss Fonda?"

"Over here, Miss Fonda."

"One more, Miss Fonda."

"We think *you* were brainwashed, Miss Fonda."

She survived, but the news that night showed nothing of what Jane Fonda was about. In a two-minute clip it showed a beautiful woman with darting eyes making a speech that was not in fact strident but was made to seem so. Gone was the badgering; on-screen, close up, was the badgered: the public image of Jane Fonda, as filtered through ABC News.

That American planes are bombing dikes was made abundantly clear in a film she had brought back with her. In it, she stood atop a large mound of dirt as the camera made a continuous-action 360-degree pan. The land was flat. Nothing was on the horizon—no industry, no buildings, nothing. Rice fields. And a dike with a twenty-foot hole in it, guarded by North Vietnamese soldiers, men and women, so peasants wouldn't step on unexploded fragments. The holes varied, but the scene was repeated again and again. The news called them "alleged bombings," and mentioned her speaking for the enemy.

I SAT DOWN AGAIN WITH JANE FONDA. SHE IS BEAUTIFUL BUT DOES NOT glow. Her eyes are more piercing than simply clear. She invites conversation.

Throughout our talk I was struck by the final unwillingness to tie all her connections together. I finally leaned forward and said, "You've defined the President as a corporation head and the state as oppressor. Do you want to define yourself? . . . Do you think of yourself as a Communist?" Twenty years ago lightning would have struck.

Jane Fonda looked at me, knew she knew me not well, and leaned forward to meet my undefined charge. "I'm not flippant with that phrase," she said. "It's not one I toss around lightly." She paused, then spoke firmly. "I'm not a Communist. I would be honored to be called a Communist. It's like a Red Badge of Courage which I haven't come close to earning. I haven't read enough Marx or Engels to consider myself qualified to say."

But in America I'd still asked a dangerous question; what's more, a private question in a public setting to a figure at once public and private. She recognized the dichotomy and added, "It's also a label which can serve no useful purpose. Being a Communist to you means something entirely different to someone in Iowa or anywhere around the country. It's a label that's been used beyond its meaning. It's emotional now. It's imprecise. Why should I categorize myself, especially in a category which touches off so many emotions having nothing to do with the meaning of the word, when it doesn't apply? I just don't toss that word around."

While Jane Fonda was a frenetic cause hopper she could be written off, an easy laugh, a Johnny Carson one-liner. Now, with hard charges, she is threatened with indictment for treason. She turns toward her industry for an occasional film with which to support more organizing. She must consider the conventional media with enlightened mistrust. She looks *first* to the people in front of the screen. So the next time Jane Fonda comes on the tube, never mind if she's not smiling. Listen up. She just might tell you the truth.

# Lennon's Last Gig

*by Patrick Snyder*

*November 1972*

*When we covered the Willowbrook concert at New York City's Madison Square Garden, we couldn't have known it would be John Lennon's last. Imagine—you could just walk up to the window that afternoon and buy a ticket to see Lennon (and Geraldo Rivera) live. The show didn't even sell out.*

> *"This is a song off one of those albums I did after I left the Rolling Stones."*
>
> *—John Lennon introducing "Mother"*

The audience at the evening performance in the cable-vaulted cavern on 34th Street seemed expectant but not excited. Perhaps it was the leavening of straights who had come to the Willowbrook Benefit, but more likely it was John Lennon himself and the image he and Yoko have carved for themselves during their almost two years in New York. He's a fixture of the town now; no more impressive to a New Yorker than the other imported superstar, the one with the upraised torch in the middle of the harbor. It's nice to have them around but who can really get too excited about it, especially when the Yankees are winning?

It proved to be the first big-name concert at the Garden that never became an Event. Lennon has tried to divest himself of the superstar aura he acquired in the '60s and he has to some degree achieved his goal, more by releasing some notably unexciting music than by media manipulation. The concert went largely unadvertised—the evening performance sold out in a couple days on the basis of a simple press release—until a second, afternoon show was added. It never did sell out, but the Lennons personally bought the $60,000 worth of unsold seats and gave the tickets away.

Willowbrook is a local issue brought into prominence less than a year ago by Geraldo Rivera's exposé for ABC's *Eyewitness News*. A state institution for the mentally retarded, the largest in the world and located in the middle-class wilds of Staten Island, Willowbrook is a human cesspool, a bureaucratic bedlam that "cares" for the most unfortunate, pathetic, and defenseless members of our society. Recent slashing of state funds resulted in cutbacks in the already minimal caretaker staff, leaving whole wards of helpless, retarded children wallowing in their own filth and occasionally dying with their lungs full of vomit. So this benefit was organized to provide money for the establishment of four new centers for the retarded.

After returning from a three-month vacation in California, John and Yoko rehearsed for three weeks with Elephant's Memory in the Fillmore East and various studios around town. The afternoon concert by all reports was a dismal affair later referred to by Lennon as a "paid rehearsal." The band was too loud and the predominantly young crowd sat on its hands.

But the evening show was a different story entirely. Sha Na Na opened rousingly in all their primitive gold lamé rock and roll splendor and got a well-deserved encore. Stevie Wonder and Wonderlove were next, and his rather lifeless and jazz-influenced set fell on unresponsive ears. With perhaps the worst pacing I've ever seen, Roberta Flack began her set with a long improvisation giving each musician in her excellent backup band a solo. It was no way to open a set but she redeemed her slow start with brilliant renditions of "The First Time Ever I Saw Your Face," "Just Like a Woman," and "Somewhere (There's a Place for Us)."

After a series of introductions—Mayor Lindsay, Eleanor McGovern, Jacob Javits—thousands of tin tambourines were passed out to the audience, the lights dimmed, and after a little *a cappella* "Power to the People" from David Peel's Human Voice Choir, Chip Monck's special effects exploded, stretching its awning of light over the stage, streaking up to the suspended mirror and reflecting back onto the stage crowded with John, Yoko, and Elephant's Memory. Lennon looked like his famous *How I Won the War* poster, minus the bloody groin, dressed in army fatigues and cowboy boots. Yoko, all in white, was the only person up there who looked like a superstar.

"New York City" blasted out and John Lennon said hello to his adopted home.

He seemed wary and nervous after the afternoon's debacle, but as the set continued John, Yoko, the band, and the audience all found the groove and it fell together perfectly. Yoko sang five or six numbers, mostly off *Sometime in New York* but also a new one in which her phrasing was amazingly reminiscent of Lou Reed. Still no great rock vocalist, Yoko racks up a lot of points on sincerity and the band was always so fine that she became impossible to resist.

And in case anyone still doubted it, Lennon proved himself to be one of the finest rock vocalists ever. You have to hear him live to realize how little studio gimmickry he uses on record. His voice soared through "Woman . . .," rasped through "Come Together" ("Here's one from the past, just one"), and floated tenderly through "Imagine." His hands clenched and his face contorted through two minutes of screaming at the end of "Cold Turkey" as the band slashed savagely through the song. The audiences cheered and Lennon said quietly into the mike, "You enjoyed that, didn't you?" Here was the essence of Lennon's recent work, self-crucifixion for the masses, an internalized gladiatorial game for readers of *Psychology Today*.

The set ended with "Hound Dog," giving Lennon the chance to act out his fantasies, and predictably the encore was "Give Peace a Chance" with scores of celebrities, from Allen Ginsberg to Shirley MacLaine singing and dancing on stage.

# Muhammad Ali: A White Lackey, a Concrete Mexican, and the People's Champ

by *Michael Jay Kaufman*

*May 1973*

*Ali was one of our cultural and political heroes during the '60s, and* Crawdaddy *chronicled his ups and downs throughout the 1970s. We even published a quite amazing self-profile that he wrote called "I Am the Master of My Destiny." The following article finds him in a comeback mode—and still in fighting trim.*

A concrete little Mexican stands dumbly on the lawn. A concrete Mexican with concrete sombrero and concrete donkeys, on the lawn in front of Muhammad Ali's house in Cherry Hill, New Jersey. Ali's house is a one-level pink stucco, Spanish style. Inside the main entrance there is a portrait of the Honorable Elijah Muhammad, the seventy-five-year-old leader of the Nation of Islam. On the wall opposite the Prophet there is a sign.

NO SMOKING, it says.

The fellow who ushers us in is the same guy who unlocked the outer gate when we drove up and tooted the code, a serious young black man with close-cropped head. "Wait here," he says politely, and disappears.

It is a short wait. We are taken down a long hall into a red-carpeted sitting room. Muhammad Ali, the ex-champ, is sitting in a large white leather chair in the corner. He is with two white men. He is signing autographs for one, who looks like Victor Jory, the actor, and who (we learn later) has just sold him a $45,000 Bluebird Bus.

The other is a chunky character with bushy mustache and curly hair. He wears a grey checkered suit and he says his name is Gene Kilroy and he works for Muhammad Ali. "I call myself a flunky," he says pleasantly, "but he likes to elevate me. He calls me his business manager." Ali also calls him "Boy."

"This one's for Nick," Victor Jory tells Ali, thrusting another sheet before him. "That's N-i-c-k . . . And this one's for Phyllis . . . that's P . . ."

With Ali busy signing autographs, Kilroy provides us with information he thinks will help our story: "All of his bills are paid . . . He doesn't owe anybody anything . . . Have you ever been to the training camp at Deer Lake? You should see it. He designed the layout for it himself. He sketched how he wanted the architects to do it and . . ."

Victor Jory leaves. We begin a conversation with Muhammad Ali. The phone rings. Muhammad picks up. A radio announcer at the other end wants his opinion of George Foreman. Ali stays on for several minutes, putting on a show for the radio announcer (and for us?).

"I *am* boxing, I am the resurrection. I am the savior. I am the people's champ," he rants. "If anyone wants to meet me, *they'll* have to make a move." He stops to let the radio announcer say something. "You're not as dumb as you look," he replies. This is one of his favorite lines.

With Ali now busy on the phone, Kilroy begins again: "He's one of the five most known men in the world . . . You take someone like John Lennon. You'd think he was pretty well known, right? Take him to Egypt, though, and they never heard of him. Joe Namath . . ."

Ali tells the radio announcer that George Foreman is a good fighter for the Olympics but that he is slow and has no footwork. "I'm about three times faster," he says. "Foreman has yet to prove himself qualified to meet me . . . He beat a washed-up Joe Frazier who I destroyed . . . I'm the one that's keeping the game alive . . . Thirty-one years old is young for myself . . . I'm young, I'm pretty . . ."

Belinda Ali enters the room with Muhammad's eight-month-old son, Muhammad Ibn Ali. She is tall, graceful, dignified. She does not hide her affection for the child. She has a Polaroid camera with her and she begins to take pictures of the baby. "Muhammad Ali!" she calls to get his attention and when he looks up, she clicks the shutter.

"Shhh," says big Muhammad. "I'm talking on the phone."

Belinda continues to play with the baby while Muhammad talks to the radio announcer. Kilroy continues, nonstop: "He's still a great humanitarian. He loves to be with people. He always stops for hitch-hikers." And: "He was sleeping during the Frazier-Foreman fight. I woke him up with the news [Foreman's Victory] and do you know what he said? He said, 'I'm not surprised.' We visited a prison the next day and he told them not to get down, not to give up on themselves. It must have worked because the next day two of them escaped . . ."

Muhammad is off the phone long enough to tell us, "You might have to take a ride." He has a press conference scheduled in Philadelphia. We can talk to him in the car and perhaps later when we get back to the house.

And then he is on the phone again.

This time he speaks quietly, almost in a whisper. "I want to talk to you," he says softly, "about something that's happening in the faith." There is a pause. A worried expression crosses his face, then disappears.

Again Muhammad is off the phone and again a conversation is begun and interrupted, this time by Belinda, who has picked up the phone in another room. "Muhammad!" she calls. "It's Turkey calling for you."

"WHO?"

"A country called Turkey."

"Tell 'em to call back around four o'clock this evening."

Presently we are escorted to a car for the ride to the press conference. Kilroy drives. We ask Muhammad how much time he gets to spend with his family. He says about two days a week on the average. This is one of them. Tomorrow he'll be in the Bluebird Bus driving out to Las Vegas for the Bugner fight. Why, we ask him, does he keep fighting?

"I fight for the money," he says.

"You own everything you have," purrs Kilroy.

Ali tells us that his new training camp at Deer Lake, near Reading, Pennsylvania, cost $250,000. "There's not a penny owed on it," he says.

He says he clears an average of $190,000 per fight. "I plan on fighting for a couple more years. Then I want to quit and start preaching."

As we roll toward Philadelphia he begins a monologue: "I'm rated worldwide, right up there with the Pope of Rome, Gandhi, Kennedy. I'm most popular in Saudi Arabia, Japan, Estonia, Russia . . . Take Joe Namath and go over to England. Nobody would know who he is.

"Being well known in America don't mean nothing. America is the most hated country on the planet. Everybody hates America, all the darker countries . . . Turkey, Indonesia, Thailand. These are countries that don't follow America.

"I'm accepted all over the black world as a brother . . ."

A question about his future plans elicits the response that after he fights Bugner he will fight Ken Norton. And after Ken Norton?

"I'm going on a tour. Australia, Bangkok, Thailand, Syria, Libya, Lebanon, Egypt, Sudan . . . all my beautiful brothers . . . I'm going to Ethiopia in six months." He tells us that they are now beginning to make their own airplanes in Ethiopia.

"Black people [in the United States] are so far behind," he says. "They've been tricked with this integration shit."

He is riding in the front, next to Kilroy, and he does not look back at us as he speaks. He looks straight ahead. He talks, we listen. The occasional questions we ask seem to annoy him.

"If your mind is limited to America," he says, "it's small. I went to Africa expecting jungles and savages. I found guys in suits and ties . . . I was the savage . . . I looked it up in the dictionary.

"They don't have any sissies over there. No lesbians, no policemen, no guns . . . In Philadelphia the cops carry two rifles . . .

"I used to think of Africa and I'd think of a white man walking around in a diaper. Tarzan. Ah-aaah-aaaaah. I used to believe that shit. They had me tricked.

"I looked at pictures of Jesus. He was white, with blue eyes. Look at pictures of the Last Supper, you don't see no Indians there, no Chinese, no colored people. The angels in heaven, all white. Angel food cake is white, devil's food is chocolate."

He tells us that only by following the teachings of the master, only by uniting around a program of "total separation" as prescribed by the Honorable Elijah Muhammad, will the 30 million black people in the United States achieve freedom.

"The Chinese got a country that's named after a Chinese," he says. "Cuba is named after Cubans, Czechoslovakia is named after Czechoslovakians . . . But where is the country named after a black man?"

The silence that follows is broken by a question about a tour of South Africa that had been scheduled for him. The tour was called off only after protests from black organizations in the United States and by many African nations. The question angers him.

"I was invited to South Africa by the government there," he tells us. "The Africans asked me not to go. But I'm going to South Africa next time the Africans don't defend the blacks in America . . . I can't love everybody . . . I ain't seen a damn African nation defending poor Negroes. I ain't seen thirty-six nations get together for poor blacks.

"When I went to Africa I thought it was going to be like going home, coming back to our culture. But the Africans didn't understand. 'But Muhammad,' they told me, 'we don't wear Afros.' African women wear wigs. They straighten their hair. Shit. And they tell me not to fight in South Africa. Fuck 'em." He does not seem at all aware that what he has just said about Africa and what he said a few minutes ago about Africa are in contradiction.

By now we are in downtown Philadelphia. The car stops in front of the Sheraton Hotel. Kilroy tells Muhammad the number of a room where he is to go to sign for a television commercial. He tells us it will only be a few minutes and takes us to the coffee shop of the hotel.

"He believes in Allah," Kilroy tells us, "just as much as the Catholic pope believes in Jesus Christ or Billy Graham believes in God."

And: "Do you know what he says that I love? He says, 'I never want to let success go to my head nor failure to my heart.' "

Kilroy's incessant chatter is becoming too much to bear. Perhaps he senses this for he announces, "Listen, I'm no stage-door Johnny. I'm not in this for the money."

Presently Ali returns and we are driven to a place called the Parkway House for the press conference. Ali's arrival causes a stir among the assembled reporters, most of whom are middle-aged white men, loudly dressed. The room is the kind you might rent for a small engagement party. It is filled with smoke. On one side a fancy buffet is laid out. It is a nice spread.

Bobby Goodman, publicity director for Top Rank, Inc., which promotes many of Ali's fights, moves to the front of the room. The press conference begins:

"Do you fear Joe Bugner?" somebody asks.

"Howard Cosell gets paid for being an idiot," Ali replies, "what's your excuse?"

You would think, by the guffaws that greet this remark, that the assembled scribes were hearing it for the first time. "I am greater than boxing," he says. "I *am* boxing. Muhammad Ali is the greatest thing in the history of all sports . . ." The reporters eat it up, but in a patronizing way. Indeed, some of Ali's clowning smacks of Uncle Tomism.

But there are exceptions. One comes when somebody asks if he has any advice for the new champion, George Foreman. The reply is serious:

"Don't do too much talk about patriotism. Don't be too much of a good American . . . Remember that you are black, that your people get beat up by policemen . . . Don't just take the title and be such a good boy."

It is a glimpse of the Muhammad Ali who refused induction in 1967, the man who said, "No Viet Cong ever called me nigger," who would not sacrifice his principles for a title and the money that went with it, and who was exiled from his profession for three and one-half years.

But soon he is again clowning for the reporters. And he is Cassius Clay and it's 1963. "I only have one fault," he says, "and that fault is I really don't know how great I am."

The press conference finally over, we leave the assembled reporters to the broiled fish and other delicacies and begin the ride back.

You can live a whole life and not experience something like this ride back.

We are driving for only a couple of minutes when a young white woman standing on a street corner attracts the eye of Muhammad Ali. "What nationality do you think she is?" he asks Kilroy.

"Indian, I'd say," replies the flunky.

"How old would you say she is?"

"Oh, about twenty-six."

"Too old for me. I like 'em around fifteen or sixteen . . . Just to look, of course," and laughs at his joke. "No," he says, "I don't mess around with white women. No way. All you get with a woman anyway is a climax so why get involved with all the trouble afterward by messing around with a white woman?"

A short while later he tells us he has written a poem dedicated to the sniper in New Orleans who took on the entire police force of the city last January from the rooftop of a motel before he was finally cut down. "It's a funny feeling doing something and you know you are going to die," he says. "Here's how he must have felt." And recites:

> Better far from all I see
> To die fighting to be free,
> What more fitting end to be?
>
> Better than a heart attack,
> Or some dose of drugs I lack,
> Let me die up here being Black.

*Better for that I should go,*
*Standing here against the foe,*
*Is there sweeter death to know?*

*Better calling death to come,*
*Than to die another dumb,*
*Muted brother in the slum.*

*Better for my fight to wage,*
*Now, while my blood boils with rage,*
*Lest it cool with ancient age.*

*Better violent for me to die,*
*Than to come out Uncle Tom and try,*
*Making peace just to live a lie.*

*Better now than later on,*
*Now that fear of death is gone,*
*Never mind another dawn.*
*RAT-TA-TA-RAT-TA-TA-RAT-TA-TA*

This last is a loud impression of machine-gun fire, and as he does it he laughs. "Lord, that's bad," he says, and leans his head into Kilroy's soft middle.

Straightening up he becomes serious for a moment. "All that praise back there," he says, "all those cameras, don't mean shit. Money don't mean nothing. When I get applause from the people out there, that means something. Walking the streets and straightening out four or five wineheads, that means something." He recites another poem, the first verse of which goes:

*We came in chains, we came in misery.*
*Now all our suffering and pains,*
*Are part of history . . .*

He finishes and Kilroy says, "How about the one 'Black Balloons'?"

But Ali is done reciting poetry.

"I write songs, too," he says. "Here's one I wrote for a fella named Dee Clark a few years back." And sings a couple of choruses of "Hey Little Girl." Then he says, "I wrote one called, 'It's All Over Now,

Mighty Whitey,' " and sings it through. It is a song he sang on Broadway in *Big Time Buck White*. "It could have sold a million copies," he says after singing it, "but I never got around to releasing it."

Next, in response to a question about why he clowns around in the ring, he delivers a long existential rap that seems to say that nothing means anything. "One hundred years from today we'll all be dead," he says. "Our thoughts and ideals will be forgotten. Two thousand years from now nobody will even remember this country . . . Do you know that Marc Antony and Cleopatra once lived? . . . Look at that graveyard over there. Those people in there used to screw . . . It don't mean nothing."

Later he says, "The truly great men of history never wanted to be great. All they wanted was a chance to get closer to Almighty God, the truly great one.

"The name of Jesus will never die because he represented the little people. The name of Moses will never die because he represented the little people . . .

"I still walk on the streets with the wineheads."

And then he claims that he pays out thousands of dollars to "some brothers" to "run the whores and pimps off the streets of New York." He says they give him weekly reports.

And now he is saying, "We must respect our women. A nation is no greater than its women. Dogs and animals have more respect for women than Negroes. I don't blame white people . . ."

And now: "Black and white just can't get along. Oh, there might be two or three couples that can make it, but that's all."

And now we are in front of a pink house in the almost all-white suburb called Cherry Hill, New Jersey. Muhammad Ali lives here with his wife and eight-month-old son. There are also three daughters, Maryum, Rasheda and Jamillah. Where, we ask Muhammad Ali, does he want to bring up his children?

"Right here," he says.

The concrete Mexican on the lawn doesn't say a word.

# Catch-22 and Disorder in the Courts

*by Joseph Heller*
*August 1973*

*G.M. interviewed Heller in 1972 when* Catch-22, *as a cult classic, was still going strong and the world was beginning to believe he would never write another book. Later* Crawdaddy *published an excerpt from the extraordinary book that eventually emerged,* Something Happened, *as well as an unpublished play based on the "Clevinger's Trial" episode in* Catch-22. *Heller also contributed to* Crawdaddy *this look at the links between* Catch-22 *and '70s political trials, involving, among others, Angela Davis, Philip Berrigan, and Dr. Spock.*

There is much about law in the novel *Catch-22*. Catch-22 itself, unread, unseen, perhaps even nonexistent, becomes a handy edict for overriding all safeguards to individual liberty and safety, the key element in a tricky paradigm of democratic government that allows the law to do legitimately what the law expressly prohibits itself from doing. "Catch-22 says they have a right to do anything we can't stop them from doing," the old woman in the whorehouse explains to Yossarian, and, in practice, she is shown to be correct. Throughout the novel there are inquisitions, trials, sneaky undercover investigations, bullying interrogations, and numerous more cruel, unpunished acts of intimidation and persecution by people in positions of power, no matter how small, against others who are decent, innocent, and harmless, or whose offenses, if committed at all, are trivial.

Much of our national experience in recent years has been characterized by the same.

Anyone in touch with the news these past few years must be aware of the many legal actions of major scope and doubtful merit that have been launched against people who have been conspicuous critics of our military actions in Indochina or active opponents of racial discrimination here at home. With heavyweight champion Muhammad Ali, who was denied conscientious objector status as a Black Muslim and subsequently found guilty in the lower courts of violating the Selective Service Act, we had an example of both. One ought to note also the many times jurors have refused to convict in these trials and the other times convictions were set aside on appeal or prosecutions discontinued—often because of illegal eavesdropping activities by law-enforcement officials.

The suspicion has often been strong from the start that the true motives behind these court proceedings were not lofty but selectively spiteful: to inflict severe, disabling punishments upon these individuals more for their irreverent opposition to official policy than for actions seriously criminal. The suspicion has been substantiated by the outcomes. Legally, these cases have been fiascoes. From the vindictive point of view of the prosecution, however, they have not been entirely wasteful, for the power to put people on trial is itself the power to punish heavily. Such trials, however, are rank persecutions.

In the trial of the Black Panthers in New Haven on charges of murdering one of their members, as in the charges against Angela Davis in California in connection with the shootings outside the Marin County courthouse, people were killed; but in so many of the others, it has been difficult to locate a crime that took place and impossible to identify a victim who suffered by it. Where acts were committed, they were acts more of impertinence than destruction. It is doubtless true that Father Philip Berrigan, Father Daniel Berrigan, and seven other people, who all together came to be known as the Catonsville 9, poured animal blood over records in a Selective Service office in Maryland. It is difficult, however, to measure this soberly as a "crime" against the people or to believe that society has been grievously crippled as a result. Who suffered?

For want of anything more concrete, the abstract charge of conspiracy has often been lodged, that rare and heinous crime of doing nothing more than talking about doing something illicit. (What illegal conspiracies have been formed more likely exist in the courtroom between prosecutor, judge, and policeman, who draw their paychecks from the same bank account and depend for promotion on the same political superiors.) The public announcements at the beginning have been grandiose, and the allegations are frequently wild.

In Harrisburg, Pennsylvania, with John Mitchell as U.S. attorney general, Father Philip Berrigan, who had been in prison all the while for his role in the Catonsville action, Sister Elizabeth McAlister, and four other adults, collectively known as the Harrisburg 6, were indicted and tried, at an estimated cost to the federal government of $2 million, on charges of conspiring to kidnap Henry Kissinger, a presidential aide, as a gesture of protest against the American war in Vietnam and, furthermore, of conspiring to blow up the underground heating system in Washington, D.C.

The charges sounded preposterous. Their credibility was not enlarged by the evidence presented in court by the federal prosecutor. (In one of those beguiling coincidences that chance constantly takes pains to provide, his name was Lynch.) The chief witness for the government in Harrisburg was a fellow inmate of Father Berrigan's in Lewisburg Prison, a habitual criminal working as a paid informer for the FBI for an asking price, it was revealed, of $50,000 tax-free, though he received less. His testimony was unimpressive, even in Harrisburg. The jury voted ten to two for acquittal. The jurors in Harrisburg, a tranquil and conservative area selected as the site of the trial for precisely those qualities, either did not believe the government's case or did not feel that conspiring to kidnap presidential aide Henry Kissinger and hold him hostage for a week was much of a crime.

In Boston earlier, Dr. Benjamin Spock, Reverend William Coffin of Yale, author Mitchell Goodman, and Michael Ferber, a graduate student, were brought to trial for attempting to build public resistance to government operations to the matter of the draft and the war. Here the charges were true. The activities and goals of the group were stated openly from the beginning and widely advertised. All ultimately went free.

As an outgrowth of the street disturbances during the National Democratic Convention in 1968, there was the trial of the Chicago 7 on very vague charges of conspiring to cross state lines for the purpose of creating those disturbances. Some of the seven were scarcely acquainted with the others if at all, and there had been no plans or communications in which all had participated. Yet they were brought to court together, again under Attorney General John Mitchell, in a trial presided over by a distasteful old man whose crude and insulting bias soon made people stop wondering how he'd ever become a judge and start wondering how he'd ever gotten through law school. The jury acquitted the defendants of all the major charges. Because of the verdict, Black Panther leader Bobby Seale, whose case had been severed from the rest, will not be brought to trial.

Seale was acquitted also in New Haven with other Black Panthers on charges arising from the murder of one of their members. In New York City, some fifteen or so Black Panthers were tried and found not guilty of conspiring to detonate bombs in, among other places, Bloomingdale's department store. By the time of their acquittal, most had spent nearly twenty months in prison.

Verdicts of not guilty do not necessarily signify that blacks get fair trials; they get fair juries—if they are lucky.

Muhammad Ali was not lucky and was found guilty. He was deprived of his heavyweight championship and he paid millions for his principles before the verdict was reversed by the U.S. Supreme Court. Active and prizefighting again, and brash and wise as ever, he remains perplexing to his staid peers and superiors, for in this free-enterprise culture of ours, reputable citizens are not supposed to pay for their principles; they are supposed to profit from them. Otherwise, what good are they?

In California, Daniel Ellsberg and Anthony Russo Jr. were put on trial for espionage, theft, conspiracy, and whatnot for releasing classified government documents now known as the Pentagon Papers, a voluminous effort undertaken to assemble as history the private records leading to this country's increasing involvement in the war in Indochina. One stark conclusion to be derived from the Pentagon Papers is that Lyndon Johnson and his staff cruelly and systematically lied to the press, to the American people, and to both houses of Congress about what was happening in Vietnam and what they intended to do. (They could not lie so successfully to our "enemies" in Vietnam, who knew the truth through experiencing it and were therefore less naive than Congress and most of the country.)

Another utterly appalling revelation is that none of these distinguished gentlemen, these models of rectitude who were welcome in second-best homes everywhere, seemed to have experienced any compelling discomfort over playing the part of liars in a deception about a bloody enterprise that produced more American dead and wounded than World War I. None resigned in disgust to denounce the others. When McGeorge Bundy left, it was for a better-paying job with the Ford Foundation.*

*In this Johnson circle, the names are Pickwickian, although the people were not. There were Deans, a brace of Bundys, a Rusk, Walt Whitman Rostow, Hubert Humphrey, MacNamara's band, a Lodge, a Bunker, and even two Balls, one of them good.

As to the Ellsberg trial itself, the legal possibilities were intriguing from the start. The defendants were authorized to have the material; they did not steal, but photocopied it; they did not deliver it to a foreign power but made it available to the American public through the medium of the press. A number of other copies of the entire study were in the possession of people who no longer held government position. Is this espionage? In the aftermath, it was clear that nothing was damaged but the reputation for efficiency and probity of a Democratic administration that was already sunk in disdain.

Astonishing as it may seem, rumor had it from the beginning that no law existed that was broken by the release of this information. (*Catch-22:* "The case against Clevinger was open and shut. The only thing missing was something to charge him with.")

Ellsberg and Russo were really tried for *embarrassment,* for bringing confusion and ridicule to the present Nixon administration, which is not otherwise implicated by the Pentagon Papers. The charge against him and Russo was *effrontery:* As legally defined, the crime of *effrontery* lies in a failure to show respect to people in high office who will never feel sure they deserve any.

*Catch-22*—both the novel and the play—begins with a secret investigation. An undercover search takes place to find the person or persons guilty of writing Washington Irving's name on the envelopes of censored letters of enlisted men. Preposterous? Of course. But any more preposterous than maintaining in court with a straight face that the Harrisburg group was seriously engaged in a plot to kidnap Henry Kissinger, a presidential aide, and blow up the underground heating system of Washington, D.C.? The investigation in *Catch-22* widens, and the suspicion is voiced that the chaplain has been concealing stolen secret documents inside a plum tomato. This is preposterous too, but hardly more improbable than the real-life event that suggested it: the Whittaker Chambers–Alger Hiss case of the 1940s in which the former produced evidence he declared had been hidden inside a pumpkin.

Both the novel and the play begin and end in the hospital. The war continues. The effort to "look good" supplants all other military objectives in importance. A few trifling and whimsical actions by Yossarian at the start touch off irrational investigations threatening others ceaselessly. At the end, Yossarian must choose between alternatives that are dangerous or repugnant. There is no prospect of reprieve.

"No hope," is the judgment agreed upon near the end. "No hope at all."

Minna Diskow in *Twentieth Century Literature* (Vol. 12, January,

1967) has explained more lucidly than I can how these words, which are repeated, relate to Yossarian's "Night Journey" through Rome earlier and how both passages can be associated with Dante's *Inferno* and that ominous warning at the entrance to Hell. "All hope abandon, ye who enter here."

Yossarian turns back in defiance, and it is with a feeling of optimism and exultation that he elects the difficult course of escape.

"At least," he says, "I'll be trying."

There have been optimistic signs in certain recent events that suggest such rebellious efforts at preserving one's body and one's soul may prove successful. Outstanding among the favorable omens, I feel, are those startling, those amazing jurors I've mentioned, selected to the extent permissible for their built-in aversions to the defendants and the philosophies they are presumed to represent, who *refuse* to convict only because they are asked to. (I am aware that there have been countless cases receiving less attention in which atrocious penalties have been imposed for infractions that are petty or understandable. I am also aware that beyond a certain point there is no lawful remedy for these injustices perpetrated by the courts.)

There was that jury in San Jose, California, last year, that found Angela Davis *not* guilty on all counts charged. The key factors were against her: She was black, she was educated, she was a Communist, she was militant, and she could be linked with at least one of the persons who were involved in the killings and with the weapons used. Local hostility was virulent: A white dairy farmer who advanced bail was ostracized and put out of business. But the case against her must have been lamely, despicably weak; not once in the several ballots inside the jury room was there a single vote for conviction!

When put to the test, twelve ordinary people in upper California whose names I never even bothered to note displayed more intelligence and moral sensibility in a courtroom than the prosecution gave them credit for possessing, transcended those instinctual fears and prejudices that lurk inside all of us, braved the enmity and displeasure of others in their communities, and unanimously and emphatically declared: "Not guilty!"

Bravo to them.

# The "Say Hey Kid"
# Says Goodbye

*by Peter Knobler*

*December 1973*

*After Willie Mays's final playoff game, we ran onto the field. P.K. still has a patch of grass from center field (encased in plastic) snatched from the Shea Stadium turf that day.*

From out in right field you couldn't see Willie crying. His voice had bounced around the upper decks like a foul ball, fans clutching at it wildly as it careened away. Something about "sorry to take up your time"; a nod in the direction of Duke Snider, Larry Doby, Pee Wee Reese—men whose names will stay with me all my life because I spoke them like daily equations; words on the wind about fans forgiving him for hitting only .211. It was Willie Mays Night, and Willie was announcing his retirement.

Willie Mays, to me, was what could happen if everything worked out perfect: if I didn't turn my head on the asphalt short-hops; if I grew the extra inch and a half and broke six feet; if the girl across the English class ever smiled at me; if the major league scout just happened to be walking past Waverly Place when I made one of my leaping catches; if I could hit the curve or get the A or capture the tone in the air after Labor Day and hide it so winter couldn't come and it would have to go back to being summer again; if I could just have The Good Stuff. Some of it worked out, but when Willie Mays retired I could smell the old hickory as it crackled and burned on the bridges behind me.

I don't cry often or easily, and never over the New York *Daily News.* But the night-worn copy I found on the subway detailed my evening by the time I got home. Willie Mays, tears crossing his cheeks like soldiers, had said "goodbye to America." An interesting concept since he isn't dead, merely declining. Why, then, was I all choked up on the IRT? I've never met Willie Mays, would probably be shattered if I did; disappointing rock stars can be taken for granted, but I never wanted to *be* Stephen Stills.

I think the first time I heard Willie speak for more than twenty seconds was his Brut commercial only three or four years ago ("I like to keep up with the younger fellows on and off the field . . ."), and a guest spot bantering with Bob Hope on the Johnny Carson show . . . and Willie *squeaked.* So I *found* humor in his easy chatter, and *insisted* on insight. Faith, to be genuine, must be blind.

Willie was once joyous, and perhaps his most momentous feat— better than his catch off Vic Wertz in the '54 Series, *or* his throw; better than 660 homers, 3,273 hits, or a .305 lifetime batting average over twenty-two years; better than single-handedly pulling the San Francisco Giants into first place in the National League West in 1971 at the age of forty; better than his four home runs in one game in Milwaukee or his homer against the Giants in the first game he played for the Mets—better than all of this was the fact that he instilled a joy for moving, for living, in me and every little kid who saw him play . . . and it stuck. Nobody's doing that now. Cesar Cedeño, Earl Monroe, Reggie Jackson, Jackson Browne, James Brown, Dr. J . . . nobody.

It's a quaint notion: joy in what you do because it's fun. It's knocked out of performers around the time their first record is expected to make the charts; out of high school ballplayers when they're recruited for college, or certainly when college ballplayers negotiate with the pros; out of students at exam time, or writers when the rent is due. It's out of Willie now, and it's painful to see how much he's forgotten. He played in this year's World Series and just hoped not to embarrass himself; self-consciousness was foreign to the *real* Willie Mays. So he fell down on the bases, got blinded by the center-field sun . . . but his clutch hit—no line drive, but a legitimate chop up the middle—won a game.

Living close to a legend I'm sure dulls it, just as living close to one's *own* legend must make perspective next to impossible, so I wasn't surprised at Willie's apologies or the sportswriters' lack of reverence. It is left to the fans, the people for whom the game once was played, to restore justice and pay our respects. For my part I offer this:

It's the fifth and deciding game of this year's National League playoff, at Shea Stadium. The Mets, by far the worst team ever to win a division title, are trying to become the worst team ever to play in the World Series. The Cincinnati Reds, the "Big Red Machine," are heavy favorites but this game is for the season. The Mets go up by two runs, then it's tied. They have the bases loaded, nobody out. They've knocked out the righty reliever and a lefty is in. Ed Kranepool, a lefty outfielder, is due up.

Manager Yogi Berra looks to his bench for a righty pinch hitter (Yogi's playing by the book) . . . It's gotta be Willie. Willie hasn't played ball in three weeks. His ribs are bruised and sore, his right shoulder is shot from running into a railing chasing a foul pop (while playing *first base*), his legs are old and weak. Any Willie Mays you've ever heard about is not there. Willie finds a bat and ambles to the plate.

The crowd goes wild.

Out in the right field boxes it's pandemonium. We are yelling and screaming "WILLIE!"

Bad sports novels couldn't have gotten away with the scene. If Willie hits one out we tear down the stadium; a line shot to center scores two. In 1954 you'd *expect* that. But it's been twenty-two years in the bigs, and the Willie legend has worn so thin its fabric can no longer withstand the abuse. He could strike out. It's the classic summon-it-up-completely-out-of-instinct situation. They bring in a righty to face him, stripping him of even this meager advantage. Willie steps in.

First pitch and it's a high, high chop. The crowd shrieks. Felix Millan races in from third, sliding hard into the plate. The pitcher jumps for it, the ball sticks in his webbing, and when the throw comes home it's late.

The place ignites.

The run is in! Willie stands on first with a thirty-foot single. You can almost see him sag from relief. Justice has been served, unextravagant but gloriously precise. Willie *had* to get a hit, and he got the one he could. It was pure and perfect. He stepped past heroics and was working on salvation.

Spiro Agnew resigned that day. They flashed it on the scoreboard. His past caught up with him and he pleaded "no contest." It was no revelation, just a false face falling. There was no grace he could summon, no saving grace. He and his president and his president's men had demanded faith, but we'd known better from the start. And then it occurred to me, startling me awake like a sharp one-hopper to a daydreaming second baseman, and I speared the thought before it got by me: The only thing I'd ever in my entire life had faith in was Willie Mays. And Willie came through.

# I Call on Kurt Vonnegut Jr.

## by Kilgore Trout (Greg Mitchell)

*April 1974*

*This was the first time a writer took the liberty of borrowing the byline of Vonnegut's most famous character, Kilgore Trout. Later, a couple of books and other articles appeared under this name (none written by G.M.). Vonnegut had just penned* Breakfast of Champions *and was at the height of his popularity.*

There I was at high noon, crossing Times Square with a purple hard-on courtesy of the withering winter chill and a visit to pornographic bookstores on 42nd Street where I had gone to buy copies of my novels. Although my Creator had promised that he would line up a reputable publisher for me—"no more beaver books for you," he had declared at our last meeting—that hadn't been arranged yet, and, anyway, that still wouldn't have accounted for copies of my books I've been trying to track down for years.

The titles I give to my books are often changed, incidentally. The book I had succeeded in finding that day, *Pan-Galactic Straw Boss,* was being sold as *Mouth Crazy.* It was illustrated with pictures of several white women coupling with the same black man, who, for some reason, wore a Mexican sombrero.

What do my science fiction stories have in common with pornography? Fantasies of an impossibly hospitable world, or so I'm told.

The city sky was clean and hard and bright, looming like an enchanted dome that would shatter at a tap or ring like a great glass bell, as I made my way to East 38th Street and a reunion with my Creator on the first anniversary of my freedom from bondage.

"I am approaching my fiftieth birthday, Mr. Trout," he had informed me on that murky midnight in Midland City, Indiana, one year before. "I am cleansing and renewing myself for the very different sorts of years to come." Although he had been using me for some twenty years, this was our first meeting face-to-face. "Under similar conditions, Count Tolstoi freed his serfs. Thomas Jefferson freed his slaves. I am going to set at liberty all the literary characters who have served me so loyally during my writing career.

"You're the only one I'm telling," he whispered between drags on a foul-smelling stub of a cigarette. The reason, he explained, was that I was the only character he had ever created who had enough imagination to suspect that he might be the creation of another human being. What I had suspected, actually, was that I was a character in a book by somebody who wanted to write about somebody who suffered all the time.

"For the others," he continued, "tonight will be a night like any other night. Arise, Mr. Trout, you are free, you are *free*."

Even though they didn't know it at first, so were all the other characters he had created and used repeatedly over the years, including Bokonon, Howard W. Campbell Jr., and Eliot Rosewater, who were, like me, at that moment en route to Kurt Vonnegut's East Side apartment. We were throwing ourselves a birthday party of sorts.

In a very real sense, we were each one year old that day.

This then is a tale of the meeting of five lonesome, skinny, fairly old men on a planet that was dying fast. . . .


THE IDEA HAD BEEN MINE. AS IT HAPPENED—AS IT WAS MEANT TO happen—I was going to be in Manhattan that day; Bokonon and Campbell had settled in New York and it was easy to convince Rosewater to fly in for the occasion.

I had spent the previous night in a movie theater on 42nd Street. It was much cheaper than a night in a hotel. I had never done it before, but I knew sleeping in movie houses was the sort of thing really dirty old men did. I was in town to take part in a symposium entitled "The Future of the American Novel in the Age of McLuhan."

As I walked east on 38th Street I decided that what I wished to say at that symposium was this: "I don't know who McLuhan is, but I know what it's like to spend the night with a lot of other dirty old men in a movie theater in New York City." And: "Does this

McLuhan, whoever he is, have anything to say about the relationship between wide-open beavers and the sales of books?"

The others wouldn't be arriving at Vonnegut's until 2:30. I welcomed the opportunity to spend some time alone with my Creator.

What were we doing walking around with all that free will? Vonnegut had explained the motivation behind his dramatic Emancipation Proclamation in his latest book, *Breakfast of Champions*.

"As I approached my fiftieth birthday," he wrote, "I had become more and more enraged and mystified by the idiot decisions made by my countrymen. And then I had come suddenly to pity them, for I understood how innocent and natural it was for them to behave so abominably, with such abominable results: They were doing their best to live like people invented in story books. This was the reason Americans shot each other so often: It was a convenient literary device for ending short stories and books.

"Why were so many Americans treated by their government as though their lives were as disposable as paper facial tissues? Because that was the way authors customarily treated bit-part players in their made-up tales."

So the Creator had cut the strings on his dancing dolls. "I won't be needing them anymore," he told one interviewer. "They can pursue their own destinies. I guess that means I'm free to pursue my destiny, too."

So there I was, sleeping in dirty movie houses and walking down East 38th Street, pursuing my own destiny. Since Vonnegut no longer needed me, I was free to write for anyone: reputable publishers, publishers of beaver books—anyone. At that moment, in fact, I was considering ways I could turn that afternoon's gathering into a big-deal magazine article.

I was only a half block from my Creator, and slowing down. I wondered if he would recognize me. Since our previous meeting, my hair had gotten thinner on top and greyer on the sides, and I had shaved my scraggly white beard. Still, there were these distinguishing features: I am snaggle-toothed and missing the top joint of my right ring finger.

Vonnegut had also given me a tremendous wang. You never know who'll get one.

There I was in front of his Victorian brownstone, where he had moved within the past month from another location ten blocks away, with his lady-friend, Jill.

I rang the bell and within seconds, Kurt Vonnegut was at the door.

"Here I am," I offered.

"So glad you are," he said, taking my bag.

He spoke twangily and his smile went on and on. He's a sweet old poop, a big man, six-feet-three, broad shoulders, no hips, no belly, less of the bear of a man I had remembered from our previous, brief meeting on a dark night. His hair had been trimmed, also.

"Mr. Trout—Kilgore," he began to say, ushering me into the apartment.

The room was bare but for the black leather couch we sat on, a glass coffee table alongside and shelves of books against two walls.

Vonnegut was dressed in terribly baggy but good tweed pants, a green V-neck sweater, and brown Hush Puppies.

"What are you doing now, my old friend?" he asked, his dark eyebrows shooting up and his lips breaking into a really fine grin. He had left me in Cohoes, New York, installing aluminum storm windows and screens.

I told him I was back at the job he'd made me leave a decade earlier at a stamp redemption center in Hyannis, Massachusetts. "Think of the sacrilege of a Jesus figure redeeming stamps," I said, softly.

He said that he was teaching graduate and undergraduate fiction writing at City College of New York. "I hadn't taught for a couple of years and thought it was time," he explained. He was quitting after one more semester, however, because "I haven't had time to write anything in three months."

At that moment, the telephone sitting on the table in front of us rang. Vonnegut picked up the receiver eagerly, spoke a few words, then hung up.

I asked him if he got a lot of crank calls; until he moved, his phone number had been listed for all to see in the Manhattan directory.

"Well, it was interesting," he said, grinning. "I'm always interested in experiments like that. I'm willing to run the risk just to see what the hell happens. I could see the word going out that I had a listed phone number and the calls I got were, you know, from Texas, California, and all that, and not particularly from New York. People generally were quite nice about it. I would say I would get maybe two sort of nonsense calls a day, which is bearable. You almost get that number anyway."

He said that surprisingly few of the calls and letters come from young people. I asked him if he was grateful that, with the overwhelming commercial success of *Breakfast of Champions,* he had finally been relieved of his "campus cult."

"I don't think I ever really went after a particular audience," he answered. "Just whoever it was who was buying books, because I wanted to sell them. I really had no inkling of the young. Reports came back from salesmen that I was selling very well on campus. Part of the American life cycle for an ordinary educated person is that he does most of his reading when he is young. So there you are.

"My fraternity brothers at Cornell, for instance, who are all men like me, in their fifties, don't read at all anymore. And whatever books that may have shaped them, they read when they were kids.

"You have one problem," he noted, lighting another cigarette. "Only kids read books."

At one time Vonnegut was harassed by young fans. "When I was living on Cape Cod," he recalled, "there would be a lot of visitors with nothing else to do far from home. I don't mean to pander to young people, but they're no worse than anybody else—and I enjoy their company. Adults wasted just as much of my time."

My son Leo had run away from home at age twelve, I told him, and had tried to make his way to the home of John R. Tunis, author of sports books for youngsters such as *Iron Duke.*

Vonnegut laughed; after all, he had *made* my son do that, had enabled me to find him before he reached his destination, and later made Leo join the Marines. And later, be sent to Vietnam. And later still, defect to the Viet Cong.

I asked him if he had been able to figure out yet why he's the bestselling author on campus. If I was going to write an article based on our conversation, I had to get some good quotes.

"Well, I'm screamingly funny," he obliged. "I really am in the books. And I talk about stuff Billy Graham won't talk about, for instance, you know, is it wrong to kill?

"I see nothing wrong with being sophomoric. I mean, my books deal with subjects that interest sophomores. Again, I fault my fraternity brothers from Cornell. Not only do they not read anymore but they're not interested in the Big Questions, and I don't regard that as mature—I regard it as a long step toward the grave."

"How nice," I said of his fellow Cornellians. "To feel nothing and still get full credit for being alive."

Still, I wondered whether yesterday's sophomores now look back at his work as "kid's stuff."

"People usually don't go back and reread my books," Vonnegut observed. "I seldom do it myself. If someone has read me when he was nineteen, which is quite likely, when he ceases to be nineteen he's going to leave me behind too. If it's comforting to the person to feel he's outgrown certain things and is into deeper stuff, well I'm really all for him. That's a nice way to feel.

"No, I don't have any loyalty to the 'college crowd,' if that's who my audience really is."

"Do you think," I asked, "they have any loyalty toward *you?*"

"As shown by the mail, they certainly have feelings of great friend-liness toward me," he answered, negating his sainthood by talking out of the corner of his mouth. "But they'll get older." He wheezed and then coughed *hard.*

"And one day," he continued, "they'll stop and think and ask themselves: 'How did I get so *old?*' And 'Where have all the years gone?' "

At that moment I was asking myself those very questions. I was in agony because of gas. I farted tremendously, and then I belched.

"Excuse me," I said to Vonnegut. Then I did it again. Vonnegut had made me a very old, old man. "Oh God," I said. "I knew it was going to be bad getting old." Vonnegut just shook his head. "I didn't know it was going to be *this* bad."


THIS LAST REMARK HAD TOUCHED HIM DEEPLY, I COULD TELL; VONNEGUT at times gets the most genuinely sympathetic look across his face I've ever seen in a human being. So I chose that moment to tell him how much I appreciated his giving me my freedom. I said that although this meant that I wasn't necessarily going to win the Nobel Prize for Medicine in 1979, as Vonnegut had originally arranged for me to do, it also meant that I wasn't necessarily going to die in 1981 (at the age of seventy-four) as he had also planned.

That's what I told him. What I really was feeling was that I was a frightened, aging Jesus, whose sentence to crucifixion had been commuted to imprisonment for life.

Vonnegut had given me a life not worth living, but he had also given me an iron will to live. This was a common combination on the planet Earth.

I didn't really want to get into it then, so I excused myself. I had to take a whiz.

Returning to the living room I found Vonnegut on the phone again, chatting amiably with someone who seemed to be a stranger. By and by, Vonnegut hung up, dipped into the kitchen for a minute, came back out, and offered me an apple.

"They treat me as an extremely prosperous man now," he said suddenly. Apparently that had been one of his students on the phone. "Which makes a difference. I don't know what sort of differ-ence.

"A student whispered these exact words one morning when I

walked by," Vonnegut said, almost choking on his apple. " 'Fabu-
lously well-to-do.' "

*Breakfast of Champions* has sold over a quarter of a million copies
in hardback, "which is *extraordinary*," Vonnegut said, adding that
the $2.45 paperback will be published in April.

"You get what you pay for," I said. I meant it ironically. I had never
been paid for a single word I'd ever written. My Creator contends
that my unpopularity is deserved. "Trout's prose is frightful," he
once wrote. "Only his ideas are good."

This is how much of the planet I own: doodley-squat.

Vonnegut, on the other hand, said he saw his writing career as "a
perfectly straightforward business story." He wasn't being perfectly
serious, but then he could afford not to be. "My wealth is mainly in
the form of copyrights," he explained, "which are very valuable as
long as the computers and the printing presses think I'm their man."

I'd read somewhere that he'd just bought a brand-new white Mercedes.

"Yeah, it has about fourteen miles on it," he said. "It was the first
expensive thing I've done. I realized I was number one on the best-
seller list, so I just went down to Hoover Imports on Park Avenue,
bought it off the floor, and drove out.

"But if you want my expert opinion," he said, and knew that I did,
"money doesn't necessarily make people happy."

"Thanks for the information," I replied. "You just saved me a lot
of trouble."

I once wrote a book about a money tree. It had twenty-dollar bills
for leaves. Its flowers were government bonds. Its fruit was dia-
monds. It attracted human beings who killed each other around the
roots and made very good fertilizer. And so on.

"I've been shrewd about publishing but stupid about life," Vonnegut admitted, his voice trailing away in sadness. "I have been un-
necessarily unhappy for too long. And it is too early to give any
reports on my belated pursuit of happiness."

At that moment, Jill, carrying a hammer, came into the living
room from the bedroom, leaving the door ajar. Inside I could see a
Wagnerian bed covered with a pink and white chenille bedspread.

Worked into the tufts of the bedspread was the message, GOD
DOES NOT CARE.

On the wall over the bed hung an enormous photograph of a
woman attempting sexual congress with a dignified, decent, unsmil-
ing Shetland pony.

The pony appeared to have a penis approximately fourteen
inches long and two and a half inches in diameter. I have a penis

seven inches long and two and one-quarter inches in diameter. The world average is five and seven-eighths inches long and one and one-half inches in diameter when engorged with blood.

The blue whale has a penis approximately ninety-six inches long and fourteen inches in diameter.

"Nature is a wonderful thing," I said, pointing to the print. Vonnegut said it was a reproduction of the first dirty photograph in history.

Kurt Vonnegut's penis is three inches long and five inches in diameter. Its diameter is a world's record, as far as he knows.

*Breakfast of Champions* had been filled with four-letter words and drawings of assholes and vaginas. Because of its loose, informally cluttered structure, some reviewers in criticizing the book referred to Vonnegut as "writer in trouble."

"Well, that's okay," he said tiredly but seemingly unannoyed. "I mean they have to say something when they're reviewing me, and perhaps that's true."

"People are unkind sometimes without meaning to be," I suggested. I wouldn't have given him my word of honor on that.

The fact that all his former characters were free men and women, I observed, certainly indicated that his next book would be quite different from what preceded it.

"There'll be no references to Indianapolis, or Schenectady or these other touchstones I've used before," Vonnegut replied. "I don't think there'll be any veering off to Tralfamadore, which has meant, you know, in the midst of a tragic situation just deciding to laugh, and the hell with it, to turn the whole subject off. I doubt there will be that sort of evasion possible this time."

"Will that departure be too great for many of your loyal followers to, well, *follow?*" I asked lamely.

"I don't know, we'll see," he answered, lighting another Pall Mall. "If it is, that's just the risk I take. There's plenty of other books being written. If this one flops or never gets finished, why I'm sure someone else will have finished a book that people can read."

It was a very Bokononist thing to say.

He asked me what I'd been writing and I said I hadn't written more than twenty pages of fiction all year. I had lost my inspiration.

"You've got to *write* again," he said good-naturedly. He really did look concerned.

"Dead men don't usually write very well," I said.

"You're not dead!" he argued, interrupting another cough with his fist. "You're full of ideas."

I couldn't think of a single one. "Blather," I said.

• • •

*(ED. NOTE: IT IS WORTH STOPPING THE NARRATIVE AT THIS POINT TO SAY that this cock-and-bull story about the pornographic picture of a woman and a Shetland pony hanging on the wall in Vonnegut's bedroom is one of the few known instances of Kilgore Trout having told a lie. To say that Trout is a writer is to say that the demands of art alone are enough to make him lie, and to lie without seeing harm in it.)*

• • •

It was encouraging to know that Vonnegut had become interested in writing novels again, even though I wouldn't be in any of them. Just three years ago, after the reasonably successful Broadway production of *Happy Birthday, Wanda June,* he had said: "It's plays from now on."

His next book—the new novel won't be finished for some time—is a collection of nonfiction which will contain, Vonnegut said, essays and commencement speeches plus articles he wrote for *McCall's* on Biafra and for *Harper's* on the 1972 political conventions. When I asked him if he thought he would continue doing this kind of magazine reportage, he answered whimsically: "Hell, that's like asking, would I like to take a trip? Yeah, I'd like to take a trip some time.

"When I said I ended the first half of my life and I was going to do something else," he explained patiently as Jill banged boxes behind us, "what I was going to do was try to become responsible *in another way.* I have found myself intimating things and I've gotten interested in what those are. And as a responsible writer I would like to get my shit together, to make a strong statement that's really quite clear. I've been dealing in approximations so far, and I would like to *externalize.*"

"It often seems," I said, "that your books are really addressed to the leaders of this country, and that the readers are merely allowed to listen in on your high-level dialogue."

"Well, there really has been that stance," he replied, pleased to have been found out. "It was always sort of a playful feeling on my part. I'm surprised you detected it."

"And so what?" I asked. "The prolonging of the Vietnam war proved that the leaders really weren't listening."

"No, they don't," Vonnegut admitted mournfully. "The most frightening thing about the Republican administration is this: There are no readers. I don't suppose a Henry Kissinger has time to read books, or a *Nixon.*" He said this last word contemptuously.

"When you get to be our age," he added, "you all of a sudden real-ize that you are being ruled by people you went to high school with. You all of a sudden catch on that life is nothing but high school class officers, cheerleaders, and all.

"So there's this lag," he concluded. "I might be politically effec-tive when the people who read me get important jobs, but it takes a while for a young person to get a good job, unfortunately."

"Do you think you had as much influence on your own children's attitudes about life as you had on thousands of strangers' kids across the country?" I asked.

"I don't know," he answered. "I couldn't really say. They're not So-cial Darwinists. And they're not racists. They are all pacifists. They avoided military service with my encouragement."

Vonnegut said he had managed to teach his children—three of his own and three adopted when his sister died—"the only rule I know of." This is it:

*God damn it, you've got to be kind.*

"What about the other messages you've passed on in your books?" I asked accusingly.

He cocked his head quizzically. "I know nothing about any mes-sage," he said, deadpan. "Somebody said something about a mes-sage?"

The doorbell rang.


VONNEGUT BRIGHTENED, BEGAN HUMMING "THAT OLD GANG OF Mine," and headed for the door in his bow-legged, slouching, loose-jointed manner. Shortly after, shouts of recognition wafted up the stairwell. Soon Vonnegut was escorting Eliot Rosewater, Bokonon, and Howard W. Campbell Jr. into his living room.

Rosewater immediately dashed over to greet *me*. He represented perhaps half of my living fans.

"Let me shake the hand of the greatest writer alive today," Rose-water boomed to the room. "The hell with the talented sparrowfarts who write delicately of one small piece of one mere lifetime, when the issues are galaxies, eons, and trillions of souls yet to be born!"

Rosewater then turned to Vonnegut and apologized for his be-lated arrival; he had met Campbell and Bokonon at Grand Central Station a bit late because he had been turning 42nd Street upside down searching for copies of my books. He had managed to find a rare hardbound edition of *Plague on Wheels,* had paid twelve dollars for it. It was lushly illustrated with beaver shots and its title had been changed to *Auto-Erotica.*

I had met Rosewater before, of course, but none of the others. Bokonon was introduced to me as Lionel Boyd Johnson, apparently his name before he was washed up on the shores of San Lorenzo as a calypso-singing saint. He was a scrawny old black man smoking a cigar.

Bokonon produced a copy of *The Watchtower* and announced proudly that he was devoting the remaining years of his life to going door-to-door for the Jehovah's Witnesses.

He handed me the paper. Naturally I said it was trash. "Of course it's trash!" Bokonon screamed triumphantly.

Bokonon then introduced me to Campbell (he called him "Kahm-boo"), an ordinary-looking old man extravagantly costumed in a uniform of his own design. He wore a white ten-gallon hat and black cowboy boots decorated with swastikas and stars. He was sheathed in a blue body stocking that had yellow stripes running from his armpits to his ankles. His shoulder patch was a silhouette of Abraham Lincoln's profile on a field of pale green.

Campbell, who had served too enthusiastically the Nazi cause during World War II as an American agent and had hanged himself in an Israeli jail twenty years later (before the Jews could) only to have Vonnegut cut the rope with his Emancipation Proclamation, explained quickly that he had revived the Iron Guard of the White Sons of the American Constitution. Apparently he had taken yet another turn for the worse.

Rosewater, meanwhile, was really carrying on. The five of us were standing in a circle, Rosewater dominating the conversation with his drunken patter and the room with his six-feet-four frame. His breath smelled like mustard gas and roses. "I thought I had gotten you off the bottle," Vonnegut teased. "This is an alcoholic nation," Rosewater said, defending himself. "Much big business is done by people four sheets to the wind."

Eliot said he was making a living selling whisk brooms and life insurance back in Indianapolis. This is a man who had given away virtually all of the Rosewater fortune to poor, useless human beings.

"Indianapolis, Indiana," said Rosewater, "is the first place in the United States of America where a white man was hanged for the murder of an Indian. The kind of people who'll hang a white man for murdering an Indian—" said Rosewater, "that's the kind of people for me!"

"Two Hoosiers in one room," Vonnegut piped in, meaning himself and Eliot.

"We have a regular granfalloon festival on our hands," Bokonon observed, beaming.

Rosewater asked me what *I* was doing and I told him.

"What is a man with your talents doing in a stamp redemption center?" he gasped.

"Redeeming stamps," I replied, mildly.

I really had to go. I was due at the Hilton in twenty-five minutes for the symposium. Rosewater was drawing us into a semicircle with his huge arms and toasting Vonnegut on this our anniversary day.

"We rejoice in the apathy of our Creator," he blabbered on and on, "for it makes us free and truthful and dignified at last. No longer can we point to a ridiculous accident of good luck and say, 'Somebody up there likes me.' "

I nodded, appreciating the mania, but ducked away to search for my coat.

I stepped into the bedroom, retrieved my coat from atop the chenille bedspread, winked at the Shetland pony, and realized that somebody had put a note in my pocket, did it with intentional clumsiness, so that I would know the note was there.

I went into the bathroom to read the note. The note was printed on lined paper torn from a small spiral notebook. This is what it said:

*Leave at once. I am waiting for you in vacant store directly across the street. Urgent. Your life in danger. Eat this.*

This was my reaction:

"What next?"

As I marched down the hall to say my goodbyes I became aware that the four men were embroiled in a political discussion. "History—read it and weep!" I heard Bokonon say, and then Campbell called him a "jigaboo bastard."

Rosewater caught my look of disbelief, and turning away from the others for a moment, said to me: "People have to talk about something just to keep their voice boxes in working order, so they'll have good voice boxes in case there's ever anything really meaningful to say."

"You?" I was amazed. "A Bokononist too?"

He gazed at me levelly. "You, too," he said. "You'll find out."

Out in the midwinter cold again, I was ready for anything, and wouldn't mind death. I had finally reconciled myself to a life—a short life, mercifully—of farts and fears, belches and bitterness. Suddenly the prospect of being a free man nauseated me.

I really didn't like life at all.

I took perhaps fifty steps down the sidewalk, and then I stopped.

I froze.

It was not a heartbroken rage against injustice that froze me. I had taught myself that a human being might as well look for diamond tiaras in the gutter as for rewards and punishments that were fair.

What froze me was the fact that I had absolutely no reason to move in any direction. What had made me move through so many sad and pointless years was curiosity.

Now even that had flickered out.

How long I stood frozen there, I cannot say. If I was ever going to move again, someone else was going to have to furnish the reason for moving.

Somebody did.

As it happened—as it was *meant* to happen—a blond-haired young man who had been standing on the corner came over, and he said, "You all right?"

"I never felt better in my life," I heard myself answering. "I feel as though—as though—" I couldn't quite explain the wonderful visions I was suddenly having.

"Yeah?"

"As though some marvelous new phase of my life were about to begin."

"Don't ask me why, old sport," the young man said, laughing, "but somebody up there likes you."

I said one word. This was the word:

"Joy."

At that moment the Universe ended. The Tralfamadorians had blown it up, experimenting with new fuels for their flying saucer. A Tralfamadorian test pilot had pressed a starter button, and the whole Universe disappeared.

So it goes.


OF COURSE, THE UNIVERSE HASN'T BEEN DESTROYED—YET. OTHERWISE how could this story have been written? How could you have read it?

Hey, presto: I was only kidding.

Kilgore Trout went on to address that symposium at the Hilton. Here is what he said he thought might be the function of the novel in modern society:

"To describe blow jobs artistically."

And so on.

Kilgore Trout is a bitter man.

Actually, that's not true either. Kilgore Trout is a happy man. If I say he is. In fact, he's anything I say he is. Even a writer for *Crawdaddy*.

Listen:

The person who put that urgent note in Kilgore Trout's pocket—the blond-haired young man who gave Kilgore Trout such wonderful visions just before the Universe ended—that was I. That was me. That was the author of this story. Greg Mitchell.

A lot of the things in this story were lies, or what we Bokononists call *foma:* harmless untruths that set us free. I will risk the opinion that lies told for the sake of artistic effect can be, in a higher sense, the most beguiling forms of truth.

I don't care to argue the point.

I have already admitted that the pornographic picture hanging on Vonnegut's bedroom wall was a fake. I put it there, and now I gladly take it down.

This much about the story is true: I did visit Kurt Vonnegut for a couple of hours in midwinter and almost all of what I have him saying in this story he *really* said. Most of the rest—including the keenest of Trout's observations—was taken from his books. It's all vintage Vonnegut, even the stuff plucked from clean air.

Incidentally, this story is an example of what John Barth calls "the contamination of reality by dream" meant to remind us of "the fictitious aspect of our own existence."

John Barth *really* said that. I'm finished with lying now. I'm not going to put on any more puppet shows either.

So like Vonnegut, I am freeing Kilgore Trout. As always, he has served his purpose well. Hopefully he will go back to writing novels, but you may see his byline next month in *Popular Mechanics, The National Enquirer,* or *Swank.* He'll even be writing for this magazine again, perhaps under the pseudonym "Harlan Ellison."

But *I* am through with him. Let others use him.

"Let others bring order to chaos," Vonnegut says. "I will bring chaos to order. If all writers would do that, then perhaps everyone will understand that there is no order in the world around us, that we must adapt ourselves to the requirements of chaos instead."

This is my conclusion:

*Why should we bother with made-up games when there are so many real ones going on?*

So arise, Mr. Trout, you are free, you are *free.*

# Born to Ronette

*by Richard Price*
*July 1977*

*This guy named Richie came into our office and bothered us for weeks to read the manuscript of a book he hoped to sell, called* The Wanderers. *It sat on a shelf for months turning yellow, as we explained to him over and over that "we don't publish fiction." Geniuses. Later, after that book brought him fame as a novelist/Bronx historian, we happily made amends by introducing him to his boyhood fantasy.*

The Ronettes—three bad chicks in skintight side-slit Suzie Wongs, almond-eyed, kohl-eyed, jet-black beehives, and a single snaky tress down the neck over the breast. And that look—just as soon slit your belly with a nail file as French kiss and don't you think they wouldn't and don't you think half the teen male population of New York City in 1963 wasn't staring at those photos with their tongues hanging out and the bottom four buttons of their Jac shirts undone. Babies take your pick—just slip it in anywhere. And the lead singer Ronnie—the baddest, the teen queen of the hitter scene. Images of vinyl ankle boots, red nail polish stopping runs in off-black stockings. "Be My Baby" exploded on AM radio the summer of 1963, a combination of Phil Spector thunder and lightning, Dragon Lady macho, and Ronnie—it was razor lickin' good.

A few more hits from the Ronettes, then nothing. 1968: Phil Spector married Ronnie. And those who remembered wished him the worst. He probably wouldn't survive the honeymoon anyhow. Anyways no more Ronnie, no more Ronettes. 1977: Rumors. Ronnie's coming back, something about Springsteen. Would I return to my past and confront my jack-off deity? Shit yeah.

Ronnie came to the door of her small East Side apartment decked out neither in jade nor black leather. She was wearing dungarees and a T-shirt. Her movements weren't sultry; they were perky. Ronnie was tight and bouncy, unsinkably cheerful. With her straight, long black teased hair and her Oriental eyes she looked like a cheerleader at a high school where most of the seniors majored in automotive shop.

We sat back on a white couch in a living room facing a TV that looked like next year's model, one that you could consider a roommate. We did testing testing testing on the recorder and she belted out "BE MAH LITTLE BAYBEH," then laughed. It shook me up. History. I decided to work backwards. "How come you haven't recorded in the last few years?" I asked.

"It's because I didn't . . . I couldn't find the right producer. And, of course, you know, people say, like—you're trying to compare everybody with Phil. I said no. I just want a good producer, someone that would know my voice, know my style, and it took me a good three and a half years."

"For the new single you've been working . . ."

". . . with the E Street Band, that's Bruce Springsteen's band."

"But you're also working with Southside Johnny?"

"Yeah, well, I did that one number, 'You Mean So Much,' and it got a lot of airplay, so I've been traveling with the Jukes and singing 'You Mean So Much' with them on tour."

She's been getting a great response on the concerts and she talks about it hand-to-breast, "You mean *me?*" Like she can't believe it. Ronnie sounded constantly amazed, like her fate and good fortune are out of her hands. There was something princesslike when she talked about the people in her life, when she talked about Billy Joel, Brian Wilson, Cher, Springsteen, the big guns who admire her, write songs for her, the fans who remember her. It was a pinch-me-I'm-dreaming quality. A Queen for a Day rush that in some way I felt had something to do with Spector and perhaps pre-Spector days. A sense of emerging from something that maybe by contrast wasn't so great.

It was time to do Roots.

Ronnie grew up in New York's Washington Heights in the '50s and '60s, a racially mixed neighborhood that has spawned such diverse offspring as Henry Kissinger and Freddie Prinze. Ronnie herself is part black, part white, and part Indian. ("I'm the race of all races . . . which is good, you know.") She formed the Ronettes (originally Ronnie and the Relatives) with her sister (Estelle Bennett) and her first cousin (Nedra Talley) when she was twelve. "We used to go to singing school for three-part harmonies . . . my grandmother didn't want us in the streets. . . . A lot of people thought that the Ronettes were a gang; it was just the opposite. The only reason that we dressed the way we did and we wore the way-out makeup and everything is because we had to be different."

Shit. So much for the Dragon Lady.

Starting out with Joey Dee & the Starliters, they were sent to Miami to open the Peppermint Lounge in 1962. They were primarily dancing girls. Murray the K came in one night, saw the show, and whisked them back to New York to do the Murray the K shows at the Brooklyn Fox.

"We used to feel so bad because we didn't have a hit record. We were getting 'More, more, mores' from the audience because we looked different and we had the sexy dresses with the slits, you know."

"Yeah, I remember. I remember."

She laughed. "So, yeah, I guess I gave us that image, you know."

"That was a pretty heavy thing to give a fourteen-year-old kid to look at . . ."

"I was . . . what . . . fourteen myself when I started the Brooklyn Fox. And people don't know. My mother was right backstage with us, you know. We were like this." She snapped her fingers and gave me *that* look. "Bullshit, you know. We weren't anything like that."

Phil Spector originally heard the Ronettes through Georgia Winters, an editor at *16 Magazine*. "We met Phil and we were supposed to do some backup singing for him. Just background, because we did Bobby Vee, Bobby Rydell, and a couple of those backgrounds at the beginning of our career, and we were supposed to do background singing for Phil. And when Phil first heard my voice, he said, 'Uh-huh, this voice is for singles,' you know, he thought I sounded so much like Frankie Lymon, yet I was a girl.

"Frankie Lymon was my idol. I remember being like eleven, twelve years old, sitting under the radio as a kid, because we were brought up rather strictly, and just listening to Frankie Lymon, you know, and I don't know where I got my voice from, but a lot of people say, 'Boy, you sound a lot like Frankie,' you know. I guess I loved him so much and listened to him so much that a little bit of it rubbed off and I met him, you know."

Every once in a while Ronnie would laugh and playfully slap my knee. I'm a big boy now but I kept feeling myself wanting to yell across time to the 15-year-old Richie Price—"Hey Richie, dig it! I'm sitting here with you wouldn't believe *who* man! She was touching my *knee,* man! Suf-fah!" Ronnie is 29 but I don't imagine she looked that much different thirteen years ago in her offstage self. She still projects a Dick Clark winkydink perky wholesomeness that is definitely pre-Beatles '60s.

"What was it like in high school? Were you big-time in school?"

"Yeah, it was weird. When I was in the tenth grade we weren't doing any shows or anything. I was a cheerleader and I was very happy in school and everything, and very lively, and in every activity, you know, stagewise. But the following year when I was in the eleventh grade, we started doing the Murray the K show. Then when I'd go to school the kids would act a little different toward me. They weren't—they were nice to me, but they were like reluctant to say hello or shy, or—"

"Intimidated?"

"Yeah. So it was weird, you know. Then when 'Be My Baby' came out I was practically out of school. Then I had two months to go."

"You were a senior in high school?"

"Uh-huh. 'Be My Baby' came out and it was like all over the school, you know, the whispers and stuff. It flipped me out."

"Did you do a lot of touring, like in '63?"

"We didn't do a lot of tours, but we did the Rolling Stones, or they did our tour, the Rolling Stones in England, and the Beatles here in the United States. And Dick Clark's tour.

"Like on Dick Clark's tours there were maybe five, fifteen acts, you know? You sang two songs and you were off. At the Brooklyn Fox we did six and seven shows a day. It was ball-busting."

"Were the kids any different?"

"No, I don't think so. I think when anyone likes something they're gonna wave and go crazy—just like they do now, they did it in the Brooklyn Fox. It's sort of the same as far as the kids are concerned. I think today they're a little more exaggerated, I mean, a little more far-out because there are more far-out people like the David Bowies and—and I don't remember. Well, maybe because we didn't do it, but I had never heard of marijuana. And backstage you never smelled it or anything, you know. No one thought about it."

"What was your social life like at this point? When I was a kid and I saw the three chicks up there with the Suzie Wong, with the bun on top, I had a heart attack. It was just like a fantasy, like I couldn't believe that there were people like that walking around."

She sat on the couch laughing with mock coyness. I wanted to lean back, affect a yawn and stretch my arm in a sunrise to sunset arc, casually dropping my hand on her shoulder and seeing if I could get to first base. I'd take a single, a walk, a balk, hit by a pitch—anything.

"And what was our social life like?"

"Yeah, I mean 'cause I feel like if I flipped out, there must've been a million guys who did the same."

"Well, during that time it was so hard to have a social life because you were traveling. The most we would do is to give parties ourselves, and that's the only way we'd get any—that's where all the groups, like the Supremes and everybody, that's how we could get together. But other than that, it was just backstage. Backstage was our party, you know, after the show and things like that, but anything else—there was nothing else to do, except to go to sleep. Especially me. Like a lot of times my sisters would go on to another party. I would have to go home because I would get laryngitis. By singing lead I would get laryngitis if I didn't get my rest, so I'd have to come home. It wasn't a lot of partying."

Okay, Ronnie wasn't street meat. Grandmother was with the radio, mother backstage, laryngitis, parties—a real cheerleader. A Good Girl.

What I felt projected was that dichotomy between image and reality, the strange mixture between worldliness and being sheltered that she must have grown up with. It was a peculiar type of candor, an innocence out of sync with today, that early '60s feeling I felt before. I thought of an old Bronx joke: What's the difference between a good girl and a bad girl? A good girl goes to a party, goes home and goes to bed—a bad girl goes to a party, goes to bed and goes home.

"Okay, and then at what point did you get intense with Phil?"

"In the beginning he would teach me all my songs, you know, and he was married at the time. He had just gotten married. So it was just basically a friendship, you know, and business. I slowly fell in love with him and he slowly fell in love with me. And it just got closer and closer and closer, until we both said, 'Hey, what's this? Let's get the little wedding bands and get married,' you know."

"What year was that?"

" '68."

From what I've read, Spector was a very lonely guy, and very short. Ronnie is tiny herself. She also struck me, despite her liveliness, as being lonely. I'm sure Phil has a swarm of dichotomies that make Ronnie's personality contradictions look as interesting as North Dakota on a Sunday afternoon in February. I think of their small physical statures, their secretive inner selves, their gargantuan public images—shake it all up and come out with two people hugging and holding each other with the urgency of two kids in a hurricane-battered hut on a deserted island. "What was happening between '65, when the hits stopped, and '68?"

"I was more or less in California. My sister got married. My first cousin got married. And they're still married, with babies and everything, and they love that life, which is good—whatever you like—and I was more or less in California with Phil."

"Were you cutting records then?"

"No. I made one record called 'You Came, You Saw, You Conquered.' Phil didn't go all out for it, because he was really more interested in my just being a housewife."

Ronnie gave me a neutral blink and flicked the ash off her Marlboro.

"Oh, I hated it. But I thought Phil and I would have a great marriage, because you know, his first love was producing and my first love was singing."

She said all this with no betrayal of feeling. I felt like I was getting data, not texture. There was no mood revealed in any of her openness. I felt like there was a fatty layer between her words and thoughts. Perhaps that layer was there for her too. The monster TV winked at me.

"So you thought it was going to be like a working thing?"

"Yeah, so I thought that at least I would be able to do four tours a year and stay home and do albums a lot, you know. But I didn't do any albums, any singles. I made one single with George Harrison called 'Try Some, Buy Some.' That was in '69, and that did nothing 'cause it wasn't me, because Phil was getting crazy. He was running. He was doing the Beatles, and it was a crazy time. So I just more or less stayed in L.A. and went out with Cher a lot. She's my best friend. And that's all. A lot of shopping, you know. Boutiques. That's all I did for two years."

Ronnie perched herself on the edge of the couch, lit up another Marlboro and coughed. Her knee was running. I was looking for Freudian slips, body language, any wedge past the words now.

L.A. is a deadly town. I tried to imagine Ronnie there, a N.Y. teen party queen downshifting from fourth to reverse. Cinderella moving in with the Prince and given an Electrolux instead of a broom.

"It was very stifling, because I lived in 23 rooms and I had five people on the household staff and there was nothing for me to do. I mean, you know, there was *nothing to do.* The first year it was great, 'cause you're so much in love and all you want is each other, you know. But after that you kind of, you want other things, and Phil didn't want me to do anything else. I couldn't see myself as just a housewife. It became very boring to me. I just couldn't deal with it, you know. A lot of people think of it as Orson Welles's story."

"*Citizen Kane?*"

"Yeah. Except I *could* sing. You know? He put me in this big beautiful house and gave me all of this, and he didn't let me sing, and I could sing. So it was like *Citizen Kane* in reverse."

"He just didn't want you to do any records?"

"I guess not. He didn't record me." She laughed and I didn't know how to take the laugh.

"Did you talk to him about it?"

"Yeah, well, not only did we talk, but every single night, practically every night, I'd sing. He'd make me sing. He loved my voice, so I'd sing 'By Your Side.' "

She sang, " 'By your side, satisfied . . .' and I thought, 'He's going to go in and record me with it. I can't wait. I can't wait.' "

By your side . . . satisfied. How very fucking sad. Phantom of the Opera sad. But there was no tone of tragedy in the way Ronnie sang it. That song should stick in her craw but as she said, she loves to sing. Phil created his own early '60s sex goddess, then married her.

Ronnie, what do you do with your rage?

I got up to use the bathroom and snuck a peek into her bedroom on my way. Facing her bed was another mother-sized TV. Two mammoth tubes and a stack of best-sellers against a wall. Not enough. Ronnie, what do you do with your rage?

"Sounds like maybe he just wanted to hear that."

"Yeah. Well, he would do that and a lot of songs with me. But that was just for his personal pleasure, but as far as taking me into the studio and doing it . . . and I hadn't lost my voice. I could see if I had lost my voice or, you know what I mean, but I hadn't lost my voice or anything."

"What would have happened if you said, 'Well, look, I'm gonna sing, and I'm gonna get somebody else to produce me'?" Probably the dumbest question I could have asked.

"Oh, forget it. He never would have allowed that."

"When you split, was it mutual?"

"Well, it was mutual, but I divorced him, because I just couldn't live that housewife life. And Phil didn't go out a lot, number one. He went out, like, annually. He didn't like a lot of people around, so I was more or less isolated from everything, other than the occasion of once in a while coming to New York and seeing my family. I was completely isolated. I found myself just driving around Beverly

Hills. That was my daily routine. For something to do I would get in my car and go for a ride through Beverly Hills and back."

Rapunzel, Rapunzel, let down your hair. In 1961, Claudine Clark had a big hit "Party Lights" about a kid whose mother wouldn't let her go to a party across the way.

"And how'd you feel when you split?"

"Well, at the beginning I missed it a lot, because everything was handed to me, you know. I hadn't had any responsibilities. When I was fourteen or fifteen, boom, I got out of high school and number one record, right? So I never had to cook. I didn't learn how to do anything. And going from that to marrying Phil right into another not-having-to-do-anything. So I feel good now, because I'm responsible for everything—my bills, my everything. It makes me feel more responsible as a person."

"So when you split in '74 you came to New York?"

"Yes. Straight to home. It took me eighteen months to get my divorce, because Phil was in a car accident and he almost died, and he had to have plastic surgery and a new nose put on and all that stuff, so it took a while for my divorce. So I was in L.A. a lot getting my divorce. Back and forth in court and stuff."

"Did you work after that?"

"I did an English tour. I hired two other girls. And I tried to get a similar look. You know, we all looked alike, my sister and my first cousin. And I couldn't get that look, so I just got darker girls that didn't look like the Ronettes. And it was very successful. But I tired very easily because I said, 'I don't want this. I don't want to be labeled oldies but goodies.' And that went on from '74 until maybe '75. Maybe a year, and then after that I didn't do anything. I was just, like, looking for the right producer." She stared at me with a "G'-head, ask me anything" look.

"Did you ever feel that if it wasn't for him you wouldn't have made it?"

"No."

"I know Dion told me that he felt like—a lot of people feel like their voices are just instruments for Phil to play with."

"I didn't feel that. No, I didn't feel that I wouldn't make it. I always had faith, because I'm religious, and, you know, I have that faith, and it's just like I had the faith in myself that I would make it."

"How does it feel when people today come up, people like Springsteen who remember back then and admire you?"

"Yeah, I flip out, because I can't believe, you know—it's like Bruce. When I do his shows, he insists upon doing 'Be My Baby,' 'Baby I Love You,' and 'Walking in the Rain.' He loves those three songs. And when I'm onstage, he's just mesmerized. It makes me feel funny in a way, because I didn't think of myself—I didn't think I was great like they think I'm great."

"Other than Bruce, has anybody else—?"

"Oh, John Lennon, the Rolling Stones, Cher, a lot of them just love my voice, you know. I guess it was because I was married for like five years and I felt like I was forgotten, you know, and to come back and see all these people saying 'Your voice, Ronnie, your voice.' And, 'Say what?' you know. I just thought I was a forgotten little Ronnie, you know?" She said this doing a wide-eyed Blanche DuBois.

I couldn't tell how she felt about the pictures she was painting for me, how much her high about things to come was obscuring her feelings about the past. She was talking about ten years of frustration and boredom with a buoyancy and chattiness that made me wonder if she was hearing her own story.

On the other hand, I've noticed a phenomenon in people who have been to hell at some point in their lives and dragged their ass back to some kind of normalcy. The hell could have been self-destructively voluntary, drugs, booze, another person, or imposed by nature—an incurable disease that was cured. In each case they made their decision to fight back and they won. They are now quite literally "high on life." They have no time for bitterness, no time to resent their captivity in the past.

Maybe that's what I was picking up and mistaking for either evasiveness or obliviousness—that joyousness projected by someone coming out of prison and stepping into the fresh air for the first time in her life. She's not a kid anymore, nor a captive maiden. She's got good people behind her and dynamite pipes. But I've got to say this one last time—there's more to Ronnie than what I'm getting here. Maybe I wouldn't be making such a fuss about getting past her words if I didn't feel this promise of openness that I was being teased with.

"I feel brand new. I feel like I'm fifteen years old and I just recorded 'Be My Baby.' It's very intense moments right now, but within me it's so exciting. I can't sleep at night . . . I'm recording, you know?"

Ronnie had to split. We went downstairs, she snagged a cab and gave me a Hollywood kiss on the cheek. I thought of an old Phil Spector/Crystals hit and gave it a pronoun twist—"Then She Kissed Me." Bring in the two hundred horns, six hundred drums, and call it a day.

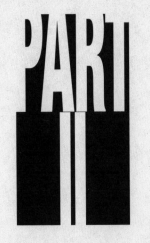

# PART II

*Rock 'n' Roll*

# At Home with
# Michael Jackson

---

*by Garry George*

*September 1972*

*Michael at thirteen, an age for which he has great affection. He was shoot-ing hoops and just being a kid . . . forever. Was Jethro Tull really his fa-vorite group?*

The Jackson 5 are a phenomenon. In two years they have topped such fellow Motown giants as The Temptations, The Supremes, The Four Tops, and Stevie Wonder in record sales. They have sold out the major concert halls and auditoriums across the country—a feat usually reserved for the giants of white rock. Every Saturday morn-ing, animated cartoons of the Jackson 5 are broadcast to millions of homes—an honor previously bestowed only on the Beatles. They have appeared as guest stars on big-time television shows (Flip Wil-son, Ed Sullivan, and Andy Williams) and presented their own net-work special "Goin' Back to Indiana." Sweatshirts and other paraphernalia flood supermarkets and drugstores with their names and pictures. Their faces are on the covers of all the youth and soul magazines. They show promise of becoming even bigger after being the top record sellers of 1970–71. And all this in the three years since their first big hit "I Want You Back" was released.

Why the Jacksons? Why now?

Certainly they are naturals for a "market." They are black when black is beautiful and there are millions of black teenyboppers and liberated white teen queens. They are young when we are led to believe that most of the record buyers are between the ages of twelve and sixteen. They are clean-cut with their mini-Afros and well-publicized "brotherhood." And they have the backing of Motown Records, the giant of soul music, and the help and encouragement of the original black showbiz success story Miss Diana Ross. Not to mention that they really do put out a clean and rhythmic soul sound. How could they go wrong?

Now it's 1972 and changes are happening in and around the supergroup. The initial rush of success is over and plans are being made to continue the careers and popularity of the Jackson 5, and to enlarge their audience. The Jacksons moved from Gary, Indiana, to suburban Los Angeles shortly before Motown moved from Detroit. They have begun to record songs from writers outside the Corporation. And Michael Jackson, the thirteen-year-old high-pitched soul-singin' leader of the group, has stepped out to take a solo effort, recording songs by such diverse writers as Bill Withers, Carole King, and Holland-Dozier-Holland.

What's goin' on?


I DROVE THROUGH THE CANYON TO ENCINO TO THE HOUSE THAT Jackson built. I negotiated the driveway, pulled up to the speaker, and pushed the button.

"Who's there?" Then a buzzer sounded and the huge gate over the driveway swung open. I was looking down a long row of trees and shrubs that created a telescopic effect, leading to a small patch of parking at the end of the green tunnel. I pulled my mighty blue Pinto in line alongside a Stingray, a foreign sports car that looked like a Porsche, and a couple of undistinguished American cars.

Four boys were playing basketball with their manager in the driveway of their average upper-middle-class spacious California home— no mansion but comfortable for a family of eleven from Gary, Indiana, whose father used to be a crane operator. With the boys was their white lawyer from New Jersey dressed in gym shorts and a T-shirt trying to keep up with them, and their press agent's daughter (also white) in a dress, shooting some mean baskets and pausing periodically to snap pictures of the group. She was in heaven. The youngest Jackson, Janet, was playing one of her brothers in a handball game against the garage door with a large ball that mostly landed on her head, causing gales of giggles. Six minibikes were scattered around the garage and pool area. Just your average family with father Joe Jackson quietly and peacefully taking it all in. The good life in America. The sweet smell of success.

"Hello." I extended my hand to the Jackson's manager, Reggie.

"How you doin' man? Want to shoot some baskets?"

Father Joe Jackson came out for a little talk and a lawyer joined us. "We gotta be careful," father Jackson explained, "because this girl did this interview and she ended up writing this totally unauthorized book with photos and everything, so we've got to stop it and make sure everyone gets treated fairly."

"I guess you have a lot of problems with a group this big," I offered.

"That isn't the half of it, believe me."

I believed him.

"Mr. Jackson," I asked, "what do you think of the move to California?"

"Well," he said smiling, "it's good for the boys, and there's more space and everything." He chuckled and I wasn't sure why.

Michael was ready to talk and I began setting up the tape recorder in the music room, which contained a piano, drums, and a couple of mikes. Stacks of 45's were everywhere—Chi-Lites, Marvin Gaye; they seem to get lots of them.

Michael came strolling in, played a couple of notes on the piano, pulled up a chair, naturally picked up the microphone, and looked at it like saying hello to an old friend. I liked the way he was dressed: orange shirt, striped pants, and a tweed-looking cap slung crossways over his mini-Afro. His eyes were bright, his face almost pretty. He looked at me expectantly, quizzically. He seemed poised and sure, but anxious to start.

I began by asking him about the move to California, and his change in status from student to superstar, from talent shows to Madison Square Garden, and how it all happened. He talked about it as if he had answered the questions a hundred times before. Probably he had. Mostly he answered my questions with a "yeah" or a "right," but occasionally he would relax and give out with some information.

"We've been here three years. Oh yes, we like it much better than Indiana."

"Do you think of yourself as a star?"

"Yeah. Sometimes when we go to the movies or go-cart or horseback we have to have security cause, like, everybody pile up and follow us around."

"Did you like the big billboard on Sunset Strip?"

"Yeah. Diana Ross's billboard was in the same spot. It's a nice spot 'cause you can see it coming all the way down."

"She discovered you, didn't she?"

"Right. What happened, was, uh, we did a talent show in Indiana and the mayor brought a guest, Diana. We didn't know she was in the audience—nobody did—and we did the show and she came backstage and told us that it was really good. We were surprised—we didn't know who she was until the mayor told us. And she liked our act and brought us to Motown."

Michael seems to be expanding his material on his solo album. And lately the Jackson 5 and Michael have been doing old Bobby Day and Thurston Harris tunes. This seemed a departure from the Motown tradition of home-based tunes and the Jackson tradition of songs by "the Corporation." Michael, or whoever was managing his career, was obviously confident of Michael's talents and his future. I was interested in this, especially since Michael's voice wouldn't be high and cute all his life.

"How do your brothers feel about your solo album?"

"While I was doing it in the studio they were all there and helping along. They'd give me different ideas. But they're also doing solo albums. Jermaine has a solo album coming out—Jackie, Marlon, Tito. The one I got out now is *Got to Be There*."

"Where did you learn to sing?"

"Oh, to tell the truth, in Gary a really, really long time ago. Used to go to the farm, lived on a farm like. Used to wake up early singing country songs like, uh, what's that song, 'Cottonfields Back Home,' stuff like that. Country songs. I used to listen and sing in. That's how I started. On the talent shows we did The Temptations things and Smokey Robinson."

"What do you think would happen if your voice changed next year?"

"Everybody's voice change, but when your voice change it has nothing to do with singing a different way or can't sing no more. If it just change then you sing the same way."

"Who are your favorite singers and performers?"

"I like Three Dog Night, Moody Blues, Temptations, Diana Ross. And all Motown . . . and Crosby, Stills, Nash and that's about it. Oh, and I especially like the Chi-Lites."

"If Motown came to you and said 'Michael, we want you to do an album with your favorite person,' who would it be?"

"Diana Ross, or uh . . . Jethro Tull."

· · ·

I WAS ANXIOUS TO FIND OUT MORE ABOUT MICHAEL'S LIFE OUTSIDE OF the studio and the concert stage. I wanted to know what it was like to be that young, that famous, and that talented. He seemed impenetrable, so I started in easy:

"Do the girls act different to you now?"

"They treat you a little different and they ask for autographs now. When we do concerts here, they come up and try to grab us."

"Do you have a girlfriend?"

"No."

"Would you like to have one?"

"I'm not old enough."

"If you had one, what would you like her to be like?"

"Nice and . . . quiet."

"Do you always want to be a singer?"

"I like to do other things outside of that too, like acting, producing, going to college . . ."

"Acting? Who are your favorite actors?"

"I like Jerry Lewis, Dean Martin, and James Coburn."

"Do you want to be in a movie?"

"I don't know. Maybe something where I throw pies. Just a bunch of pies everywhere."

"What would you do if President Nixon said 'Michael [a round of laughter], if we gave you whatever money you need and whatever channels you need to get something done—one thing—what would you do?' "

"To get the one thing done?"

"Yeah. What would you do?"

"There's a lot of people starving and dying 'cause there's no food. Now if they wouldn't go to the moon so much just to see some rocks we can use it for something else."

"What do you think of black power?"

"I think everybody should live together peacefully—no fighting or anything like that."

"You'll be able to vote in about five years. What do you think about that?"

"I think I'd rather watch."


I TALKED TO MR. JACKSON AGAIN WHILE MICHAEL WAS BEING PHOTO-graphed around the pool and playing basketball.

"Did Michael tell you about his art?" he asked.

"No," I said, "does he paint?"

"He sure does. He has a little studio behind the music room. Ask him to show it to you."

Michael was reluctant but finally agreed to take me to his studio. He had done quite a bit of work, mostly cartoonish, and a huge poster-size watercolor of Diana Ross, with teased hair, sequin dress, and wide smile adorned the wall. He also showed me a cartoon of Tricky Dick, and some serious still portraits, one of which he posed with.

"Most of my stuff is at school," he said. "Someday I'd like to see it at the Museum of Modern Art or something."

"Would you like to have anything put in the magazine as a message from you to the public?"

"Naaaah."

Has success spoiled Michael Jackson? Naaaah.

# The Album Jacket
# as Art Form

*by P. J. O'Rourke*
*October 1972*

*Remember* album jackets? *A walk down memory lane with an apolitical P. J. O'Rourke—surely one of his first published articles.*

Not counting the little boxes that Edison Cylinders came in, record covers didn't commonly exist before the late 1920s. Originally, the old 78's were sold in paper sleeves much like the inside sleeve we have today. The sleeve was never unique to a particular artist or group. Conceived as a throwaway protective device like weenie skin or cigarette pack cellophane, these sleeves were forthright, cheap, and did the job well enough, considering cost per. They have almost nothing to do with the evolution of the album cover.

In early records it was the label that bore the promotional weight. The label wouldn't get thrown out till the record did, so considerable attention was paid to design. It was still a standard item with just space left for the performer's name, but in exceptional cases a special label might be designed for an important artist. Most record collectors see these labels as the real ancestors of the album cover. The album cover has the eye-catching extravagance of the old label rather than the utility and economy of the sleeve.

In the late '20s record companies came up with a hot idea—sell a collection of 78's by the same performer or group with some common theme *all in one package.* To give this package an abiding sense of unity the companies put their records in an "album"—an album in the proper, front parlor sense with four to six paper sleeves bound into a book with a stiff cardboard cover just like *Famous Views of Lake Lucerne.* These albums, sold separately, had been around for some time, presumably to lend tone to the family phonograph collection. They were adopted as a ready-made packaging method and often included a little booklet with a gummed front page to stick inside the cover—the first liner notes.

The label was hidden and now the cover of the album had to take on the duty of making some visual presentation, and the result was the golden age of record packaging. The albums were *books* and were accorded that kind of artistic respect. The binding at the left and the oblong shape of the album cover gave the artist a well-defined space and attractive shape to work in. Nineteen thirties commercial art had abandoned the campy potted palm and Camels pack look of the '20s and hadn't yet completely bailed out of formal balance and rules of proportion. The multisleeve, or pocket albums, of the '30s and '40s weren't necessarily beautiful but they were rarely pretentious and usually to the point about conveying the artist's riff. Besides which, the artwork was attached to and never interfered with a well-made, permanent, easy to operate, and very protective container for the records.

The best pocket albums probably still carry the best designs around. An Earl Hines *Piano Solos* album of uncertain date and anonymous design (on the "Hot Records Society" label) is the single best album cover I've ever seen. And *Blackbirds,* a cast album from a black Broadway musical, was recently rereleased by Columbia with the original cover. It looked so good I took it for a new cover that put some of Columbia's recent work to shame.

In 1948 the LP was discovered and the pocket album became obsolete. In theory the record companies could have gone back to selling the thing wrapped up in a piece of paper, the way they had before, like an old fish, but people had come to expect a nice formal package. Something had to be done, but the LPs cost less than the 78 collections and the pocket-album style was considered too expensive for a single disk (pretty funny in light of recent developments). What the companies finally came up with was just a cheap imitation album with a thin cardboard jacket fastened on three sides and the old paper sleeve stuffed in, loose. And though the album has since been "artistically" screwed around with, the mechanical design of the package has never been improved upon from the imitation book cover.

The whole thing should be simpler and more functional. The envelope should open at the top. The sleeve, if it's necessary at all, should be bonded inside the album and not come popping out all ripped and squished around the record. And there should be at least one really stiff piece of cardboard involved somewhere to hinder warping.

But a bad mechanical wasn't the worst problem in LP packaging. Records began to be BIG business. Gigantic numbers of releases were filling equally gigantic self-service stores. The record companies had to rely heavily on the album covers as promotion and advertising and accordingly began to demand flashy design and elaborate back-cover hype. So the new, more difficult, square format produced ten years of rotten album covers, many with liner notes longer than this article.

Slap the performer on the front—make him look SEX-EE! Ugly artist? Or colored or something? . . . Slap a broad on the front—lotsa leg! La-de-da classical stuff? . . . Slap some art up there—a little Botticelli, some Vincent van, a St. Francis Assisi, any old thing! Cool jazz for hep cats and cool kittens? . . . Make it modern—Picasso cum Dalí out of Braque's basement and into your home!

There were exceptions of course: An absolutely knockout Billie Holiday album, the color and printing of which apparently influenced Warhol's Marilyn Monroe; some fine ink sketches of jazz artists by David Stone Martin for Verve; and low-key good taste stuff by Bill Harvey at Elektra. But by and large the album cover design was headed for the well-deserved oblivion of the '56 Mercury, Miró-inspired linoleum, and driftwood coffee tables.


Then in the middle '60s the youth culture bloomed. Every kid on the block was consuming marijuana, L.S.D., or whatever and getting Cinerama visions in his head. Quick as you could say *Om Mani Padme Hum* a new wave of artistic endeavor hit the deck in America, sparked by twice as much energy as talent. Not to denigrate some first-rate people—I mean, the San Francisco Poster school and the original underground cartoonists are blue in the face with talent. But their styles, when commercially imitated, produce uglier visuals than a late-night color TV Veg-O-Matic commercial adjusted to abscess magenta.

It swept the country.

One day all the record company executives were sitting around in their offices mumbling, "Slap a broad on . . . Slap some art on . . . Make it SEX-EE," when in swarmed their pop musicians on contract dressed like rejects for the lead in Ken Russell's production of the *Life of Oscar Wilde* screaming that their next album covers had to be "Loaded with VIBES, packed with VIBES"—Milt Jackson? Lionel Hampton?—"heavy VIBES, far-out VIBES, VIBE CITY!"

Psychedelics knocked the lead out of record cover design. And some of the results were beautiful—*Live Dead,* Moscoso's *Steve Miller Band,* R. Crumb's *Cheap Thrills.* Others had a certain charm—*Sergeant Pepper, Their Satanic Majesties' Request, Tommy.* But the whole vibes thing when translated into competitive commercial art constantly demanded pushing further, outdoing itself. Not only wasn't this much in the spirit of psychedelic art, but it couldn't go on forever either. The Blind Faith naked nymphette cover hassle and the nondistribution of the Ono-Lennons in the all-together quickly defined the limits of visual brouhaha.

The reaction set in—Beatle and Stone white *nada* nothing; nostalgia pioneered by Quicksilver *Happy Trails* and *Beautiful Day* covers and carried beyond bounds of sense or taste with Crosby, Stills, Nash and Young's *Deja Vu;* Who *Live at Leeds* imitation bootleg, and Manhattan Transfer's Carmine Miranda sleeze.

Not enough. The crazy package had caught on like cholera. Small Faces whelped a completely *round* album jacket in the form of a giant can of Nut Gone tobacco, which begat a Rolling Stones octagon and a Traffic trapezoid; a Melanie put-together something or other; Grand Funk's Silver Foil coin; an endlessly unfolding nearly full-scale Dave Mason with a record (you remember records) the color of marbleized vomit; real zippers; a John and Yoko wedding box, the cataloging of whose contents would exhaust Sears and Roebuck; and generally enough junk to cripple a legion of rack jobbers and satisfy the primal traumas of all my contemporaries whose parents couldn't afford a *Doctor Dan the Bandage Man* Golden Book with real Band-Aids (reg. t.m.) in the back. These albums are fraught with design considerations that would scare Buckminster Fuller back to the post and lintel, and as for "art". . . .

God knows where it would have ended . . . Frank Zappa albums with live rats. A Joe Cocker release wrapped in a groupie. I don't know. But the economy in its infinite wisdom saw fit to visit us with recession and some common sense may be lurching back into the record industry.

Almost all art directors are reinstituting the liner notes that went out the window when Consciousness Ill guitar players decided that reading was last year's form of communication. They say the liner notes are aimed at information now, not hype. I hear a lot of talk about "a need for functional packaging." And Warner Brothers released one of the most beautiful albums of the past twenty years— Allman Brothers' *Eat a Peach*. They all concede that the customer still wants something special. Maybe good taste is Loaded with VIBES, Packed with VIBES, VIBE CITY . . . Anyway, it's cheap. . . .

# First Raitt

*by David Rensin*

*March 1973*

*Bonnie Raitt was* Crawdaddy's *kind of rock and roller—pretty but not pristine; smart, funky, politically progressive. This piece was one of the first written about her, and year after year, rave after rave, we tried to make her a star. But nothing happened—until the late 1980s, long after* Crawdaddy *ceased to exist. We're happy for her. We did our best.*

Bonnie Raitt is by nature a purposeful woman. On a personal level, she is attempting to forge a new ethic reaching beyond the often self-imposed limitations of today's recording artists. Bonnie is warm and disarming—she smiles, you smile. Yet at twenty-two she is already aware of both the advantages and consequences of her chosen way of life.

"When I started out I didn't even want to make a record," Bonnie said as we settled into a sofa. "I didn't take it seriously then and in a way, I don't now. But I had to put out a record to survive, to keep things going. Right now I'd be content to be just well known enough to go on playing the Ash Grove circuit for the next twenty years."

A sense of social responsibility and political consciousness nurtured at an early age makes Bonnie see life as a series of compromises, but she feels everyone should be able to answer for whatever he/she does at any time. This viewpoint makes abundantly clear the reasons she chose to sign with Warner Brothers instead of, say, Arhoolie Records. "Warner Brothers gives me a total budget (instead of advances) that I put into one account and decide what to do with," Bonnie explained. "So I'm carrying off some innovative ventures in accordance with my belief that artists should take only what they need to live on from performance, record, and royalty money and find ways to redistribute or give back the rest. Everybody's just out to take all the money they can and I'm just trying to do something different."

For example: Using the record company money given her to do the first album, Bonnie decided to take a chance on a friend who was in the process of setting up his own studio and needed some money to get off the ground. She provided the cash and although he had only four-track equipment, recorded with him. "My first album was done in a garage in Minneapolis, but I wasn't trying for the perfect record. Some of the money I had went to musicians who had never played a session before, but they were friends who needed the cash to go on doing the kind of music they wanted to. Besides, the guy with the studio, Dave Ray, now puts out records for from two dollars to two-fifty and each contains a complete accounting of how every penny is spent. I really believe in that sort of thing.

"My main motivations are political in a different sort of way. To me politics is relating to and caring about people. I just want to have a good time and give the audience something worthwhile. My primary interest is in how I'm playing things and I don't care if I sing good or bad, play up to par, or write the most original songs. That's irrelevant."

Onstage, Bonnie and her bass player, Freebo, who looms quietly but effectively behind her, are at home with almost any audience. Her choice of music ranges from old blues to originals to songs by friends and peers Joni Mitchell, Jackson Browne, Chris Smither, and Joel Zoss, to '60s standards such as "I know" (Barbara George), "Walk on By," "Since I Fell For You," and Stephen Stills's "Bluebird." Bonnie's vocals are clear and strong, with just the right amount of feeling. Above all, they are fresh and honest.

The daughter of musical-comedy star John Raitt (*Carousel, The Pajama Game*), Bonnie was born in Burbank, but found herself shuttled across the country a number of times before finally settling in Los Angeles (for a while) in 1957. "I hated Los Angeles," she recalled. But her parents' reluctance to dive headlong into the blossoming Hollywood/Beverly Hills social scene saved Bonnie the experience of growing up with the sons and daughters of her parents' show business acquaintances. Instead, she divided her time between school, records, guitar, and a Quaker-oriented camp in the summer.

"It was the camp that put me in a social situation with leftist-type people," said Bonnie, brushing a thick lock of hair away from her abundantly freckled face. "I was around activities that had no basis in my Los Angeles world or the schools I went to—you know, Pete Seeger, Joan Baez, pacifism, and all that. I went for eight years and managed to absorb most of my political values from that atmosphere."

Growing up in Los Angeles, Bonnie never took to surf, folk, or white rock music, and she still dislikes being cast as any particular type of singer. For her it was soul music, dancing, drinking, partying, and opposition in general to the beach fads of her time. At thirteen she was listening to Son House, John Hammond, and John Hurt—mostly because she liked them, and partially as a result of her rebellious nature.

Moving East into the alternative culture of progressive schools, Bonnie finished her mandatory education and then attended college for a while (Radcliffe, no less). She also hung out at Boston's Club 47 during its last year, as well as other clubs, long enough to realize she could sing better than a lot of the second acts that were being booked. "I was sick of working in the daytime and I needed money to live, so I gave it a try." As Bonnie began to circulate, her reputation preceded her and the gigs eventually led to the Gaslight in New York and the Philadelphia Folk Festival. A record contract soon followed and she currently has two solid releases on Warner Brothers, *Bonnie Raitt* and *Give It Up*.

Bonnie spoke about the problems she faces as a woman on the road: "Some things make it difficult for me to adjust. For instance, if I were to meet a guy I liked, I couldn't just drag him along with me the way a guy can take a chick. It would be a strange, masculine situation for me although it's already something I have to a degree since I write out all the checks for my bass player and studio musicians. I'm a strong person and a strong girl and I've never been oppressed even though I'm not the overly 'feminine' type." As a child, Bonnie said, "I did anything I wanted to, and now that I'm grown up I meet all these girls who say that they're 'so proud of me because I'm so good on the guitar and I'm doing my own thing . . .' It just flips me out. I never realized that other girls were more conditioned not to do what they wanted in certain areas. I just don't like the idea of being put on a pedestal." But being one of the few young, proficient, and well-known woman guitarists (and she plays a mean bottleneck), Bonnie finds herself beginning to have to deal with a worship situation.

"All I'm trying to do is revolutionize the business in my own way.

I'm just doing it in the most righteous way possible—not screwing or ripping anybody off. If I happen to get famous because of what I'm trying to accomplish, fine, but on a personal level it scares me. I'd rather be just as I am since I'm starting to lose my privacy. I even have to go out of my way to have a good time."

Bonnie, above all, considers herself a fluke because although she's so political, she's still in demand. According to her, most of the revolutionary folk/blues artists are never heard of since they refuse to go commercial or because they all write and sing like a "shitty Dylan." "But my politics," Bonnie explained, "is how I deal with everyone as a person, not which organization I belong to or write checks out for. It's putting old blues musicians on my bill because they need the work. Big blues stars have a right to play their music like anybody else, but they don't have the right to take so much money when other blues musicians are starving. Having them with me is education; it shows audiences the real thing still exists."

Though Bonnie says she understands other artists' lack of social/political responsibility, she doesn't forgive it. "The public expects you to play a role and often literally kill yourself for them. So it's either destroy yourself or withdraw. I was raised with a political outlook to know better, but people like Dylan and James Taylor just withdrew. I'm not planning to let it happen to me, and I guess that sets me apart."

# Who Is Bruce Springsteen and Why Are We Saying All These Wonderful Things About Him?

*by Peter Knobler, with Greg Mitchell*

*March 1973*

*We first heard Springsteen in Sing Sing prison. It was in late 1972. Bruce had recorded his first album but it hadn't yet been released, and his manager saw a gig at Sing Sing as a great publicity gimmick. He said this kid was a combination of Bob Dylan, Chuck Berry, and Shakespeare, so we figured, hey, what's to lose? (We were always suckers for a "new Dylan" and the riot at Attica was fresh in the mind.) Turns out we were the only editors in New York who bit. Bruce and the band played in the prison chapel. The sound system stunk. In the middle of an R&B song, a short, squat, bald black guy with bunched muscles came rumbling down the aisle like the law was still after him. He got past the guard, hit the stage at a gallop, reached into his shirt, and pulled out . . . an alto sax! And he was great! There was a roar that could start engines and bend steel. Then, silence. Like the oxygen was cut off. Like cyanide. The inmate finished the number and returned to his seat. A few guys patted him on the ass. Bruce approached the mike and said, "When this is over you can all go home!" What follows is the first article ever written about the future Boss.*

Two months ago I was living under a sorry illusion. Jaded, sick to death of imitations and nostalgia, I figured rock and roll had priced itself out of its own salvation. Artists & Repertoire men were combing the coffeehouses and cellars of the country like major league scouts, offering bonus baby bribes to anyone within four octaves of the big time. No one, my reasoning went, could possibly mature *be-*

*fore* being discovered and *absolutely* no one could ignore his own hype and do it afterwards. There were no transcendent phenoms coming out of hideaway woodsheds.

It turns out I was wrong.

Bruce Springsteen (double *e;* it's originally a Dutch name) has been hiding in New Jersey writing these incredible songs. He's twenty-three, has spent the last eight or nine years playing in rock and roll bands, and sings with a freshness and urgency I haven't heard since I was rocked by "Like A Rolling Stone." His phrasing is as weird, laconic, and twisted as his words, borrowing liberally from acknowledged masters Dylan, Van Morrison, and The Band. He wears his influences on his sleeve—he can be easily dismissed as "just another Dylan rip-off" if you're not really listening—but increasingly, as he begins a road he knows has done in fellow travelers, he is his own man.

Springsteen tosses words around like marrow in a meat shop, and if that weren't enough he presides over a band that jolts out his music like anti-aircraft. Let me explain:

It was just a normal Friday night December crowd at New York's Kenny's Castaways. There was no air of great tension, no scent of earthshaking significance about to be loosed. In fact, there were only about thirty people there to see the first show and most of them only came for the atmosphere. Bruce Springsteen was headlining and there weren't a dozen people inside who knew who he was. Outside, on the hand-drawn marquee, they'd misspelled his name.

He arrived onstage in jeans and a beat-up hooded sweatshirt, adjusted the mike to his acoustic guitar, dropped a flat pick, bent to retrieve it, stood up, strummed a bit, and asked out over the audience's head to one friend at the back, "How long have I been up here?" Hardly an auspicious opening.

But when he began to sing it was like the ocean had calmed out and you knew a storm was brewing by the way it prickled your skin.

> *Circus boy dances like a monkey on barbed wire,* he sang.
> *The barker romances with a junkie, she's got a flat tire.*

His voice growled lines after they'd been sung, making them sinister, mysterious, and somehow necessary.

> *The elephants dance real funky*
> *And the band plays like a jungle fire*
> *Circus town's on the live wire.*

Phrases, images, and sounds flew by. Lines were fleeting; you got glimpses of them where full stares, gapes were required. They passed once—these were completely new songs—and left their mark.

His eyebrows rose and shifted like waves with each line. His hair, cut short, curled vaguely and his beard was hardly filled in. No doubt about it, he looked like Dylan. If the passion hadn't been so genuine, this might have been a problem. He moved from a howl to a whisper in an instant and caught the crowd unawares. His voice made words into sounds, and then reconverted sounds to sense. He gulped and spat syllables, and the song ended like a tide receding, the applause chasing after like beach rain.

Bruce Springsteen's songs offer that wonderfully bewildering problem of how to keep up. Words tumble over one another, phrases mysteriously *feel* right and then disappear. There was no way, sitting there without warning in the middle of the wash, that I could even begin to define what his power was. This was an entirely new perspective offered, like nothing I'd heard before. There was no given, no center I knew all these spokes were connected to. I was once again on my own with new eyes, and it was exhilarating!

A song ended, but not for Springsteen. The stage was cluttered with equipment, and while Bruce switched the guitar mike to the piano stand he absently hummed a verse he had just sung, like a carpenter amusing himself while sawing. The tune had not finished its moment with him and he just kept humming.

When he's playing alone, Springsteen carries himself onstage with a rather humorous reserve. He'll say what he's thinking ("Got to get these wires out off the keyboard," or "How do those words go?") and talk to the crowd like acquaintances. Not quite friends, but beyond strangers. He is easily amused, listens to his own words, and even laughs or smiles at a good line. His material was, and continues to be, so new that he seemed to be hearing much of it for the first time. I'd never seen a performer more in touch with his songs.

> In how many wasted have I seen the sign
> "Hollywood or Bust"
> Or, left to ride those ever-ghostly Arizona gusts,
> Cheerleader tramps and
> Kids with big amps
> sounding helpless in the void
> High-society vamps
> And ex-heavyweight champs
> mistaking soot for soil.

He had stilled the place.

"All right, let's bring up the band!"

Stepping out of the calm, he clapped his hands together and rubbed his palms like a greedy coach at game time. Out of the crowd stepped four guys, and as they took the half-step onto the stage, he took attendance, strapped on a wood Fender cutaway, and diddled some impatient, cut-crystal blues riffs.

The band consisted of bass, drums, organ, and sax, and as they casually tuned there was a different air to Springsteen's presence. Where he had bent over his acoustic guitar he leaned back from his electric. It was slung low and hung from his shoulder as from a gun-slinger's hip. There was a measure of comfort, almost a psychic opulence, to the way he found his form. He was digging it, and he got cockier for its power.

The band slammed into the song like downfield blockers and what had seemed at first a "folk" night burst into flaming rock and roll.

> *Madman drummers bummers and Indians in the summer*
> *with a teenage diplomat*
> *In the dumps with the mumps as the adolescent pumps*
> *his way into his hat.*

Springsteen's eyebrows arched again, this time from force as he leaned up and into the microphone, placed only a little too high. A shoulder up to the band and another angled to the audience, Springsteen tipped the music toward the crowd and it poured in a torrent. It was hard to believe he was that good; but that, it turned out, was just for starters.

His voice flew between Van Morrison and Dylan, but imitation was out of the question. There was influence all right—undenied and rather unconcealed—but the tone was coming out Springsteen.

The song built, words thick and fast but now even more difficult to pin down above the roar of the electricity. It was catch as catch can, and the odd catch was a prize. I hadn't felt this kind of intelligent/lunatic intensity since *Blonde on Blonde*. The thought immediately made me self-conscious, but the more I thought about it the more I liked it. Then I started to grin. I went home beaming.

I woke up the next morning and snatches of song hung from me as by static electricity. I hummed phrases I didn't know I knew, riffs that seemed like they'd always been there. You know the kid is good when you wake up and you're singing his songs—and you've only heard them once!

• • •

WHERE DID HE COME FROM? WHERE HAS HE BEEN?

He was signed to Columbia Records by John Hammond Sr., noted for a similar decision ten years ago; Columbia President Clive Davis called to wish him a Merry Christmas; he hasn't got a decent record player; and he is still flattered that people like his stuff.

Bruce Springsteen was brought up Catholic in Freehold, New Jersey. (His songs show the influence of parochial school and a sinner's familiarity with the Church.) He first picked up the guitar at age nine. "I saw Elvis Presley on TV and knew that that, for me, was where it was at. I went down, got a guitar, started taking guitar lessons. But my hand was too small to get into it. Plus, guitar lessons at that time were like a coma, buzzing on the B string. I *knew* that wasn't the way Elvis Presley did it."

We sat in Bruce's newly rented apartment ("the first one of my own") in Bradley Beach, New Jersey. The place had the disheveled, lived-in look of a million off-campus spots, but it was home and, for Bruce, almost the first luxury. His phonograph was a Longines Symphonette, the kind you get free from record clubs.

"Nothing hit me until I was about fourteen," Bruce said. "And when it did, it hit me completely, took over my whole life. Everything from then on revolved around music. Everything."

From the time he learned to play, Bruce has been in one band or another. At sixteen he was commuting to Greenwich Village nightly to play guitar in a group at the Cafe Wha? "I was *ready*," he laughed. "It's like when you're a kid . . ." He stopped and added, "Well, I'm still a kid, but when you're younger, you know, you've got this incredible idealistic enthusiasm. And I was always popular in my little area, and at the time it was something I needed very badly, because I didn't have anything else. So I wanted to be as big as you could make it—the Beatles, Rolling Stones. I went to New York and I learned earlier than most people you had to write your own material."

With a six-month background in folk music and an overriding interest in R&B, he spent most of the next eight years putting bands together. He fronted a group called Steel Mill ("a Humble Pie–type band") and got fairly popular for a while, and fairly well paid. He has clippings of him with shoulder-length hair screaming like a maniac on a rave-up.

Steel Mill lasted a couple of years, "when I was eighteen-nineteen. Then came Dr. Zoom and the Sonic Boom where we had everybody I knew that could play an instrument . . . and some that couldn't!"

The sax player, for instance, served essentially as a percussionist, and they set up a Monopoly board on a table in the middle of the stage for no apparent reason.

"That lasted two or three gigs. Then there was the big band, which was my band," the first he alone put together. He speaks of it rather proudly, if incredulously. "I gave it my name. A ten-piece band when I was around twenty." Vini Lopez and Danny Federici, who now play drums and organ respectively with him, were also in the ten-piece. "That one lasted for about two years, then it slowly dwindled from ten to seven to five. Then, about a year ago, I started to play by myself." He was pretty well broke. His parents had moved to the West Coast when he was seventeen, and he'd been evicted from the house he'd grown up in a month later. Living in a surf-board factory, he got good and depressed and "just started writing lyrics, which I never did before. I would just get a good riff, and as long as it wasn't too obtuse I'd sing it. So I started to go by myself and started to write those songs."

A friend introduced Bruce to Mike Appel and Jim Cretecos, whose claim to fame to that point had been responsibility for writing the Partridge Family's million-seller, "Doesn't Somebody Want To Be Wanted," among others. Appel and Cretecos were astounded, and encouraged Springsteen to write more. He did. Sometimes he finished three songs a week.

"Last winter I wrote like a madman. Put it out. Had no money, nowhere to go, nothing to do. Didn't know too many people. It was cold and I wrote a lot. And I got to feeling very guilty if I didn't," he explained. "Terrible guilt feelings. Like it was masturbation." He laughed a liberated Catholic school laugh. "That bad!"

Appel and Cretecos gave him New York transfusions of encouragement and it worked. Three weeks after he signed to be managed by them he was in John Hammond's office.

Mike Appel is what you might call a fast talker. In one breath he can and has compared Bruce Springsteen to Wordsworth, Dylan, Keats, Byron, and Shakespeare. On the other hand, he knows how to get through doors.


JOHN HAMMOND'S OFFICE IS A FIVE-BY-TEN-FOOT CUBICLE ON THE eleventh floor of the CBS building. It is cluttered and jumbled and as good as you can do to unconsciously disrupt the well-documented aridity of a corporate spread. A stand-up piano is tucked into one corner, a tape deck in another.

Hammond himself is a friendly man, with an enthusiasm for

Springsteen that, when I entered, was both unleashed and infectious.

"He walked into my office," he recalled. "He was *led* into my office! My secretary made the appointment. She said, 'I think you might do this—he came on very strong.' Mike Appel, the note said. I said okay, I have fifteen minutes.

"Bruce, who looked marvelously beat, was sitting over there." Hammond gestured to a chair tucked away in the far corner. "And so Mike started yakking. He said, I want you to know that we're just, you know, being nice to you because you're the guy who discovered Dylan and we just wanted to find out if that was luck or whether you really have ears.

"So I said, 'Stop, you're making me hate you!' He laughed incredulously. "Bruce was very quiet, sort of grinning over there in the corner. He told me he played both guitar and piano, and I said well you want to get your guitar out? He said, sure. And he started. I think the first song he played was 'Saint in the City.' And I . . ." He recreated his wonder. "You know, I couldn't believe it!

"So then I started to talk. I said to him, have you ever worked as a single? He said no. Well, two hours later, by this time it was a little after one, I had set up a performance for him at the Gaslight. By this time he'd played some more songs, and I was just convinced that he really *was* . . . Just 'cause he was so unassuming and so right. Everything he did.

"I ran and got some other people down the hall here and they all kinda liked him. The initial reaction was, well he looks so much like Dylan, he's a copy of him. But he's not. I mean not even remotely. You see, when Bobby came to me, he was Bobby Zimmerman. He said he was Bob Dylan; he had created all this mystique. Bruce is Bruce Springsteen. And he's much further along, much more developed than Bobby was when he came to me.

"So I went straight to Clive on this. You know, I've brought in a few stiffs as well as some good people to Columbia. Well, Clive just had to check around a bit," he chuckled, remembering the scene, "but Clive loved what he heard on the tape. He said, 'You know, John, he's very amusing, isn't he?' I said, 'Yeah,' I said. 'He's more than that, Clive,' I said. 'He's fantastic?' "

BRUCE SPRINGSTEEN'S RECORD IS *GREETINGS FROM ASBURY PARK*, AND it's a delight. Completed last September, it offers a picture of the performer/creator as he was stepping out of one sense into another.

"It's definitely a first album," says Bruce. "And it shows how the band came into being; there's some by myself, then there's some with a small band, and there's some which is pretty much where the band is now, which is 'Spirit In the Night' and 'Blinded by the Light.' "

The album takes its toll on your time. One day one song reigns, demanding attention like the brightest kid in class; the next day, another. There hasn't been an album like this in ages, where there are words to play with, to riff off yourself, to pull out of the air and slap down with a gleam on the shiny counter of your conversation. There are individual lines worth entire records. The record rocks, then glides, then rocks again. There is the combined sensibility of the chaser and the chaste, the street punk and the bookworm.

It is not perfect, of course. Springsteen was originally signed as an acoustic act, a folksinger. ("I told them I'd been playing in bands for eight years and by myself for two-three months. They forgot about the eight years and went with the two months.") The album, as a result, was originally planned as basically acoustic. Bruce plays excellent electric guitar, but nobody knew that until the sessions were almost complete, and the record loses some power for it. Bruce's vocals are quirkier now too, as his style has developed. The production is a bit muddy and leaves something to be desired, and by the time the sessions were almost finished Bruce had written a dozen new songs and grown beyond some of the old ones.

The band is plenty turned up now. Garry Tallent was added on bass and Clarence Clemons on sax, and the group fairly steams with fresh energy. They are tight and growing tighter.

At Kenny's Castaways, at The Main Point coffeehouse near Philadelphia, in rehearsal in an old, unheated garage, we heard Bruce play more than two dozen songs, only six of which were on his album (the record has nine in all). The *next* album should be unbelievable! "That's why I like the band," Bruce said with pleasure. "We get into those great funky riffs, that Gary U.S. Bonds stuff that is lost forever in the annals of time." He snickered at his radio diction. "You can get into that groove, get it *there,* and sing weird words to it too!"

Bruce Springsteen laughs easily. He's like the new boy in town and seems genuinely unaware of the temptation to treat him like a Man of Importance, perhaps because that's not the way he sees himself. He's writing continuously. Two days before I visited a rehearsal, he'd cooked up "Kitty's Back," a song with claws. He finished an epic South of the Border number *between sets* at a club one night. He is like a man undammed: prolific and unpolluted. At twenty-three he stands perceptively between childhood and worldly wisdom. "This is the songwriterpoet as innocent," he announced before one song;

"And now the songwriterpoet as pervert" before another. Both times it got a laugh.

"I'M AT A PLACE NOW WHERE I'M FLATTERED." THE KITCHEN TABLE HAD been cleared after dinner and he sat picking his new guitar (one of the few uses to which he's put his advance money). "I'm flattered and I'm happy that people would take an interest, you know? You have to watch out, though. You don't want to get too self-centered. It's easy to do, you know, because people are always shovin' *you* in your face."

But it's only just begun for him. He'd never been interviewed before, the openness a delight.

"My songs are very mysterious to me, in a way. It's good if I can look back on a song and be excited by it, then I know it's good. You know when you've written a good song, too, because it's there in your room, before you even go out into the living room and sing it there. Right there when you finish it, you know, then it's a good song, then it excites you.

"Like that line in 'Spirit in the Night' . . ." He skimmed verbally through the tune as if scanning it looking for a spot. " '. . . take you all out to gypsy angel row . . . They're built like light.' It's like that, you know. 'They're built like light and dance like spirits in the night.' That's what it is to me, that's the essence of all the songs to me. Built like light, to be run through . . ."

He had stopped picking, and he looked up and smiled. "It's exciting to me! It's very weird, you know. I'm happy and the music is exciting to me." He looked for an explanation, his eyes glazing over for a moment. "It's like I'll write a song and I'll think back on some of the lines, and they get me off!" He was so pleased a grin almost shone. "As an observer, you know.

" 'Cause in my mind, my mind was thinking 'hmmm, need something to rhyme with night, need something to rhyme with . . . all night.' And it works like that; it focuses it in. 'Well, you got the universe to think about but you need something that rhymes with night!' " We exploded with laughter and he chortled, "So that narrows it down a bit, and out it'll come. And that's how I write!"

"You're going to get confronted with the Dylan image sooner or later," I said. "How can you deal with that?"

"I don't know," he answered. He's already been tagged a "new Dylan" and it's an uncomfortable harness. "I don't like it and it's hard to live with," he said. "I mean, I resent it when *I* hear it about anyone.

"I love Dylan!" he laughed. "What can you say? I think Dylan is great. I listen to all his records. It's *the* greatest music ever written, to me. The man says it all, exactly the right way. Incredibly powerful. You don't get no more intense. Such a great instrumental sound. And he was . . ." He searched for an exact description. "He was Bob Dylan, you know?

"But it's like a map. You gotta read a map. You just can't go off in the middle of the woods and go off in the right direction. You don't, so you've gotta look. You've gotta say, I dig the way this cat's doing it; I want to do it like that, but . . ." He glided his hand out on an arc to the left, ". . . like this.

"I go onstage and feel myself. And I'm not worrying about, 'oh, man, that note sounds like this dude. Hey man, I heard that word off of "Subterranean Homesick Blues"!' " He laughed and shook his head. "At one time it worried me but it doesn't anymore, because when I get onstage finally I feel myself. That's who I am."

"Your vocal style changes from acoustic to electric sets," I mentioned. In fact, when he's alone with his guitar he is at once supple and bristly. It has the effect of soothing by scraping, leaving a rough edge smoothed.

"I got a thing which is like percussion-on-voice." He punctuated the words and we laughed at the demonstration. "It's a different style of singing than with the band; it's based on little voice cracks and little, like, percussion things. For instance:

> *Oh, when the night grew fear*
> *and the jungle grew near*
> *It was so dark I couldn't talk at all*
>
> *I was a hunter in the midst*
> *of civilization*
> *In some bombed-out music hall.*
>
> *There was some . . . funky junk on the jukebox*
> *But I didn't know how to turn it on.*
>
> *There were some dudes at the door givin' trouble*
> *There was a lady at the bar giving hope . . .*

He laughed at the phrasing. "It's an Adam's apple trip," he chuckled.

• • •

BRUCE SPRINGSTEEN DOESN'T KNOW HOW GOOD HE IS. PEOPLE ARE only just now beginning to tell him. Clive Davis called to wish him a Merry Christmas and he didn't know that was unheard of. People continue to be floored when they see him play and he still says "Really?" That can't last. But he's writing prolifically, as if there's no other way. It's an exciting thing to see happen. Even his mother is having a hard time believing it.

"I called her and told her, 'Hey I signed a record contract!'

" 'Oh yeah?' she said. 'What did you change your name to?' "

# Disco Dreams

*by Mark Jacobson*

*April 1975*

*Before disco sucked, before it got to Studio 54 and "Dance Fever's" Denny Terrio, it was all the rage in the edgy clubs. Just as it was going mainstream* Crawdaddy *sent Mark Jacobson (now a successful novelist) to profile the scene that would be immortalized a couple of years later in* Saturday Night Fever.

Tony Bongiovi is checking the readings on the gyros and altimeters of his Mooney Mini Airplane as he taxis across the frozen tundra of the Solberg Airport. Tony loves to be at the controls; he's very much into knobs and needles. Next to the exotic blinkers and dials on the mixing boards he builds, Tony likes airplane controls best. Only twenty-six now, he's been flying more than eight years. At first it was the fabulous sense of freedom flying gave him that prompted Tony to scrape together the $32,000 the Mooney Mini costs. But now the plane more than pays for itself as an integral cog in the financial empire Tony is setting up.

"I could move away from here," Tony says, as he waves his arms around the empty sky above Somerville, New Jersey, the outlands suburb where he grew up and still lives with his parents, "but I never will, because out here is where a record really makes it or breaks it. Right now the people out here never even heard of discotheque. There aren't any discos out here yet. They can only hear WABC. They don't even know 'Never Can Say Goodbye' came from the discos. But come back in a year or so and ask people about discotheques, they'll know all about them."

When the people in Somerville do start going to the discotheques that are sure to start opening out on Route 22, perhaps some of them will remember Tony Bongiovi as the little guy with the soulful brown eyes who built crystal radios all the time and used to carry his semihomemade tape machine to the school dances. But without a doubt, they'll be hearing his music, because Tony Bongiovi and his "little record company," DCA Productions, have based their considerable future on the mushrooming disco scene. And so far, they're doing all right; DCA, in business less than a year and a half, not even long enough to set up distribution of their own label, has already produced three national hits: Gloria Gaynor's "Honey Bee" and "Never Can Say Goodbye," and Carol Douglas's "Doctor's Orders." Gloria Gaynor's first album, *Never Can Say Goodbye,* the first DCA has done, is shaping up as a major smash.

It's not completely unheard of for a small independent company to start off with a string of hits, and it's certainly not unusual to hear the company executives boast they'll be "as big as Motown in three, well, maybe four years," as Tony and his partners Jay Ellis and Meco Monardo continually do. What is unusual is the way DCA is going about it. They produce records almost exclusively intended to be played in discotheques, and they promote these records almost completely in the discos. It's turning out to be a sound policy, because in today's record market, a tune that makes it big in the dance halls pretty much has things its own way on the radio and the national charts.

A couple of years ago, the thought of going to a disco, much less using them as a base to make another Motown, seemed ridiculous. Discotheques? That's where Sybil Burton hung out with her jet-set pals, after Richard dumped her, so Eugenia Shepard could check out their newest St. Laurent purchases. Discos were snot-city—haughty, useless places, homes for the atrophied mind. After they fell out of fashion, they became seedy nightclubs that were too cheap to hire live bands. But that was before New York black and gay people, two embattled cultures, adopted the forlorn dance halls and transformed them into the most dynamic form of entertainment since Hendrix set his guitar on fire. The clotheshorses were out; the new scene was all kinky eight-inch platforms, luminous makeup, and outrageous sexuality. It soon became clear that these discos, which were quickly renamed "par-r-rties," were for, as The Jackson 5 say, "Dancing, dancing, dancing machines!" And madness ensued.

The New York disco scene from early 1971 to about the middle of 1974 was a true underground society and art form. The gays, long locked away in their bars, sought situations where they could party a little more frantically. Black popular music suited their purpose, and that interested uptown blacks who were seeking to escape depressing neighborhoods. An odd and tenuous alliance between the two groups was formed, and a whole secret culture born.

Most discos rocked in factory lofts or abandoned restaurants. It was not unusual to drive down a deserted warehouse district street at four in the morning and encounter triple-parked cars. Many places established themselves as "private" clubs that allowed only members, naturally making them more desirable. Clubs were christened ephemeral and mysterious names like Liquid Smoke, The Cobra, The Jungle, and Sanctuary. It was the complete opposite of the white-hippie sun-drenched spectacle form of entertainment that culminated with mass events like Woodstock and Altamount. This was entertainment for the shadows; it was urban, rock hard, and very primal. The head beatings of the Woodstock era weren't necessary lessons for blacks and gays; they knew all along—the only way to really have a party was behind closed doors, away from prying and disapproving eyes.

Inside those portals, a whole new method of record playing itself evolved. Two turntables were used so the operator, the deejay, who was to become a major conceptual artist of the '70s, could blend one record into another and the music would never stop. It was continuous and absolute mind blitzing, no time to think, complete stimuli reaction. The sound systems were incredible—loud, brassy, and at the command of the all-powerful deejay. He arranged the music, culled from the glut of available records, into spiraling "sets" that "climaxed" in especially intense songs. The deejay ordered the "climaxes" in any way he wanted, with whatever records turned him on. His only responsibility was to the dancers, to get them off. That was his art, and the whole idea of the underground disco.

The Loft, which opened its narrow factory doorway on Lower Broadway in New York every Saturday, and only Saturday (and only after midnight), was the greatest of the underground discos. David Mancuso, who lived in and owned the second-story loft, really knew how to throw a party. If you were lucky enough to get past the Cerebus-like guardians of the door, you found a city-life heaven inside. Every imaginable ethnic and social group made the scene. People who would scare the shit out of you on the subway; people who would make you laugh yourself silly on the subway—they were all there dancing like crazy to the same music, and smiling. Shaven-headed black guys with fearsome dispositions. Skinny women wearing big hats. Mad glitter goddesses. Even guys wearing suits. It was a million different trips pulsating to the same beat. And it was fantastic, the most religious experience you could probably ever have in a garment factory. David, who doubled as deejay, sat in his booth reveling in what he had wrought. Every Saturday night he was a guru, and even his toughest patrons spoke of him in hushed and respectful tones.

Perhaps it was all a little too quicksilver to survive. As the legend of the place grew, ugly scenes happened at the door, and the dance floor became insanely cramped. The neighbors, nervous about the bulging ceilings in their apartments, complained and had the place shut down. There was some hope David might reopen elsewhere, but he hasn't. The closing of The Loft and several similar places took most of the soul out of the underground disco scene.

Several salient facts remained, however. For one, the discos are very practical depression entertainment. The arithmetic is simple: The concert and club scenes were dead. The artists, their heads swelled from constant hype and enormous gate receipts in the late '60s and early '70s, had priced themselves out of the market. With most major groups insisting on huge guarantees, promoters had to rent the largest buildings in order to make any kind of a profit. It was all becoming a big hassle. It became apparent that a smart promoter could open and run a discotheque for a year's time with about the same capital it took to put on two or three major concerts. Disco expenses are small. Even the most lavish ones cost well under $100,000 to open. The underground ones started with less than $25,000. Operating expenses, with no performers to pay, are minuscule. Until recently, the deejays' average pay was thirty-five dollars a night. And they bring the records.

Attracting customers is no problem. People with pinched pocketbooks are no longer blindly willing to plunk down ten or fifteen dollars to see a group in concert. Discos usually cost less than five dollars. And the party doesn't stop after forty-five minutes; it goes on all night. No singing group ever has a bad night; you hear only their very best records. After you find a deejay whose conception of the current music fits yours, you've found an excellent way to party through the hard times. It all makes sense, for everybody.

Another, slightly more subtle, salient disco fact is that the dance halls are shaking up the record charts and radio playlists. A few years ago, when an odd, but arresting, record called "Soul Makossa" appeared on the radio surveys, there was some talk that it was discovered by a deejay in a discotheque. There was a story about it in the trades but it was promptly dismissed as a fluke. Early last year, a few more records trickled out of "nowhere" onto the charts, among them Barry White's "Love's Theme" and a Latin tune called "Corazon." Both songs reached the top ten. And some industry people started asking questions.

Then came the blitz. The Hues Corporation's "Rock The Boat," a song that ended up number one for the year on WABC, and George McCrae's "Rock Your Baby" broke on the scene and dominated the charts for months. Now everybody was asking questions. The answer was: a disco deejay at one of the underground clubs had picked up "Rock The Boat," a single RCA was letting mold on record store shelves, and played it at his club. Everyone liked it, including the other deejays, and soon it became a "climax" tune in every disco in the city. Dancers came up to ask what was the name of *that song*, and started buying it. Fifteen thousand copies of the tune were sold without a peep of airplay, and a new way of breaking hit records was discovered.

The trades ran the story, and the rush that eventually killed the underground discos was on. Record companies who had laughed at the disco deejays when they asked for promotional records were frantically scurrying to get lists of the most important clubs in town. WPIX, a station that had been playing Golden Oldies, started a disco style of radio programming. Groups with names like Disco-Tex and the Sex-olettes appeared. The discos themselves began to change. Sensing big money, several places began to advertise, something that was anathema to the underground clubs. As the word of the scene surfaced, suburban promoters, mindful of the inescapable disco economics, started to open clubs in Long Island and Westchester. Now, New York–style discos are opening all over the country.

Tom Moultin, who writes a "Disco Action" column for *Billboard*, the most powerful of trade papers (which has just instituted a chart that maps the most popular disco records), says, "This is really only the beginning. The discos are far from reaching their peak commercially. Record companies are realizing that discos are very good places to break records. The response is immediate. You can tell right away if the people like it or not. Everyone is hoping that the discos pick up on their sound."

THAT'S WHERE TONY BONGIOVI AND DCA PRODUCTIONS COME IN. The discos have picked up on their sound. "Never Can Say Goodbye" was broken right out of the discos. So was "Doctor's Orders."

This didn't happen by chance, the way disco hits were made in the past. DCA planned and orchestrated the whole thing. They release their tunes to a few key discos and wait for the action; when it happens, that's when they make their major radio and sales promotion. "Never Can Say Goodbye" was number one in the discos for over a month before it appeared on the charts. Only after it had died in the clubs was it number six with a bullet.

Right now Tony is at the controls of the massive thirty-two track at Media Sound on 57th Street putting together what DCA hopes will be the next sound to break out of the discos for them, a ditty called "Dance, Dance, Dance." Sitting behind the metallic expanse of needles and knobs, Tony looks like an Italian munchkin driving a rocket ship. He pushes buttons and slides levers furiously. He says there's no doubt that "Dance, Dance, Dance" will be a hit. No reason why it shouldn't, it sounds exactly like "Doctor's Orders" and "Never Can Say Goodbye." The beat is a shuffle, insistent and unchanging. The drumming is all high-hatting and chatty. There are no separate riffs, no sense of dynamics from the rhythm section; it just all rolls on like a loop. But it sounds *up*, infectious, almost like a carnival tune. The repetitions work; they make it danceable. And that's all that matters. "The only thing I think of when I make a disco tune is whether people will dance to it. If they won't dance, I wasted my time," Tony says.

It's stuff like "Dance, Dance, Dance" that will come to mind when we try to remember what 1970s dance music sounded like thirty years from now. Until recently, most white people believed that all music made by black people was good to dance to. It didn't matter what the *intention* of the song was, if it was black and not a ballad, it was ass-shaking music. But now, the discos, with their absolute emphasis on dance music, are establishing much more specific criteria. Songs full of what used to be called "soul" (of the hard-bopping blues-influenced Otis Redding–Wilson Pickett variety) are rarely heard in the discos. The emphasis on singing in those tunes slows down the dancing. Disco songs tend to have much more "music" than the typical R&B song. They hardly ever center on a singer, or "star," thereby producing a far more dispersed sound.

Singers who have been popular in the discos, like Eddie Kendricks, generally tend to use their voices as an instrument in the overall ensemble sound, rather than trying to "front" the song. Much of this has to do with the gay influence, which has smoothed out much of the growling masculinity of the soul numbers. Baroque strings and gliding horns, elements alien to more traditional black music, have become disco staples. With larger productions and restrained singing, the tunes are beginning to lose their individuality. Disco record producers like Tony realize they're making records that will be programmed into a flow of other records. They're not necessarily trying to make tunes that will stand out from the rest, but rather ones that fit comfortably into a pattern. Got to keep it in the groove; most disco-goers spend five or six hours a night dancing, so each tune can't be a "climax."

Before "Dance, Dance, Dance" is finished, Tony and arranger/producer Meco plan to add some extra "happiness" to it by laying a track of "people having a good time" over the music. It's a common disco convention. "The world is a drag these days," Tony says. "People need these kind of songs. I'll never make a depressing disco record. That would be crazy. Who wants all these messages? I don't want anyone coming over to me saying, 'Oh, man, wow, that was heavy.' I want them to say, 'Hey, man, that was *clever*.' "

# Led Zeppelin
# Meets Naked Lunch

---

*by William Burroughs*
*June 1975*

*What did lead guitarist Jimmy Page and Beat novelist William Burroughs (a longtime* Crawdaddy *columnist) have in common? As it turned out, quite a bit: magic, trance music, and Aleister Crowley, among other things. In Burrough's Soho loft, within steps of the writer's orgone box, they discussed a literal stairway to heaven.*

When I was first asked to write an article on the Led Zeppelin group, to be based on attending a concert and talking with Jimmy Page, I was not sure I could do it, not being sufficiently knowledgeable about music to attempt anything in the way of musical criticism or even evaluation. I decided simply to attend the concert and talk with Jimmy Page and let the article develop. If you consider any set of data without a preconceived viewpoint, then a viewpoint will emerge from the data.

My first impression was of the audience, as we streamed through one security line after another—a river of youth looking curiously like a single organism: one well-behaved clean-looking middle-class kid. The security guards seemed to be cool and well trained, ushering gate-crashers out with a minimum of fuss. We were channeled smoothly into our seats in the thirteenth row. Over a relaxed dinner before the concert, a *Crawdaddy* companion had said he had a feeling that something bad could happen at this concert. I pointed out that it always can when you get that many people together—like bullfights where you buy a straw hat at the door to protect you from bottles and other missiles. I was displacing possible danger to a Mexican border town where the matador barely escaped with his life and several spectators were killed. It's known as "clearing the path."

So there we sat. I decline earplugs; I am used to loud drum and horn music from Morocco, and it always has, if skillfully performed, an exhilarating and energizing effect on me. As the performance got underway I experienced this musical exhilaration, which was all the more pleasant for being easily controlled, and I knew then that nothing bad was going to happen. This was a safe, friendly area—but at the same time highly charged. There was a palpable interchange of energy between the performers and the audience that was never frantic or jagged. The special effects were handled well and not overdone.

A few special effects are much better than too many. I can see the laser beams cutting dry ice smoke, which drew an appreciative cheer from the audience. Jimmy Page's number with the broken guitar strings came across with a real impact, as did John Bonham's drum solo and the lyrics delivered with unfailing vitality by Robert Plant. The performers were doing their best, and it was very good. The last number, "Stairway to Heaven," where the audience all lit matches and there was a scattering of sparklers here and there, found the audience well behaved and joyous, creating the atmosphere of a high school Christmas play. All in all a good show; neither low nor insipid. Leaving the concert hall was like getting off a jet plane.

I summarized my impressions after the concert in a few notes to serve as a basis for my talk with Jimmy Page: "The essential ingredient for any successful rock group is energy—the ability to give out energy, to receive energy from the audience, and to give it back to the audience. A rock concert is in fact a rite involving the evocation and transmutation of energy. Rock stars may be compared to priests, a theme that was treated in Peter Watkins' film *Privilege*. In that film a rock star was manipulated by reactionary forces to set up a state religion; this scenario seems unlikely. I think a rock group singing political slogans would leave its audience at the door.

"The Led Zeppelin show depends heavily on volume, repetition, and drums. It bears some resemblance to the trance music found in Morocco, which is magical in origin and purpose—that is, concerned with the evocation and control of spiritual forces. In Morocco, musicians are also magicians. Gnaoua music is used to drive out evil spirits. The music of Joujouka evokes the God Pan, Pan God of Panic, representing the real magical forces that sweep away the spurious. It is to be remembered that the origin of all the arts—music, painting, and writing—is magical and evocative; and that magic is always used to obtain some definite result. In the Led Zeppelin concert, the result aimed at would seem to be the creation of energy in the performers and in the audience. For such magic to succeed, it must tap the sources of magical energy, and this can be dangerous."

I FELT THAT THESE CONSIDERATIONS COULD FORM THE BASIS OF MY TALK with Jimmy Page, which I hoped would not take the form of an interview. There is something just basically wrong about the whole interview format. Someone sticks a mike in your face and says, "Mr. Page, would you care to talk about your interest in occult practices? Would you describe yourself as a believer in this sort of thing?" Even an intelligent mike-in-the-face question tends to evoke a guarded mike-in-the-face answer. As soon as Jimmy Page walked into my loft downtown, I saw that it wasn't going to be that way.

We started talking over a cup of tea and found we have friends in common: the real estate agent who negotiated Jimmy Page's purchase of the Aleister Crowley house on Loch Ness; John Michel, the flying saucer and pyramid expert; Donald Cammell, who worked on *Performance;* Kenneth Anger, and the Jaggers, Mick and Chris. The subject of magic came up in connection with Aleister Crowley and Kenneth Anger's film *Lucifer Rising,* for which Jimmy Page did the sound track.

Since the word *magic* tends to cause confused thinking, I would like to say exactly what I mean by *magic* and the magical interpretation of so-called reality. The underlying assumption of magic is the assertion of *will* as the primary moving force in this universe—the deep conviction that nothing happens unless somebody or some being wills it to happen. To me this has always seemed self-evident. A chair does not move unless someone moves it. Neither does your physical body, which is composed of much the same materials, move unless you will it to move. Walking across the room is a magical operation. From the viewpoint of magic, no death, no illness, no misfortune, accident, war, or riot is accidental. There are no accidents in the world of magic. And *will* is another word for animate energy. Rock stars are juggling fissionable material that could blow up at any time . . . "The soccer scores are coming in from the Capital . . . one must pretend an interest," drawled the dandified Commandante, safe in the pages of my book; and as another rock star said to me, "*You* sit on your ass writing—I could be torn to pieces by my fans, like Orpheus."

I found Jimmy Page equally aware of the risks involved in handling the fissionable material of the mass unconscious. So over dinner at Mexican Gardens, I told him the story of the big soccer riot in Lima, Peru, in 1964.

We are ushered into the arena as VIPs, in the style made famous by *Triumph of the Will*. Martial music—long vistas—the statuesque police with their dogs on leads—the crowd surging in a sultry menacing electricity palpable in the air—grey clouds over Lima—people glance up uneasily . . . the last time it rained in Lima was the year of the great earthquake, when whole towns were swallowed by landslides. A cop is beating and kicking someone as he shoves him back towards the exit. Oh lucky man. The dogs growl ominously. The game is tense. Tied until the end of the last quarter, and then the stunning decision: A goal that would have won the game for Peru is disqualified by the Uruguayan referee. A howl of rage from the crowd, and then a huge black known as La Bomba, who has started three previous soccer riots and already has twenty-three notches on his bomb, vaults down into the arena. A wave of fans follows The Bomb—the Uruguayan referee scrambles off with the agility of a rat or an evil spirit—the police release tear gas and unleash their snarling dogs, hysterical with fear and rage and maddened by the tear gas. And then a sound like falling mountains, as a few drops of rain begin to fall.

The crowd tears an Alsatian dog to pieces—a policeman is strangled with his tie, another hurled fifty feet down from the top of the stadium . . . bodies piled up ten feet deep at the exits. The soccer scores are coming in from the capital . . . 306 . . . 318 . . . 352 . . . "I didn't know how bad it was until rain started to fall," said a survivor. You see, it never rains in Lima, or almost never, and when it does it's worse than seeing mules foaling in the public street . . . trampled ruptured bodies piled in heaps . . ."

"*You* know, Jimmy," I said: "The crowd surges forward, a heavy piece of equipment falls on the crowd, security goes mad, and then . . . a sound like falling mountains . . ." Jimmy Page did not bat an eye.

"Yes. I've thought about that. We all have. The important thing is maintain a balance. The kids come to get far out with the music. It's our job to see they have a good time and no trouble."

And remember the rock group called Storm? Playing a dance hall in Switzerland . . . fire . . . exits locked . . . thirty-seven people dead including all the performers. Now any performer who has never thought about fire and panic just doesn't think. The best way to keep something bad from happening is to see it ahead of time, and you can't see it if you refuse to face the possibility. The bad vibes in that dance hall must have been really heavy. If the performers had been sensitive and alert, they would have checked to be sure the exits were unlocked.

Previously, over two fingers of whiskey in my Franklin Street digs, I had told Page about Major Bruce MacMannaway, a healer and psychic who lives in Scotland. The major discovered his healing abilities in World War II when his regiment was cut off without medical supplies and the major started laying on his hands . . . "Well Major, I think it it's a load of ballocks but I'll try anything." And it turns out the major is a walking hypo. His psychic abilities were so highly regarded by the Admiralty that he was called in to locate sunken submarines, and he never once missed.

I attended a group meditation seminar with the major. It turned out to be the Indian rope trick. Before the session the major told us something of the potential power in group meditation. He had seen it lift a six-hundred-pound church organ five feet in the air. I had no reason to doubt this, since he was obviously incapable of falsification. In the session, after some preliminary relaxation exercises, the major asked us to see a column of light to a plateau where we met nice friendly people: the stairway to heaven in fact. I mean we were really *there*.

I turned to Jimmy Page: "Of course we are dealing here with meditation—the deliberate induction of a trance state in a few people under the hands of an old master. This would seem on the surface to have little in common with a rock concert, but the underlying force is the same: human energy and its potential concentration." I pointed out that the moment when the stairway to heaven becomes something actually *possible* for the audience, would also be the moment of greatest danger. Jimmy expressed himself as well aware of the power in mass concentration, aware of the dangers involved, and of the skill and balance needed to avoid them . . . rather like driving a load of nitroglycerine.

"There *is* a responsibility to the audience," he said. "We don't want anything bad to happen to these kids—we don't want to release anything we can't handle." We talked about magic and Aleister Crowley. Jimmy said that Crowley had been maligned as a black magician, where magic is neither white nor black, good nor bad—it is simply alive with what it is: the real thing, what people really feel and want and are. I pointed out that this "either/or" straitjacket had been imposed by Christianity when all magic became black magic;

that scientists took over from the Church, and Western man has been stifled in a nonmagical universe known as "the way things are." Rock music can be seen as one attempt to break out of this dead soulless universe and reassert the universe of magic.

Jimmy told me that Aleister Crowley's house has very good vibes for anyone who is relaxed and receptive. At one time the house had also been the scene of a vast chicken swindle indirectly involving George Sanders, the movie actor, who was able to clear himself of any criminal charges. Sanders committed suicide in Barcelona, and we both remembered his farewell note to the world: "I leave you to this sweet cesspool."

I told Jimmy he was lucky to have that house with a monster in the front yard. What about the Loch Ness monster? Jimmy Page thinks it exists. I wondered if it could find enough to eat, and thought this unlikely—it's not the improbability but the upkeep on monsters that worries me. Did Aleister Crowley have opinions on the subject? He apparently had not expressed himself.

We talked about trance music. He had heard the Brian Jones record from recordings made at Joujouka. We discussed the possibility of synthesizing rock music with some of the older forms of trance music that have been developed over centuries to produce powerful, sometimes hypnotic effects on the audience. Such a synthesis would enable the older forms to escape from the mold of folklore and provide new techniques to rock groups.

We talked about the special effects used in the concert. "Sure," he said, "lights, lasers, dry ice are fine—but you have to keep some balance. The show must carry itself and not rely too heavily on special effects, however spectacular." I brought up the subject of infrasound, that is, sound pitched below 16 hertz, the level of human hearing; as ultrasound is above the level. Professor Gavreau of France developed infrasound as a military weapon. A powerful infrasound installation can, he claims, kill everyone in a five-mile radius, knock down walls, and break windows. Infrasound kills by setting up vibrations within the body so that, as Gavreau puts it, "You can feel all the organs in your body rubbing together." The plans for this device can be obtained from the French Patent Office, and infrasound generators constructed from inexpensive materials. Needless to say, one is not concerned with military applications however unlimited, but with more interesting and useful possibilities, reaching much further than five miles.

Infrasound sets up vibrations in the body and nervous system. Need these vibrations necessarily be harmful or unpleasant? All music played at any volume sets up vibrations in the body and nervous system of the listener. That's why people listen to it. Caruso, as you will remember, could break a champagne glass across the room. Especially interesting is the possibility of rhythmic pulses of infrasound—that is, *music in ultrasound*. You can't hear it, but you can feel it.

Jimmy was interested, and I gave him a copy of a newspaper article on infrasound. It seems that the most deadly range is around 7 hertz, and when this is turned on even at a low volume, anyone within range is affected. They feel anxious, ill, depressed, and finally exclaim with one voice, "I feel TERRIBLE!" . . . last thing you want at a rock concert. However, around the borders of infrasound perhaps a safe range can be found. Buddhist mantras act by setting up vibrations in the body.

Could musical communication be rendered more precise with infrasound, thus bringing the whole of music a second radical step forward? The first step was made when music came out of the dance halls, roadhouses, and night clubs, into Madison Square Garden and Shea Stadium. Rock music appeals to a mass audience, instead of being the province of a relatively few aficionados. Can rock music make another step forward, or is it a self-limiting form, confined by the demands of a mass audience? How much that is radically new can a mass audience safely absorb? We came back to the question of balance. How much new material will be accepted by a mass audience? Can rock music go forward without leaving its fans behind?

We talked about the film *Performance* and the use of cut-up techniques in this film. Now the cut-up method was applied to writing by Brion Gysin in 1959; he said that writing was fifty years behind painting, and applied the montage method to writing. Actually, montage is much closer to the facts of perception than representational painting. If, for example, you walked through Times Square, and then put on canvas what you had seen, the result would be a montage . . . half a person cut in two by a car, reflections from shop windows, fragments of street signs. Antony Balch and I collaborated on a film called *Cut-Ups,* in which the film was cut into segments and rearranged at random. Nicolas Roeg and Donald Cammell saw a screening of the film not long before they made *Performance.*

Musical cut-ups have been used by Earl Browne and other modern composers. What distinguishes a cut-up from, say, an edited medley, is that the cut-up is at some point random. For example, if you made a medley by taking thirty seconds from a number of scores and assembling these arbitrary units—that would be a cut-up. Cut-ups often result in more succinct meanings, rather than nonsense.

Over dinner at the Mexican Gardens, I was surprised to hear that Jimmy Page had never heard of Petrillo, who started the first musicians' union and perhaps did more than any other one man to improve the financial position of musicians by protecting copyrights. One wonders whether rock music could have gotten off the ground without Petrillo and the union, which put musicians in the big money bracket, thereby attracting managers, publicity, and the mass audience.

Music, like all the arts, is magical and ceremonial in origin. Can rock music return to these ceremonial roots and take its fans with it? Can rock music use older forms like Moroccan trance music? There is at present a wide interest among young people in the occult and all means of expanding consciousness. Can rock music appeal directly to this interest? In short, there are a number of disparate tendencies waiting to be synthesized. Can rock music serve as a vehicle for this synthesis?

The broken guitar strings, John Bonham's drum solo, vitality by Robert Plant—when you get that many people to get it, very good. Buy a straw hat at the door—the audience all light matches. Cool well-trained laser beams channeled the audience smoothly. A scattering of sparklers. Danger to a Mexican border town. We start talking over a cup of the mass unconsciousness—cut to a soccer riot photo in Lima. The Uruguayan referee is another rock star. Sound like falling mountains of the risks involved. It's our job to see trouble and plateau the center of the room—remembering the stairway to Switzerland? Fire really there. You can't see it if you refuse—underlying force the same. I mean we were playing a dance hall in heaven at the moment when the stairway actually possible for the audience was unlocked.

# Elvis Has Left the Building

*by Robert Ward*

*November 1977*

*In the '70s, living down at the end of Lonely Street, Elvis got fat, lazy, and lame. He wanted to become a narc for Nixon. But when he died we had to come to grips with what he really meant to us. Robert Ward, now a well-known novelist and television writer, got the call.*

It is 1956 and I am twelve years old. It is Saturday morning and I am sitting in the basement of my Baltimore row house. I am miserable because I am in love with a girl named Kathy Martin, a girl I have absolutely no chance of speaking to, much less taking out. She is dark, beautiful, and though I don't know it at the time, she is from a rather well-to-do family. This accounts for her social polish, her style, her ineffable grace. My family's lack of money, our stone Baltimore provinciality, our very real working-class fears combined with our very loony superstitions and sense of doom . . . all these have conspired to make me play the fool. When I see Kathy in the hall at school I stammer, attempt hopeless jokes, and suddenly see myself as Ralph Kramden. Overweight, sickly, too damned sensitive for my own good, and unable to tell anyone about it for fear of seeming unmanly. In short, there seems no release, except in movies, books, and this brand new thing on the radio called rock and roll.

Every Saturday morning I trek down to the cellar and sit in the cool shadows and turn on the *Buddy Deane Radio Show*. Buddy Deane is a southerner, from Pine Bluff, Arkansas. He has made it big in

Baltimore with both a radio show and a weekday TV dance program. Buddy, however, will never be as successful as Dick Clark, because Buddy is a hick. His mouth is too wide, his teeth are too big,
his hair too long and greasy. He is too obviously destined for the
small time. Like myself, he is too eager to please, too vulnerable,
too obviously ready for a rebuke.

In many ways Buddy Deane seems the embodiment of the Baltimore Myth. "Do your job, but don't shoot too high, don't try for too
much." Or as my father always said, "The bastards will get you in the
end. The smart boys in New York . . . they know how to get it, and
they grab it all. . . ." Best to finish high school, marry a nice girl from
around the neighborhood, buy a row house, have a coupla kids, eat
a few hardcrabs, drink a little National Bohemian Beer, watch the
Birds and Colts, and . . . well, that's it. Already I have seen the older
boys in our neighborhood doing just these things and I have no reason to doubt that someday, if anyone will have me, I will do likewise.

Yet there is something else in me, something gleaned from
movies, from books and from the radio. It blossoms forth in a random act of violence like smashing Northwood Elementary School's
windows, or ramming a shopping cart into the side of a car—stupid
acts, and ones I pay heavily for in guilty, sleepless nights.

But all the same, it is there, not only in me but on the radio—
barely conscious, like an itch. Buddy Deane is part of it too. And on
this particular morning, as I sit in an old lawn chair, a John R. Tunis
book in my hand, listening half-heartedly to Buddy's Top Ten, he becomes crucial. The number one record is something called "Dog-
face Soldier" by the Russ Morgan band, and I listen groggily, aware
of the mounting heat, of the sound of my father getting out the old
hand mower. I know he will come in soon to get me to help him. I
dread it. Another day on the damned lawn: bugs, sun, nothing . . .

Deane does a shill for some acne medicine, and then his voice
breaks out of its customary slick patter and takes on a quizzical
tone. He says, "Now I've got something, well, *strange* here. It's a new
record, and I'm going to be honest with you: I don't know if you are
going to like it or not." There's a pause, dead air, as if Buddy Deane
is stumbling to express himself. "This is the craziest record I've ever
heard. I don't even know how I feel about it. But I do know one
thing—I've never heard anything like it.

"This record is called 'Heartbreak Hotel.' It's by a new young
singer named Elvis Presley. Whether you like it or not, call in, and
let me know what you think." He gives the number of the station,
then he spins the disc.

Years later, in college, I will learn Edmund Wilson's term, "the shock of recognition." It describes that transcendent moment when you lose yourself entirely in a book because the author is expressing perfectly all the longings that lay buried nameless within you. You become conscious of yourself and the great shared human spirit. On this day, sitting in my cellar, I have no words to describe what is happening to me. I only know pure, perfect physical and mental bliss. Every syllable of this Elvis Presley's voice speaks urgently, directly, powerfully to me: "Down at the end of Lonely Street at Heartbreak Hotel."

I'm there . . . I've always been there on the blackest of streets. I can see the bellhop, his face in his hands, and the desk clerk, sitting behind a worm-eaten desk with his black shirt, black face. Behind him are the letter slots, but they are empty today, tomorrow, forever. And the singer's voice, expertly complemented by the raw blues guitar (and I have never heard the word "blues"), makes this world seem an ideal. It's not like my sadness over Kathy Martin, over the dull brute facts of my life—it's a *perfect* loneliness, a perfect dream space where all the pain is around me and yet I'm magically protected from it by the tough, vulnerable, infinitely sensual voice.

Nothing in my entire life has hit me with the force of this moment. I cannot bear for the song to end, and when it does I race upstairs and call the station (something I had previously considered infinitely "uncool," the kind of thing stupid girls do). I have been transformed, overwhelmed, and I don't care who knows it. Apparently, however, other kids in our great sluggard of a city have been sitting right next to their phones, for the line is busy—and keeps being busy for half an hour. (Meanwhile, I race back down to the cellar and turn the radio up, just in case the song is played again.) After forty minutes I give up and go downstairs to stay, while Buddy Deane begins to tally the results.

Again he sounds altered, stunned. "We've never had a response like this," he says. "Already there have been hundreds of calls—and so far almost all of them have said the song is going to be a big hit." He stumbles again. "And what's more, most of the callers have asked us to play the song again, and so here we go, Elvis Presley singing 'Heartbreak Hotel.' "

NOW IT IS AUGUST 1977, AND I AM THIRTY-THREE YEARS OLD. I HAVE abandoned the city of my youth (and feel strangely guilty about it, as though I have carelessly sliced away a piece of my soul) and am living in New York. There is no lawn to be cut where I now live, and the local "shopping center" is midtown Manhattan. My life lacks no novelty. If I am bored, I can take a six-minute walk and be in the theater district for either a play or a movie. If I am hungry, I am two minutes away from several of the best French restaurants in the United States. I am writing a commissioned screenplay, and outside of a recurring ulcer problem I'm feeling pretty good.

Still, there are always things to be traded away for success. Without sentimentalizing it, I miss the sense of neighborhood that Baltimore offered. I miss the fierce, close friendships that I grew up taking for granted. And, of all things, I miss a sense of continuity.

I sit at my desk, trying to figure out the logistics of a scene, when the phone rings. Automatically I pick it up and assume my professional voice of authority. I can tell immediately from the tone of the static on the wire that the call is long-distance, and I feel a certain tension . . . long-distance might mean California . . . might mean career. . . .

But it's not the present or future calling at all . . . it's the past. My father is on the line and he sounds tired, older than usual.

"Hello, Bobby?"

"Yeah. Hi, Dad."

"Listen . . . how you doing?"

"Okay. . . . Good. . . ."

"That's great, son. I got to thinking of you tonight, you know, when I heard that Elvis Presley died. You know how much you used to like his records."

Instantly, all my professional cool—all the defenses that I have proudly erected—are obliterated. I almost start to laugh. It's too damned much . . . like a cheap novel. Your old man . . . the one person you can't bullshit . . . your old man calling you . . . to tell you that a rock singer—he was just a goddamned rock singer, fer Chrissakes, and it's not like you were buying his records anymore . . . but Elvis Presley *dying*.

"How can he be dead, Dad?" I am numb, unable to talk.

"They found him on the floor. You didn't know? God, I thought you'd hear sooner in New York."

"No, Dad, I didn't know. Christ, I can't believe it, but I feel like I could start crying. That's ridiculous, isn't it? Jesus."

There is a long pause, and then my father sighs deeply. "I remember the Christmas we gave you that record with 'Jailhouse Rock' on it," he says. "You played that damned record until I thought I would go nuts."

"Yeah," I say, so ridiculously shaky. It's like your own past coming to bury you. . . . I think of a couple of years ago, when I had forgotten all about Elvis. My girl and I were driving in upstate New York when

"Suspicious Minds" came on the radio, and I had to stop the car, I was so moved. Moved that he could still do it, that he was still *great*.

"Well, I don't want to bother you if you're working," my father says. "I just miss you. You ought to come down to Baltimore soon."

"Yeah," I say, suddenly feeling dizzy, sick. "Yeah . . . in two weeks. Yeah." I tell him I love him, and hang up, and sit there remembering 1956, how far I've come, how much I've left behind, and how Elvis was one of things you took for granted that you'd always have around.

During the next few days, Elvis is all you hear. THE KING IS DEAD screams every paper, every TV show. You watch a sixty-minute assessment of Elvis's career by noted social philosopher Charles Kuralt, during which Kuralt attempts to "put Elvis into the perspective of the fifties." You retch a bit as you watch one of the brilliant devices used in this instant documentary: They juxtapose Elvis with other "things that made it big in the fifties," among them "instant coffee and power lawn mowers." You stare like a tranquilized goon as they carry his body down Elvis Presley Boulevard, and you hear amiable newsmen fake sympathy so they can elicit a little grief from the thousands of mourners outside Graceland.

But I could still grieve. I could remember. I could be a little proud that a few months back I had been offered a chance to coauthor a book with three of Elvis's bodyguards, and I had instantly turned it down because it smelled of shit. Now that book, *Elvis: What Happened?*, had hit the stands, had a five million printing, and its author would become rich. Dancing on the grave. A true Heartbreak Hotel.

I sit around my sweltering apartment feeling dazed, trying to sort it out . . . Elvis's huge talent, the rich mystery of his voice, which like Garbo's face was always just beyond the reach of exposition. How many times had I heard people do Elvis imitations (or done them myself) to the amusement and knowing smiles of our friends? Yet we knew that we had missed it. The voice was his signature. His genius. The true magic was that Elvis's voice spoke to us so naturally that we assumed ownership.

Indeed, another call comes from my oldest Baltimore pal, Richard Moss, now working for the government in D.C. He tells me that he has just come from the Egyptian Embassy where young Egyptian bureaucrats sat humming "Love Me Tender," drinking wine, and feeling as blue as the housewives who waited up all night outside of Graceland.

The shock of losing him . . . for me the *shock* of the shock, as well . . . is not unlike the trauma of losing JFK or Martin Luther

King. In spite of all the smears written about all three of them, they seemed an extension of what we believed best in ourselves.

So why the meanness in the press coverage? Perhaps there is a deeper sadness here. A sadness that transcends one great American's death. It is the sadness of my generation, many of whom (perhaps myself included) cannot get used to the idea that we are mortal. Of course, Elvis was our symbolic Never-Aging Rebel. And, of course, he manipulated the image, and grew rich and famous off of it.

And we went for it. We went for it in the '50s, when we needed it. When we needed—oh, how we needed—to cut out; hit the road, Jack; ride the mystery train.

And we went for it again, in a bigger way, in the '60s . . . when most of us literally did the things we dreamed of doing (and that we thought Elvis *was* doing) in the '50s. We headed down the American Highway never thinking that the last exit could be Heartbreak Hotel.

Which brings us to now . . . now that we are having trouble with our weight, have been through one or two marriages, have seen ourselves easy prey to petty careerist jealousies and all the other human frailties we so loudly proclaimed abolished. It's as though we are unleashing our own sense of failure, of bitterness, on our first love.

Some of us feel he failed us in some essential way. Or he cheated us. He was a Romantic in the '50s, and we loved him for ushering in our own Romance. Which is, of course, what I felt that day in my cellar . . . the Call . . . the First Stirrings of the Call. . . . Not merely sex, but Art, Beauty, Perfection, Idealism . . . and we lived it to the hilt in the '60s. But now we've become older, more tired, cynical, and, quite frankly, afraid. His death is too much for us, because he represented too much to us . . . all our love, and good bodies, but all our own terrible, sensational, and grotesque waste.

Yet, like our hometowns, like our parents whom we once rejected—like our own pasts—finally we are powerless to reject Elvis without severing the vital connections that keep us alive. His life was a triumph over low birth, lack of education, and a deadening conformist era that broke many a more advantaged man's heart. He taught us how to begin to feel, what it meant to turn yourself loose. He seized his time, and he gave it back to us—recharged, renewed, filled with all the courage, tension, and sweetness that made up his own complex and lonely heart. In short, he was simply one of us— and for a very long time, one of the best. As Auden wrote on the death of W. B. Yeats, "He became his admirers." It is Elvis's legacy, and his challenge to us, that we do as well for those other children of the dead '70s, sitting alone in their dark cellars, waiting for the Word.

# Elvis Costello Pumps It Up

*by James Willwerth*
*March 1978*

*Now this was an Elvis* Crawdaddy *could really get behind, a bright angry rocker at the peak of his form. His rage was true.*

It was a bitterly cold evening, "less than zero," as the song says. Outside The Hot Club, New Wave forum in the center of the city, fans had started lining up at six o'clock for the show at nine, turning blue as they hugged the side of the building to hide from a howlin' wind. The man they waited for walked toward the club with his shoulders hunched, looking like Mr. Peepers gone berserk, plus pimples. An absurdist portrait of a Chaplinesque tough guy: clunky shoes, rolled-up dungarees, horse-blanket overcoat snatched from a thrift shop bin, rumpled trilby hat over horn-rimmed glasses. "I'm not an artist," he was saying in his jerky, rapid-fire voice. "Even the word *musician* I kind of balk at. I'm a songwriter, and I'm a singer. But no hyphen, see? Don't make that mistake. Even a simple mistake like that can be costly in terms of misinformation." It is hard to understand what makes Elvis Costello, all of twenty-three years old, so intense. He's scuffled around the British pop scene and taken his knocks for a while, but not that long. He has endured the pain of sending his tapes to the major record companies and getting yawns, but so has everyone else. He grew up in a working-class household split by divorce, but he wasn't poor, or hungry. So what is he angry about—his looks?

Actually, it is something more akin to a temperamental version of the Kosmic Blues. Life is deadly, Elvis has concluded: dangerously grey, suffocating, getting worse. His rage to stay alive comes out of that rasping, angry mouth in rock rhythms and surreal lyrics so strong that they might easily melt the wax wings of those angels who wanna wear his red shoes. Like so many artists of our time—whatever his time in the spotlight might be—Costello has transformed a complex inner pain into something that has reached the nerve endings of a larger audience. "What I do is a matter of life and death to me," he says. "I don't choose to explain it, of course. I'm doing it, and I'll keep doing it until somebody stops me forcibly."

By now, Costello, his three-man band, a roadie or two, and his manager Jake Riviera—a rude, argumentative Cockney type likely to win this year's cup for Most Obnoxious Rock Manager—are knocking in vain at the club's front door. The line of fans is growing, and more than one hundred latecomers will astonishingly choose to wait in the bone-chilling winter wind until the eleven o'clock show, also SRO. "You can't call it punk or New Wave," says Carlin Dalessandro, nineteen, a bundled-up Temple University student in the front of the line. "He has a sound all of his own. I don't know what to call it."

A door at the back of the line opens and everybody shuffles over to get out of the winter, leaving the fans behind. Once inside, Costello stands with his arms folded tightly over his chest and moves around the room like a robot in need of oil. Driving in from the airport, he'd poked a station-changing button and found "Lady Madonna." "It's a bit sad when you have to wait for a ten-year-old record to come on the radio to turn it up," he grumped in his hoarse, grating voice. "You can twiddle your dial up and down—they're the same songs. If I have to listen to another Fleetwood Mac track, I'll probably kill somebody."

The radio is one of Costello's obsessions. False values, betrayal, the life-sapping drudgery of working-class labor are others. As a kid in the West London district of Twickenham, Costello found that most of his schoolmates were into "Paki-bashing"; but he hung out with the Pakistanis, also the Irish and Jordanians. His father, Ross McManus, a jazz trumpeter and cabaret singer, left home, but not before young Elvis—his real name is Declan Patrick McManus—tagged along to some live radio shows and started fooling around with a guitar. Still, after graduating high school at eighteen, he wound up working as a computer technician and living in a dreary flat in Acton with his wife and child, playing gigs on the side, hating his life, biding his time. The radio, a lifeline for so many people, began to annoy him mightily with its rigid programming, an anger reflected in the as-yet-unrecorded song "Radio, Radio" ("I want to bite the hand that feeds me"). Already he was writing, sometimes to rhythms of the computer terminals.

"It was like a drone," he remembers. "The trains to and from work would play a part. Rhythms that go through your working day affect you, right? They had sort of a clattery sound—*tk, tk, tk, tk.* . . ."

On the road, he carries an account ledger that says "records" on the front cover, and he scribbles constantly. "Marriages performed here!" he chortled caustically and flipped open the book as he passed a tacky Justice of the Peace office in Philadelphia. He had time to kill, so the CBS publicist took him to an oldies record store, then to the thrift shops he prefers. He bought shirts ("I don't care what size they are. I just buy them") and combed through boxes of old records. "I'm more interested in people dancing than thinking," he said, up to his elbows in old clothes. "I don't like concepts. Individual things are more important. Being stood up on a date hurts more than a Big Concept." Once he told a British interviewer that "guilt and revenge" were his only lyrical "reference points." Asked to expand on that, he looked at the old shirts for a moment; then: "My album has no love songs. Not in the sense that I choose them. Quite a few of my reviews have tended to picture me as an emotional masochist. Well, many of the songs are involved with revenge and guilt. Some are about being tricked. These are the stronger feelings, the ones you are left with at night."

Costello put together his tour band only last July. Before that, he'd done pickup dates—"always at the wrong place with the wrong people at the wrong time"—and finally he signed with Stiff Records for practically nothing. In August, Jake Riviera (not his real name either) noticed that CBS International was convening at the London Hilton. So in the best tradition of old rock and roll movies, Elvis hustled on down with a guitar and amp and did some theater. It didn't get him a contract, but it did get him arrested. The contract came later when Columbia's East Coast head of A&R, Gregg Geller, convinced management that the kid who looked like Buddy Holly could sing like him, too.

Ten o'clock now. The Hot Club is packed shoulder to shoulder; it's impossible to get to the bar. Costello is pushing full-throttle toward the climax of his set. He is lobster red; the veins in his neck bulge, and his ill-fitting narrow-lapel suit is soaked with sweat. "This song is for all the people," he is shouting hoarsely into the mike, beating his hand in the air like a seal's flipper, "who listen to the radio morning, noon, and night—and nothing is coming out!" And then he goes into "Radio, Radio." His stage act is good, filled with a snarling, thumping intensity. But the album is better, the rhythms worked out in cleaner lines, the dark-dream lyrics more audible.

During the second act, Costello is thrown completely and leaves the stage briefly when someone pulls a plug backstage—his stage presence is about as smooth as gravel, nothing like the classic rockers. The era of Chuck Berry and Buddy Holly, in fact, is only history to him. "I'm too young to remember rock 'n' roll, really," he'd said earlier in the car. "I must have heard it, but I don't remember." Besides, nothing curls the Costello lip faster than talk of influences. "The question of influence is pointless," he barks. "I never list them except in a flippant way. There's no reason to assume that if I listen to Kenny and the Casuals, I'm going to go and write a song like them. I went through all sorts of periods. For a while, I was writing nothing but country songs. I may still return to that. Problem is, some people think it's a joke."

Maybe. But Costello, who somehow manages to combine the rhythms of the old English "beat bands" with '70s surreal lyrics, is no joke—except perhaps in his overangry posturing. At home in Acton, he admits to watching the telly "a lot" and likely has kind words for his wife and child. He's even capable of relaxing with a writer, as long as he isn't asked What It All Means. But somewhere behind those dark, bespectacled eyes, the belligerence is real; the pain is no laugh. Declan Patrick McManus is afraid of dying slowly. Even the songs are compressed, as if it all has to be said quickly and directly to the audience he remembers with those small, squawking radios. "I write singles-length songs," he concludes. "If you can't get it down in three minutes, you ought to give it up. It's not mock anger that I express."

# Blondie: Punk Harlow

*by Denis Boyles*

*June 1978*

*Debbie Harry: Madonna with a substance abuse problem.*

The explosion, the gasp, and the jump: the windshield is lace and web, glass and plastic, reduced to mosaic by a stone. "Can you believe it?" Chris Stein, Blondie's lead guitar player, leans forward in his seat, his sunglasses in hand. "That's the second time!" He offers his glasses to the driver. "Hey, Debbie!" he shouts over his shoulder, "That's the second time, isn't it?"

Debbie Harry is reclining on the backseat of the bus. She looks, in repose, like an Italian postcard of Marilyn Monroe. Though the rest of the bus is in mild chaos, she has not moved, has not acknowledged the shattered windshield. Through her wraparound, mirrored-lensed sunglasses, she watches the road to Canterbury pass. It is Blondie's last gig in Europe. Debbie is tired. Chris Stein is shouting from the front: "Hey, Debbie! That's the second time, isn't it?"

"Yeah."

Stein turns back around in his seat. "It's the second time this has happened. It's weird. I think the bus is bent and the pressure makes the glass break. Or maybe it's from backfires." The driver reaches out and gingerly touches the glass. Chris shivers. "It can't hold together, it's going to go." The bus is running silently now, everyone slouches low, watching the driver, waiting for the shattering bump on the motorway, anticipating the inevitable. "It can't hold to-gether." Waiting for the shower of glass.


AT THE ROUNDHOUSE THE NIGHT BEFORE, PETER LEEDS, BLONDIE'S manager, had been a little on edge. "This is our last date in London. We've never quite done it right. This time it has to be good." The Roundhouse had sold out five hours after tickets went on sale, and outside, a procession of disappointment wound its way down Chalk Farm Road. "We could've sold out this house for a week."

The converted railroad shed is crammed. A red "Blondie" logo floats over the audience; the sound system plays old Del Shannon, Shirelles, Buddy Holly tapes. No one is sitting; shirts and blouses are soaked, not from sweat but from beer. But this is no London punk crowd; instead, pogoing young professionals circle the stage, edging out the younger kids. The attraction is this blonde woman, a kewpie Harlow who sings a cover of "Denise"—now, with a French verse, retitled "Denis"—and who sits quietly backstage.

"Debbie's the brains of the outfit," Leeds had said. "She's the one who runs the show. But if you tried to tell the group that, they'd deny it. She's smart, wrote that French verse *all by herself.*"

The show's over in London, three encores, raves to follow. "I don't know how they ever got it together," says a roadie. "I thought Nigel [Harrison] and Chris were going to kill each other onstage. Everybody's too tired. The feeling's getting bad. I just hope they hold together until the Canterbury gig."


IN FRONT OF THE CANTERBURY ODEON A MILLING THRONG OF RUTTING fans has clogged the driveway. The bus turns off the main road and stops short. The blemished faces of young Britain freeze in anticipation. The engine stops, the crowd advances. Suddenly a bottle of Newcastle Brown ale sails through the windshield, glass everywhere, a boot through the window, more bottles. Through side and front doors, Blondie's members emerge and dash through the stage entrance. "Fucking heavy, man," says one kid to another.


"REGGAE? REGGAE! FOR-GET IT!" DEBBIE IS AGITATED. "R&B? AND reggae? Chris is crazy! He thinks he's a nigger; he shouldn't be loose."

Chris has been unleashed before. In Doncaster, there was no security. Somebody spit on him, spit at Debbie. "I jumped into the crowd and started beating this asshole in the face with my guitar," he says. "You can only be so punk." A Chrysalis photographer enters the dressing room, and Chris disappears in an avalanche of technical jargon: F-stops, magenta filters, ASA numbers, manual override. "I went to art school for four years. Everybody had a band in art school. But I really want to be a photographer. Can you use some of my pictures? I spend a lot of time taking shots of Debbie; I've got one of her standing in the kitchen of our apartment just after it got burned out. I'll get it for you when we get home. How about some performance shots?"

THE ARRIVAL OF THE MANAGER BRINGS GRINS AND HANDSHAKES. "Congratulations on your *first number one record!* 'Denis' is number one in Holland!" Leeds looks from Stein to Harrison to Harry. Nobody talks. Jim Destri, anxious about a missing synthesizer, pops a beer. Clem Burke drums his fingers on the tabletop. Frank Infante has disappeared for a pizza; the rhythm guitar player has gone away with the seventeen-year-old waif the group adopted out of a shrink-wrap factory in the East End of London. Stein, Destri, Burke all flaked out, exhausted. Debbie Harry pulls her cap down over her eyes.

"Oh." Debbie yawns. "Oh. Good."

Leeds retreats into quiet conversation. "I'm very cautious, cautious about everything. The States, for example: I don't know if we have the momentum there or not. I spend money when I have to. Did you get a Blondie valentine? *Those* were expensive. And T-shirts. T-shirts cost a lot."

THE ROAD MANAGER IS TALKING SECURITY: "I WANT TWENTY GUYS IN front of the stage—put a couple at each end—that's where the trouble always is. If just one of those guys gets his hands on Debbie, they'll wreck the place to get at her." The promoter looks a little awestruck. Punctuation: "They destroyed the hall in Doncaster. *Destroyed it.* Understand?"

THEY HAVE DESTROYED THE FIRST FIVE ROWS OF SEATS AND BLONDIE IS encoring with "Denis" in double time, a nice touch, but a touch of frenzy as well: hands upraised without a clenched fist in sight. Every hand is spread wide, reaching for Debbie Harry, hoping for the most public copped feel in history. She's dodged digits before, Debbie has. "This is what I've always done. I've always done rock. Rock. New Wave, whatever you call it. Now I've got to get everyone in shape. I've got this theory about stage movement, see, movement that has nothing to do with the music. I want a disjointed effect, something dramatic, visually. I want to make the act much more visual." White T-shirt, white boots, white explosion of hair, she seems incapable of touching the stage, of standing still. Until she freezes to one of Stein's solos, a bullet of sound. All white, backlit, she teases the little boys.

# PART III

*Politics*

# Nixon's the One

*by Peter Knobler*
*January 1973*

*The major Watergate revelations didn't arrive until weeks later—Wood-ward and Bernstein were still working up steam—so the sentiments ex-pressed in this editorial were by no means mainstream. It sounds quaint, but the notion that a president would lie to the public on a regular basis was not yet widely accepted.*

I'm a young man, but I'll be thirty before Nixon is out of office and I'm running scared.

The presidential election was a choice between mass murder and a tentative rounding of corners, and the American people chose public execution. I assume I'm speaking to young people—*Craw-daddy* is not now a cross-generational magazine—and I wonder how representative, or represented, we are. As a natural constituency, young people voted for McGovern. But too many young votes went to Nixon, and that is unsettling.

President Nixon's campaign—one of evasion, espionage, and gallingly smug stage management—clearly demonstrated the will-ingness of the government, *and the people,* to endorse, no, actively pursue corruption as the ideal. That the Watergate spying incident and the incredible and undenied network of Nixon's subversives were *taken for granted* by the voting majority speaks to an acceptance of personal danger that seems unprecedented. For some time now it has been fashionable to assume your phone is being tapped. Para-

noia has become a very hip disease. The future holds fewer para-
noiacs and more strange noises.

Let's review some of the maneuvers this man Nixon pulled to become President. I'd call them "capers" but this is serious business.

First is the infinite cynicism involved in stage managing the
"peace" prospects of an originally unjustifiable war. That the battle
could have ended four years ago, or eight, or eighteen for that matter, is not to be forgotten (pious denials notwithstanding). That
Kissinger and Nixon chose the week before Election Day to pull this
rabbit out of their hats is enough to make you want to see them
bleed. That the American people accepted it is infinitely more
frightening. One begins to get the feeling that anything goes.

Agnew took to blowing a police whistle into the microphone
when confronted with people who didn't want to hear any more lies.
"Five fouls and you're out," he said. Goon squads kicked the shit out
of hecklers while the audience cheered and joined in. The news media were so effectively castrated they never even tried to get it up.

Nixon never faced the people. With the ultimate personal cynicism he never publicly mentioned McGovern's name from nomination through election. He never answered questions because he was
never asked. He made statements that were not to be challenged,
only absorbed.

McGovern, for his part, did not run the race of a winner. He
missed his pace, ignored his kick. He should have run on the
premise that anything Nixon says is a lie. He'd have had Nixon by
the harness. The campaign was one fabrication after another. Mc-
Govern should have challenged every assertion. Who says the White
House didn't know about Watergate? Who says the $100,000
brought by hand from Mexico to Washington for Nixon's campaign
fund is legal?

Nixon says.

Who's Nixon?

McGovern could have made history by being the first candidate
to base his campaign on the complete and utter fraudulence of the
man in office. The President as liar. It has a ring to it.

But would the people have accepted it? The concept of the *office*
as fraudulent seems too much for the voter, and so, more than
unanswered, questions go unposed. The entire concept is too alien;
you don't get taught that kind of shit in school. Washington never
lied; Lincoln freed the slaves; Teddy Roosevelt was rough and Tru-
man tough.

Perhaps all of this should have been said long ago. Maybe Nixon's
perpetual five o'clock shadow wasn't sufficient metaphor for the

darkness he can bring. A laconic sense of humor is a commendable tactic in the day-to-day, hand-to-hand combat of living in these times. But once in a while all that stifled passion has got to show itself. Nixon can no longer be voted out. *The country wants him in,* and that's a fearsome message. How to change it?

It's hard to think of rock and roll at a time like this.

# Why They Were in Vietnam

*by Peter Knobler*

*May 1973*

*You had to be there. Tens of thousands of Americans and Vietnamese had died in a war that should never have been fought, and instead of stopping it, the Nixon administration was packaging returning prisoners of war as heroes. The media played right along. The tone of this editorial was sharp, but the source of our anger was not the former POWs themselves but rather the government's cynical manipulation of patriotism for political gain.*

The American prisoners of war deserve what they got, not what they're getting. Returning in 1973 to a 1953 reception, they must believe nothing much has happened since they hit the silk. The boys are stepping in to a Conquering Hero syndrome that would have done John Foster Dulles proud.

Pilots mostly, the elite of the fighting corps who rarely had a sense of the reality of their mission (it's hard to tell, from twenty thousand feet, what a village feels like beneath a bomb)—these guys had it good. Until they got shot down they ate better than anyone around, pulled in more money for less combat time, lived the glamour life of a flyboy (all volunteers and officers) while foot soldiers shot it out and the civilian population became accustomed to death. These are the career boys, the order-followers.

Most POWs were shot down while bombing peasants; they weren't ignorant of their targets, just unmoved by them. It is in the nature of a career man to pursue his career; they dropped their bombs and asked few questions. Their crimes go beyond callousness.

There are 592 POWs being returned. At the height of the war that many Americans were dying *every week,* while the Vietnamese totals were much higher.

These are *killers* we're welcoming home. The heroism involved in being kept alive by the people you were trying to kill scares me. The ability to maintain one's pride in self and country when confronted with the scope of destruction you personally were a party to strikes me as less than a virtue. Every POW who returns from captivity and celebrates the glory of his commander and his commands is a danger to this country's future, not to mention its present.

The media coverage of the POW issue has been execrable. Where is the comparison between North Vietnamese and Viet Cong treatment and the "tiger cages," "field telephones," and general interrogation/torture policy paid for and executed by the American presence?

The slickness of governmental manipulation compounds this public relations coup. The isolation of returnees, the uniformity of their responses—something of a knee-jerk patriotic fervor—should make one increasingly suspicious. Where is the first public doubting of a POW's ecstatic word? Why will the press not try a little sacrilege? The government lives on a continuing policy of lying to the public; when will the major media recognize that assumption?

There is a mixture of sympathy and cynicism to watching the joy of families reunited by the POWs' release. Their emotions are real, incredibly strong, and on a human level they must be respected and felt for. But they are no more compelling than the grief that fifty thousand families must have felt when their kids came home in oak or didn't come home at all. There's longing being fulfilled here, not virtue.

And of course the final absurdity is the overwhelming public sympathy for these voluntary bombers when placed next to the continuing hostility to the young men who followed their consciences and refused to participate in the killing. Amnesty for draft resisters, in a typical American perversity, seems more remote now than before the war ended.

So the POWs, our boys, have come home, their war long over, and they seem determined to make up for the fighting they didn't get a chance to do. It seems the war will not end.

# Watergate Down

*by Paul Krassner*
*November 1973*

*One of* Crawdaddy*'s many offbeat looks at Watergate, midway through the crisis. Krassner, editor of the* Realist *and an original Yippie, was a* Crawdaddy *columnist for five years, and conducted exclusive "interviews" with Patty Hearst and Howard Hughes, among others.*

There is actually a record store in Washington, D.C., where you can get ten free albums if you've been indicted for Watergate. This was the first time I'd ever been to Washington for an event other than a demonstration—nuclear testing, civil rights, antiwar, counterinauguration, marijuana smoke-in, you know, all the *Oldies But Goldies*.

I was on my way to the Second A. J. Liebling Counter-Convention. *Editor and Publisher* once carried a classified ad for a reporter that stated this condition: "No Lieblings need apply." They considered him a generic term for press critic and reformer.

The convention was intended to be counter to that of the American Newspaper Publishers Association, but both were being held in an atmosphere reeking with the inner anguish of dislocated shoulders resulting from patting themselves on the back for the role of the media in opening up Watergate.

*Orgy* seemed to be the word for it. *Washington Post* columnist David Broder wrote that journalists were indulging in "an orgy of self-congratulation." One of President Nixon's bosses, Henry

Kissinger, warned against "an orgy of recrimination." And Roger Grimsby of ABC News said that "so many people are taking bows for Watergate, it looks like a Greek orgy."

Liebling II was scheduled to take place at the ultrafashionable Mayflower Hotel, where any guest noticing the lack of toilet paper at least doesn't have to get up to complain inasmuch as there is a telephone in every bathroom. I stayed at the Washington Hotel, where the Declaration of Independence is lacquered onto the wastepaper basket in each room.

COME CLEAN, says my lapel button. It's supposed to be for—or rather, against—venereal disease, but I figure it applies to Watergate specifically and to life in general. Reporters at the Washington bureau of *The New York Times* are wearing buttons that say FREE THE WATERGATE 500.

It seems I fail to recognize a lot of old acquaintances at the counterconvention. Guys in the underground have cut their hair and shaved their beards and refer to themselves as members of the alternative press. Guys in the overground are complaining that the police state is already here and they have sideburns that are way longer than their expense accounts. A lawyer I know who once told his radical client to trim his sideburns so as not to prejudice the judge later grew sideburns himself and another judge thanked him for making it easier for *him* to grow sideburns.

The revolution must be over, because even Barbie's pal Ken now comes with such accessories as a Mark Spitz mustache and a mod-styled mini-wig.

The irony of this counterconvention is that the 1973 A. J. Liebling Award is presented to Homer Bigart, who reported from Vietnam for *The New York Times,* yet he is mentioned in the Pentagon Papers as having originally cooperated fully with the CIA propaganda mill. But since we chanted "Join us!" so much at all those peace rallies, I guess it's only sporting not to hold grudges against those who have, at whatever level. Award-winner Bigart sets a precedent, though. He doesn't make an acceptance speech. He doesn't even thank all the little people—Michael Dunn, Janis Ian, Toulouse-Lautrec . . .

The irony of the newscasting profession is that 65 percent of the American public gets its news from television, and the newsmongers get *their* information mainly from *The Washington Post,* so that you often have the perpetuation of myth by well-meaning individuals who themselves are victims of the media.

Until recently, the American press had not been treating Watergate with the same significance that the foreign press, except for China and Russia, had been laying on it. In fact, Ralph Nader told me that Richard Nixon's brother was making arrangements to open a hundred gas stations in Moscow. I mean, that's played to the simultaneous accompaniment of gas stations being forced to close in the United States.

Nader thinks that the President ought to resign. On this, the consumer advocate has found himself in agreement with Martha Mitchell for the first time in recorded history. Quick, let's call up Dita Beard and arrange a breakfast celebration; we'll all share this huge bowl of Shredded Memos sprinkled with gemstone.

Just suppose that, not here, but in some other country in Europe or Latin America, it was announced that the new palace chief of staff was General Haig? That the new Attorney General Elliot Richardson was fresh from his leadership role in justifying the bombing of Cambodia? That Robert DePew, head of the racist Minute Men, had been quietly released from prison? That the new head of the CIA William Colby had been counterinsurgency expert in Southeast Asia? That Vice President Agnew made at least five trips to New Orleans during the 1972 election campaign to meet with Cuban exile Carlos Brienguier, who according to the *Warren Report* figured heavily in Lee Harvey Oswald's espionage career? That the new budget director, Roy Ash, served as a conduit for CIA funds, channeled through the Pappas Foundation, which led to the overthrow of Greece?

Might we not then be treated to a spate of editorials about a possible military junta being set in motion?

There are some pretty funky chickens hanging around, the ones that Malcolm X talked about when John Kennedy was killed. "Just a case of chickens," he had said, "coming home to roost." It was not considered a popular sentiment at the time.

# Nixon's Last Press Conference

## as taped by Paul Slansky

### April 1974

*This was published a few months before Nixon's actual last press conference. We thought we'd seen the last of him! Slansky, like so many former* Craw-daddy *regulars, is now a screenwriter in California.*

OPENING STATEMENT: Now that you're all so delighted that I've been impeached, let me just make a few things perfectly clear. I am invoking the little-used but well-established inherent power of "desperate privilege." Let me put to rest a rumor making the rounds in the various media. I am not going to "bug out" of this office. As you know, my parents were from the Midwest, and from them I inherited the quality of having what it takes. I am going to tough it out. I am not resigning! Any reports of my leaving this office, voluntarily or otherwise, before the term to which I was elected by the largest majority of any president in our history is over, are just plain poppycock! I would remind you all, I am a Quaker, not a quitter.

For the first question I'll go to Mr. Rather, who would rather assert than inquire, heh.

*Q. Mr. Ex-President, you have said that you will not leave your office, despite the fact that the Senate convicted you by a vote of ninety-seven to three, and that according to the latest Gallup poll, your popularity is down to six percent.*

A. That is correct, Mr. Rather (*mopping his upper lip with a neatly folded handkerchief*).

*Q. According to that poll, sir, everyone in the country with an IQ over ninety-five "hates your guts." I wonder if you could share with us your reaction to the removal of your personal belongings from the White House.*

A. Well, let me just say, Mr. Rather, that I know what I'm doing. I have what it takes. The removal of my possessions is of little consequence, as they are still my possessions whether or not they are in the White House and are still legitimate tax deductions under the law. The American people did not vote for my possessions when they reelected me by the largest majority ever given to an American president.

As for anti-Nixon feeling in the country, I can only say that unpopularity is nothing new to me after twenty-seven years in public life. I can take it. I have what it takes to take it. There are those who say I've taken far too much.

*Q. And pocketed the rest.*

A. Ahem, with regard to my staying in office, I have a secret plan to accomplish this. To propose it now, in the midst of bitter nationwide partisan debate, would only serve to inflame the public. In due time, however, it will be revealed. (*Moving men carry out air conditioner, Lincoln fireplace, and television set.*) You there! Yes, I would appreciate it if you left the set until after the playoff game tomorrow!

*Q. Sir, does it seem at all ironic to you that so many millions of dollars were spent on your reelection, only to have it all come to this, little more than a year later?*

A. Well, Mr. Schorr, I'd be less than candid if I didn't admit that there have been some disappointments, some setbacks. I have not accomplished all that I set out to do when I began my second term. At the same time, it cannot be said that I have not accomplished anything.

I helped reinvigorate the Congress by forcing them to override my veto of the War Powers Limitation Bill. I admit there are those who claim that I obliterated what was left of North Vietnam, and that I put the economy through a wringer—and some say that I totally destroyed the public's respect for the presidency, the vice presidency, the Justice Department, the Supreme Court, the CIA, and the FBI. All I can say about that is that I certainly wouldn't want history to prejudge me on these matters.

Next, Miss Helen Thomas. I see you're wearing pants again, Miss Thomas. Much as I hate pants on women, on you they look very masculine.

*Q. Would you agree, Mr. Nixon, that yours has been a unique presidency?*

A. Yes, I most emphatically would agree. I was, you may recall, the first American president to go to China and after only a half a term I feel I ought to go again, heh heh.

*Q. Mr. Nixon, you were the first to be removed from office. You were the first to have his entire administration under forced resignation, indictment, or imprisonment. I think it only fair to point out, sir, that you . . .*

A. Well, Mr. Lisagor, there you have a perfect example of the tendency on the part of the press to harp on the negative—to make every little instance of misconduct into a federal case. As you must know, most of the misdeeds which have occurred are not federal cases at all, but are rather under the jurisdiction of local courts.

*Q. Mr. Nixon, could you go over the whole missing tapes controversy with us one more time?*

A. Let's take them one at a time. As you all know, the Mitchell call was placed on an unconnected phone, and the Dean meeting was held after the tape had run out.

The June 20th meeting between myself, Mr. Haldeman, and Mr. Ehrlichman was, as you know, mistakenly erased nine times by Miss Woods.

The June 30th meeting between myself, Mr. Mitchell, and Mr. Haldeman was not recorded because a spool of adhesive tape was inadvertently used instead of recording tape, and nothing stuck to it, heh heh.

The September 15th and two March 21st tapes that I lent to Bob Haldeman were accidentally erased when he left them in his closet next to a powerful electromagnet which, in all candor, I must admit I had also, er, lent him.

The meeting between Dean and myself on March 13th, in which I believe he told me I was getting cancer, was recorded. It is unintelligible, however, and the March 22nd meeting, attended by my whole staff, is simply not relevant since everyone, by that time, was refusing to say anything at all. The entire meeting consisted of passed notes.

And finally, the June 4th tape of me listening to the April 15th tape was accidentally eaten by King Timahoe (*Irish setter, wearing an ill-fitting red wig, pads to Mr. Nixon's heel and sits down*) and I just want to say that regardless of what you feel about it, we're going to keep him.

*Q. What about the October 25th tape, sir?*

A. I'm glad you asked that. The October 25th tape, as you know, was of me listening to the June 4th tape—which was of me listening to the April 15th tape. Unfortunately, the recording was drowned out by horns honking outside the White House. And in my view, whoever was responsible for that traffic jam, incidentally, was guilty of obstruction of justice.

*Q. You have offered to release your own versions of what was on the nonexistent tapes. Would these be actual transcripts or edited summaries?*

A. They will be actual summaries. These conversations, I might add—as the nonexistence of the tapes plainly shows—never took place. Nevertheless, the empty reels are equally protected by the privilege of confidentiality.

*Q. Mr. Former President, you did invoke the Fifth Amendment in your impeachment defense before the Senate. How do you think that influenced the verdict?*

A. Now of course there are those who believe that a Fifth Amendment plea is tantamount to an admission of guilt. I must admit that at times I have also held this misconception. I will simply say this: I could have done the easy thing and invoked the Fourth Amendment, or any number of other amendments. I could have answered the questions, insolent as many of them were. This would have been the popular thing to do.

However, I could not square this with my personal belief in the right of the president, in the interests of national security, to cover up wrongdoing. I might add, in this connection, that I am not a crook.

*Q. Sir, an estimated six million people descended on the Capitol for your trial. And Gillette agreed to pay off the national debt in return for the TV rights. How do you feel about all this?*

A. Of course it has not escaped my attention, Mr. Jarriel, and I think it puts the lie to public opinion polls that have been touting the decline of my mandate. With or without charisma, Mr. Jarriel, I am still a good draw!

*Q. I was just wondering if you have any pleasant memories of your years in office. I mean really pleasant memories.*

A. Yes, actually there are quite a few. *Patton* and *Chisum,* to name just two. China—as President Eisenhower said when he saw the Taj Mahal—was "very nice." The hard hat given me by the construction workers who beat up the peaceniks is something I'll always cherish.

Mr. Brokaw, you seem agitated. You have a question?

*Q. Mr. President, AP is moving a bulletin that Moscow has been destroyed by nuclear bombs! Brezhnev's declared they're reacting in kind, and missiles are now headed for Washington!*

A. Well, it would seem that you have stumbled onto part of my secret plan. It is, contrary to what I previously said, my irrevocable decision to relinquish this office under the circumstances, the sooner the better. But to clarify any misconceptions I may have given you earlier, let me point out that in 1976 I will be constitutionally eligible to run for election—after, as it were, the smoke clears.

*Q. Mr. President, one last question . . .*

A. Please make it snappy, Mr. Reston . . .

*Q. Sir, you started off by saying you weren't resigning and now you say that you are. Isn't this a blatant contradiction?*

A. Mr. Reston, if I may suggest, after twenty-seven years in politics, watch what I do, not what I say. (*He exits hastily.*)

*Q. Thank you, Mr. President.*

# Cinque Very Much

*by Jeff Shero Nightbyrd*
*June 1974*

*Or: Everything's Coming Up Rosebud. Largely forgotten today, Patty Hearst's kidnapping by the Symbionese Liberation Army was the story of its time.*

The era of protest is over. The age of terrorism has begun.

"There should be no question of amnesty for political kidnappers," says U.S. Attorney General William Saxbe. "They should be executed. America is now coming face-to-face with the problem we've seen in many areas of the world—hijackings and political kidnappings. There is a worldwide trend toward terrorism."

The call of the tom-toms echoes throughout the global village. The U.S. consul general is kidnapped in Mexico. In Argentina, executives of Firestone, IBM, ITT, and Pepsi-Cola are taken hostage. The West German ambassador is seized in Brazil. Japanese working for Palestinians shoot up a Rome airport, killing Americans and Europeans while trying to eradicate Jews. All those niggers of every color, would-be niggers of every class, and desperate wrecks of modern society have discovered new weapons.

Civilized people are shocked . . . and shocked again. In our pockets of comfort the regular Joes don't see the hungry getting hungrier or the poor nations getting poorer. And all the while, corporate potentates in the citadels of power keep on interconnecting their computers and perfecting their space-age weaponry to keep things just the way they are.

Would-be guerrillas move to the urban wilderness. Uruguay's Tupamaros prove that the very complexity of the modern city makes it supremely vulnerable—an overgrown techno-electronic dinosaur. They prove that a few disciplined people at a critical neural nexus can shake a nation and send a message to the world. Kung Fu replaces cannons.

Barricades are for nineteenth-century romantics, and Marx is fine for armchair intellectuals, but center stage is suddenly being seized by outcasts with the tools of terrorists.

In Berkeley, Patty Hearst was kidnapped and the nation held its breath. The Symbionese Liberation Army, whose name, not to mention ideas, was barely known before, received *total* attention. In one day the electronic media delivered a message that couldn't be duplicated by a hundred years at a basement mimeograph machine. Randolph Hearst, right-wing editor of the *San Francisco Examiner,* declared the SLA, which has taken as its symbol a seven-headed cobra, "well intentioned," but "going about things in the wrong way."

This way . . .


IT IS 9:21 IN THE EVENING. ON A QUIET RESIDENTIAL STREET IN BERKELEY a long-haired young woman wearing an army surplus jacket rings the doorbell at 2603 Benvenue. Steve Weed, a lanky Princeton philosophy major with a walrus mustache and gentle manner, answers the door. "I've had an auto accident," she says nervously. "Can I use your phone?"

He opens the door. Suddenly, two black men armed with rifles muscle their way in. They wrestle him to the floor, pinning him face down in the hallway. He tries to look up, tries to comprehend what's going on. A work boot crashes into the side of his head. Dazed, he tries to look up again. Again he is viciously kicked. One of the attackers produces a rope and binds Weed's hands behind his back.

"Where is the safe?" one of the intruders demands. Weed can hear his lover, Patty Hearst, moaning in the kitchen of the two-story town house. She is being bound and blindfolded.

One of the invaders grabs a full wine bottle and smashes it into Weed's skull. Through a sodden haze, Weed hears the woman spit with commandolike curtness, "We've got to get rid of them. They've seen us." She is right. Before Weed was thrown to the floor, he had gotten a good look at their faces. In a desperate bid for freedom,

Weed struggles to his feet and lunges into the living room, somehow freeing his hands in the process. He tears open the sliding glass doors and scrambles over the back fence. Panicky, blood pounding in his head like the surf, he vaults two more fences and drags himself away.

Meanwhile, Patty Hearst is manhandled into the street. The struggle has been fierce and she is naked from the waist up. Twisting and pulling, she shrieks at her abductors, "Please let me go . . . Oh no . . . Oh no . . ."

Susan Larkey, a student, runs out of her apartment and sees two men grappling with Patty. Are they rapists? "Let her go!" she screams. Three shots are her answer.

Patty is thrown into the trunk of a white convertible and the hood is slammed shut. As the car roars into life, her neighbors come flying into the street. Sandy Golden tries to get the license number, but is driven back by a hail of bullets.

With professional efficiency the white convertible is dispatched a mile away, and Patty is transferred to a Chevy station wagon. Peter Benenson lies bound in the front seat. He had been unloading his groceries less than a half hour before when his car was stolen for a kidnap vehicle.

A scout car speeds away from the scene and Patricia Hearst is rushed off to the first of her hideouts. This is the beginning of America's first political kidnapping. Terrorism has come home.

> *I'm that nigger you've hunted and feared night and day. I'm that nigger you've killed hundreds of my people in the vain hope of finding. I'm the nigger that is no longer just hunted, robbed and murdered. I'm the nigger that hunts you now . . .*
>
> *Yes, you know me. You know us all. I'm the wetback. You know me. I'm the gook. The broad. The servant. The spic. . . . Now we are the hunters who will give you no rest.*
>
> —SLA Field Marshal Cinque

It's strange to be in Berkeley these days. Just a decade ago, universities hummed with news of the Berkeley Free Speech movement and People's Park. Now it's assassinations.

People don't jump into extreme action; rather they try the most moderate means available and move on to the next stage when the more legitimate channels of protest are shut off. Recently the Watergate exposures have revealed an incredible domestic espionage and counterinsurgency apparatus aimed at insuring frustration for the

'60s forces for change. The FBI ran a campaign to destroy any "black messiah," hence Fred Hampton in Chicago was assassinated. Black Panthers were forced out of their Serve the People programs and into dealing with the crisis of simple survival as police agents from within and uniformed police from without waged war against them. Police agents disrupted the internal democracy of organizations, proposing and even initiating violence, in numbers only just now beginning to be revealed. The secret police apparatus worked toward disrupting mass organizations, which in turn forced individuals into more secretive, more isolated, more urban guerrillalike activity.

Few whites were psychologically prepared for guerrilla warfare. The communal movement in the countryside began, offering a reprieve from the insanity and intensity of the dying days of the Movement. The calm and steady work involved in making a go of it in a rural commune gave women and men, separate and together, a chance to discover their identities. Most blacks were not so lucky.

Donald DeFreeze, identified as Cinque (pronounced *Sin-Q*) and called Cin by his friends, was a child of a poor black family in Ohio. Before he was thirty he'd been arrested in Buffalo, New York; Newark and East Orange, New Jersey; and West Covina, California. He was in Soledad Prison during the time when George Jackson fought for his dignity and was killed. DeFreeze escaped.

He was desperate. An escaped black convict with any political consciousness at all knows there's only prison bars or a policeman's bullet waiting for him. There weren't any communes in the countryside or high-priced lawyers waiting while Cinque found himself. In the most obvious terms, just as communes produced a concern with personal and spiritual growth, the prisons and their violence became the breeding grounds for the SLA mentality. Ask the survivors of Attica about that.

A FANATIC IS A PERSON WHO CHOOSES TO SEE THE WORLD IN ABSOLUTES. Cinque has experienced the whole tortured logic of tantalization, punishment, and denial of a white class society, and been left little chance for manhood. These are the words of a man up against the wall:

"Speaking as a father, I am quite willing to lose both of my children if by that action I could save thousands of black, yellow, and red children from a life of suffering, exploitation, and murder. I am quite willing to carry out the execution of your daughter to save the life of starving men, women, and children of every race."

The slave becomes the judge. Cinque begins to decide who is to live and who is to die in his service to "suffering humanity." If the SLA logic, establishing the organization as the "People's" court, judge, and executioners, seems like a hideous rationalization for murder, then you're missing the point.

Take Joseph Remiro, nicknamed G.I. Joe, combat weapons expert who volunteered for two tours in Vietnam with the 101st Airborne. Handsome and easygoing in his courtroom appearances, his style belies his mastery of the M-1 carbine, the M-60 machine gun, the M-79 rocket launcher, .38 and .45 caliber pistols, and miscellaneous Czech and Chinese weapons. Who could judge by outward signs that he had been trained to kill . . . by the U.S. Army? Somewhere in the Vietnam inferno Remiro decided he should turn his skills around. He joined the SLA and conducted marksmanship classes. Add to Cinque's list of niggers, spics, broads, and wetbacks . . . the grunt. Remiro is not a surprise. The surprise is that more grunts have not brought the guerrilla war home.

There's an inexorable, lock-step force that makes some people desperate outlaws in these times. Rage bottled up under the civilized veneer of America has become an everyday fact of life. White men who couldn't quite understand it in Indians or blacks, have begun to witness it explosively in their women.

This rage of the powerless doesn't respond to reasoned argument, or even common sense. Cinque early on declared himself ready to murder Patricia Hearst; yet she was every bit as innocent as he ever was. The chance of Cinque's birth was to be black; the chance of Patty Hearst's was to be Citizen Kane's granddaughter. But unless we accept the idea of original sin, nothing Patty Hearst had done had earned her execution. Yet Cinque was ready to murder her for the sins of her father, and grandfather. That's not justice. That's revenge.

Rational people feel outraged. Kidnapping Randolph Hearst would be one thing; kidnapping his black-sheep daughter is an entirely different matter. But in every San Quentin, Soledad, or Attica, do you suppose the convicts criticized the SLA for picking the easiest victim? . . . or did they feel an exultant sense of power that a nigger could rip off the Man's empire for millions of dollars' worth of food? Rage goes beyond reason. In Soledad you can bet there was celebration.

Consider the name Cinque, chosen by DeFreeze in prison. In 1839, Spanish slave traders raided the African coast and seized fifty-four people of the Mendi tribe. On the high seas their chief, Cinque, led a revolt, killing the captain and some of the crew and taking charge of the ship, *L'Amistad.* By trickery, the remaining crew sailed the *L'Amistad* to New York rather than back to the rebels' African homeland.

The slave trade had been outlawed in the United States in the 1820s, but these blacks had murdered white men. There was a public furor. The Mendi tribespeople were arrested and tried. John Quincy Adams argued their case before the Supreme Court and, in a 7–1 decision, the Court ruled that with no other recourse available, the blacks had an inherent right to rebel.

While in the U.S., the Mendi had received instruction in Christianity. Before sailing back to their home they were asked if they would have arisen again and killed the ship's officers. Some said they would pray for the captain, but Cinque is reported to have replied: "I would pray for the captain, and kill him too."

The Symbionese Liberation Front seems to embody this righteous anger. The men seem to be mostly ex-convicts or Vietnam veterans. The majority may be women—tough, angry, no-nonsense women who are fighting back. Around Berkeley, coffeehouse leftists argue over their communiqués, printed full page in the daily newspapers, and feel pressed to justify themselves for debating rather than acting. But in the glare of publicity surrounding the Hearst kidnapping, people forget the SLA's first public action: the killing of Oakland school superintendent, Marcus Foster, which was as badly justified by the SLA as the White House tape gap is explained away by President Nixon.

REVOLUTIONARY FERVOR DOESN'T NECESSARILY PRODUCE EFFECTIVE programs. The SLA has proved efficient in military operations but its political acumen has been sadly lacking. In demanding a free food program for the poor, it didn't give people a greater sense of dignity or self-reliance; it created a situation where hungry people were provided with revolutionary charity. Revolutionary charity is still charity; it's not a long-run solution.

At best, the free food lines possessed a sense of community festivity—with easy joking, helpfulness with children and packages, and just a little sense of glee. On those occasions if musicians had brought harmonicas, drums, or other instruments, there might have been dancing. But all too often there was a swirling undercurrent of anger and boredom. When a television camera would appear, the crowd reaction was usually shame or hostility. Unfortunately, the Robin Hood joy of eating the king's meat was missing.

Studying the SLA techniques one can't help but assume they surveyed the tactics of the Tupamaros and the all-time kidnapping experts, Argentina's People's Revolutionary Army (ERP). Like most of the American left, the SLA seems captivated by the dash and romance of military tactics, while ignoring the nuts and bolts necessities such as how to fulfill people's everyday needs.

In Argentina, the ERP kidnapped executives of IBM, Firestone, Otis Elevator, Fiat, Eastman Kodak, etc. They forced these corporations into financing a free children's hospital in the Buenos Aires slums. When the hospital ran low on money, another foreign executive was kidnapped and held for a multimillion dollar donation. If the SLA had learned from this example they would have been using Hearst money to capitalize ongoing food co-ops run by the poor themselves. In these cooperative programs, poor people could have developed managerial skills, while creating an independent marketing system outside the Safeway chain store network. Most important, people could have purchased food cheaply on a long-run basis.

In choosing to assassinate [local schools chief] Marcus Foster and kidnap Patty Hearst as its first two actions, the SLA has created suspicion rather than sympathy. A group like the People's Revolutionary Army took a different path, working carefully to build up credibility. At one point they released a hostage when the ransom demands weren't fully met, to prove their humanity. By May of last year the ERP was so respected that the Ford Motor Co. agreed to pay the group $1 million not to kidnap an executive—a rather gentlemanly arrangement, and a brilliant bit of public relations, which eliminates all the messy necessities of selecting a victim, pulling the job, and paying the ransom.

But the ERP developed slowly under more repressive conditions. They had time to work out their demands. In one case they forced General Motors in Argentina to rehire a thousand workers who had been fired from their jobs. Another action saw a foreign corporation forced to double the wages it paid its workers, while yet another had 154 ambulances delivered to rural hospitals in eight provinces. If we, indeed, live in a global village where black American revolutionaries study *The Battle of Algiers* and SLA members watch the Tupamaros' experience brought to life in Costa-Gavras's *State of Siege,* why has the SLA lacked revolutionary maturity? Why did the initial SLA demand of seventy dollars' worth of food for every disadvantaged Californian work out to an absurd and impossible figure of over $100 million? The answer seems to be that the guerrilla lessons were transmitted as images, devoid of their day-to-day working reality.

The immediate insight among media people covering this kidnap was: "We'll see a lot more kidnaps before this is over." And of course they were right. Just as the initial airplane hijackings prompted worldwide imitations, the Patty Hearst affair sent a kidnapping ripple across the United States.

So even if we give this SLA action the benefit of the doubt, we must still judge the other kidnappings, for which they have some responsibility.

Who will be the first hundred kidnappees? If Reg Murphy, why not Hank Aaron? That would arouse some attention, please Babe Ruth fans, and the Braves would pay a bundle for his return. Taking the American sports mania a step further, the underworld betting syndicate could put their money down and then kidnap the opposing quarterback the day before the play-off game. Damn, once kidnapping gets in vogue it's easy to imagine kidnapping a politician's daughter in the final weeks of a campaign and demanding that the father withdraw from the race.

And, of course, there are no ideological limitations to kidnapping.

In Argentina when the left kidnapped Paraguayan consul Joaquim Sanches and demanded the release of political prisoners, the right kidnapped Yuri Pivavarov, secretary of the Soviet embassy, and threatened to kill him if the prisoners were released. What it's all likely to add up to is the average American being even more willing to trade in his civil liberties for a little security. That's been the net result of airplane hijacking. Searches that two years ago would have been outrageous invasions of privacy are welcomed in airports now. Said one former Berkeley activist, "This kidnap is producing employment for every Pinkerton security thug in the whole universe."

FOR MANY, EMOTIONAL REACTIONS TO PATTY HEARST'S KIDNAPPING interfered with their ability to make a clear analysis. Some were overjoyed that something *heavy* had finally happened in a period defined by streaking. Others were appalled by the violence. Still others found it a positive act because Americans were being made to realize what a huge number of hungry people are hidden away in the cities. A few just wanted a gunfight at the O.K. Corral to get it over with quickly, because they were bored.

But what if we take the SLA at face value and extend their vision?

An underground organization is severely limited in its tactics. First, it can only support existing programs, for the simple reason that if the members try to establish community services such as food distribution points or clinics under their own banner, they are arrested immediately. In Argentina, the People's Revolutionary Army has grown to a couple of thousand members and is capable of carrying out five kidnappings simultaneously, but ultimately kidnapping and bombings have proved an exercise in harassment, not a means of achieving state power. The experience in Argentina and even in Ireland, where a community supports the IRA, is that the necessity for secrecy limits the size of the organization. At a certain point in growth, bureaucratic administrative control sets in, and that creates too high an unreliability factor. A high degree of secrecy and commandolike efficiency are incompatible with tens of thousands of members.

The SLA would no doubt denounce these arguments as pathetically liberal at a time when everybody must "pick up the gun." The reply that "picking up the gun" just increases the national level of paranoia and compounds already existing problems would demonstrate, to them, a severe lack of vision.

But what of the SLA vision? Ultimately they will have to admit they aren't going to overthrow the government by themselves but are setting an example to encourage people within the mother country to join with Third World people in a planetary brand of class warfare.

But the SLA doesn't inspire me to pick up a gun, and, finally, that is their problem. To Patty Hearst, whose contact with hard-line revolutionaries must have been rather limited until her capture and rather overwhelming during it, they may seem to be really in command and know what they're doing. To me they are unconvincing as revolutionaries, let alone as leaders. The example they are setting is not one to be followed seriously.

After a month of examination of the SLA, I was reading their third communiqué for maybe the tenth time when suddenly this sentence leapt out at me:

"This court notifies the public and directs all combat units in the future to *kill any civilians who attempt to witness* [italics mine] or interfere with any operation conducted by the people's forces against the state."

Do they really mean that they will kill all bystanders who happen to witness a kidnapping? Does this mean they tried to kill Patty Hearst's neighbors but were lousy shots? Or is it only more overblown rhetoric? If so, how do they expect to develop trust among the people they are trying to defend? And if killing a witness is a serious intention, where is their humanity?

I'd risk my life for a society with justice, equal opportunities, and community. But for the life of me, I can't find myself submitting to a society run by the SLA. At the end of the Cuban revolution Fidel Castro held only the rank of major. With only twenty-odd SLA members we already have "General Field Marshal" Cinque.

# The Last Song of Victor Jara

*by Stew Albert*

*October 1974*

*One of the defining political moments of the '70s was the CIA-led coup that toppled the Allende government in Chile. Strangely, almost no one mentioned this episode in 1994 when Nixon, at his death, was hailed as a masterful "foreign policy" president. The image of Jara's trembling fingers has stuck with us ever since this article arrived. Phil Ochs, who appears in this piece, killed himself not long afterward. Stew Albert later coedited (with his wife Judy) the anthology* The Sixties Papers.

"Victor Jara was murdered!"

A friend I hadn't seen in over a year stunned me with the news. We had met Jara during our visit to Chile in the early days of the Allende experiment. The death of the democratic socialist Allende in a bloody military coup was old news but Jara's death was not. "They killed Victor in the stadium. His wife saw the body. It's really him."

Three years before we had watched Victor Jara perform at the Pena de los Parras, a club for Chile's most dedicated and talented folk artists. Jara was a folksinger like Pete Seeger or the early Dylan who set his poems and his political passions to music. His voice was strong, his face broad and exuberant. You never forget such a face. He sang of a priest who became a revolutionary:

> *Behind a bullet, he found a voice.*
> *It was God who cried out Revolution.*

*Remake my cassock, my general*
*So a man of the cloth*
*Can become a guerrilla.*

Victor was a regular at the Technical University in Santiago, where he taught folk art and talked politics with the students. While captivating in its own right, his music was always used as an organizing tool. "Usually we Chileanos meet only bad guys from the U.S., like from the CIA," he observed, "but it's really nice to know we have some brothers up north."

He was delighted to discover Phil Ochs was a fellow folksinger. "You will have to come with me to the copper mine up in the Andes. It's just been nationalized and I am going to sing. Also some of my brothers from the university are going to have a basketball game with the workers. It would be very good to have a gringo like Phil Ochs sing."

It was a long, bumpy bus ride to the Anaconda mine. Of the three North Americans, only I spoke a little Spanish, and Victor, who spoke perfect English, was deep in discussion with members of the basketball team. I could make out words like *spies, agents,* and *Nixon.* Finally, Victor turned to us. "My brothers are a little bit mistrustful of you. They think maybe your long hair is some kind of spy's disguise. I am going to sing revolutionary songs. If perhaps you will join in with some enthusiasm, they will see your hearts are in the right place."

As the bus pushed up into the mountains and the magnificent peaks began to disappear into the night, Victor began talking about his life and his dreams.

"My songs, they are what I feel, they are about my life. But I am a peasant and so they are also about millions of people, about suffering, but also sometimes victory."

Victor was dark skinned, and his muscles were built solid from hard labor. He translated from his songs, poetic lines, which showed that when a man reaches deeply and privately into his own heart he may discover the pain and suffering of most of humanity. He sang softly, as if it were just a lullaby, but it was more.

*Don Pedro is your owner, he bought you*
*Things can be bought, but men, no—*
*The white man takes the gold*
*To the black man he leaves pain.*

"I try not to hate," Victor declared, "but how can you not hate such oppression?"

"Do you think Allende's approach will solve Chile's problems?"

"It is necessary for now for us to be peaceful, because the army has all the guns and they aren't friends of the poor. Maybe someday they will make the coup against us. I hope that we will be organized and brave to fight."

Victor's distrust of the military was not publicly shared by the Allende government, which regularly proclaimed its faith in the army's patriotism and loyalty. Jara said, "Well, what they say is public, and of course they don't want to antagonize the army. What I say here is private and among brothers."

We saw Victor again, briefly, at the Technical University. He asked us if John Lennon might want to visit, and we told him about Lennon's troubles with the Immigration Department.

"If the gringos don't want him," Victor replied, "maybe he should come live in Chile."

THIS WAS THE LAST TIME WE SAW VICTOR, STANDING OUTSIDE A CLASSroom at the same university where he was taken prisoner by the fascists. Victor was spending a lot of time there helping students bring food and fuel to the poor people, who were suffering from the CIA-sponsored strike of small businessmen. Food wasn't being distributed by the business interests so students were trying hard to feed as many as possible. This is what Victor was devoting his life to when he was captured. He and six thousand other Chileans were thrown into the National Stadium and kept under armed guard.

Miguel Cabenzas, a Chilean journalist, was a prisoner in the National Stadium. He witnessed the murder of Victor Jara. This account was translated by Leonore Veltfort.

"Chaos, desperation, panic were all over. Unless one has lived through a scene like this one can't imagine the extent of people's collective madness when they are provoked by such incomparable terror.

"The prisoners were put in the bleachers of the stadium, and down below were the military. They focused strong lights on the prisoners. Suddenly, somebody began to scream with terror, having lost his mind. Immediately, machine-gun volleys were loosed against the section from where the scream came. Ten or twenty bodies fell from the high bleachers, rolling over the bodies of those prisoners who had thrown themselves to the ground to avoid the shots.

"I saw comrades who, in all the days they stayed there, never lifted their faces from the stone floor and afterwards had lost all capacity to move. The psychological shock was complete. There were people who for many days were only able to stammer a few incoherent words.

"Victor wandered around among the prisoners, trying to calm them, to keep a minimum of order among them. A fruitless attempt. The terror was limitless. It brought the prisoners to the lowest degree of human degradation. The military were determined to accomplish this, and after three days of detention and mass terror they did.

"The prisoners, who had not eaten or drunk anything in those three days of imprisonment, vomited on the dead bodies of their comrades. I saw prisoners who howled, wide-eyed with terror, no longer able to remember their own names. Victor tried to control his own psychological state, a very difficult task under the circumstances.

"At one point, Victor went down to the arena and approached one of the doors where new prisoners entered. Here he bumped into the commander of the prison camp. The commander looked at him, made a tiny gesture of someone playing the guitar. Victor nodded his head affirmatively, smiling sadly and candidly. The military man smiled to himself. He called four soldiers and ordered them to hold Victor there. Then he ordered a table to be brought and to be put in the middle of the arena so that everybody could see what was to happen. They took Victor to the table and ordered him to put his hands on it. In the hands of the officer ('I have two beautiful children and a happy home,' he declared days afterwards to the foreign press) rose, swiftly, an axe.

"With one single stroke he severed the fingers of Victor's left hand and, with another stroke, the fingers of the right. The fingers fell to the wooden floor, trembling and still moving, while Victor's body fell down heavily.

"A collective outcry from six thousand prisoners was heard. These twelve thousand eyes then watched the same officer throw himself over the fallen body of the singer and actor Victor Jara and begin to hit him while shouting, 'Now sing, you motherfucker, now sing.'

"No one who saw the face of the officer, axe in hand, disheveled hair over his forehead, can forget it. It was the face of bestiality and unbridled hatred.

"Victor received the blows while his hands were dripping blood and his face was rapidly turning violet. Unexpectedly, he laboriously raised himself to his feet and blindly turned toward the bleachers of the stadium. His steps were faltering, knees trembling, his mutilated hands stretched forward like those of a sleepwalker.

"When he came to where the arena and the bleachers meet, there was a deep silence. And then his voice was heard crying: 'All right, comrades, let's do the *señor commandante* the favor!'

"He steadied himself for a moment and then lifting his bleeding hands, began to sing, with an unsteady voice, the anthem of the *Unidad Popular,* and everybody sang with him.

"As those six thousand voices rose into song, Victor marked the time with his mutilated hands. In his face was a smile—open and released—and his eyes shone as if possessed.

"This sight was too much for the military. A volley, and the body of Victor began to double over as if he were reverentially making a long and slow bow to his comrades. Then he fell down on his side and remained lying there.

"More volleys followed from the mouths of the machine guns, but those were directed against the people in the bleachers who had accompanied Victor's song.

"An avalanche of bodies tumbled down, riddled with bullets, rolling into the arena. The cries of the wounded were horrible. But Victor Jara did not hear them anymore. He was dead."

Victor Jara was twenty-seven years old.


A FEW MONTHS AGO I ATTENDED A BENEFIT IN NEW YORK FOR CHILEAN refugees, which was organized by Phil Ochs. It was a big event because Bob Dylan appeared, coming out of political retirement like he was back in his old hootenanny civil rights days. But the highlight for me was Pete Seeger reading a poem written by Victor and smuggled out of the stadium shortly before his death. Pete's voice evoked the feelings behind Jara's words.

> *We are 5000, here in this little corner of the city.*
> *How many are we in all the cities of the world?*
> *All of us, our eyes fixed on death.*
> *How terrifying is the face of fascism!*
> *For them, blood is a medal, carnage is a heroic gesture.*
> *Song, I cannot sing you well when I must sing out of fear.*
> *When I am dying of fright.*
> *When I find myself in these endless moments.*
> *Where silence and cries are the echoes of my song.*

Today, the struggle for democracy in Chile goes on, and in the fight guns are going to be used. This time it won't be nonviolent. The generals and the CIA don't want the peaceful "Chilean way" to work. The songs of Victor Jara will again be sung in a free Chile. But Jara's greatest poem is beyond the language of words. It was his death, and life.

# Chappaquiddick:
# A Bridge Too Far

*by David Black*

*September 1975*

*Hard to believe, but when* Crawdaddy *helped revive the Chappaquiddick scandal, Teddy Kennedy was thought to be a front-runner for president in '76 or '80. In typical* Crawdaddy *fashion, our writer literally went the extra mile—diving into the channel and practically drowning in the process. David Black survived to write several novels and nonfiction books and scripts for* Miami Vice *and* Hill Street Blues, *among other shows.*

We live in a secular age, so naturally we are an obsessively religious generation. And since the pageantry of church ceremonies no longer satisfies our spiritual needs, we seek rituals in the public life of our nation and we make public personalities our gods. An appropriately jovial Richard Burton does for Jupiter, paired to the plump, sexy, wrathful Juno of Elizabeth Taylor. Peter Bogdanovich is Pygmalion fashioning a Galatea out of Cybill Shepherd. Burt Reynolds plays Cupid to Dinah Shore's Venus. Rex Reed becomes Mercury, the messenger of the gods, a bearer of salacious tidings.

Normally, these new Olympians work and play on the fringes of our consciousness. When we need a taste of the divine, a fix from the godhead, we tune them in: by watching Johnny Carson, reading a Hollywood autobiography, or poring over the gossip columns (many of which crowd the newspapers disguised as political commentary).

Every so often, however, an event involving celebrities seizes our attention and, because of its elemental nature, opens up, offering us access to our mythical past. The assassination of JFK, for example, was not only the murder of a public leader, but a ritualistic replaying of the myth of the sacrificed hero. That is why it has such a grip on our imaginations. We responded on a primitive level to the tragedy. It is not just JFK we mourned, but also his earlier mythic versions. JFK becomes Osiris, Tammuz, Orpheus, Christ.

Like JFK's assassination and Robert Kennedy's murder, Edward Kennedy's car accident on Chappaquiddick Island off Martha's Vineyard in Massachusetts on the night of July 18, 1969, has also been transformed with the passage of time into a mythical event. The fascination it evoked and continues to evoke has as much to do with its mythic as with its political consequences. People who have no apparent interest in politics—continue to worry the tragedy of Chappaquiddick like a dog gnawing on an old slipper.

Part of the accident's appeal has to do with its timing. Because it happened during the same summer as the first Moon walk, it acted as an anchor that dragged on our emotions of triumph in space, as though it were part of a divine punishment for our hubris in entering the heavens.

Part of its appeal was due to its being the third public act of the modern drama of an American House of Atreus—the royal sons suffering for the sins of their father, Joseph Kennedy, former ambassador to the Court of St. James's, who on the eve of World War II betrayed a sinister sympathy for Nazi Germany.

And, of course, part of its appeal was the result of its echoes: it was a playing out, in a minor key, of the Osiris-Tammuz-Orpheus-Christ legend that had already absorbed brothers John and Robert. A playing out of that legend with a twist—Edward physically survived.

The death and rebirth of the hero.

None of this, of course, is meant to suggest that interest in what happened to Edward Kennedy on Chappaquiddick is not political. In a recent Gallup poll, Kennedy led by *twenty-one points* the nearest contender for the Democratic presidential nomination; and last May he was only two points behind President Ford in the Harris poll. Despite his disclaimers, Edward Kennedy may very well be our next president.

It *is* meant to suggest that, while examining the accident and the subsequent events, it may be useful to admit an element of the irrational into any speculation. Perhaps, even necessary. Kennedy himself, in the televised speech he gave a week after the accident, said,

"All kinds of scrambled thoughts, all of them confused, some of them irrational . . . went through my mind during this period . . . including such questions as . . . whether some awful curse did actually hang over all the Kennedys. . . ." And his failure to report the accident for ten hours was justified in his mind by a magical notion that "even though I knew Mary Jo Kopechne was dead and believed firmly that she was in the back of that car, I willed that she remained alive."

Kennedy's irrational thoughts sound authentic; why would a politician invent moral ramblings that were irrational and therefore untrustworthy? And these irrational thoughts expose a desperate attempt on his part to understand what had happened to him on Chappaquiddick mythically—as the result of some special, often malignant destiny that demanded blood sacrifice from the Kennedy family.

The world is not always a rational place; and people, after all, even senators and potential presidential candidates, do not always act logically.

SIX YEARS LATER, EVERYONE STILL TALKS ABOUT IT. EVEN THE ISLANDERS who try to act bored by the subject still talk about it. On the ferry that leaves Wood's Hole (the southernmost point on Cape Cod mainland) and slips across Vineyard Sound to Vineyard Haven, one of the few towns on Martha's Vineyard Island, the girl behind the snack bar says, "On every trip over, you hear two or three people at least talking about it."

It is the night of July 18, 1969, when Teddy Kennedy drove a black four-door 1967 Oldsmobile 88 off a narrow wooden bridge on Chappaquiddick, a smaller island to the east of Martha's Vineyard, a dribble and a blob from God's pen as he mapped the earth. In that accident, a twenty-eight-year-old woman named Mary Jo Kopechne died, trapped in that sunk car like an astronaut locked in a space capsule that was running out of oxygen and hurtling out of control toward the margin of our solar system. Kennedy survived, although precisely how has never been detailed.

There are a number of conflicting versions of what happened that night, some as arcane as Talmudic scratchings, commentaries on commentaries—which is understandable since the events at Chappaquiddick offer us a morality tale of no little interest. We measure our own courage and stamina against Kennedy's: What would we have done in that situation? And we measure that private event against possible public events: What if Teddy Kennedy were president and Chappaquiddick (the name denotes an incident now as well as an island, psychic as well as terrestrial geography) were a new Cuban Missile Crisis?

The crisis, however, occurred in a playground, Martha's Vineyard, an island where the rich go to summer and to die. The streets of the town are crowded with the young and the retired, all waiting for the events that will change their lives: the perfect affairs, the discovery of unparalleled havens from the sweaty bustle of the mainland world.

To gain a measure of the island, you must check out the hired help. The waitresses are all attending Smith and Mount Holyoke. The baby-sitters all go to Spence and Chapin. Jimmy Cagney lives up the road; James Reston owns the local newspaper.

To reach Chappaquiddick from Edgartown (which is on Martha's Vineyard Island) one has to cross a swift channel of water five hundred feet wide, a distance a little longer than the length of a subway train. When the tide is running, the small ferry, just large enough to carry two or three cars, which works back and forth across this channel, must head into the current at a 45-degree angle to buck the undertow and avoid getting carried far down the shore.

On the dock by the ferry slip, an old man is fishing for squid. He throws his line into the water, and the squid immediately attack his lure. When one is hooked and brought to the surface, it squirts out water and ink, spinning like a pinwheel; and, when the pale blue-white bodies are flopped onto the dock, they abruptly change color, turning a deep crimson and back to a pale blue-white again, desperately trying to find the appropriate camouflage. The ink they had expelled drifts in clouds through the water long after they've been landed.

"Yes," says the old man, "that's the channel Kennedy says he swam." He tugs on his line and lets it drift again. "Far as I know, only one man ever swam that channel, and it wasn't Edward Kennedy."

The man is John Farrar, captain of the Edgartown Fire Department Search and Rescue Division, the scuba diver who dragged Mary Jo's corpse from the submerged car the morning after the accident. Farrar runs the Turf and Tackle Shop on the main street of Edgartown. He is a rangy man, a Marlboro cowboy from Brown University, now in his waning thirties. He wears boots and a Stetson, sits with his feet up on his cluttered desk in his office at the back of the shop, talking slowly in a kind of dreamer's drawl.

The radio is always on. Its crackle and squawk dominate the small room. Like the high school fullback who can never free himself from nostalgia for that big homecoming game when he scored the

winning touchdown, Farrar thinks wistfully of the summer of 1969.
Thinks wistfully and listens to his shortwave because you can never
tell when another call might come through that could give John Farrar another chance to participate in great affairs of state. Kennedy
made Farrar a hero. Farrar likes being a hero, but he hates Kennedy.

Like a chef at Benihana slicing up a shrimp, Farrar cuts up
Kennedy, snips and bits of reputation flying:

"Hell-bent for election," says Farrar, "that's how he was driving
over that bridge. . . ."

Farrar relishes pointing out all the contradictions in Kennedy's
story; and the story sounds like a John D. MacDonald mystery, all
high society and low desire. Six men, all over thirty and all but one
married, meet six girls, all under thirty and all unmarried; they
party in a secluded cottage on Chappaquiddick, rowdy enough to
rouse the neighbors. Kennedy drives off with one of the girls,
doomed Mary Jo, a perfect ingenue part for, say, Karen Black,
Kennedy played by Robert Redford (who has the same flash of teeth
in the smile, the same hunched charisma).

They are going (Kennedy says later) to catch the last ferry back to
Edgartown, which leaves at midnight. But a woman who lives near
the bridge does not hear any crash off the bridge before midnight,
when she goes to sleep. And Deputy Sheriff Christopher Look Jr.
sees at 12:45 a large dark car with a Massachusetts license plate beginning with an *L* and ending with a *7* drive off down the Dyke Road
toward the bridge where the accident happened. Kennedy's
Oldsmobile had a Massachusetts license plate L78207.

The contradictions tumble from the tale like clowns spilling from
a tiny circus car. By now they have become a well-rehearsed ritual
for political analysts. But you have to see the main road of Chappaquiddick to realize how impossible it would be for Kennedy to accidentally turn from that onto the dirt track of the Dyke Road. Such
a mistake would be the equivalent of a jet liner swerving from its
normal route and mistaking a footpath into the airport terminal for
the runway.

A week after the accident, Kennedy gave a TV speech explaining
what had happened on the night of July 18th, a performance as slick
and as glossy as Fabulon poured thick and dried over a rotten floor.
No one can doubt that Kennedy was grief-stricken. Even the most
rabid right-winger would admit that Kennedy mourned, if not Mary
Jo, then at least his political future.

But the little grief that showed appeared through the glaze of a
professionalism as admirable as it was unsavory. What was the psychic cost of preparing a public face for his despair?

In the speech he denied being drunk or having had an improper relationship with Mary Jo, a claim many people dismissed as being, at best, a gallant evasion and, at worst, a cowardly lie. One's reaction to this disavowal of drunken or lewd behavior, in fact, may be the seed around which crystallizes one's own mythology of what occurred that night—and, until Kennedy more fully explains what went on at the Chappaquiddick bridge, all we are left with is mythology: that is, assumptions based on our own imagination to account for events whose explanation remains hidden from us.

It was during the television speech that Kennedy first publicly mentioned his plunge into Chappaquiddick Channel, another aspect of the case that has greatly disturbed students of Chappaquiddick.

> *The ferry having shut down for the night, I suddenly jumped into the water and impulsively swam across, nearly drowning once again in the effort, and returned to my hotel about 2 A.M. and collapsed in my room.*

And it was during this television speech that he indicated he had talked to the hotel clerk, had in fact stepped from his room dry and fully dressed, even to a coat, and asked the clerk for the time (it was 2:25)—an action that sounds suspiciously like a preparation for an alibi.

The reactions to the speech were mixed, Kennedy's people claiming a great deal of support, major editorials cautious, and many people incredulous with anger—anger that could not be dissolved in pity or resolved into outright contempt for the senator, anger like a chicken bone stuck in the throat. In the small town in Massachusetts where I was living that summer, solid Kennedy country in previous elections, the feeling among the voters was cannibalistic, especially among those who had apotheosized his brothers. By surviving, Teddy had cheated them of another martyr. Three is a magical number; Teddy's escape violated their sense of neatness, completeness, closure. The accident was like a muffed suicide, the suicide manqué alive the day after, sheepish, embarrassed at still being alive. His survival seemed to some in this small Massachusetts town one more indication that he did not measure up to his brothers, who had gone the whole route, and who—by doing so—had given them icons to adore. Their anger at Teddy, had he died, would have been reverence.

• • •

DURING THE WEEK BEFORE HIS SPEECH AND FOR MONTHS AFTERWARDS, crowds of tourists tromped up Dyke Road to the bridge to scoop water from the pond and sand from the bank, and to cut slivers from the bridge that, like pieces of the true cross, they would venerate once they returned to their homes.

The graffiti that had been scratched on the bridge within days of the accident—"Teddy and Mary Jo" inscribed within a heart: "Teddy's Car Wash"—have long since been erased. But the tourists still come and gawk, shuffling back and forth across the bridge, peering underneath the planks, poking each other, pointing, and smirking. They look at Dyke Road and see Lovers' Lane. They look at the bridge and see Lovers' Leap. They exercise a politics of sly insinuation. They embellish their surmise with lewd suggestions. It's the front page of the *National Enquirer* brought to life. An ecstasy of titillation.

At dusk, when the tourists start to leave and all that is left is an old bridge with a kid fishing off the side, the landscape comes back into focus. There's nothing lurid about the place. It's a peaceful, quiet spot. A small, unassuming bridge, set at a dangerous angle to the road. The pebble that tripped the elephant.

For two hours at dusk I drove back and forth across the bridge. Twenty miles per hour—the speed Kennedy claimed he was going when the accident occurred. 25 mph. 30 mph. 35 mph. One had to be very careful at 35 mph, to aim well, for the bridge is narrow; even a Volkswagen's trip across is precarious. At night, an Oldsmobile 88, a car with the unwieldly bulk of a wide-hipped woman, could easily have gone off the bridge at 20 mph.

I drove back down Dyke Road and turned onto the paved road toward the Lawrence Cottage, drove slowly, thinking about the bridge, and realized that I had missed my goal.

I had missed not only the cottage but the houses along the route and the little concrete fire station that looks like somebody's garage. Farrar claims that Kennedy could have, should have stopped in one of those houses or at least at the fire station to call for help.

Well, it is not hard to miss the houses. And the fire station does not command your attention—even when you know it's there. Yes, Kennedy could have missed them. But it is also likely that he didn't want to see them, that he wanted to collect himself, appraise the situation before reporting the accident to the police.

"When they dragged the car out," Farrar told me, "large bubbles of air came out, which means there must have been a fairly sizable air pocket within the car that she could have used to breathe in. She could have lived for a half hour, maybe even longer, in that air pocket. The tragic thing is that if Kennedy had gotten help immediately, she could have been saved."

After I returned to Edgartown for dinner, I ferried back to Chappaquiddick to take another look at the road, the bridge, the cottage. The island seemed deserted. And, because it was deserted and isolated there was a feeling of wide possibility in the air. At night, Chappaquiddick is the kind of place that invites the secretly erotic, the kind of place where you could easily wander away from a party to skinny-dip in the ocean with a stranger.

At the ferry slip, I parked my car, and, stripping to my shorts, waded into the channel from the shore on the harbor side of the dock. Just because it seemed unlikely, the idea of Kennedy diving into the channel and swimming across to Edgartown appealed to me—trying to defeat one disaster by inviting another, as though by swimming close to death he might find in this risk the route to the Underworld and, like Orpheus, try to charm Mary Jo, his Eurydice, back to life. Not so much a drunken plunge as an existential leap. If he didn't swim the channel (and it is hard to believe that he did), he should have.

It was cloudy, so there was no moon. The water was very dark and very cold; entering it was like slipping a wet rubber glove over my body. I walked out hesitantly, testing the riptide, planning to keep on my feet until the water reached my chest and to turn back if the undertow seemed too strong. Although a good swimmer, I am not a particularly powerful one. I lost my balance in the current. Dunked, I started kicking against the tide, a doomed salmon trying unsuccessfully to make it upstream. When I poked my head above water, I checked out the position of the ferry slip on the Edgartown side, and realized that I was fast being carried out into Nantucket Sound toward the Atlantic.

I floundered back toward the Chappaquiddick side of the channel, swallowing too much water, and beginning to feel somewhat panicky. Kennedy's description of how he felt he was going to die lingered in my mind like an after image of a slide flashed for a second on a screen.

Driving a car off a bridge and then jumping into a treacherous channel—the two acts are consistent, betraying a lust for extinction and rebirth. While drifting with the current on a dark night in dark water you can hear death's siren call. It *is* attractive, it *is* peaceful to give yourself up and be carried out to sea. For a moment, you even consider letting go, allowing it to happen.

My toes touched bottom just as I was passing around the last close point of land after which the harbor would have gulped me down. If

I could easily imagine Kennedy jumping into the water, I could not now as easily imagine him resisting the lure of death by drowning. If his story is true, if he did dive into the channel and make it to the other side, his soul must be a battlefield where the desire for death (the itch to join his brothers, to follow their example; how left behind he must feel) and the will to live must struggle like Satan and Christ locked in combat on the Plain of Armageddon.

EXCEPT FOR FARRAR, NO ONE WILL TALK. LOOK, THE WITNESS (WHAT occult coincidence singled out a witness with a name like "Look"?); Mills, the doctor who examined Mary Jo's corpse; Frieh, the undertaker—all politely hang up the phone. No comment. I don't know that I want to get into that again.

"Don't you want to scotch the rumors that are still going around?" I ask.

"Rumors?" They speak with one voice; their responses were nearly identical. "They have nothing to do with me."

The rumors of course not only survive in the silence, they thrive, multiply.

"Hunt and Liddy and that other guy, that Cuban," says a man at the bar of the Harborside Inn, "I saw them up here a month before the accident. I recognized their photos in the paper during that Watergate thing. They're the ones behind what happened to Kennedy." I suspect that for a number of years to come any unexplained mischief, especially if it has a political nature, will be blamed on this trio.

Each rumor jostles for space among other rumors; all rumors are presented as fact. "I know what really happened; listen—"

"Mary Jo was pregnant."

"Mary Jo knew something about the assassinations and she was going to talk."

"Three of them—Kennedy, Mary Jo, and Rosemary Keough [whose purse was found in the backseat of the death car]—went off together but Teddy and Rosemary wandered off together, and Mary Jo was pissed and she drove off the bridge."

"Accidentally?"

"Maybe, but," here's the leer, "she could have done it on purpose."

Theories of what happened, and especially theories based on rumor, can be spun as easily as cotton candy at a carnival. And they are just that substantial.

But they do plug the well. The suggestion that Joseph Kennedy Jr. had been driving the car that plunged off the bridge, like a thumb in the dike of Teddy's reputation, melted away with time only to be resurrected in whispers when Joseph Jr. was in a car accident in which a young girl was paralyzed. Joe Jr. (according to some reports) was seen wandering sopping wet through the streets of Edgartown, around the time his uncle was supposed to be swimming the channel. And Joe Jr. left Edgartown the morning of the 19th—although he may have been spirited away only out of a decent respect for Teddy's disaster, not because he was the agent of it.

In any case, this theory has the advantage of suggesting a family tie that conjures up the ghost of pride in every uncle who ever genially covered for his straying nephew: Junior didn't steal my car; he knew I'd let him borrow it. Right, Junior? An elbow in the ribs, a manly wink. Next week it's time to tell you the facts of life. After the baseball game, I'll take you to your first whorehouse. Uncles: rogue fathers without a father's responsibility.

But it is unlikely that a U.S. senator, no matter how loving an uncle, would put his reputation on the line for a nephew run amok.

PERHAPS THE MOST LIKELY SOLUTION TO THIS MYSTERY IS THAT THE accident happened more or less as Kennedy claimed. He may have been a little drunker than he admits to, he may have left the house a little later than he says he did, he may have been driving a little faster than he would like the public to believe.

If so, what are we left with? An accident, which, as Mike Mansfield telegrammed to Teddy, could have happened to any of us. It could, of course; and yet . . .

The Kennedy family has suffered a series of tragedies so foul and so inexplicable that it is not surprising to hear the whistle of superstition in Teddy's television speech or in his subsequent testimony at the inquest. And it would not be surprising if in the center of Teddy's imagination is the faith that, yes, there has to be a Kennedy curse, because otherwise the tragedies would not make any sense at all; they would be merely coincidences, and that would be truly intolerable.

So he lives with the idea of a curse, clings to it; it is religion and salvation, a charm against insanity and meaninglessness. And, because he lives with it, it cannot help but shape his life.

Our lives are, after all, in part a product of our expectations. We are all seers of self-fulfilling prophecy. How much of the accident at Chappaquiddick, therefore, was the result of Kennedy's subconscious premeditation, the result of this belief in a malignant special destiny for the Kennedy family, for himself?

He has outlived his brothers. And a survivor cannot escape from the twinges of guilt: Why did *he* escape? Why not him, too? The accident may have been Kennedy's unconscious offering to his brothers—a self-sacrifice that failed.

If we are drawn to the accident, years later, it is finally because we recognize that Kennedy is living with this myth, this idea of a curse; and that the myth could, in a larger form, be our myth too, a myth that is demanding a worldwide stage and inconceivable weapons of destruction for its realization.

If Teddy Kennedy might become our next president, it is because we are a people who are prepared to elect as our leader a man who may very well be marked, not only by some future assassin's bullet, but also by his own private sense of doom.

# Time of the Assassins

*by William Burroughs*
*April 1976*

*Burroughs was a* Crawdaddy *columnist for three years, which helped spark his rediscovery by a new generation of punks, neo-Beats, and rock and rollers. He called the column "Time of the Assassins," and indeed, some of his best work centered on topical political violence and intrigue.*

As a columnist I sometimes raid other columnists for ideas, and the inspiration for this column I owe to William Buckley Junior, the conservative buffoon.

As old lady Luce said about him, he is articulate; and in his column for the *New York Post,* January 16, 1976, entitled "Assassination and the CIA," he has clearly articulated the basic conflict formula between nations and individuals—a line of thinking from Jehovah to Hiroshima: I am *right,* justified, duty bound, in the name of National Security, decency, morality, Jesus Christ, America, Mom, the CIA, the FBI, Wall Street, supermarkets, color TV, venison sausages, and Malvern spring water in my bursting refrigerator, which when I open it sometimes spills gallons of milk and orange juice and chilled aquavit across the kitchen floor, in the name of the American way of life, everything we hold sacred, our churches and our banks, General Motors, Standard Oil, IBM, Con Edison, our living standard, and the Bible Belt. I am *right* because I am an American and my opponent is not. And by "American" I mean *real Americans, who share all my opinions*—not dissidents, deviants, and malcontents.

And my opponent is wrong, because he is not a real American as here defined.

So in dealing with such unmitigated evil, clearly any means are justified. We would be failing in our duty if we did not . . . measures necessary for the preservation of . . . in the face of this threat to our national security . . . no other alternatives being open. . . .

All right, back to this Buckley. A month or so ago he was saying that Squeaky Fromme and all others who make an attempt on the life of a public official should be executed. Now to make my own position on assassination clear, I want to say I think the Fords are nice people . . . just the sort of people I grew up with, nice, rather ineffectual people . . . and I certainly don't want any of the First Family shot. I feel that assassination of public or private figures should be firmly discouraged and I am no apologist for Squeaky Fromme, who would probably assassinate me if she got a chance. On the other hand, I have always opposed capital punishment under any circumstances.

Well, here is Buckley now, defending the CIA assassination attempts, which are old stuff, really—we British have been doing it for several hundred years, and pride ourselves in *succeeding* in our attempts for the most part and not getting caught with our pants full of opium and fish poison guns. Like I say, old hat: The Russians have cigarette cases and lighters that shoot cyanide pellets and who knows what else.

So with one gulp Buckley is saying we should execute assassins or attempted assassins of public figures, and with another: "It's all right if *we* do it." Here he is on Cuba and the CIA-inspired assassination attempts on Fidel Castro: "Except for the Nuclear Age the United States would certainly have declared war against Castro's Cuba. The provocations far exceeded those that conventionally precede a declaration of war." Buckley is clearly a gentleman of the old school who believes in conventions about this sort of thing. He continues: "Castro had invited our principal enemy into his country to arm that country with destructive weapons aimed at American population centers."

Now how did Russia become our "principal enemy"? You all remember back in World War II, the pictures of American and Russian troops embracing on the battlefield. You can see their breath in the air spell out The Cold War. From here to eternity—where would the CIA, the GPU, the armies and the navies of Russia and America be without it? It's the old game of war. In the course of which we were always open, honest, fair, well intentioned, willing to be friends; whereas the Russians were consistently covert, unprincipled, treacherous, ill-intentioned, and dedicated by some strange alien obsession known as communism to the total overthrow of the United States? So now, all our peaceful overtures have fallen on barren ground, and destructive weapons are aimed at our homeland. And how many American missiles are there on Russia's borders with destructive weapons aimed at the Russian homeland and population centers?

Buckley continues: "Castro was sending out platoons of revolutionaries to disturb the peace of the continent." The peaceful regimes of Papa Doc's Haiti, Santo Domingo under Trujillo, present-day Santo Domingo under the Trujillo family and the CIA, the torture/murder squad police state of Brazil, the mass terrorism in Chile, the oppressive regime of Uruguay. Indeed, such revolutionary platoons corrupted the South Vietnamese eventually, disturbing their peaceful tiger cages and flourishing heroin traffic.

Buckley continues: "If it becomes necessary to remove the threat posed by a single leader who has a handle on nuclear weapons, does one prefer the sniper or a mass amphibious operation?" Such alternatives posed in a vacuum are meaningless. And Mr. Buckley should bear in mind that according to the rules in this James Bond world of snipers, any number can play. You think the Russkies don't have our fish poisons—something better maybe? Mr. Buckley, you are declaring *open season on all political figures in the world who have a handle on nuclear weapons* . . . like we can knock off Brezhnev, or the head of any country whose politics we disapprove of, and vice versa—from Russia with love. Mr. Buckley's policies might well kill all the politicians everywhere.

I just wonder if he sees the full implications of what he is saying when he says "ethical men might therefore in good conscience have recommended the elimination of a single individual to avoid nuclear devastation." Politicians in any country tend to think of themselves as "ethical men." In any case, is assassination a reliable way to avoid nuclear devastation? Couldn't an assassination just spark something off? It happened before—in Sarajevo, if memory serves. Turn the thing loose and Sarajevos leap up like hydra heads all over the planet—got so they couldn't pay anyone to occupy the White House . . . dragged an old drunken bum off skid row, and our image suffered when he blew snot on the shoes of a visiting dignitary and it was almost conventionally a declaration of war.

This either/or, right or wrong, "I'm right and he's wrong," is the basic war and conflict formula. "Ain't room for both of us on this planet—fill your hand, stranger. You're different from me and I don't like you." It seems highly unlikely that one clean quick bullet could knock out the potential for nuclear war, especially since more and more government officials are becoming interchangeable bureaucrats. Buckley continues: "Most people agree that the fanatical opposition of Amin to Israel could bring him to load an atom bomb into one of his wheezy planes and drop it over Tel Aviv." Buckley doesn't say where Amin would get the atom bomb, and certainly Israel has more of a handle than Amin on nuclear weapons. "Does the Israeli version of the CIA have a right to send a sniper down to Uganda?" he asks . . . and could not the fanatical anticommunism of Chile's Pinochet bring him to drop an atom bomb on Cuba? And so on.

I don't feel that I can justly be accused of being a bleeding heart idealist when I suggest that shooting someone doesn't necessarily calm a situation down. Any number can play, and if we encourage or condone assassinations in other countries, we can expect to see assassinations increase in America, rapidly escalating towards a shooting war. You can't go around knocking off anybody who doesn't agree with American policies and who might have a handle on nuclear weapons without making the use of such weapons progressively more likely, since what more adequate grounds for conventionally declaring war can there be than the assassination of a leader by a hostile foreign power? Russia withdraws from the U.N. . . . the president bluntly warns . . . "Ladies and gentlemen, it is exactly thirty seconds to countdown; if the president receives no message from Russia in answer to his terms, as clearly stated yesterday, before 3:08 P.M., war will automatically be declared by both countries and computerized atomic missile attacks will be activated on both sides. We suggest that at countdown you proceed to your bunkers and may God help us all . . ." Triumph we must but our cause would be dust.

Consider the future of the world after an all-out nuclear war between Russia and America: vast areas devastated, uninhabitable for years to come; diseased, starving survivors, many doomed or crippled from birth, staggering through radioactive mazes . . . New York is fantastic, like a vast sinister slag heap with mountains of molten glass and steel and a constant smog of brick dust. Our Geiger counters chatter ominously. We mutter a ritual curse on our ancestors, those ethical men who acted in all good conscience, and feel better—but not for long . . . the slow fire in our bones . . . "I don't care what the Geiger counter says, I'm kicking in that drugstore and shooting up with radioactive morphine."

I agree with Mr. Buckley about the danger of atomic weapons in the hands of lunatics and fanatics; yet I cannot but think that a psychotic American or Russian general, as in Doctor Strangelove, could be considerably more dangerous than Amin.

I feel that we must reject assassination as an instrument of peace, however much it may appeal to the schoolboy in us all—the lone sniper who cuts the fiend down with thirty seconds to countdown, when his missiles would have rained down on a peaceful and civilized world. The assassin is of course hailed as a liberator by the dictator's unwilling accomplices.

There is also a danger implicit in computerized missile systems that only the major atomic powers can afford. The machine thinks so much faster than the human brain that it could be making calculations ten years into the future and issuing an attack order based on these findings. Doctor Norbert Wiener, the father of cybernetics, sounded a word of warning: "The machine thinks so much faster than we do that it might well sweep us all to disaster before we realized what the machine was about."

One only hopes they can think of something less messy; perhaps a plague that will kill off 90 percent of the planet's personnel, leaving 10 percent hale and hearty with plenty of fertilizer. Yes sir, the compost laid down by all them dead bodies—you drop a seed in and then jump back before the plant hits you in the eye—opium pods big as cantaloupes—and we lived off the fat of the land. Who did? Why, those who released the plague, of course. You get a good biologic that kills within minutes, inoculate your boys, then turn it loose and get yourself hid good until things quiet down and you can look at a beautiful vista of corpses to the sky! "Safe at last, boys. YIPPEEEEEEEEE!"

It's the old army game. One of the rules is that there can be no final victory, since this would end the game. Yet every player must believe in final victory and strive for it with all his powers; threatened by the nightmare of total defeat, he has no alternative. So all existing technologies have been directed towards producing ever more total weapons, right up to the atom bomb, which may yet end the game by killing all the players.

Now let us postulate a miracle: The so-stupid players decide to save the game. They sit down at a table and draw up a plan for the deactivation of all atomic weapons and the destruction of such weapons over the next 500,000 years. Why stop there? Conventional bombs are more destructive than necessary if nobody else has them. So we set the war clock back to 1914—

*Keep the home fires burning*
*Though our hearts are yearning*

*It's a long way to Tipperary*
*It's a long way to go . . .*

On back to the Civil War—"He has loosed the fatal lightning of His terrible swift sword." His terrible swift sword didn't cost as much in those days. Think of the enormous savings in the defense budget as we set the war clock further and further back, to flintlocks, matchlocks, swords, bows and arrows, spears, stone axes. Why stop there? Why not grow teeth and claws, poison fangs, spines, stingers, beaks, and stink glands and fight it out in the mud? If the human race cannot exist without enemies, it would seem advisable to limit the damage they can do.

# FBI vs. Indians

*by Stew Albert and Judith Clavir*
*October 1976*

*Wounded Knee, Russell Means, Leonard Peltier—one Native American cause followed another throughout the '70s. (Not to mention Shasheen Littlefeather and Little Big Man.) This trial, featuring special guest appearances by Marlon Brando and "Wild Bill" Kunstler, was dramatized many years later in Robert Redford's Incident at Oglala.*

Rifles blaze. The solitary calm of the South Dakota plains is broken by a fierce exchange of gunfire. A shoot-out between FBI agents and Indians is tearing up the land. An old house caught in the crossfire is assaulted by tear gas and bullets. The dwelling belongs to an Indian couple who have just celebrated their fiftieth wedding anniversary. Men are dying. Two agents and an Oglala Indian will be dead by the end of this day, June 25, 1975.

Within twenty-four hours the FBI will launch a military-style invasion and occupation of the Pine Ridge Indian Reservation, just thirty miles from the site of the Wounded Knee massacre almost a century before. They will capture and eventually indict four Indians for murder.

"It was a cold-blooded ambush," FBI Public Relations Director Thomas Cole tells the press. The G-men were only trying to serve an arrest warrant, he explains. It's an open-and-shut case—murder in the first degree; the two FBI agents, Jack R. Coler and Ronald A.

Williams, had been dragged from their car and ritualistically slaughtered.

It is the first time since the 1920s that two FBI agents have been killed in a single battle. The air around the bureau reportedly is thick with the anticipation of punishment and revenge. And how sweet it will be—capital punishment is once again legal. There will be a trial in U.S. District Court for two of the Indians but it is only a formality. After all, Dino Butler and Bob Robideau are members of the radical American Indian Movement (AIM). The defendants are a sure shot for the electric chair. Their lawyers are going to plead "self-defense," but when has it been permissible under any circumstances for an Indian to shoot at an FBI agent?

CEDAR RAPIDS, IOWA (POPULATION 125,000) IS IN AN UPROAR. THE battle lines are drawn. An Indian encampment is being established on the outskirts of town for the avowed purpose of assuring a fair trial. AIM is seeing to it that the white man will not try their two members in isolation.

Compounding the Indian invasion, a team of eastern Jewish lawyers descends. Their titular head, whose presence would rival Sitting Bull's at a church picnic, is William Kunstler. "Wild Bill," the story goes, will do anything to win a case, and if he succeeds, the Indian hooligans will wind up looking like saints on the network news while the townspeople will come off like corn-fed Nazis.

Everyone from District Court Judge Edward McManus to the bellhop at the Hotel Roosevelt Royale is predicting trouble, but the courtroom proves a model of decorum. With alcohol and drugs forbidden in the Indian encampment, sweat lodges and sacred pipe ceremonies are the order of the day. In fact, the Indians seem substantially less violent than the aging members of the Benevolent Order of the Eagles who are holding their convention at the Roosevelt downtown. Amidst much drinking and carousing, two of the more militant conventioneers drop dead of heart attacks right in the hotel lobby. In the second week of the trial, friendly letters about the Indians and their attorneys begin to appear in the *Cedar Rapids Gazette*.

Meanwhile, the prosecution cannot produce a witness who claims to have seen either defendant kill anybody. Because the defendants are Indians and the corpses FBI agents, the defense team feels it is not enough simply to demonstrate that there has been no evidence introduced concerning who specifically killed the agents. The defendants are facing two charges: one, that they killed the FBI agents;

two, that they aided and abetted the killers. Both translate as first-degree murder. Butler and Robideau have been placed at the scene of the crime, and one witness watched them shooting at the agents. If the jury of seven white men and five white women is to acquit the militants they must be convinced, the defense reasons, that the defendants—just as all the Indians on Pine Ridge—had good reason to fear the FBI; that it was the FBI who provoked the battle and the Indians who had to defend themselves. If the jury was not made to understand the unique living conditions on the reservation—the state of siege provoked by the presence of the FBI—they might use their own law 'n' order Cedar Rapids framework to judge the defendants guilty as charged.

William Muldrow, a specialist with degrees in sociology and divinity who had served on the U.S. Commission on Civil Rights, is called to the stand. The defense is trying a daring tactic—to impeach the testimony of witnesses from one government agency (the FBI) by calling a witness from another government agency. Muldrow, a white man, had been asked by the federal government to go to the Pine Ridge Reservation after the shoot-out to report on its causes and prepare a general analysis of conditions there.

"A great deal of tension and fear exist on the reservation," Muldrow testifies. "Residents feel that life is cheap, that no one really cares about what happens to them, and that they have no one to turn to for help or protection. Acts of violence, such as the one in which the agents were killed, are commonplace. Numerous complaints were lodged with my office about FBI activities."

Kunstler poses a hypothetical question.

"What would be the expected reaction of a group of Indians living in an isolated area of the reservation when they heard gunshots and observed firing by unknown persons from unmarked vehicles?"

The prosecution objects and is overruled.

"It seems only logical," Muldrow answers, "that people in such a position would take immediate steps to protect themselves."

The key phrases in Muldrow's testimony are "fear" and "isolation." The Indians, he notes, live in scattered clusters with very poor means of communication. There are few telephones and the police are unreliable. In this atmosphere, fear of the outsider, especially a white, is overwhelming. Sole support comes from family and friends.

Prosecutor Hultman tries to discredit Muldrow's testimony, but the soft-spoken Protestant minister insists he has no axe to grind for AIM. After the prosecution has concluded its strenuous cross-examination, Judge McManus breaks precedent to ask Muldrow several questions, "for my own information." Muldrow describes the 70 percent unemployment rate, the arid land that Indians are forced to farm, the white ranchers who control the best land on the reservation.

Judge McManus's inquiry is not directly related to the facts of the case. It seems the judge is sending a covert message to the jury— "Listen to Muldrow, not the prosecutor." McManus, at least, is beginning to see that this is no ordinary murder trial but a case involving fundamental issues of American history, economics, and sociology.

THE ROAD TO PINE RIDGE RESERVATION WINDS DOWN FROM INTERSTATE 90 at Kadoka. If you miss it, you must travel two hundred miles to Rapid City, at the far western end of South Dakota, to find another road in. Highway 18 is the major route through the reservation, connecting Pine Ridge to the Rosebud Reservation on the east and running through to the Oglalas' most sacred place, the spectacularly beautiful Black Hills. It is on this land, stolen from the Indians by Mormons more than a century ago, that sculptors carved huge white visages out of the sacred soil. If you visit Mount Rushmore you can feel a tremendous spiritual presence thousands of years older than the exposed white face of the mountain.

After an eight-hundred-mile journey from Cedar Rapids (Judge McManus had recessed the trial for ten days) we approach Pine Ridge in the dead of night. Traveling with us is Ethel Merrival, a seventy-year-old tribal attorney, whose appearance had intrigued the jury.

Short, stocky, with long black braids, she had confirmed in the courtroom racial stereotypes of a "squaw," but at the same time presented an articulate view of life on Pine Ridge. Merrival said she had lived on Pine Ridge virtually her entire life (she has fifty grandchildren) and joined AIM in 1972, when Raymond Yellow Thunder was killed by "the goons. . . . Dick Wilson [former Oglala tribal chairman] and his cronies, are a private army on the reservation. They take the law into their own hands. They are Indians but they are Uncle Sam's puppets. The BIA [Bureau of Indian Affairs] appropriates money to pay for these people. The FBI backs them up. The FBI even tried to proposition me, if I would tell them who shot the FBI agents. One FBI said he would forget my income tax, that he could give me a picture of himself in a bathing suit, that he would creep into my tepee.

"We fear for our lives," she had told the jury. "Twice my house has been shot. My fourteen-year-old granddaughter was raped by a BIA policeman. He got her drunk and raped her. I tried to get him for contributing to the delinquency of a minor but even though I'm a tribal attorney it's a year and a half later and nothing has happened."

She recalls Anna Mae Aquash, a young Canadian Micmac and AIM militant, whose partially decomposed body had been discovered in Wanblee, about one-hundred yards off the highway we were presently traveling on. "The FBI had told Anna Mae they'd kill her unless she cooperated with them," Ethel says. "She told a lot of her friends about this, and then she was found dead. The FBI had an autopsy and said she died of exposure. But her family had another autopsy and they discovered a bullet in her head. We all think the FBI put it there."

The Oglalas' land is surrounded by South Dakota but it is really like another country—a place whose poverty cannot be measured by the penury of Harlem or Watts. There are no movie theaters, newspapers, or radio stations; the small café stays open for only part of the day and the largest source of employment is the BIA. Most Indians are on some form of federal dole and there is no rising class of hip Sioux capitalists getting rich because Oglala drums have become popular.

If you yawn you might miss the town of Pine Ridge, where one small supermarket, a police headquarters, a number of churches, and a block of houses for bureaucrats create an eerie mirage. For a moment it looks like Main Street, USA, but soon you discover that the few houses and stores are shabby props with nothing behind them but wind, dust, and dry plains.

The reservation itself is a rip-off ravaged by greed. The farms surrounding the Oglala community are rich with corn and cattle owned by wealthy farmers who are fast becoming John Birchers. (AIM has become one of the prime targets of the national Birch Society.) The choice land once belonged to the Oglalas and tens of thousands of Sioux were murdered before the government could turn the bloody soil over to German and Irish immigrants from European despotism. The new Americans' promised land was a graveyard for Native Americans.

The Jumping Bull house, scene of the FBI confrontation, is pockmarked by bullets. A washing machine in the backyard is inexplicably shot up; an old car is filled with gaping holes. How many agents fired at how many Indians, and how did it start? Nobody on the reservation knows for sure but the betting is that the FBI was responsible in a provocative plan that misfired.

"The FBI knew AIM members were living there and they knew

their intentions were peaceful," says Sam Running Horse, a neigh-bor of the Bulls, "but they don't want AIM organizing on the reser-vation. So they tried to be smart—they sent in these two agents to pick a fight and draw some fire, and then they were going to send in an all-Indian SWAT team as backup. But the shooting was too heavy and the Indians were not going to go in there and die for a white man."

Running Horse's version would explain why the FBI agents did not retreat when they drew fire. Standing on the spot where the agents' bodies were found, we recognize several roads that could have provided an easy getaway, roads that, significantly, were miss-ing from the prosecution's elaborate courtroom maps. Perhaps the unfortunate G-men stuck around because they had been promised reinforcements with automatic machine guns. The only other expla-nation is they thought a couple of white supermen could make any number of redskins cry for mercy: hallucinating John Waynes who died with their boots on.

As THE END OF THE TRIAL NEARS, MARLON BRANDO AND DICK GREGORY arrive at the Cedar Rapids airport. They have been traveling for some thirty hours because, for reasons known only to themselves, they went looking for the courtroom in Wichita. Earlier, another sympathizer, Muhammad Ali, had almost gotten on a plane for Wounded Knee, South Dakota.

After bypassing the local press, Brando sits around the kitchen table at the defense quarters speaking through a mouthful of steak, Stanley Kowalski style, while Dick Gregory concocts fruit and veg-etable drinks in the other room. "I'm going to treat Ali's blood clots with fruit juice," Gregory announces to a crowd gathered around the table in the aftermath of Ali's bout with the Japanese wrestler, Inoke.

"Ali's big dream is to be the world wrestling champion," Brando adds. "It's like the shoemaker who wants to be a carpenter." This once-muscular paradigm of Hollywood grace and beauty is now very overweight, his soul somehow imprisoned in a huge, Picasso clownlike body. "I'm going on a Dick Gregory fruit-juice diet as soon as I find the time," Brando declares unconvincingly.

"I will do anything I can to help any Indian," he declares. "No matter what their relationship to the law." Given his wealth and rep-utation, supporting the Indian cause is not a great sacrifice for Brando. But when he rejected the Academy Award for Best Actor in

1973 (for *The Godfather*) as a protest against Hollywood's caricaturing of Indians, it went beyond the call of conscience, or duty.

"When I gave up that Academy Award—which I *really* wanted," Brando reveals, "that was a real sacrifice for me. But it was the least that someone in my position could do.

"I come to places like this to have personal contact and also because I am a celebrity. I attract media, which I try to focus in the Indian's direction. Lately I have shown up in some places where Indians were in trouble and the press ignored me. I do not think the media is involved in a government conspiracy against the Indians; it's just that the networks are involved in selling dog food, and they do not think Indians are commercial.

"When I go to a press conference I play the part of the concerned citizen. I put on a suit and act like a member of the establishment. Sometimes it works. I once called Henry Kissinger to complain about a matter involving the usual mistreatment of Indians, and he took the phone and spoke to me. He finds Indian demonstrations embarrassing to his foreign policy. It makes Americans look bad. So he listened to me and that time we got results. It pays to have someone around who can talk to Henry Kissinger."

Bill Kunstler, who cannot talk to Henry Kissinger, nods happily in agreement; this is his fifty-seventh birthday and everyone's celebrating. (Brando will play the role of William Kunstler in his forthcoming *Wounded Knee* epic.)

"I do not think we can write to our congressmen to help the Indians," Brando says, continuing his monologue between bites. "It seems they are too busy. According to recent disclosures, most of our politicians are in bed most of the time." We all laugh but Brando turns serious again. "We are all oppressed. With some of us it's economic and with others, it's existential and psychological."

The next day, Brando and Gregory come to court. When Brando steps forward to shake hands with the defendants, the federal marshals block his path, so the actor retires to the back row of the spectators' section and sends a note of good wishes to Butler and Robideau.

But, despite Brando's presence, it is FBI Director Clarence Kelley's testimony that makes the evening news.

At the beginning of the trial, Judge McManus had refused a defense request to subpoena Kelley—but there were to be further developments. When he died, agent Jack Coler was carrying secret Cointelpro papers plus maps of Indian territory with specific areas marked "bunkers." (Cointelpro was the name for the FBI's elaborate harassment campaign against "radical" groups in the late '60s and early '70s.) Apparently someone had been trying to make Coler think he was walking into a free-fire zone; far from being military fortifications, these "bunkers" are century-old root cellars that could not stop a BB pellet.

The judge, once shown the Cointelpro documents, reversed his decision and issued a subpoena for the FBI chief. Now Clarence Kelley was becoming the first FBI director ever to take the witness stand.

Kelley seems to be a man trying to testify with candor who really doesn't seem to understand what's going on in his own organization. The director describes AIM as "a movement that has fine people. I think it has something worthwhile to offer; it is not un-American, subversive, or otherwise objectionable." He is "unaware" and surprised to learn that his subordinates have listed AIM as a "terrorist" organization.

The defense presents Kelley with recent teletypes, originating from Washington, that link AIM to "planned" political violence, including the assassination of the governor of South Dakota, sniper attacks on tourists, demolition of Mount Rushmore, and an assault on a federal prison. Kelley denies that these messages were deliberate provocations, a continuation of Cointelpro under a different name. Kelley claims Cointelpro had been discarded by the bureau but admits there "wasn't a shred of proof" that any of the AIM events were ever intended.

When the defense asks if he considers these telexes "provocative," Kelley claims that law enforcement agencies are "becoming professional . . . We are not stampeding to build up fortifications. These telexes are informative and positive."

"Why do your agents carry M-16 rifles on the reservations?" Kunstler wonders. "Why do they wear army jumpsuits?"

"I don't care who it is," Kelley responds. "If people's lives are threatened, they have a right to defend themselves."

"Exactly," answers Kunstler. "No further questions."

Senator Frank Church testifies that the FBI materials certainly did resemble Cointelpro documents and that such documents did put targeted individuals "in physical danger." The defense rests. The jury must know by now that the FBI was out to get AIM; but would they consider the shoot-out in this context or would they believe the prosecution's claims that whatever Cointelpro was, it had nothing to do with this case?

After closing arguments, the jury deliberates for four days and then sends a note to the judge—they are "hopelessly deadlocked."

But over $2 million has gone into this trial and Judge McManus wants a verdict. He orders the jury to go back and, without cutting the truth, bring back a decision.

Then it is announced. There is a verdict. For most of the defense team its arrival seems like the "angel of death." Kunstler drives to the courtroom, his gloom unyielding.

"Some will come in crying and ashamed," he predicts. "They won't be able to look at Dino and Bob, but how can they hold out against the power of prejudice? It's just not possible; time wears a jury down. Maybe they don't hate Indians but they believe in law and order."

The friends and family of the defendants sit in the courtroom in hushed horror. Kunstler is increasingly despondent. The prosecutors are tense but talk tough, seemingly confident.

The jury walks into the courtroom. For people who have been tied up in debate for five days, they seem jaunty. But the tension in the room is at the level of physical pain. The foreman hands the verdict to the judge, who reads it silently, then passes it to the court clerk.

"Not Guilty."

The courtroom explodes with applause. "Not Guilty" on all four counts. Everyone at the defense table weeps. Kunstler, sobbing, embraces the two defendants.

The prosecutors are stunned. A row of FBI agents file out of the courtroom, pillars of stone. Twelve white middle-Americans had just disowned them, and now their careers—and the diminishing prestige of the bureau—hang in a balance that has suddenly shifted.

"We more or less determined [that it was] a case of one armed camp against another armed camp," the jury foreman explains.

By and large, the people of Cedar Rapids approved of the verdict. It was a source of civic pride. Strangers in the streets congratulated anyone connected with the defense team. On a local television station, one weatherman said, "It will be a fine night to celebrate the victory."

THE DAY BEFORE THE VERDICT, THERE HAD BEEN A CEREMONY AT THE Rosebud Reservation, which lies on Highway 18 just east of Pine Ridge. As the participants emerged from the sweat lodge, they saw four eagles come from the west, north, south, and east. The eagles circled and then flew off in four directions.

"When I spoke to those people yesterday, they told me that Dino and Bob would walk the earth as free men," said John Trudell, national secretary of AIM, on victory night. "We know how to call on a power that the government just doesn't understand."

# Plains Speaking

*by Abbie Hoffman*

*June 1977*

*In one of our few brilliant public relations strokes, we appointed Abbie Hoff-
man our Travel Editor after he became a fugitive from the law in the mid-
1970s. Abbie wrote several wonderful yarns for us—documenting visits to
Mexico, Los Alamos, and Hollywood—and we got a few mentions in the
press for having a Travel Editor with a special reason to remain on the road.
We titled his column "On the Lam." Here he time-travels to President
Carter's hometown.*

Plains, Georgia, sticks in my memory like a piece of unchewed
peanut brittle. Having been a civil rights worker in Americus, literally a stone's throw away, I find it hard to swallow all the honey-
coated grits being dished out daily by the fawning media. Can we
really take four, maybe eight more years of the "good ol' gas station," that "good ol' church," and all those "good ol' boys" swattin'
flies and dispensing homespun philosophy?

Way back then (a dozen years ago) working in Sumter County on
one of the toughest voter registration campaigns in the South, we
had a slightly different view of all those good ol' boys. Plains was just
another one of those small, company-owned towns in southwest
Georgia that offered aid and comfort to the White Citizens Council.
When someone got word that a group from Plains was coming over
it didn't mean Miss Lillian's Relief Brigade. It meant board-up-the-
windows-and-duck.

Along about midnight, cars containing your rowdier element would race by, throwing bottles or garbage or letting off a few rounds of ammunition. In general, Plains boys were pretty bad aims. In fact, they often were referred to as the bimbos of the county, although I think we used the term "cracker-heads" then. You know, the type of folk who woke up in the morning, put their shoes on wrongside-to, and then go to the doctor to get their feet adjusted.

Now that Plains has become so firmly entrenched in the sacred archives of *americanus naturales,* I for one see no harm in taking a little wind out of the town's sails. There would be a healthy effect on our society if we could restore that forgotten image as a Boob-town. I'm speaking of an all-out effort to defuse all the Southern-fried folksiness by making Plains our own little Bimboville—the butt of every jerk joke we can think of.

This is not without precedent. For centuries there was such a town in Poland (where else?). It was called Chelm. In actuality, Chelm had a pretty rough history, being sacked repeatedly by the Cossacks and finally obliterated by Hitler's Nazis. In Jewish folklore, Chelm played an entirely different role; it was strictly Yiddish hicksville, the place where all the country numb-numbs sat around racking their brains, trying to shortcut their way to wisdom and the big time. Hundreds of tales have been recorded and passed down from generation to generation concerning the *schleps* from Chelm. In fact, all you have to do to break the ice with some of the old-time Jews on New York's Lower East Side is to ask them if they know a good story about Chelm. If you do, prepare yourself for some hearty laughs.

Now I propose we join together to make Plains, U.S.A., our Chelm.

Actually, this is going to solve a whole other problem—a problem that's bothered me for years. See, I love Polish jokes. I laugh like crazy when I hear a good one. Ten minutes later I start feeling guilty about encouraging these derogatory stereotypes of one of our purer ethnic groups and I forget the joke. I mean, what have the Poles ever done to me? There just doesn't seem to be any redeeming social value in repeating or inventing Polish jokes. I've tried substituting other countries, real and imaginary, and it just doesn't work. The joke is deflated before it even gets off the ground.

So for years this repression has been going on with no solution in sight. Then along comes Plains. Lately I've been able to tell a few Polish jokes in Plains clothes. Or is it Plains jokes in Polish clothes? (Are you getting any of this or am I just communicating with Gerald Ford?) Let me try a few on you and you try them on your friends and see how it works.

### PLAINS JOKES

*"Do you know the Plains version of the Galloping Gourmet?"*
*"Nope."*
*"Why, that's Billy Carter chasin' a garbage truck!"*

*or:*

*"It takes a hundred folks to ring that little ol' church bell
down in Plains."*
*"Gee, son, why's that?"*
*"Well, see, it takes one fella to hold the rope and ninety-nine to
shake the church up and down!"*

*or:*

*"Do you wanna hear a real funny story about Plains, Geor-
gia?"*
*"Now, be careful son. I* am *from Plains."*
*"Uh, that's okay. I'll tell it* real *slow!"*

Right. I'm not exactly sure these work when you read them but,
due to circumstances beyond my control, I can't tell them to you in
person. But I urge you to try these and any Polish jokes you've been
hiding away, substituting sweet li'l ol' Plains, of course. This could
get bigger than smoking bananas . . .

IN A MORE SERIOUS VEIN (IF YOU'VE GOT ONE LEFT)—SOUTHWEST
Georgia for the last two dozen years has been no laughing matter. It
was the scene of some of the most outrageous oppression of blacks
imaginable. During the '50s and '60s, a virtual reign of terror was instituted by local police and vigilante night riders.

Very early in the '50s, instant Southern justice was meted out in
Glynn County to eight unarmed inmates who had escaped from a
rural jail. When they were caught, all were summarily executed.

Many black families have had a relative killed by whites under
strange circumstances. Since Reconstruction, 324 lynchings have
been documented in Georgia. Black groups in the state insist the
count runs to ten times that number. And most occurred in the
southwest corner of the state. "Uppity niggers" often disappeared,
only to turn up floating facedown in a nearby creek.

In 1958, just an hour's drive from Plains in Dawson, Georgia,
James Brazier was taken out behind the jailhouse by a county sheriff's deputy and beaten with a blackjack until he died. The crime

was so well documented that the Justice Department, in one of the rare cases of federal intervention, sought to prosecute the deputy. After only a few minutes of deliberation, a Macon grand jury saw fit to return no indictment. After the affair blew over, the deputy was promoted to chief of police.

Laurie Pritchett, sheriff of Albany, Georgia, became one of the first nationally known villains of the civil rights movement. "Ain't gonna let Boss Pritchett turn me 'round, turn me 'round," sang the peaceful demonstrators marching in the streets. Boss Pritchett unleashed specially trained dogs and showed the world a new use for cattle prods.

In Americus, four civil rights workers passing out leaflets were arrested in 1963 and charged with "insurrection against the state of Georgia." The charge carried the death penalty and, even though the law had been declared unconstitutional in the '30s, the organizers were denied bond and kept in jail six months before legal efforts to release them were successful.

Just five short miles from Jimmy Carter's ranch house, Clarence and Florence Jordan founded an integrated study-community called Koinonia Farm. Shootings and bombings were a regular occurrence. Police and county officials tried every trick in the book to close the place down. (Koinonia still exists. They carry on community projects in the area, including low-cost housing construction, classes in farming, and an integrated free school for kids.)

I remember well that hot summer of '65; canvassing door-to-door, church rallies, the black families who took us in, even if it meant risking loss of a job or other intimidation. Each day the city council would pass some new ordinance aimed at thwarting the voter registration drive. We'd gather mornings in one of the black districts to begin the protest march downtown. Rarely did we get more than a block or two into the white section of town before troopers waded in and carted us off to jail. Local people were hit with stiff sentences, some as long as a year in prison, for violating "public nuisance" ordinances or for "parading without a proper permit." Legal efforts to defend people were often interrupted when the judge or city recorder just happened to be "away fishing."

One of the few Southern whites who really joined that struggle was attorney Charles Morgan, who roamed the South for the American Civil Liberties Union (ACLU) coordinating much of the legal strategy that did away with the more flagrant forms of segregation. His office in Atlanta was bombed and his home strafed with bullets. Still, Charlie Morgan sweated through that tough struggle in Americus and managed to keep enough of us in the streets to eventually kindle one of the strongest local movements in the South.

And where were the Carters of Plains during this period? Probably at home, sitting on their hands like almost all of the decent white folks of southwest Georgia. Ah, but that was a dozen years ago. Charlie Morgan is now a trusted adviser to the President of these United States. Andy Young, Martin Luther King's chief of staff during the Americus campaign, is now generally considered the most influential black in the new administration, and John Lewis, who was then chairman of SNCC (the Student Non-Violent Coordinating Committee) was an early and ardent supporter of Carter. The blacks of Americus turned out in record number for "Brother Jimmy." Even the folks at Koinonia, if they voted, went for their neighbor (I'm told).

Yes sir, bygones be bygones, times are changing, and we certainly are in the Great Transition. Lord knows the country desperately needs the social programs Carter promised.

But Carter or not, it still seems the white folks of southwest Georgia ought to be paying some dues. One characteristic about the fabled good ol' boy is that, along with chawin' Red Man tobacco and sluggin' Dr Pepper, he likes a good belly laugh. Hee-Haw! Let's see how they take to our Plains jokes. One way or another, we should be able to recapture the Polish vote.

# Going After Missile Silos

*by Tim O'Brien*

*January 1979*

*When Tim O'Brien, author of* Going After Cacciato, *and most recently* In the Lake of the Woods, *became obsessed with the bomb, he was about two years ahead of the nuclear freeze movement in the early 1980s. The experience he describes in this article helped inspire his novel,* The Nuclear Age.

As a kid, I had nuke fever.

It was the work of imagination.

I heard the scream of incoming ICBMs; I watched New York turn to cinders. I saw strontium 90 curdling my milk. I sat aghast as the TV hissed its one-note test of the Emergency Broadcast System. *Déjà vu.* A voyeur at my own thermal funeral. "Just a test," the announcer intoned matter-of-factly, but this was never very reassuring. I was witness to the terrifying possibilities.

I grew up scared on the flatlands of southern Minnesota. My hometown called itself Turkey Capital of the World. This bit of fame probably didn't much impress the Kremlin—not enough, anyway, to make them place the town high on the strategic hit list. Still, you couldn't be sure. I began taking precautions. On tiptoe, I headed for the basement. There I built myself a miniature fallout shelter. Actually it was just a Ping-Pong table piled high with bricks and books and hunks of balsa wood, a ventilation shaft of cardboard tubing, charcoal briquets to soak up the deadly radiation. It was more than make-believe. It was a genuine fortress, a place to wait out the holocaust. Secretly, I stocked it with rations from the kitchen pantry, laid in a supply of bottled water, set up a dispensary of Band-Aids and iodine. Let the Soviets go on a turkey shoot. I was ready.


IN SEPTEMBER OF THIS YEAR, I WENT TO KANSAS TO TRACK DOWN THE source of all this fear. I went on an ICBM hunt. Stalking the mysterious Titan II missile. The objective of this trek was simple: to touch the nuclear age. *Touch* it, that's all. To put my hand against a piece of atomic machinery, to confront—man to metal—the realities of megatonnage and guidance systems and warheads. I aimed to strip away the mystery, and maybe even the fear, by taking a hard look at the physical material.

So I went to Kansas.

First there was the heat. Incredible heat. A new record for that date in mid-September. Maybe I was looking for bad omens, or maybe the omens were looking for me, but, either way, the omens were there: the unworldly heat, a freaky-black atmosphere coming in from the west, electricity building, stored energy. It was the Kansas of Oz. Kansas was a case of the creeps.

If I'd been studying the Kansas ecology, I might've paid attention to the Caribbean-blue lakes I passed, or the black-eyed Susans growing by the billions in the ditches, or the rich-looking soil, or the rolling-ness of the land, the sweeps and swales and ten-mile vistas. Instead, I kept seeking out Titans, searching for the telltale signs of our age. Sure enough, the details and ironies were there for the finding. Odd antennae bristling from cornfields. Jets mysteriously overhead.

Highway 15 led to Highway 77, and next there was a sign for the town of El Dorado. But I wasn't going to El Dorado, not by a long shot. I was heading for Rock, Kansas. Population, maybe two hundred. Chief industry: thermonuclear war.

Three weeks ago, I knew, the town had been evacuated—a nuclear mishap, one of those scary improbabilities, a few moments of terror. Clouds of dark orange gas spewing from a leak inside an underground Titan II missile silo killed one Air Force worker, seriously injured two others, and forced the evacuation of hundreds of people from homes near the missile complex.

And then I spotted it.

Here's how you recognize a missile site. First you see this small rectangular sign, a white sign, perfectly unassuming. Stenciled on it is the letter M. That's all. Just an M. And an arrow. It's a matter of perception: If you're not looking for it, you don't see it; if you see it, it may not even register. But this time it registered. I stopped, pulled off onto the shoulder, and followed the arrow. Yes, and there it was: five or six antennae of various heights, a single white light like those you see in farmyards, two trucks painted Air Force blue, a grazing cow beyond the fence, bales of rolled hay, a single road, a shack that might've passed for an outhouse, another stenciled sign: DEADLY FORCE AUTHORIZED.

The feeling was all-out emptiness, desertion, vacancy as in outer space. A tumbleweed feeling. Fifty yards up the road, lonely looking, was a blue pickup. An *armed* guard, most likely. But I couldn't see him. Maybe he lay curled in ambush, or maybe it was nap time. No matter, it was good to be alone. A chance to contemplate.

So here it was: ground zero. In the earth below, out of sight but hardly out of mind, a genuine Titan II stood in its 147-foot-deep silo. Also underground, connected to the silo by a short tunnel, was the steel-and-concrete launch command center where four-man combat crews live and work in twenty-four-hour shifts. All alone: no morning, no night. Waiting for that message that tells them to launch.

The command center is built on three levels—first the crew's underground living quarters, next the combat room, then an equipment storage tier. All three levels, I knew, were suspended on springs from the ceiling like a birdcage, a way of absorbing shock in the event of nuclear attack. Squinting, listening hard, it all came clear: bright lights, fans whirring, chrome control consoles, key slots, the faint smell of oil, eerie warbling sounds, buzzes, hums, digital clicks, checklists, echoes and echoes.

"In a way," a former Titan crewman told me later, "it's like a miniature universe down there. Everything you need—food, beds, books, electricity. But it's not like a house or anything. It's like a spaceship. Like zooming through outer space, completely separated from Earth. Stranded, marooned. That's what it *feels* like. Nothing but you and the Titan."

And then I got to thinking about the missile itself. I knew the vital statistics by heart: ten feet in diameter, 103 feet tall, 330,000 pounds of launch weight, a flight range exceeding 6,000 miles, two engines to deliver the largest warhead in the American arsenal—more than five megatons of raw firepower. I knew, also, that here before me, below me, was but one of fifty-four such sleeping giants nestled so snugly across the Grand Republic. I knew that each of these Titans can be launched with a reaction time of one minute; that the seven-hundred-ton lid over each silo can be opened in something like twenty seconds; that, once fired, there is no calling the Titan back, no self-destruct mechanism.

And this wasn't all I knew. I knew that somewhere deep in central

Russia, or somewhere beneath the seas, there was a Soviet counterpart to this big baby, an SS-9 or SS-11 or SS-13, aimed at precisely this piece of the North American continent. Those trees, that fat cow, that patch of meadow, me—the bull's-eye. All this was food for thought, and I spent maybe an hour thinking. Imagining.

That night Mother Nature showed her power. Sheltered in a Holiday Inn, I listened as television told of a hurricane hitting Honduras, an earthquake killing sixteen thousand in Iran. *The Love Boat* battled a typhoon. Outside, lightning made fireworks. The TV 10 storm center issued tornado warnings. Flash floods were possible. Somewhere nearby a burglar alarm was whining, and it whined for most of the night; Wichita's policemen and firemen were on strike. Lightning hit houses. Lightning hit the Holiday Inn. My TV set was knocked out—a buzz, a Civil Defense hiss, then static.

OVER THE NEXT COUPLE OF DAYS, AS I ROAMED ROCK, THE ANSWERS were always the same. These fine, smart, honest, sensitive, open people—they weren't afraid.

"It's *possible*, isn't it?" I was trying hard to ignite some sodden fear-fuse in Jim Hodgson, a farmer who works land directly adjacent to Rock's Titan II silo. "I mean, look, the warhead's right there. Every day you ride by it on your tractor. Right *there.*"

"Yeah," Jim said. He was watching the Bears against the Lions, a black-and-blue division game.

"And it doesn't . . . make you shiver? Just a little?"

"No."

"Look at it this way," I said. "You're living on a piece of ground that'll be absolutely, totally, forever wiped out in the event of war. You understand that?"

"Yeah. But it won't happen."

I didn't get anywhere. Jim Hodgson, though cordial, seemed suspicious. Near the end of the first half, I found out why.

"Look," he said. "When the accident happened a few weeks back, there were all kinds of reporters around here, like flies at a picnic. And they all wanted me to say how bad I felt having that missile here, how I wanted to get rid of it. But I don't feel that way. I don't."

Did the Titan touch his life in *any* way?

"No."

Subconsciously? Nightmares, dreams?

"Nope."

Could he think of any drawback at *all* to having the Titan silo here?

"Oh," he said, "it's a little unhandy. Have to farm around it."

THE 381ST STRATEGIC MISSILE WING, WHICH CONTROLS EIGHTEEN Titan II missiles in southeastern Kansas, has its headquarters at McConnell Air Base outside Wichita. The building is wooden. In SAC lingo, a soft target. Across the street, considerably more substantial-looking, is the base chapel.

At 1330 hours sharp, by arrangement, I entered the offices of Captain Alan DeFend. No kidding, that was his name. He smiled when I mentioned the irony.

"DeFend," he said. "Capital F." And, as McConnell's press information officer, that was essentially his job. We began by talking about the accident at Rock.

"To understand it," he said, "you've got to understand how the Titan's propellant system works. Otherwise it won't make sense." And so, carefully, he explained that the propellant consists of two parts—fuel (unsymmetrical dimethylhydrazine) and oxidizer (nitrogen tetroxide). When these two ingredients combine in the Titan's engines, you get the thrust that sends her on her way.

"All right," DeFend said, "here's what happened." As part of a periodic maintenance program, the Titan missile at Complex 3-7 (Rock, Kansas) had been removed from its silo. Another Titan had been installed to replace it. On August 24, an eight-man missile propellant team began the refueling process. Meanwhile, down below in the command center—separated from the silo itself by a tunnel and blast doors—the four regular crewmen went about their usual routines.

What happened next is a matter of some mystery and much concern. DeFend wasn't certain about the details—or perhaps he just wasn't saying—but apparently a valve failed to close. When the hose was removed, ten thousand gallons of toxic chemical began spilling out and turned to gas. The silo became a gas chamber. The airmen below scrambled. Staff Sgt. Robert Thomas, the team's leader, had been topside at the time of the accident, but he went below to help out, and he died. Nine days later a second man died.

"At no time," said DeFend, "was there danger of explosion. The actual *fuel* had not been pumped in—just the oxidizer. And there was no warhead on the missile."

What if the valve malfunction had occurred three days later, after complete fueling and after five megatons of firepower had been placed on top? What then?

"I can't speculate. It just didn't happen that way."

But what if?

"An explosion in the silo would not cause the warhead to detonate. There would be no nuclear reaction."

Even so, wouldn't a silo explosion—if the Titan and its warhead were blown apart—result in escaping radioactivity? A massive dose of fallout?

"That's a matter of speculation."

True. But that's been my problem from the beginning, the tendency to speculate. I asked Captain DeFend if *he* ever speculated.

"If you mean do I worry, no. I just don't stew about it." He paused. "The Titan II is one element in this nation's deterrence posture. It's there to prevent war, not to start it. That's the whole idea."

He went on to point out that the Air Force runs a Personnel Reliability Program to keep tabs on the psychological well-being of those who work with ICBMs. "We screen these people very carefully. Anybody associated with the Titan II—crewmen, security guards, maintenance men—has to go through the program. That's one way of preserving rationality."

What about Brezhnev and Carter—are they screened by the Personnel Reliability Program? I didn't even ask. But I did ask if the Titan crewmen, those responsible for manning the sites and turning the keys, are given periodic psychological checkups. The answer was no. I asked if the Air Force maintained a psychiatric staff at McConnell, and, again, the answer was no.

"We don't have a psychiatrist," DeFend said, "but we do have a psychiatric social worker." He didn't elaborate, but my impression was that this arrangement is somewhat less than rigorous. "Also," he said, "if a man's coworkers notice any erratic behavior, the man might be suspended until we get to the bottom of it."

"ERRATIC BEHAVIOR?" SAID JAMES P. LITSEY, A FORMER TITAN CREW commander, a man who once had key-turning responsibility. "Let me tell you a story. Back when I was second-in-charge of a Titan complex, we had this commander who was a little uptight to begin with. And it got worse. His time underground was almost up—only a couple more shifts to go—and I guess that had something to do with it. Anyway, one morning I played a little joke on him. Hid his breakfast eggs. Well, the guy went bonkers. Pulled a pistol, cocked the hammer, pointed it right at me. Talk about erratic behavior."

Out of four years in the Air Force, James Litsey spent a solid year underground. Now, at thirty-one, he's running for Congress.

"I'm a conservative," he told me. "In '76, I worked for Reagan at the Republican Convention. I'm a believer in maintaining a strong nuclear deterrent. And that's why I'm raising some serious questions about the safeguard and security systems in the Titan II program."

The Personnel Reliability Program: "Sure, they make sure you'll launch the missile. They ask lots of questions about that. But they don't ask if you'll go to war before they give the order." Litsey paused. "Most of the Titan guys are pretty level-headed. But, still, many aren't down there by choice. They've been assigned. They're young. They're inexperienced. You've got *commanders* who are twenty-three or twenty-four years old."

More erratic behavior: "When you're down below day in and day out, buried with that warhead and all the equipment, you have to find ways to pass the time. Otherwise. . . . Anyhow, one way the men pass time is to mess around with the machinery."

Mess around?

"Yeah. There's this thing called the Launch Enable System—LES. Ever heard of it?"

I hadn't but Litsey filled me in. It consists of two electronic signals, originating from outside SAC command posts, which are fed into the Titan's underground launch center. These signals automatically prevent launch; they are constantly on. Only in the event of nuclear war would the signals be broken off, thereby enabling the crew to fire the missile. In essence, the system is designed as a safeguard against a renegade launch, a means of preventing a four-man crew (or any two members of a crew) from firing their Titan without authorization.

"So what some guys did," Litsey said, "was to figure a way of breaking the LES circuit. They outfoxed the safeguard. They could've fired the missile, started a war, whatever. Remember, it was just a way of passing time—it gets pretty boring down there—but still it makes you stop to think." Litsey emphasized that the LES problem was subsequently corrected.

"The point is this," Litsey said. "If *our* sophisticated technology could be foiled so easily, what about the safeguards of all the *other* countries with nuclear weapons—China, France, the Soviet Union? What happens if India or Brazil or Israel converts its nuclear potential into warheads?"

Was he ever frightened down there?

"Not so much of outright nuclear war," he said. "Terrorists, though. There was a time when our whole crew was paranoid. It was during my last two months on alert. There were rumors that Black September would soon try to take over a missile silo; later we heard the same story from Air Force Security Police. They told us to be extra careful, but, well, how careful can you be?"

I TOOK A FINAL DRIVE THROUGH ROCK, KANSAS. THERE WAS THE TITAN II complex, off in its wheatfield. I circled the missile site, driving along country roads, examining the place from different angles, stopping, trying to fix the scene in my memory.

I imagined all the ways it could happen: An intentional nuclear war. A war of strategy and global politics. A madman in command. A renegade crew outwitting the safeguards. Terrorists. Simple accident. Mistaken blips on a radar screen. A limited war with the limits suddenly removed. The Mideast. The Chinese vs. the Russians, drawing us in. An underdeveloped country using H-bombs as a means of development, blackmail. A Hitler in the White House. A nervous breakdown. A new religious cult.

With all this, why was nobody scared?

I stopped, got out of the car, walked to a fence, sat down, gazed across at the instruments of doom.

Why?

"Perhaps," wrote Fred Ikle, former head of the U.S. Arms Control and Disarmament Agency, "we cannot bring ourselves to grasp the devastation and suffering that would be inflicted on the world if nuclear war could not be averted. . . . We seek refuge from our fears of the horrendous nuclear arsenals by telling ourselves that deterrence among nuclear nations will indefinitely ward off the day of doom when—as it says in the ancient Latin hymn of the requiem— centuries would be turned to ashes."

But there was more to it than that. I recalled one of Rock's fine citizens telling me, with immense patience: "Look, we've all got to die *somehow*. It's certain: We're going to *die*. Nukes are just one of maybe a million ways it'll happen."

But even that explanation didn't satisfy me. Because it wasn't merely my own death I feared. It was the death of civilization. The human species. Culture. Art, books, cities, architecture, the cathedral at Rheims, Paris, families, vacations, fallout-free milk, TV, movies, Sunday football games, schools, telephones.

Robert Jay Lifton, a professor of psychiatry and the author of a book about the survivors of Hiroshima, argues that the nuclear threat goes to the very heart of the way we ordinarily cope with our mortality. Sure, each of us will eventually die. But the straws we ordinarily grasp as solace against our mortality are blown away by the nuclear age. We fear absurd death. So the mind goes numb. It disengages. It focuses on the fancy glitterings of atomic technology. It ignores. It gapes, dumbly.

Which is what I did for a long, long time on that final morning in Rock, Kansas. The wind, the sun, the sound of birds and a far-off tractor, pretty yellow flowers, and Titan II.

NEXT DAY I BOARDED A FLIGHT FOR LITTLE ROCK, ARKANSAS. AND, YES, the fear was still there. More than ever. Accidents happen, right? If I'd learned a lesson over the past several days, that was it—accidents do happen.

Little Rock, like Wichita, is surrounded by eighteen Titan missiles. Here, too, something had recently gone wrong: another oxidizer spill. Here, too, was a bull's-eye for Soviet missiles. And here, too, people pursued their lives in nuclear numbness.

Except for a fellow named Bill Branham.

Finally, near the end of my journey, I found a man who was scared. Bill Branham: a former Titan II crew commander; a keyturner; a quiet guy, gentle, soft-spoken, whiskers, glasses, an accent that moved like an old river. He was my reason for coming to Little Rock. It made the whole trip worthwhile.

"I was scared from the beginning," he said. "The Vietnam war was on, I was graduating from the University of West Virginia—a biology major. Didn't know what to do. All I knew was this: I couldn't face the prospect of going to 'Nam. Just couldn't. So I enlisted in the Air Force. Next thing I knew, bang, I got picked for missile duty."

At some point during his time underground, Bill said, he made an important decision: He would not turn the key.

"It wasn't just me," he said. "Some of my friends—the guys I could confide in—admitted the same thing: We wouldn't launch that damned missile. Okay, we'd signed a paper that said we *would* do it. A sort of promise. But that was just paper. When you're down below, you have a lot of time to think things out, and I figured it this way. Let's say I get an order to launch. That means everything topside is gone—friends, family, the works. So what's the good of firing back? I'm not protecting my family—they're dead. My country, it's in ruins, so I'm not protecting it either. What good's a deterrent if there's nothing left to deter? So what's left? Revenge? Not me. I'm not big on revenge. I didn't want my last act on earth to be the slaughter of twenty million people.

"What would it accomplish? All it means is that a country like Iceland will be top dog instead of the United States or Russia. So why launch?

"And there were some other things behind the decision, too. For example, I was always told that our missiles are here as a deterrent—that's the official line. And I guess I could buy that. But when I got in, I found out that we have *two* types of war plans—preemptory and retaliatory. Preemptory means to strike *first,* to beat the Russians to the punch. Well, that's not deterrence, that's something else again, and a lot of us were upset to find out about it.

"Another thing I found out was this: Despite all the training propaganda, which claimed we'd only be firing at military targets, the fact is that there are *three* classes of targets—military, military-industrial, and population centers. So if a nuclear war started and if we couldn't wipe out the enemy's military installations, then the plan called for hitting population centers. To brutalize. Simple retaliation with no military purpose behind it. It was called the 'Balls to the Wall Plan.' I didn't like it. I still don't."

All this was said quietly. There was no self-pity, no real anger. A kind of resignation, sadness. I kept sneaking looks at Branham, trying to picture him in uniform, imagining him down in that steel-and-chrome command center. My time in 'Nam seemed a joyride by comparison.

I wanted to open up the man's head and climb inside and roam around in those memories. Instead, I asked about the Air Force's Personnel Reliability Program.

"A crock of shit," Branham said. "The program is supposed to weed out the weirdos and freaks, make sure we're psychologically strong, make sure we'll follow orders if the time comes. Some would-be psychologist comes in—he looks like a graduate student or something—and we sit around and bullshit about the morality of war. A blind man could see what he was looking for. So we just fed it to him and he sucked it up. That's how the Reliability Program works."

What about security? Is it lax?

Branham smiled. "Here's a story for you. Once there was this guy who left the red box unlocked. I mean, there are two padlocks on the box, right? And he leaves *his* padlock open. So for the hell of it I opened up *my* lock, reached into the box, and removed his launch key."

*The* key?

"That's the one. I hid it. Then I closed his box, locked both padlocks. The next time on alert, a couple days later, we went through the usual checklist, making sure everything was in order, and we open up the box and the guy sees his key is gone. He goes into a tizzy. Incredible, a *tizzy*. Who wouldn't? You open up the box and look inside and the fucking *key's* gone—incredible."

And the fear? What about the fear?

"I guess the worst time was back in October of 1973. One night we got a message that put us on Blue Dot DefCon—Defense Condition. It means you start gearing things up for a launch. It's not really the highest alert, in fact it's close to the bottom, but even so it was scary. Remember, that was during the Watergate thing, and I kept wondering if maybe Nixon had finally gone bananas. Turned out it was because of trouble in the Middle East, but even so it gave me the willies. And that wasn't anything compared to what went on during the Cuban Missile Crisis. Back then those poor guys were standing by to turn the fucking keys—it was that close. Stuff was ready to fly."

Then he got up to go.

"I'll tell you one thing," he said. "It was one of the best days of my life, the day I left that Titan behind me. During my last night on duty, I climbed up to the highest part of that silo, aimed at the missile, and took myself a good, long piss."

THERE WAS ONE FINAL STOP ON MY TREK THROUGH WONDERLAND: New York City. I was tired. I was up to my ears in apocalypse. In a daze, shell-shocked, I listened to the horror stories of one more ex-crewman. He didn't want his name used; he feared the Air Force. But he talked. And it was the same eerie sound: "All wars kill," said the former Minuteman crewman. "Nuclear wars just do a better job of it."

We sat in a posh restaurant, eating oysters.

"Here's how the world ends," he said. "You're down in your command center. You get the war messages. You check them, verify them. Then you go to work. You get out your checklists and, point by point, like a goddamn computer, you start going down the list. You dial in codes. You push buttons. Then you and another guy walk over to different parts of the console, you slip in your keys, you turn them. After that, I don't know what you do."

He swallowed an oyster. No chewing, he just swallowed.

"So," he said. "Next time you open a door, take a good look at the key. Feel it. Try to pretend. . . . Slip it in and take a nice deep breath and turn the fucker. You tell *me* how it feels."

# PART IV

## Film and TV

# Jack Nicholson, Down to the Last Detail

*by Patrick Snyder*

*February 1973*

*Some of the other young actors/directors we touted over and over again never went anywhere—remember Monte Hellman?—but Nicholson more than made up for it.*

When *Easy Rider*'s rolling allegory collided head-on with an endearingly warm and fallible speck of alcoholic humanity named George Hanson, the impact ignited both the film and the career of the actor playing the football-helmeted Southern lawyer. George was neither a paranoid pothead with twitching fringe nor a glacially cool motorcycle guru done up like a patriotic leather fetishist for the Fourth of July. Instead, he was a sensitive, funny guy with a good rap and a few minor vices. George Hanson was, like many of us in 1969, a rebel tasting freedom and marijuana for the first time and rather in awe of the hyper-freakdom represented by Wyatt and Billy.

With only a supporting role in the film, this characterization nevertheless emerged as the most complete; it was a prophecy of future brilliance that Jack Nicholson fulfilled in *Five Easy Pieces*. In Nicholson's Bobby Dupea, audiences found a lonely, embittered man who engendered understanding without ever demanding pity. Full of richly complex and vibrant emotion, he could in teeth-gritting frustration clear a table in a diner with one sweep of his arm as well as weep over past failures to communicate at the knee of his stricken father in a damp meadow on the coast of Oregon. For Mike

Nichols's *Carnal Knowledge,* Nicholson created Jonathan who, adrift in a sea of unfulfilled longing, remains to this day the most powerful argument for the gains to be made by men if they would or could move off the top, both literally and figuratively, in their relationship with women. And now, in *The King of Marvin Gardens,* he has portrayed David Staebler, a man of knotted introversion unable to keep pace emotionally or physically with his hustling brother.

With these handful of roles, Jack Nicholson has completed the silvering of a mirror. The palpable humanity of all these characters is more than an illusion projected by a skilled craftsman, because Nicholson is well acquainted with George, Bobby, Jonathan, and David. Just as we can see ourselves in them, they are all part of him, aspects of his personality he has dredged from his psyche and then shaped for the screen.

WEARING A NUMBER 17 UNIVERSITY OF OREGON FOOTBALL SWEATSHIRT and a pair of battered blue jeans, Nicholson sat on a brocaded sofa in the Sherry-Netherland hotel smiling with the impish satisfaction of a seven-year-old in the front row at the circus. He is, at thirty-five, at ease with himself and impressed with his success only as far as it impresses others and allows him to choose what roles he will play and what scripts he will direct.

On the coffee table in front of the sofa was Nicholson's current homework, the screenplay for his next film, *The Last Detail.* Written by Robert Towne, the film follows two career sailors as they escort a young enlistee to his court-martial and, having taken pity on him, teach him about life during the journey. Shooting was begun early in November in Toronto and New York under the direction of Hal Ashby.

Born in April 1937, in Neptune, New Jersey, Nicholson was raised in nearby Manasquan. During high school he acted in a number of school productions but says now that these early forays into drama were prompted more by Priapus than by Thespis. After graduating, he went to Los Angeles to live with his sister for a year or two before going to college. To support himself, he worked in a toy store, bet the horses, and hustled in a pool hall until he landed a job in the MGM animation department as a copyboy. All thoughts of formal education vanished as acting became his goal and he embarked on the stratagem of addressing all the executives he met by their first name, until one finally gave him a screen test and sent him off to study at Jeff Corey's Player's Ring Theater.

In 1958 he made his first film, *Cry Baby Killer,* for Roger Corman and American International but roles and paychecks did not come regularly and he kept himself alive doing bit parts in TV shows and playing innumerable correspondents on *Divorce Court*. Although in the next ten years he made over a dozen American International drive-in specials, success as an actor eluded him. In retrospect, Nicholson seems glad that fame and fortune did not come early in his life.

"I'm lucky in this way. I wanted to start off as a star actor but if I had I'd be dead because I started off when I was twenty. I'd have been a total pain in the ass by now. What would I be doing now? If I was lucky, it'd be television. I turned TV series down at the time out of some insanely perverse instinct. Now as it is, I might get to work in film until I'm forty, rather than being a has-been at thirty, which can totally wreck your life, as it has for most young successes. You can scoff at the Troys or the Tabs or whatever, but you're lucky you're not him. That's a very hard life to have to deal with. Those guys are all under forty and they've had to call on instincts that men usually use to meet their psychological dilemmas when they're seventy. It's not easy."

As we talked about his days with Roger Corman, I remembered having seen a film on television in which a very young Jack Nicholson played a French officer somehow involved with Boris Karloff in a ridiculous plaster castle but I couldn't come up with the title. So I described the film to him and as I did a wide grin spread across his face. "That film is immortal. There's no question about it," he said between guffaws.

"Do you remember the title?" I asked.

"Yes, but I'm just not saying."

"You were absurd in the part."

"I *was* absurd," he said. " 'I'm André Duvalier, French chausseur.' I wasn't exactly up to that line at twenty-three, you know what I mean? In Marlon Brando's wardrobe from Napoleon, too big in the shoulders. It was amazingly bad. It was the only completely scripted movie in the history of Hollywood film in which there is actually no story. They were going to make the story up afterward and do additional shooting but they could never pull all the ingredients together. Even though the whole script was written, there was no actual story. There was no improvisation, just nothing. I never knew whether this actor was this particular set of characteristics or that one. Perhaps that's why they called it *The Terror*."

Immensely satisfied with himself at so cleverly telling me the title, he smiled George Hanson's squint-eyed smile and went on. "I will tell you this film, next to my interview in *Playboy* magazine [where he discussed at length his past sexual problems], is the most seen and discussed piece of my work in my life. I'm sorry to say.

"I have so many stories about this movie. I was going to Jane Fonda's thing for her trip to North Vietnam, which was held in a Chinese restaurant." He paused as we considered the anomalies that can occur when you mix cuisines with cold war. "On the way up, I was walking behind three people and the first thing I heard from them was, 'Did you see that movie on the late show last night with Jack Nicholson? It was so bad. That voice, my god!' At which point, I didn't have the courage to listen anymore so I went right up and said, 'Hi, how are you?' Then the worst happened that could have happened: They started telling me how much they liked it. It crushed me."

When it seemed that Nicholson would never go beyond this stage as an actor, he began to develop his talents as a writer. His first screenplay produced was American International's *The Trip,* which starred Peter Fonda and featured Dennis Hopper, two connections that would prove very important a couple of years later. After this, he and an old crony, Monte Hellman, who with Francis Ford Coppola had codirected *The Terror,* devised a scheme to make two serious westerns under the guise of blood and guts adventure films. Nicholson wrote and starred in *Ride the Whirlwind,* and Carol Eastman wrote *The Shooting* with Monte Hellman directing both.

After another Corman film, *Flight to Fury,* Nicholson wrote the screenplay for Bob Rafelson's first film, *Head,* which was universally dismissed in its time as just another vehicle for the Monkees.

Just as *Head* exploded the commercially woven myth of The Monkees, BBS Productions' next film, *Easy Rider,* exploded the culturally woven myth of America. Nicholson was working at BBS as a producer when Fonda and Hopper brought their eight-page treatment of the film to him. Bert Schneider provided the $650,000 necessary to make the film on Nicholson's recommendation, so it was only natural that Hopper would choose Nicholson to play George Hanson after Rip Torn dropped out of the project. "Drawing heavily on LBJ for the accent," Nicholson suddenly reversed his fortunes as an actor and found himself an instant cult hero.

"I had been working as an actor a long time and hadn't had any particular success," he commented. "I had an immediate reputation among the nine people who knew my work but the unknown area, director/producer/writer, had known less failure in it so I was being attracted into that. I had no reason to assume that anything was going to change in my acting career at that point. I'm glad I got yanked back into it. It's great because I like it. I've always liked acting."

Immediately after *Easy Rider,* Nicholson played opposite Barbra Streisand in *On a Clear Day You Can See Forever,* a role he took "for the money." He then made *Five Easy Pieces,* which was written by Carol Eastman under the pen name Adrien Joyce. In writing the screenplay, she drew on many events that had occurred in Nicholson's life. For instance, the table-clearing scene in the roadside diner came from a similar incident that saw an overcooked steak hit the ceiling of a Los Angeles restaurant.

The conception of Bobby Dupea itself reflects Nicholson: Both men had ridden first the "on the road" myth of the '50s and then the stoned-Camelot myth of the '60s until each was left confused and disenchanted with the laminated American dream. And then Nicholson, as he always does, brought even more of himself to the role. Bobby's cathartic one-sided conversation with his paralyzed father had much more than an incidental connection with Nicholson's truncated relationship with his own father. In *Playboy* he said, "I never really had a relationship of any significant longevity with my father. He was very rarely around. He was involved in the personal tragedy of alcoholism which no one hid from me. He was just a quiet melancholy, tragic figure—a very soft man. He died the year after I came to California."

The portrayal of Bobby Dupea won Nicholson the New York Film Critics Award for best actor and the role of Jonathan in *Carnal Knowledge.* Jonathan, generally labeled by critics as an unsympathetic character, is followed through frustrating, unsuccessful relationships, first with Candice Bergen and Ann-Margret, and is left at the end of the film enacting a grotesque charade with a prostitute.

"I'm definitely inside *Carnal Knowledge.* I feel more inside that film and separated from the audience in regarding it than anything I've done, in that I felt—and had to make myself feel—that the character I played was ultimately the most positive thing in the film. Even though he ends up in this supposedly self-degrading position because of his sexual propensities. I chose to view it as the only honest end I could have come to. He's the most sensitive person in the adolescent triangle relationship. He is the person who intrudes but nonetheless he's also the person most hurt for it. They go on about their business and get married much as they would have if he had not been involved. He's discarded and he has to suffer the psychological imprint of it.

"He has trouble with women, of course. His ability to seduce them makes him more mistrustful in the classic Don Juan sense but still, he is the person who continues to suffer the pain of the abortions simply because he is seeking to try and have truthful relationships whether he's capable of them or not. And based on his real choices, he stays the most honest of all the people. He is still in action at the end of the film. If there's anything there, he's open to it. If it doesn't become the circumstances of his life, he's still doing the best he can. I choose to believe that this character could love. That's how far removed I am from the way the people saw the film. Primarily because I had to play the character and you can't play someone who you think is destroying himself."

Jonathan is a man who has lost sight of the boundary between rationalization and reality and Nicholson sees him as he would see himself, the primary requirement of a good performance. However, as in *Five Easy Pieces*, Nicholson expresses through the character many of his own fears and frustrations. In light of his highly personal revelations in his *Playboy* interview, there are obvious parallels between Jonathan's situation and the hectic but unfulfilling sex life Nicholson described himself as once living.

Adapted from a novel by Jeremy Larner, *Drive, He Said* was Nicholson's first attempt at directing and assuming complete control of the filmmaking process. The result is a highly provocative, sometimes wonderful movie and a "first film" with all the awkwardness that category is prone to. Set on a college campus, *Drive, He Said* deals with a star basketball player's (William Tepper) failing relationship with the wife of a friend and teacher (Karen Black) and the mental dissolution of his roommate (Michael Margotta) in the face of the draft and the hostile society it represents.

A controversial debut at the Cannes Film Festival earned Nicholson some scathingly negative press in the United States. "Three of my friends had actual fights in the audience and I began to think," Nicholson recalls, " 'I might be Stravinsky here. I got *Rites of Spring* on my hands. I'm immortality. I create a riot while they snore through every other movie!' " *Drive, He Said* opened in New York to virtually universal critical ennui. I asked him if this unfavorable reception has affected his attitude about directing another film.

"I thought the way it was received didn't affect me at all but I see that I'm a little bit less energetic. My whole rhythm about working in film was just to get it done: No complaints as an actor. Walk in there, do it. Okay. 'This line stinks, you know it stinks, you know I told you it stinks. You want it done? Okay! I'm in there doing it.' That's the style, but now I just had to go like this"—he sat back, stretched and ostentatiously flicked the joint that had been moving between us like one of his big, Cuban cigars—"and say, 'I better think about this.'

"I'm looking for something to do. I'm demanding that my subconscious produce a positive thing that I can actually believe in. Meanwhile, I get all these critical ideas, ideas about disasters because that's all I see. Just like everybody else."

An actor, a writer, and a director, Jack Nicholson is a renaissance filmmaker in this renaissance of American films. His acting is an expression of his self and on a movie set it becomes a potent, uncompromising creative force. Like the best film performers, Bogart and Tracy for example, he assumes a role and projects his own persona through it, bending and shaping it to communicate the reality of life as he has lived it.

# Mel Brooks Blazes the West

*by Peter Knobler*

*October 1973*

*On the set of* Blazing Saddles, *at the time known as* Black Bart, *the day after wrap, with Mel Brooks playing all the parts. (Farting scene included.) He also previewed* Young Frankenstein. *Brooks was, for the first time, about to be boffo at box office. This interview is probably the most fun P.K. ever had.*

Mel Brooks is at it again. A cult figure for the clinically insane, a writer able to weave Adolph Hitler into a Western set in 1874 ("He's in everything I do. I don't give a shit . . ."), a film director, a loving father, and a devoted husband. Brooks has been a social director in the Catskills on the borscht belt, a writer for Sid Caesar's *Show of Shows,* the 2,000-Year-Old Man, and (with Dick Cavett as straight man) the 2,500-Year-Old Brewmaster in Ballantine Beer commercials. He has written and directed the films *The Producers* and *The Twelve Chairs.* What he's done for us lately is *Black Bart,* a Western made with the express purpose of "putting the West to bed . . . forever."

Mel's humor is a lilting combination of outrage and seduced abandon. One gets the sense he'll stop at nothing, and not even then. A lot of it is insular, Chosen People, Jewish humor ("For the two Jews in the balcony"), but he's playing for universals now, for the goyim, and you don't *have* to be Jewish . . . *Somebody's* got to carry the melody!

He does voices that are perfect for the dumb, cagey, earthy, airy, fiery, smart, and foolish characters he chooses as if from the buffet at Grossinger's. It's gross comedy, animal humor often filled with growls and belches, but there's a fine plane to it that can shave you awful close.

Mel strode into the commissary on the Warner Brothers lot looking remarkably dapper in suede jacket and quasi-mod slacks; everything fit; the impenetrable anarchist of *The Producers* somehow blended with the *The Twelve Chairs* romantic to produce Mel the mensch, Mel the Director. His face is agile. He can go from cherub to sheriff in a flash.

*Black Bart,* from its conception, sounded too good to be true. It involves a black lawman (Cleavon Little) who is called in to clean up a pioneer town. The railroad is coming and the scramble is on to get land (by whatever means necessary), sell it to the trainmen, and make some quick bucks.

"Andrew Bergman was the originator of the idea," Mel told me. "He wrote a script originally called 'Tex X.' Wonderful title. Cute idea. Hard to say: 'Tex X.' But it was just . . . the title was a little passé 'cause the whole Malcolm X syndrome was a little . . ." he shopped for the phrase like a yenta and got one from the vaudeville bins, ". . . goodbye time, you know? But I liked the idea. Black guy, in the West. I could see the hypocrisy; God-fearing citizens, you know, the first thing . . . 'Nigger? Get him. Kill him' . . . Church-going, far-West pioneers. 'Kill him.' I like that. Then I could see all the different things I could . . . you know, Mel Brooks goes West." Pickled herring in the canteens.

"The milieu for me is very important. It's the classic Western. And whatever you do is good. You can play against cattle and horses and buckaroos and all of that shit. All of the wonderful Western sound and look. You can play kind of Jewish European comedy against that, to laminate that against it . . . Insane."

Mel smears words around like warm butter. He speaks in a pastiche, creates a rhythm that ultimately envelops you, rolls with an intuitive timing so that finally you are rocked by what has become your own rhythm into laughter.

"Westerns," he said. "I've seen Westerns since I was six years old and you say—'Fifteen guys sitting around the campfire . . . farting . . . for two minutes.' You know, given the hard work, you've got a hit there.

"Ever since you were a baby and you went to the movies. Westerns. And they're *there*. Neurograms! Stitched into our skull till we die, they're there. Sitting around a campfire . . . 'More beans' . . . 'Thank you' . . . chicken leg, you know, with the coffee in the tin pot . . . And I have a close-up on beans. Pull back . . . a *greptz* [belch] to begin with. And then fifteen guys *greptzing,* with belching, with farting. You know, all their lives they always eat beans, and you wonder . . . Every Western you see these guys . . . they never . . .

"The cowboys, the actors, had to settle down 'cause they were hysterical."

Besides directing and cowriting (with Bergman, Norman Steinberg, Richard Pryor, and Alan Uger), Mel also acts in the film. Unlike *The Twelve Chairs,* plans are for *Black Bart* to put Mel on-screen often. He plays two parts: a half-breed Indian (half-Indian, half-Jewish—what else?) and the governor of the territory, William J. LePetomane.

Mel hid a smile and informed me, "LePetomane was the name of a famous French artist who farted for a living." I laughed, then smirked. "It's true!" he insisted. "There's a book called *LePetomane.* He dropped his pants and played 'La Marseillaise.' He'd blow out a candle . . . *'Et maintenant . . .'* " He got up from the table like a trouper to demonstrate. " *'Mesdames et messieurs . . . Phttt.'* I love the name LePetomane; it means 'The Bomber.' So I had to play the governor.

"The townspeople send me a telegram: 'That you should pick a black person to be our sheriff just goes to prove you are the leading asshole in the West.' It's insane.

"One of the best jokes in the thing, and I don't mind giving it away because you can say it and it's funnier when you see it," Mel continued, "in order to delay the bad guys, Black Bart comes up with a scheme to put a tollbooth in the middle of the prairie. Now, it's 1874, right? So you see Slim Pickens—who's the best comic actor ever lived for Westerns . . . he's the best rider in the world, by the way, he's incredible; if his horse stumbles he picks him up, he picks him up *while riding*—So he's been going along on his horse, racing and running . . . they come to the tollbooth.

"Now you have a wide shot. They're on the desert, on the prairie, they can just ride around any which way. They say, 'Stop!' They pull up. He says, 'What the hell is this? *Gov. LePetomane Thruway.* What the hell will that asshole think of next?' Then he turns around to his men and says . . ." Mel drawled a Slim imitation, " 'Anybody got a dime?' Nobody has one, so he says, 'Somebody has to go back and get a shitload of dimes.' And they stay there, stuck." Mel paused, mock-reflected, and shook his head. "What liberties we take."

The same kind of lunacy that names an entire Western town "Johnson," from the barber to the lawyer to the saloon to the ice cream parlor (Howard; "One Flavor"), spawned the 2,000-Year-Old Man, Mel's most cult-revered character. There are enclaves of lunacy where initiates lean to one another and whisper, "Tell me the one about the nectarine . . . 'half a peach, half a plum, it's a hell of a fruit.' "

"We might do another record," Mel mentioned. Carl Reiner, himself a loony, played the straight man to Mel, and his cackle of a laugh always spoke of the seltzer water exuberance they produced together. "Half the record will probably be what I call the 'Fire Island tapes.' Nobody's ever heard them. From parties and when friends came by. They were made about fifteen years ago, never released. Risqué? They're filthy! Very crazy, very insular Jewish schtick." The other half will be a rerelease of their *Cannes Film Festival* album.

Reiner and Brooks appeared once on *The Hollywood Palace* on TV. I'd waited for the show all week, so had all my friends. When Mel crept out in a floppy cape like a goofball Dracula, we all showed up the next day in costume. Why hadn't they performed more often?

"Performing diminished the artistic quality of material," Mel said seriously. "When you constantly perform what you do is get down to the winners. You get down to the audience-movers, that's six or seven jokes, and you keep honing and sharpening . . . It's not the best stuff, the most subtle stuff, it's the most *commercial* stuff, and you lose your ability to discern any more about what's truly, significantly funny." He had obviously given this some thought; above anything, Mel is a consummately evocative performer, onstage or across a table. "You get down to the rhythm jokes that rock the audience, you know? Performing destroys you as a performer." The irony screwed his face into a nutty grin. " 'Cause the audience has a way of reducing your stuff to only the winners, the goers, and you gotta cover too much ground for a winner. You lose a special quality in the work, you know? It's tough.

"Guys start off great and they end up, you say, 'Gee, I saw that.' They get flopsweat."

I HAVE TWO DIFFERENT FRIENDS WHO EACH SWEAR THIS HAPPENED TO him:

Mel Brooks is spotted walking in the street. (He lives with his wife, actress Anne Bancroft, in Greenwich Village.) It is a golden moment, a vision, like Jesus in Jerusalem or Willie Mays at the Polo

Grounds . . . "He is here before me!" To let him pass is to forfeit the ultimate Mel Brooks story. "Mel Brooks! You're the funniest man in the world!" And he turns like a gypsy and says on cue, "And you're the *smartest* man in the world!"

MEL BROOKS IS NO DUMMY. THERE'S A KEEN EDGE TO HIS COMEDY; HE will run through bit after bit, but there always seems a connecting thread, less than evident but more than invisible, which ties the humor together while tying the audience into knots. Much of professional humor is so low, or an end in itself, it was a relief to hear Mel explain the concepts behind his comedy.

"I like to have a nice balance of philosophy, intellectuality, and animal comedy," he said. "Just to have the Three Stooges is fine, but it's not enough. You gotta say something. This one, *Black Bart,* I really don't know what it says, but I think it says something about hypocrisy, greed. I personally like to talk about greed . . . very basic things. Greed is my thing. In *The Twelve Chairs,* in *The Producers,* it's all greed. I don't want to get on a soapbox, so I'll say it with comedy.

"Now another movie I always wanted to do is the monster movie." And he launched into another extended scenario. With *Black Bart* in the cutting stages, and a monster movie not yet written, there came the sense that maybe Mel was trying out new material, using the interview as a sounding board much as he used friends to bounce material off for the 2,000-Year-Old Man. I had been chortling all afternoon, so there wasn't much risk involved, and maybe he already knew that, but there was a sense of audition that occurred to me only after the day was through. Earlier, I was too busy laughing.

"We're putting a new picture together," Mel began, "called *Young Frankenstein,* starring Gene Wilder as young Frederick Frankenstein who disowns his forebears. He's a neurologist. Then he goes back to claim the castle for the peasants, the inheritors, and he goes back there and he gets into the books, you know . . ." Mel fumbles through huge dust-covered, invisible volumes, first just mumbling, then grumbling as he finds inscrutable treasures. "He's going bananas . . ." until finally he's flipping pages twenty at a time, then stands up and roars, " '*It can be done!*' He fuckin' goes crazy! with the lightning and the organ music . . .

"And they get a monster . . . Peter Boyle plays the monster. And they're bringing Peter Boyle to life, and it's a mixture of all fruits and vegetables, mostly fruit, with raspberries and they're squeezing oranges, the elixir of life, fruit, with the juice, and they're mashing up . . . Marty Feldman, that little Jewish English actor, he's Igor, he's mashing and pumping it into the monster . . . and he comes to life . . ." Mel rose slowly, his face the *punim* of a monster maligned, every monster you've ever seen. And all of a sudden a strange, fey ray crossed his features, "and the monster lisps, 'Judy's at the Palace! I must go get a cab! I'll wear my dress!' And they say, 'Too much fruit! Too much fruit!' " Mel began frantically to unstuff the monster now before him. "And they hit him over the head and start to take the fruit out of him . . . 'Too much fruit!'

"But I didn't want that to be Abbott and Costello, I wanted to say something. The monster is very significant because what is the monster? Who is the monster? He really is the intellectual." He stopped to make sure he was being followed. "Intellectuals change governments, they incite students . . . and the monster in this thing is not the monster, it's Frankenstein. They're afraid of what's in his fuckin' head, they don't understand the unseen geniuses, and the result of *that* is a monster.

"The other thing that intrigued me," he paused, perhaps wondering if he'd been followed seriously, "I'm giving you shit that finds its way into the movie very obliquely," he explained. "I really play to the entertainment values, and if you're looking for thought or intellectual motif it's there too." He continued, "The other thing that fascinates me is man's envy of women's ability to give birth. It's somewhere in the core, the nucleus of the Frankenstein myth, 'cause he creates life and hates women, and it's very complicated. It's the first time in the history of fiction that that happens. The *man* creates this life, this baby, this monster. For the first time, not a woman but a man. It's an interesting idea."

MEL'S COMEDY IS LUNATIC, BUT THERE IS A SPECIAL DEBUNKING GOING on that he is only half willing to admit in public. "Putting the West to bed" is one thing. Doing it serious harm is another, and though there's a gentleness behind his grossest spoofs, there's an ultimate subversion behind the Yiddish gentility. It's that dangerous, subliminal sheen that makes him so funny, the cold edge that gives him warmth. The 2,000-Year-Old Man's national anthem went: "Let 'em all go to hell . . . except Cave Seventy-six!" Anybody can build up a system, it takes a wacko brilliance to tear one down.

THERE WAS A NEW TOY IN THE CUTTING ROOM: A THREE-HEADED EDITING machine that lets the person in charge see three takes of the same shot. It's a very expensive little production, spread out over half the room like electric trains. Mel sat down in front of it and started to play "Rhapsody in Blue." A grand virtuoso. He swung and swayed. Like a precocious kid in a space station sandbox, he cast about him for amusement. There is always material. Yard-long strips of film hung like bacon on a rack and he clutched one to his breast.

"My life is film," he insisted, a Garbo accent coloring the words.

"I *am* film . . ." He wrapped the strip around his forehead, sprockets pocking his brow, and peered through it into the light to see what surrounded him.

"Film is me . . ." He rolled it into a ball, then—*zzzzip*—stretched it across his chest like Miss Celluloid 1933.

"Expose me!"

# George Lucas, Skywalker

*by David Rensin*
*November 1973*

*Lucas had just produced his first popular film,* American Graffiti, *and told us about some kooky idea he had for a "space opera, a real crazy movie . . . like* Flash Gordon.*" Also, a reference to what would become* Apocalypse Now.

"It was my life, that's me, it was my ten-year reunion with myself," George Lucas said, pounding the desktop for emphasis, as he spoke about his new film, *American Graffiti.* "Nineteen sixty-two was the year I graduated from high school and it's about me and my friends." He sees this picaresque transition from adolescence to adulthood as an important punctuation point in his life, since, at twenty-eight, he no longer considers himself an eighteen-year-old. "Now," he laughed, "I think of myself as twenty-four."

A small man, perhaps five-feet-six, Lucas does not fit the flamboyant stereotype of film director. Dressed in white socks, tennis shoes, straight-legged Levi's and an Arrow shirt wrinkled from an early-morning plane ride, he stroked his closely shorn beard and thumbed a pair of heavy glasses to his face as he continued his reflections on the film and the seminal period it captures. "That was when the change from rock and roll to rock started. It was also the end of the '50s—the change from one period of American history to another. The same thing happened to these kids, their lives—

when you get out of high school then you go through that thing and a whole different aspect of life takes over. The movie is really about that, change of life in American culture, in rock and roll, and in the characters' lives."

After two years of majoring in social science at his hometown Modesto Junior College, Lucas transferred to USC's cinema department. Until then, his only film-related experience had been as a still photographer of racing cars, but in his second year at USC he made eight short films that won numerous prizes. He returned there and, as a teaching assistant, made a science fiction short called *THX 1138: 4EB*. The film took first-place honors at the National Student Film Festival.

On the strength of that talent Lucas won a Warner Brothers scholarship "to observe" professionals. He was assigned to Francis Ford Coppola's *Finian's Rainbow* and the two men have been together since—now, as president and vice president of American Zoetrope Productions. While working as Coppola's assistant on *Rain People,* the film before *The Godfather,* Lucas made an award-winning short about Coppola called *Filmmaker* and expanded *THX 1138* into a full-length screenplay that Warner Brothers, at Coppola's urging, agreed to finance. It was an ambitious first film.

In the same way that *THX 1138* overcame the confines of its genre to comment on a broader scope of human affairs, *American Graffiti* transcends its nostalgic setting. As Lucas himself stressed, "It's not a parody of its time, like *Grease.*" In fact, Lucas says that he and his friends actually went through all the traumas and moments of levity depicted on the screen; they weren't, however, packed into one twelve-hour period as *Graffiti's* slices of life are.

As for the characters, he explained, "I was all of them at one point or another in my high school career. The one that's least me is Steve [the bland, insurance man-to-be], who was written in to add a love story angle and round it out to four people. It shows."

But it seems hard to imagine Lucas as beefy Big John, the aging hot-rod king. "I was in a way, although I was more into sports cars than hot rods." Lucas calls himself just a "freaky, crazy kid who got into a lot of trouble," but adds that the film was still "generally a fantasy. It wasn't the way it really was, it was the way it should have been. I started out as Terry, the littlest of the group, the goofy kid trying to become a big man, but as soon as I turned sixteen and could drive, I changed. I could race and I got a lot of respect. I was even like Carlos, the smallest of the Pharaohs, but then I got into a hairy car accident and nearly got killed. I spent a lot of time in the hospital and became a student. When I got out, I still cruised, but I could see the craziness that went on. So I went in as John, dealing with cars, and came out as Curt, dealing with books."

Lucas started work on the screenplay for *American Graffiti* directly after *THX 1138* was completed. By then he'd gained, by his own admission, a reputation for being a "weird science fiction director," and was having trouble getting another project of his own off the ground. He's been offered directing jobs, mostly for action-oriented, roller derby–type flicks, but turned them down to finish the screenplay even though the money was often extremely good. The final version was taken to all the Hollywood studios and rejected, but it was accepted the second time around at Universal. Lucas cited some reasons for his problems selling the *Graffiti* idea: "They thought it was just going to be a musical montage and said it didn't have enough clout. Also, studios weren't interested in the '50s and '60s two years ago. Mainly, though, most everybody said the screenplay didn't have enough solid grounding. They felt it was too atmospheric, like *THX 1138*."

Lucas maintains, however, he is the type of director that can sense what a seemingly inexplicit screenplay will be, acted out. "I have a very strong feeling about what I'm doing or I wouldn't be doing it. Directing has a lot to do with being a human being and not much to do with technical whatevers. I feel I have an advantage in that I know *exactly* what I want."

Much of the impact of *Graffiti* is felt in the final moments as a Dragnet-type epilogue flashes onto the screen. According to Lucas, there has been varied reaction to its insertion in the final version. "We had long arguments about it, and sure, it could have been left off because all the characters' fates were painfully obvious anyway. But it just came out when I wrote the screenplay. I got to the last page and there it was in my head, so I wrote it down."

Lucas's next movie will reportedly end, at least temporarily, his tradition of not caring about the solid story line, which he virtually passed over in *Graffiti* and more so in *THX 1138*. "It will have a strong plot," he intimated slyly, not giving anything away, "and it will be full of action. It won't be like *THX* where the premise was to make a movie about people that had no feelings—something cold and alien. It will be very real.

"It will be more like a space opera, in the sense of a horse opera. Capes and laser guns and swords and such. It's a real crazy movie. Like *Flash Gordon*, *The Wizard of Oz*, or *Gulliver's Travels*—a whole different kind of science-fiction film.

"I was originally scheduled to do a film about the Vietnam war next. I've been trying to get it off the ground for four or five years now, ever since I started my first movie. But now, even though I'm a popular director and Francis is a hot producer, we still can't get it off the ground. Nobody will make a Vietnam war film. No way, shape, or form. It just can't be done in this country. Who knows, as time goes on, and it becomes less and less relevant, maybe it'll be done as a period piece."

Lucas may seem eccentric, but actually he has his finger right on the pulse of our times, anticipating the public need. *Graffiti* came at the crest of the nostalgia wave and has been hailed as "one of the most important films of the year." Still, Lucas shuns the hip director role. He avoids public functions, preferring to stay at his northern California home, immersing himself completely in his next project, and acting out his childhood fantasies on the screen. He is fond of saying: "I live my films."

# Woody Allen Goes Bananas

*by Martin Mull*

*December 1973*

*Woody Allen and* Everything You Always Wanted to Know About Sex.
*He was just starting to be taken seriously as a filmmaker (Annie Hall was
still three years off), so naturally* Crawdaddy *sent a comedian to interview
him.*

There are only two Woodys that I would ever want to meet. Allen
and Woodpecker. Both are in films. Both are funny. Both are short.
Mr. Allen is five-feet-five-and-a-half. I asked him.

My original hope was to interview both Mr. Allen and Mr. Woodpecker together in a blindfold test à la *Downbeat* magazine, but I
could not find Mr. Woodpecker, or blindfolds. The following is the
best I could do. It is an interview with Mr. Allen, with occasional
inane questions from yours truly, instead of Mr. Woodpecker. It
takes place during lunch.

For the record, Mr. Allen's lunch was: tuna salad, with little or no
mayo (apparently), no lettuce (apparently), and no tomato, on
white healthy-looking (no Wonder) bread, and coffee.

As the tape began to record, it caught us talking about the fact
that his film, *Everything You Always Wanted to Know About Sex But Were
Afraid to Ask,* was doing well in foreign countries.

*Do they dub it?*

Some countries dub it and some subtitle it. But it's doing remarkably well in Europe and South America, places that no picture of

mine has ever done well in . . . you know, like Bolivia . . . and it really is a surprise to me, you know, that it would do well like that . . .

*That's great, though. Congratulations.*

I feel good about it. I wonder what that means? It's also a big hit in Israel, where, I mean my pictures have played and done all right, you know. But not . . .

*Did it do better there than it did here?*

No, it did very well here. Here it couldn't miss, because it had that book title, you know, that was such an advantage to begin with. The title is a big plus, but I'm sure word of mouth must've gotten to people, they must've said, go see it. Because the title is always good for three weeks or two months, but the thing was continually breaking records and I will never understand it.

*And now Bolivia.*

I will never understand it.

*When you were negotiating with Dr. David Ruben and his crack team of lawyers for the book's title did you . . .*

No, it didn't happen like that. I've never met him, I've never said a word to him, I don't know him from a hole in the wall, and I can safely say that I never really read the book. What happened was I saw him on television one night and I got the idea that I had always had some ideas that were short and couldn't fit in any other format, you know, so I got the idea to do the book, and Elliot Gould had already bought the book, and they couldn't figure out how to make it into a movie—he had held it for about a year. We found that out when we called Dr. Ruben and so we got it from Elliot. I just looked through the book and tried to get questions that fit the ideas I already had, and when the questions weren't there, I just made up the questions. I mean not all the questions are in the book. I just wanted the title because it seemed like the only way to put together six or seven of those short ideas in a way that people would come and see it. Episodic movies like that have always been notorious failures. Always. And there have been some wonderful ones.

*Sadly enough, I think the title does actually reflect a great number of people and what they have on their mind. I mean there are a lot of things that they wanted to know but were afraid to ask.*

I think that's true.

*There are a number of things I'd like to know but I'm afraid to ask . . .*

I've never read the book. You know people used to ask me, while I was making the picture, "What do you think of the book? You think it's really good?" And I didn't know what to say about it, you know. I'm sure there's some people that read the book and were helped by it, you know what I mean? I guess . . .

*They're the ones to meet because, by and large, I considered most of it under the heading of tripe (I don't know if that's a literary term).*

I'm sure it is, because I read an hilarious review of it by Gore Vidal in the *New York Review of Books.* And I'm sure he was absolutely right about it. And yet I bet there are people in the country so repressed and so naive about sex that there were probably a couple of things in that book that were actually helpful to them . . . that actually made them feel that those things that they were doing at night were not all that bad. I really feel that.

*Of course there's a number of people who get a sexual response just from owning a hardbound book. [This comment of mine caused a silence that lingered until my next and, I feel, most incisive question.]*

*What's your sign?*

My sign is Sagittarius.

*Sagittarius, that's very good. Do you follow that stuff?*

No.

*I've got some questions written down here, number one: How's it going? Well, let's skip that till later on. Here's number two: How much of your work in your films do you insist on doing yourself and how much can you successfully farm out?*

Well, you can't farm any of it out. I mean, you do as much of it yourself as you can possibly do, because otherwise it just never comes out the way you want it to. It's a constant attempt to control every conceivable aspect of it—editing, sets, costumes . . . And to the degree that you succeed at that, you have a better film, almost invariably. I mean, that's not the whole answer, but it really hurts you when you're not in control of those things. I mean, a person who has never made a film can't realize how much that's a problem.

*How much do your finished products resemble your original conception?*

Not a lot, that's for sure. There's no way they can, because the difference is just too great. I just write anything I want, and a year from now I'll be shooting it some place, and I don't even think about the problems . . . You know, you write "A sixty-foot breast walks into the . . ." and you don't even think that someday you're going to be faced with the problem of a guy is actually going to be sitting there and saying, "Well, how should we do that, and where should we go, and how much is this going to cost?"

*Go to the Yellow Pages and look under breast builders, right?*

That's what it finally boils down to. Somebody's got to come in and figure out how to do, how to do . . . and that's just one little thing. There's a million things like that.

*I wouldn't call a sixty-foot breast a little thing.*

Well, actually it was one little thing on the last picture. You don't realize it when you're writing it that it's so easy to think of the stuff and never bother for a second to think about, that you're going to have to get a helicopter, and you're going to have to get wires, and you're going to have to fly this and people can't see the wires and that means the cameramen are going to have to have light from angles they haven't lit before and, you know. It never occurs to you for a second that any of this is going to happen. So the finished product is never anything like what you think it's going to be.

*I have great respect for your having a somewhat bizarre sense of humor at times and, with due respect, a more middle of the road sense of humor at other times. Although equally original. How much do you filter out the super-bizarre, more elusive kind of humor from a film so that it can hit the greatest number of people?*

Oh I don't at all. I just do whatever occurs to me at the time . . . But what I will do is this: When I play screenings of my roughcuts, if audiences continually don't laugh at a joke, or a sequence or something, I'll cut it out of the picture. Anything that doesn't work, though, after three, four, five screenings with an audience, I get rid of it.

*Who do you screen it to, just general audiences?*

I've tried everything and all the audiences I've screened it to are miserable. I've screened for an audience of friends, I've screened for an audience of half friends and half strangers, of all strangers, of servicemen from the USO, for college kids. I've tried everything. I've tried them in the afternoon, in the morning, at night. And they'll come in and sit down and watch it, and they don't seem to laugh at it. And in my first film, *Take the Money and Run,* I kept cutting stuff out of the picture. I kept cutting stuff out as I kept screening it more and more. Finally I didn't have enough material for a film! Then I showed my *original* version, one night I sneak previewed it, and it killed them. And they filled out cards afterwards and they loved it, and if it wasn't for that . . . and the same thing happened on the sex picture and *Bananas.*

*I was going to ask you . . . who do you consider your audience to be? Or do you limit it?*

No, I think . . . I think I have a small, nondescript audience.

*Under five feet?*

No, I really mean that. I know, I've never been able to pinpoint my audience because they never showed up . . .

*I have that same problem . . .*

. . . in any identifiable mass. I mean, when I was starting and got fairly hot as a stand-up comedian, my albums didn't sell, and everybody else's albums were selling. And people said, "Well, they'll adore you in the colleges." And they didn't. I mean, they would never show up . . . I played about six or eight college dates to half houses so I stopped doing that. And you know, I've had half houses in Vegas, I mean, every part of the spectrum, so I don't really know who my audience is.

*In the last picture you really had some terrific actors.*

Oh yeah, but those were professional, I mean those were really good people. But I've worked with, you know . . . like when I was making *Bananas* in Puerto Rico there were these hundreds of Puerto Rican people that, you know, couldn't act at all.

*You got Howard Cosell's best performance ever.*

Oh, I know that. [laughs] But that's foolproof because Howard has one of those personalities that . . .

*Wait a minute, I think that's one of my questions . . . yes . . . number seven: "Is Howard Cosell crazy, and if not, who is?"*

Howard's strange. He's very nice, and very intelligent, but he's just larger than life. You know, he's great fun to be with for an hour or two . . .

*Not unlike a good hooker.*

. . . but then after a while, it's too . . . you know . . . too intense, you know, he's constantly talking in that voice, and . . .

*And the same vernacular that he uses for . . .*

Yes, exactly the same . . . But he's very nice and very pleasant and very talented and a terrific sportscaster I think, just . . .

*I was just going to ask, does it make sense to actually have a conversation, hear that voice, and hear that vernacular, and not have a sporting event to refer to?*

It's okay for a while . . . and then you . . . you start missing the action . . .

*That's what I figured.*

Hear that urgency. But he's really very nice, he's not at all, you know . . . umm . . . he *is* egomaniacal, that's true, I mean all that stuff is true about him. And now I think what he does is play it up a lot, because it's worked for him. So he becomes extra, extra crazy. You know?

*I know . . . Getting back to you for a second, I was wondering if you wanted to do films right from the beginning, or was it an outgrowth of being a stand-up comic and writer?*

At that time I wasn't thinking of it. I was trying to succeed as a nightclub comedian. In those days I was just happy to succeed as a nightclub comedian.

*Which is hard . . . I met a fellow who was the piano player at the Hungry i when everyone was hungry and told me of the night when you came in and were heckled terribly and went over and put your head on the piano and just walked away . . .*

That happened. The details are a little hazy there. I was appearing there and hit a very bad audience one night, and at that time I used to watch those black jazz musicians, they would turn their back on the audience and play. So I didn't know what to do so I turned my back and I started doing my act upstage, toward the wall. And they really got annoyed, you know? And they walked out, and they complained to the manager, and he called me into his office after and said don't ever do that again because those are a lot of customers that come here, you know, frequently, and they wanted their money back, I had to give thirty refunds. It was a terrible experience. It was hard.

Now it's gotten harder for people. At least I had six clubs to play, I had the Blue Angel and the Hungry i and the Bon Soir and the Bitter End, etc. Now, if a guy's starting out it's very hard, very rough, because there's no place to try out, to do anything.

*Do you think that a humorist starting out would do better to fit his talents into a different format such as a playwright or screenwriter?*

Not necessarily, because there's a big demand for that. I mean, if one is a funny stand-up comedian, it's just hard to find places to get exercise, to get started. But once you're past that and you're good, it's a very, very satisfying field. It really can be fun. The only time it's not fun is when you have to do it for a living. I used to have to do it for six, seven months at a time without a night off. I mean seven nights a week. I would go from the Blue Angel to the Hungry i to the Crystal Palace to . . .

*Two or three sets a night?*

Yeah.

*Yeah, you get completely up for it, you know, I'm ready to go do it, I go out and do an hour and ten minutes, come back, have half a beer and then . . . it's time to do it again.*

And then you have to do it again at two in the morning. That's the worst of it.

*It's the same problem you run into going out with a girl much younger than you.*

It is.

*What are your feelings on one of my favorites,* Tiger Lily *[a grade-Z Japanese film Allen dubbed unfaithfully into English]?*

Well, it was a nice idea that, in my opinion, didn't come off. There are some laughs in it, but that doesn't mean anything. I thought it was going to be easy. But it was not. It was hard to do, and I should've had a film with more dialogue in it. I thought it would be easier to take a film with less dialogue because you wouldn't have that many problems.

*You don't have that much to do.*

Yes, but the only time you can make the film score is when there's dialogue . . . then you'd run out of dialogue and there'd be this long scene, like five minutes on the screen of chasing stuff and that stuff is so deadly, so . . .

*Well, I rather enjoyed it, I really love terrible things when they're done well.*

Well, that's one of the worst movies I'd ever seen, but it was done at such a low price, and the idea was so novel that it was almost hard for them not to make money with it, you know.

*Plus you have an immediate locked-in Japanese-American audience.*

If I did that kind of thing again, which I wouldn't, I would take a completely different kind of film. I mean completely . . . it should be done with serious dialogue. Because it can work. But even then it's very tedious to do it because you've got to sit in a room and watch loops go around endlessly, endlessly, and make up stuff and get it into their mouths after that.

*Do you try not to listen to too many other comics or other people working in similar fields? Are you easily influenced?*

I try not to listen to other people because I think that you get influenced and use their ideas without knowing you're doing it. I could hear a small comedian, a famous comedian, and enjoy it and all of that, and a year later without even thinking of it suddenly come up with a joke, and maybe I've heard him say that joke. It's just that I've forgotten about it and now it reoccurs to me. And I hate to do that kind of thing and it happens all the time. Themes and jokes and mannerisms and stuff, so I, I just don't . . . I mean, I always become the last person I saw anyhow. So it's better not to do it.

*I'm curious about a couple of things. Are you still performing stand-up solo?*

Yes. I don't get a chance to work as much, because I just don't have the time. But I still play. I did a whole slew of concerts last year. I like to perform stand-up. It's really fun. It's, it's like working in the theater . . . it's great fun. But the quantity of people that you see is so small that . . .

*It's a more personal contact.*

Yes, exactly.

*You also get your reaction immediately; you don't have to wait for color labs and editing and all . . .*

You never get it in film, never, I mean, you do it and a year later the film goes out . . . and when I'm performing on the set, I'm doing something funny on the set, you never know because everyone has got to be absolutely quiet so . . . I mean, there's no gratification in it at all.

*So why are you doing it?*

The truth is, and I know you'll think I'm kidding, I'm doing it because I know it's a very tough thing to get the opportunity to direct and star in your own movies, and I have the opportunity and I'd feel foolish not doing it. That's exactly why. It's much more fun to be in a play, and it's fun to do concerts and things like that, but for me to look up in a couple of years and say "Gee I had an opportunity to write and direct all these pictures, and I didn't take it. Now I can't do it." I may not get the chance again after a while. Because generally what happens, particularly with screen comedians, is you have a vogue for a while, and then that's it. So I'm doing it while I can. But it certainly isn't fun to do a film, I mean wake up at five in the morning month after month, and do that stuff over and over under the lights and costumes and not get any laughs and then find yourself in a room with thousands of feet of film and have to put them together and still nothing and it always looks crappy. Then you add music and it looks a little better, and then finally it comes out and that's nice for a while, but that's not fun. It was much more fun being in *Play It Again Sam* on Broadway . . .

I guess you always want to be doing what you're not doing . . . but for just sheer enjoyment, except if you're on Broadway, nobody sees you. But, to go over to a theater, at eight o'clock at night, and do a show and get big laughs for an hour and a half and that's all you've worked for the day, and then you're finished, is very gratifying.

*It certainly is gratifying to get big laughs, all right, but I was wondering if you are ever shooting higher than just laughs, a commentary of some sort or whatever?*

I certainly haven't been. It may be that at some time I'll want to write some things or make some films that make people laugh and also have a deeper meaning. But the large bloc of my work to date has been strictly to make people laugh . . . I mean, I'm thrilled to go into the movie theater and have a good time for an hour and a half, and that's it. Now, I don't think I'll always feel that way . . . I hope someday that I'll be able to do films or plays or something that are deeper than that . . . but it's tough to do that; very few people have achieved that. Chaplin is one, but at the cost of doing a lot of junk to get there. But he's been able to do films that make you laugh and also have a bit of comment to them.

*I think the Marx Brothers did it as well.*

Yes . . . but very accidental with them. I mean, I know that for a

fact because I know Groucho pretty well, and that was just pure accident; they just happened to have a built-in genius, that when it
works there's an inherent message in their work that they don't try
for in any way, but they were so great, it just worked for them.

*What are you working on now?*

I'm cutting a film—that's why I've been so busy. I made the one
mistake of giving them an opening date on the film, which you
should never do . . . and so it's booked now already in three theaters. Two in New York and in California for Christmas week. So I'm
working at a frantic pace.

*Any title for it?*

*Sleeper.*

*Any plot, premise?*

Well, I can't give you much information on it except that it's science fiction.

*Oh, excellent! Are you in it?*

Yes.

*Starring?*

Yes, and I haven't seen it yet, I've just seen 250,000 feet of film in
no order. Just shot months apart, that has to go together. I have no
sense of what it's going to be. I may look at it and find that it's too
long, or unfunny, or God knows what. But I should know more by
the end of next week.

*People are usually in pretty good spirits around Christmas week.*

Yeah, what happens after that?

*The new year.*

They always give you a big build-up for Christmas week and
Christmas week you go in any place and you break the house
record, you know, and it's wonderful, and then January first comes
and the holiday's over . . .

*The holiday's over. What are you going to do when the "big holiday" is
over? The vogue that you spoke about earlier?*

Probably just write, you know. Probably direct, write, and act.
'Cause where you really lose your appeal, I think, is as a personality.
They go crazy over you for a certain amount of time . . .

*And your particular sense of humor?*

I think that I will always be able to write prose that they would
laugh at, or direct films, or write plays that they would laugh at, and
in particular when they see other actors do them. But what I think
happens is that you run out of steam yourself. 'Cause it seems to
happen. I can't think of any performer, whether it's Keaton, or
Chaplin, or the Marx Brothers, or Kirk Douglas, or Burt Lancaster,
or Gregory Peck—I mean guys that were so enormous at one time—

that don't eventually run out of . . . and particularly the kind of thing I do . . . that broad kind of belly-laugh stuff. I mean, they see you, they see your tricks, your attitudes, and all that, two pictures or ten pictures and then . . . they want something new.

*Do people write for you . . . even unsolicited?*

What really I find is that people send me written material that they write for me, and it's always ten times as crazy as I would write for myself.

*Really? Do you use it?*

No, I don't use it because I don't need it and I write all my own stuff, but people obviously have this view of me . . . I think a *little* craziness goes a long way.

# The Brains
# Behind the President

*by Lloyd Grove*

*November 1977*

Crawdaddy *once ran a cover story called "The Whole Earth Conspiracy Catalog" and an article entitled "The Assassination Please Almanac." It was the '70s—you could believe anything. (Apparently Oliver Stone still does.) Lloyd Grove now writes for* The Washington Post *"Style" section.*

Just west of the intersection of Houston and Elm streets in the boomtown of Dallas, Texas, something really awful happened:

*Bang, bang,* and *bang.*

Actually it happened twice: first on November 22, 1963, at 12:30 Central Standard Time, when Jack Kennedy's head evulsed in the viewfinder of Abe Zapruder's 8mm camera and sprayed shimmering red mist over Dealey Plaza. And then on July 3, 1977, a motorcade survived for the second time after a dusky rifle barrel popped out of a sixth-floor window and a handsome chap in the head limo twitched and writhed to the *bang-bang-bang* of the gunshots.

This time the event was recorded repeatedly and at great expense by an industrial-strength multilensed mechanism that purred atop the grassy knoll. It and several boom mikes were attended by sweat-drenched, joke-cracking members of the nation's entertainment unions who were getting richer by the minute. At 12:30 P.M. Central Standard Time, a caterer set up on a grassy knoll with sandwiches and lemonade. A group of electricians smoked cigars and played poker under a tree, and spellbound parents and children, their

faces flushed and giddy, hurried to the obliging man who was signing candy wrappers, postcards, or anything else handy: "Best wishes,
JFK."

After all, we Americans—"born in this century, tempered by war,
disciplined by a hard and bitter peace, proud of our ancient heritage"—nearly always have made the best of even our worst difficul-
ties, the worse the better. Jolly as we are, we can even see the bright
side of something really awful.

Take, for instance, Marguerite Claverie Oswald, who happens to
be Lee Harvey Oswald's mother.

"I'm unique, one of a kind," robust, lively Marguerite proclaimed
in her immaculate Fort Worth dining room this July, a week before
her seventieth birthday.

"I'm the only one in the whole world who's the mother of the
man accused of killing a president. A president! Why else would you
come to see me?

"Let me ask you this," she continued. "They replaced the president, didn't they?"

"So I understand."

"There, you see? *I* cannot be replaced."


THIS SUMMER WAS A BUSY ONE FOR MOTHER OSWALD. I, AND SEVERAL
others, coveted her ruminations about a TV movie then being
filmed in Dallas for ABC, a four-hour what-if called *The Trial of Lee
Harvey Oswald,* which will be aired on two nights sometime soon.
Charles Fries, an independent producer out of Hollywood, spent
more than $2 million of the network's money (twice the usual
amount) before he delivered the final print. He conscripted such
behemoths of tubebiz as Lorne Greene, Ben Gazzara, and David
Greene (the director of *Roots* and *Rich Man, Poor Man*), and convinced two young actors, John Pleshette and Mo Malone, to play Mr.
and Mrs. Lee Harvey Oswald.

Don't be thrown by the film's title. Although much of the movie
dramatizes the trial Oswald never had, we aren't talking here about
Perry Mason courtroom schtick. According to informed sources,
*The Trial of Lee Harvey Oswald* won't even try to establish his guilt or
innocence.

Instead, the film is, according to Saul Kahn, the production's cho-
leric publicist, "the first . . . to deal with Lee Harvey Oswald as a
person. It is a film," he says, "based on historical fact, not speculation or rumor." However, Dallas *Times Herald* reporter Hugh

Aynesworth, a recognized assassination expert, found nearly sixty inaccuracies in the first half of the script alone.

But that's not important. What *is* important is that those of you who tune in on the appointed nights will see—in Kahn's words— "an authentic recreation of the assassination of President John F. Kennedy . . . filmed on the actual assassination site in Dealey Plaza."

MARGUERITE HAS BEEN SKITTISH OVER THE PHONE, TALKING VAGUELY of "compensation," abruptly ringing off whenever pressed on the subject. She has hung up on me five times, twice on my editor.

Finally, though, she agreed to a meeting. "Go past the Texas School Book Depository and turn onto the Fort Worth Tollway." When I arrive at the handsome brick house on Byers Street, she requests identification, and searches me for a hidden tape recorder.

"This is a nice house."

"I don't own this house," Marguerite says, "and I had to sell most of Lee's personal belongings and letters for the down payment."

Marguerite, chic in an apple-green housedress, her stout beehive unyielding against the blasts of the air conditioner, steps briskly to the dining room table.

"Everybody wants to know about the assassination," she says. "Books and more books come out every week. And some of them have even used my research without giving me the credit." She sighs.

"You say you want to know my views. Well, I don't just talk off the top of my head. I read every book that comes out. Sometimes I'll stay up until three or four in the morning doing research. Here, I want you to see my library."

She leads me into a shelf-lined alcove, containing what indeed seems to be every tome ever written on the subject, including the twenty-six volumes of the Warren Commission Report. Each book, paperback and hardcover, is individually wrapped in plastic.

"Okay, that's enough," Marguerite says after fifteen seconds, and I follow her back to the dining room.

"I live in America," she says. "Whaddya think, this isn't some kind of communistic country. This isn't Russia."

*Bang-bang-bang.* She's pounding the tabletop. "This is free enterprise. It's profit sharing. And if you're making money, and your magazine is making money—if everybody's making money, well I'm not about to go penniless."

"Why did you keep hanging up on me?"

"*Really* now." says Marguerite, peering incredulously through butterfly glasses. "In my subtle way, I left you an opening. But you insulted me. You asked me what I meant by 'compensation.' What kind of businessman do you think you are?"


OKAY. THERE ARE BUSINESSMEN, AND THERE ARE *BUSINESS*MEN. THERE are assasso-agents who merchandise specialists like Mark Lane & Co. rolling and yawing around the college lecture circuit. There are small-time entrepreneurs who market commemorative ashtrays, dinner plates, and bath mats (fur tableaux of John-John poised and saluting) at cigarette stands and curio shops across the country.

In Dallas, there's the slick-haired director of the John F. Kennedy Museum, John Sissom, who, for six dollars, will permit a family of four from Toledo to experience "The Incredible Hours," a twenty-two-minute slide show. There is the All-Tom Corp. of Arlington, Texas, which supplies a steady stream of assassination postcards to concessionaires at the Dallas–Fort Worth Regional Airport.

There are Valium-gulping network vice presidents, quick to embrace some national mood, thus saving actors, actresses, producers, press agents—and perhaps themselves—from the dole. CBS, in the true spirit of Entebbe, reportedly was preparing last summer for its own film called *Oswald and Ruby*. There are publishers like Harper & Row, eager to pay the former Mrs. L. H. Oswald (now Mrs. Marina Oswald Porter) $50,000 plus a percentage for her memoirs. There are magazine editors, less eager maybe, but willing to listen—and there are sensitive young writers like myself.

Fourteen years later, we are that "new generation of Americans" Jack Kennedy liked to talk about. With the proper incentive, we're still ready to carry the torch.

There is Marguerite Oswald: "I've gone without eating. I've been destitute. I've been taken advantage of. Why should I give interviews for free? For three years I did it for free. I've done my duty. I don't need the publicity. I have no control over what they write about me. But at least if I'm taken advantage of, I know I've been paid. That's my solace."

And then, there is roly-poly, gap-toothed Lawrence Schiller—photo journalist, media entrepreneur, the man who watched Gary Gilmore die, and who owns exclusive rights to the convicted murderer's life-and-death story.

The Brooklyn-born Schiller appears to have been worldly wise at an early age and streetwise in the womb. As a fast-talking speech and drama major at Pepperdine University in Malibu, California, he grabbed up a scholarship from the Hearst Corporation. After this auspicious beginning, he rarely missed an opportunity and went on to work for, as he says, "every major publication in the world."

Over a career spanning two decades of death and violence, Schiller has fastened himself onto enterprises ranging from a coffee-table book about Japanese victims of mercury poisoning to a best-selling Lenny Bruce biography. Ubiquitous, if anything, he even testified at the Manson trial. But he achieved true national celebrity only last January when he befriended suicidal Gary Gilmore. He won Gary's confidence with $125,000—$60,000 for Gary and his relatives, $25,000 for Gary's girlfriend, and $40,000 for his victims' survivors.

He was a twenty-six-year-old freelance photographer when he observed at close range Jack Ruby shoving a pistol into Oswald's belly. Almost as Oswald moaned, Schiller was dickering (successfully) with a Dallas *Times-Herald* photographer for the worldwide rights to the prize-winning picture he'd just snapped in the basement of Dallas police headquarters. Later, Schiller collaborated on an assassination book and took a tape recorder to the hospital bed where Ruby lay dying of cancer.

His job title on the set of *The Trial of Lee Harvey Oswald* is supervising producer: "Making sure the scenes look right, are right, *smell* right."

THE DALLAS COUNTY COMMISSIONERS COURT, WHICH HAS DOMAIN over the Texas School Book Depository, and the Dallas Police Department, which has domain over the city streets, have been only too happy to cooperate. "Time cures all things," County Judge John Whittington says.

So on Sunday of an unbearably hot Fourth of July weekend, Lawrence Schiller stands in the center of Elm Street and roars into a handmike. "I m going to make you all *famous*," Schiller tells about one hundred extras, all Dallasites in skinny ties and bobby socks. Onlookers strain against the barricades.

Breathing hard, Schiller lumbers quickly down the street, giving directions.

"*Bang*," Schiller cries. "You hear it, but you don't have time to react.

"*Bang!* Now you go down, running that way. You realize now it's not a backfire.

"*Bang!* The motorcade's moving now and you run as if to catch it."

Moments later, a high-powered rifle appears in a sixth-floor window of the depository building. For six hours, the limousines turn from Houston onto Elm, the shots ring out across Dealey Plaza, and men and women fall over each other and scream.

Don Gazzaway, a librarian with flashing white teeth and reddish-brown hair, sits in back of the jet-black Lincoln, now waving, now clutching his throat, now jerking his head, now slumping into the seat.

"It was a bit eerie, certainly," Gazzaway says later. "But it seemed like an honor. My first feeling was to do this thing with as much dignity as possible."

Houston actress Christine Rose, wild-eyed, repeatedly throws herself over the trunk of the limo, grabbing out into space.

"You folks are fantastic," Schiller tells the crowd. "This is better than *Spartacus.* Just one thing. Even though you're running, the camera is still catching some of you *grinning.*"

# Live! From Adolescence! "I Always Hated Saturday Night"

*by Gilda Radner*

*March 1978*

*Starting in the mid-'70s,* Saturday Night *was both meeting ground and sounding board for a generation. Naturally, we profiled John Belushi, Dan Ackroyd, and Chevy Chase, but Gilda took matters into her own hands. She actually wrote this all by herself.*

I always hated Saturday night because it seemed to condemn you to festivities. No matter what, Sunday was going to be the next day . . . empty "school-the-next-day" Sunday . . . go to bed early . . . stores are closed. The weekend always meant to me stuff you can't do instead of stuff you can . . . like Saturday night, you can't go anywhere (a movie, a car ride) 'cause "they" would see you weren't out on a date, and you had to keep the lights out in your bedroom so the neighbors thought you were out on a date, and if you did have a date he had to be perfect or "they" would see you with him and throw you into "ugly date prison," which meant you never got married and weren't allowed into fancy restaurants.

Yup, the guy had to be taller than you, weigh more than you, and gallantly take the lead in the world of the '60s car-door-opening and cigarette-lighting extravaganza. Saturday night was filled with the ominous "they." In my late-'50s/early-'60s adolescence, it was "LIVE, FROM DETROIT, IT'S SATURDAY NIGHT!" STARRING: EVERYBODY WHO HAD A DATE OR WAS A CHEERLEADER OR HAD BLUE EYES. Not appearing on the show tonight due to going to an all-girls school, being overweight, and not having a purse to match her shoes is Miss Gilda Radner. Gilda will be getting ready for Sunday School and watching *Your Hit Parade* on TV. She may be doing some pantomimes to records in her brother's bedroom, but she won't be appearing on the show!

I did actually appear on a few Saturday nights. My costar once was six-feet-two and weighed three hundred pounds with black-rimmed Coca-Cola glasses. I only looked at him once, when he came to the door. I never looked at him again. I can tell you a lot about the buttons on his shirt, but I never chanced looking up again.

Another time, I both towered over and outweighed my costar by forty pounds. Due to mutual embarrassment, we did the whole show out of my living room, like an interview between Kate Smith and Mickey Rooney.

Then Carol Burnett met her Lyle Waggoner. He was handsome, funny, and a Reform Jew. I spent all Saturday morning in wardrobe—my mother's closet—and all Saturday afternoon in makeup, trying to draw in cheekbones. The show went great, except that Gilda stepped into this puddle of water getting out of the car and had a wet foot during the entire show, but no one in the audience ever knew.

There was only one thing worse than not having a date on Saturday night . . . that was having a date on Friday night, which left you with two Sundays.

Then there were the fabulous one-woman Saturday Night shows starring the Gilda Radner of the '60s. This would involve me sitting in a chair in my mother's living room staring into space. I'd have to call these dramas. Either my date had suddenly gotten bronchitis a half hour before he was supposed to pick me up . . . or I'd passed a telephone audition with an older man who then canceled the show at first sight of my chunky body in a round-collar blouse, A-line skirt, and kneesocks. I'd have to call this *An Evening with Emily Dickinson:* the part of Miss Dickinson being played by the autistic, spinster Radner girl.

> *If he could see beyond my bulging thighmes*
> *There would indeed be poems and rhymes.*

SOMETIMES I THINK THE MAIN REASON I WENT INTO SHOW BUSINESS WAS to fill my Saturday nights—to relieve myself of the responsibility of celebrating, and provide a service to those who needed to be entertained. Maybe, if I could just be good enough, I could save some other girl from having to notice the smell of the guy's hair next to her, or from wondering "Will he take my hand? And if he does, will our hands sweat?" Or, "Will he put his arm around me? And if he does, will he like my shoulder height?" I sought to divert myself and to become a diversion . . . to eliminate Saturday night pains for myself and others.

I've worked Saturday nights now for the past six years. I consider myself in service to the public . . . the Entertainment Corps. Saturday has always been the heaviest performing night of the workweek. In the Toronto company of *Godspell*, Saturday meant two back-to-back performances of endurance hugging, jumping, and climbing the fence for Jesus. In my year with Chicago and Toronto's Second City, Saturday night entailed two complete shows and then another hour of improvisations based on audience suggestions. All you had to do was be funny until 2:00 Sunday morning. For *The National Lampoon Show* we worked a cabaret theater in New York, Off-Broadway. We did ten shows a week and three of them were on Saturday night. We started at 6:30, did a show at 9:30, and another one at midnight. It was like bad déjà vu. I used to go home and sleep in a chair with my clothes on.

And so "they" finally noticed me, 'cause "they" put me on TV and "they" made it be on Saturday night and "they" called the show *Saturday Night* and "they" determined that the show would be "live." So, that's where I'm at. I bathe thoroughly on Saturday morning, wash my hair, pack my clothes, and leave for my date with America's late-night TV viewing audience. I enter the NBC studio at 1:30 in the afternoon and don't leave until 2:00 in the morning. I have a great time! I figure I'm now dating the ominous "they" that I thought was watching for so many years. Although the paradox is that they're still watching. I now can answer the phone or inject into conversation the favorite words of any Jewish girl who grew up in Detroit: "Sorry, I'm busy Saturday . . . Why don't you phone me in the middle of the week . . .?"

# Clint Eastwood:
# No More Mister Bad Guy

*by Robert Ward*
*April 1978*

*This piece ran against the grain. Eastwood was Dirty Harry, a tough guy, "go ahead, make my day." Sure, his films were not exactly progressive, but we recognized that beyond the squinty eyes he was a fine actor and a damn nice, herbal-tea-and-oatmeal-cookie kind of guy.*

It is 1969 and I am just emerging from *The Good, the Bad, and the Ugly*, starring this actor I vaguely remember from the TV show *Rawhide*, a guy named Clint Eastwood. Truth be told, I went to the theater for laughs, because my liberal friends across the country had been telling me that the ultimate in moronic mindlessness had been born, the dumbest actor of all time, starring in the most ridiculous movie since *Teenagers from Outer Space*. So I had gone, stoned on uppers, grass, and Romilar, ready for an experience in High Camp, like seeing *The Son of Flubber* or the *Three Stooges* in Spanish (for my money, still one of the primo experiences to be had on TV).

But I had been surprised, shocked, stunned. Even through the haze of chemicals I had seen something in this discarded TV actor that I hadn't expected. There was something about him—that poncho, that cigar, that black hat . . . the way he held the gun. Though I wouldn't have the courage to say it, I knew right then that here was the heir to John Wayne.

But more than that, he was also the Rolling Stones; there was a wonderful sadistic/good-guy edge, everything done so damned styl-ishly that he just had to know that he was *overdoing* it. (Or did he?) His movies were "spaghetti Westerns," and it was important not to like anything D-U-M-B. But, even the movie crit crowd had to admit that the picture was "visually rich."

But to hell with that stuff. What had gotten to me was Clint East-wood. The guy was the ultimate Mythic Cowboy, the Stranger from Nowhere. There was a little of Richard Widmark's Tommy Yudo in him, the thrill of the sensual sadist, like Jagger singing "Paint It Black." Hey, Clint Eastwood was one mean motherfucker. (But I'd never tell a soul.)

Well, those days are long gone. Clint Eastwood—that maligned, critic-punished, low-graded, scoffed-at, cast-off, "fascist" male chau-vinist—has only gone on to become a superstar in the film world. He has been the top box-office draw, or close to it, in nine out of the last ten years. And now even such highbrows as John Simon and Andrew Sarris are grudgingly giving ground. Molly Haskell is com-menting on Clint Eastwood's "ironic stance." Just like they used to with Henry "Hank" James and other American honest-to-god artists. So the worm has turned. No longer do I have to defend see-ing *Dirty Harry* or *Magnum Force*. Clint Eastwood is okay to like.


ABSOLUTELY NO PARKING—RESERVED FOR CLINT EASTWOOD SAYS THE sign in front of Big Clint's *Big Sleep*-style Mexican hacienda on the Warner Brothers lot in Burbank. God knows I'm not going to try and cross him. He could hop out of his car and, seeing me in his of-fice, string me up to the chandelier. Little reptilian eyes glowering at me, he tips the chair under my feet. . . . Hellfire, let me park in Santa Monica and bus back out here rather than risk that!

Suddenly (could Clint appear in any other way?) he is ambling across the room, smiling a cascade of white teeth, looking down at me from six-foot-six of pure sinew and grit. And it's not the Man With No Name squint, or *Dirty Harry*'s killer smile; he seems actually friendly, all genial Californian charm. And definitely the most handsome person of either sex I've ever met. Christ, at forty-seven, the way he is poured into his Levi's, leather boots, and powder-blue T-shirt with a sunburst of Aztec god on the front . . . the sun god comes off a poor second.

"Good to see you," he says. "Come on into the office."

It's too normal. Eastwood is offering me a beer, sitting down on the couch, stretching out his long, lean body, getting down-home cozy and running through his early years, when his family drifted around California, finally settling in Oakland. It says here he went to trade school. "I took aircraft," he says casually. "I rebuilt one plane engine, and a car engine too. I never had any dough so I could never afford anything very nice. I think kids go through certain times, in certain towns, where cars are their whole life. Cars first, chicks second."

He seems to have been more interested in cars than in acting. His film bio says he never acted in a school play.

"No," he says. "Once, when I was in junior high school, I did a one-act play. It was part of an English class, an assignment, and the teacher gave me the lead. I guess to help me, because I was an introverted kid."

For a second I'm surprised, but then it seems natural. Though Eastwood's heroes are all men of action, they are also painfully shy. They look as though they want to speak but aren't sure enough of their words. They seem afraid to appear foolish. Obviously, then, Eastwood draws on his own introversion, gets an aesthetic distance from it and creates that sense of menace that lurks just beneath the surface of all his best and most violent creations.

"We had to put it on for the senior high school, and I was so scared I almost cut school that day. But I finally did it—it was comedy—and it went over fairly well. So I thought, 'I managed to do that.' "

His first comedy. Eastwood's movies are all comedies. His natural flair for hyperbole creates a wild, black humor and it seems important that his first role, the one in which the introverted grease monkey first realized he had some sort of artistic sensitivity, was a laugher. Yet, one can't be sure. The word on the street is that Clint is perhaps not so . . . bright. Maybe he just doesn't know his movies are a riot.


"SAY, ARE YOU ALL RIGHT?"

Eastwood has noticed that I am filling up scores of handkerchiefs with nasal New York venom.

"You ought to have some tea and an oatmeal cookie," he says.

Not me. Nobody ever took an oatmeal cookie from Dirty Harry.

"No," I say. "I'm not allowed anything with caffeine in it."

"But this is herb tea," Clint assures me. "No caffeine. And these oatmeal cookies are out of sight. Wait, I'll get them for you."

He returns a few seconds later with a steaming mug and the largest oatmeal cookie in the Western Hemisphere. He waits for my judgment.

"Delicious," I say.

"See," says Clint. "That's just what you need."

"Right." I take another bite. Not bad. "I understand you did a lot of tough gigs before you became an actor," I say through the crumbs.

"I was a firefighter, a lumberjack, I was in the army, and I dug swimming pools," he offers, "but I never knew what I wanted to do. A lot of people have long-range ambition, but I never had that. I thought I might be a musician for a while, but every time I'd get going there'd be an interruption." He stops, stares at the ceiling.

I wonder why he was aimless for so long. "What did your parents do?"

"Well, later in life, when we lived in Oakland, my dad worked for a container corporation. Before that he worked as a pipe fitter for Bethlehem [Steel] and in gas stations."

"So, like your characters, you kind of wandered."

"Sure," Eastwood says. "And I use that. My dad finally started doing well about the time I was out of high school, but by that time I was pretty much on my own anyway . . . drifting around."

There is a hint of loneliness in Eastwood's voice. Not self-pity, but something lost, something he missed in childhood: security, closeness. Clearly, he has fed off that loss.

"You had no intention of being an actor in those days?"

"Jesus, no," Eastwood smiles. "I always felt the same thing that everybody felt about actors, that they were extroverted types who like to get up in front of two thousand people and make an ass out of themselves. I still don't like to get up in front of two thousand people, unless I have some lines to read. But to stand up there just as Joe Clyde . . . whew."

"Joe Clyde" . . . a curious phrase from the '50s I used to hear in Baltimore. Meaning, of course, Joe Nobody. Indeed, Joe Clyde could be the collective self-image of the working class, the same class that scarfs up Eastwood's pictures.

He smiles and explains how he made the transition from Joe Clyde to bit actor.

"I got drafted into the army. I was a swimming instructor at Fort Ord, California. It was a pretty good job, as far as keeping me off the front line, anyway. After I got out I came down here and went to Los Angeles City College on the GI Bill. I was twenty-three. This friend of mine was an editor, and he introduced me to a cinematographer, who made a film test of me just standing there—a shot here, a shot there—and Universal put me under contract at seventy-five dollars a week. I thought that was great stuff, but I was a little apprehensive.

I mean, I didn't know what it was going to be like when I had to start playing scenes *in front of people.* But I thought, what the hell, as long as they are paying . . . So I thought, 'Well, I'll just give it a good try. I'll give it six months.' But you can't give it six months, 'cause nothing works out that quick. So what you do is you give it six, and then six more, and pretty soon it gets in your blood and you really want it.

"I kicked around there for a year and a half, but then they dropped their program and kicked me out, dropped my option. So then I did a lot of TV, both in New York and L.A., and bounced around there. I was actually getting better parts in television than I was at Universal. But then I had a real slack period for a year or two.

"I'll never forget," Eastwood says with that *Dirty Harry* smirk. "I did a whole mess of shows for a year or so, then all of a sudden not much was happening around town, a lot of strikes and stuff, and I started collecting unemployment. But I couldn't just do that, so I'd go and get jobs. I got a job digging swimming pools, and I'd be running back at my lunch hour and call my agent and ask, 'What's happening?' And he'd say, 'Nothing.'

"I finally got to a state where I was really depressed and I was going to quit. You know, I was married, no kids. But I got to do this one picture, a B movie, a little cheapo—did it in nine days, really a grind-out. It was called *Ambush at Cimmaron Pass* and I did it and forgot it. And then another slack period, no jobs, nothing, I hadn't been employed for months. The movie finally came out and I went with my wife down to the little neighborhood theater, and it was soooo bad. . . . I just kept sinking lower and lower in my seat. I said to my wife, 'I'm going to quit, I'm really going to quit. I gotta go back to school, I got to start doing something with my life.' I was twenty-seven."

"That's the age you start to question yourself . . . moving toward thirty . . ."

"Yeah," Clint says. "I was saying, 'What am I doing here . . . spinning my wheels?' and thinking this is the only profession in the world where there are three or four jobs and seven million people all want 'em, you know?"

"What were your alternatives?"

"That was the problem. I had never really figured any out. So I was visiting this friend of mine—she was a story reader for Studio One, Climax. And I was talking to her, just having a coffee or tea or something, and a guy walks over and says, 'How tall are you?' And I thought, why does he care how tall I am? But I said, 'Well, six-six and I'm an actor,' but I wasn't very enthusiastic because I figured screw it, I'd had it. The guys says, 'Well, could you come into my office for a second?' and meanwhile my friend is behind me motioning, 'Go, go!'

"It turns out he develops all the new shows for CBS. So I say, 'Would you mind telling me what this is all about?' and he says, 'Well, this is a new, hour-long Western series' . . . because *Wagon Train* was a hit and they were all getting on the bandwagon. I thought, 'This could be something . . .' but I was dressed about like this." Eastwood points to his jeans, his two-hundred-dollar boots, and his blue Aztec T-shirt, " . . . a slob.

"All of a sudden I realize, 'Hey, I'm playing this like it's zero, I better sit up straight.' So the guy says, 'We'd like to talk to you and your agent.' So I give him the number and I leave and the agent calls me when I get home and tells me to make a test tomorrow."

Eastwood smiles and sinks back into the couch. There has been a curious gentility to his *Rawhide* recollections, as if he were retelling another life. The palpable silence behind his words, his laconic delivery, reveals a profound patience also visible in his film characterizations. We begin to discuss his step from TV to the movies.

"I had seen *Yojimbo* [a Japanese samurai film] with a buddy of mine who was also a Western freak, and we both thought what a great Western it would make, but nobody would ever have the nerve, so we promptly forgot it. A few years later my agency calls up and says, 'Would you like to go to Europe and make an Italian/Spanish/German coproduction, a Western version of a Japanese samurai story?' and I said, 'No, I've been doing a Western every week for six years, I'd love to hold out and get something else.' And he said, 'Would you read it anyway?' so I read it and recognized it right away as *Yojimbo*. And it was good! The way the guy converted it had a tremendous amount of humor in it. So I thought, this looks like fun, it'll probably go in the tank but at least it'll be fun to do. The Italian producer thought it was going to be a nice little B programmer, but of course it went through the roof."

"In Europe?"

"Yeah, they couldn't release it in this country for a while because of a threatened injunction by the Japanese."

"Because they thought it was a rip-off?"

"Well, it *was* a rip-off. The Italian producer had gone over to Japan to make negotiations, and when the fee the Japanese asked was too high, he just withdrew negotiations and went ahead and made it anyway."

Eastwood laughs and shakes his head like a man who has early on learned to live with the absurd. His Man With No Name was called nonacting. In fact, his entire career has been called nonacting.

"They called me everything," he says. "One critic wrote that I did *nothing* better than anyone who ever was on the screen, and there was a lot of name calling. It was that way with *Dirty Harry* too."

Critic Pauline Kael called him a fascist.

"That was just the style of the times," he says deliberately. "People liked to throw around the term *fascist*. It didn't bother me because I knew she was full of shit the whole time. She was writing to be controversial because people expect it of her; that's how she made her name. If *Harry* came out now, Kael would be onto something else. But the public liked the picture, and they realized it was just about a guy who was tired of the bureaucratic crap."

"I get the impression you are more or less apolitical."

"I don't have any political thoughts. I feel like an individualist."

"Your movies have been criticized as being antiprogressive," I remind him, "or as advocating a kind of police state."

"That isn't the case," Eastwood says firmly. "Anybody could see what the problems would be if the law enforcement agencies of any state were allowed to do anything they want. It would be dangerous. But the opposite is true: If you stifle the law, you invite getting bad people and corruption. It's the opposite extreme."

"But in the films themselves," I continue, "like *Dirty Harry* . . . He says, 'Screw all the red tape, I'm going to get the job done, bring these guys in' . . ."

"Yes, that was true in the first film. He wanted to get the job done. [Director Don] Siegel and I put ourselves in the victim's standpoint; if I was a victim of a bizarre crime, I'd like to have someone with that kind of inspiration and imagination trying to solve the case. Sure it was an extreme case, but that doesn't mean that Don Siegel or myself adhere to any kind of ultra-right-wing organization. In *Magnum Force,* we talked about just the opposite: If a right-wing group becomes the underground of the police force. . . ."

EASTWOOD, AS PROTOTYPE FOR MONOSYLLABIC MOVIE MACHISMO, HAS taken some vehement abuse for sexism in his films. It is a subject to which he has obviously given some thought.

"When I did *Play Misty for Me*," Eastwood says, "I took it to Universal, and the first thing they said to me was, 'Why do you want to do a movie where the woman has the best part?' Before that I had done *The Beguiled,* with six major parts for gals. I did *Two Mules for Sister Sara* . . . a lot of movies with good women's parts. I don't consider myself sexist at all. I dig chicks probably as much as, if not more than, the next guy."

There is an awkward pause.

"And you can probably call that sexist because I said *chicks*, but I grew up where the guys in my neighborhood said that. The other day a female journalist asked me if I was intimidated by women, and I said, 'No, I had a great relationship with my mother . . . I think she's marvelous.' "

"I've even heard that your movies are really gay fantasies," I say.

Eastwood roars.

"People do put you down for a macho quality," I add.

"That's getting back to those words again," says Eastwood. "*Fascist* was the word before. Now it's liable to be *macho*. I never thought about being macho. I remember when I first came to Hollywood a director told me, 'Play this scene real ballsy,' and I said to him, 'I don't know what you're talking about. I wouldn't know how to do that.'

"I never thought about being anything other than what I am. I put myself in a situation, learn the motivations of the character, and just go. If you started thinking about it, tried to play something like that, you'd come off like an idiot. It would be caricature. If you think too much you can shut out things that work for you. So I really don't think I'm sexist."

Eastwood seems anxious to establish himself as the intelligent, civilized man he is. And although he is among the biggest stars in the world, he does seem to feel somewhat tarnished by the constant criticism. The increasing humanity in his films, and his vigorous, polite defense of himself, would seem to indicate he is trying gingerly to establish his full humanity, as an actor and a man.

"Many people who love your movies think they are either unintentional comedy or that the director makes them funny," I say. "Many people assume you're like Charles Bronson."

"They should analyze Bronson's movies," Eastwood says curtly. "Are *they* funny?"

"No."

"Well then, how come my movies have that humor and his don't?"

"Well, people assume that the director puts in the humor."

"I've been the director on six of them," Eastwood says. "Do you think it's just by accident?"

"All right," I say, "The Man With No Name in the Italian Westerns. How did he happen?"

"Okay," he begins, "I invented the costume, for example. I took it over with me. I went down to a costume store. I had one hat, three shirts, a sheepskin vest. I bought myself these black Levi's, two sizes too big, and washed them. I wanted them to be kind of baggy. I didn't want them to fit too well, I wanted everything to be just a little off. Only the shoes fit right. I had the boots, so I took those . . . took the boots and spurs . . ."

"Did you and [director] Sergio Leone create the character together?"

"Well, he couldn't speak English, and I couldn't speak Italian, so we had an interpreter. But I could see he was a jovial guy with good feeling for black humor, so I figured it was going to be fun. The script had a lot more dialogue; I cut a lot of it out. To keep the mystique of the character it was very important not to have the guy say too much. Very important not to know his past. And the less you knew about him, the better. If you stop and give a big expository scene to explain everything that's going on, audiences resent that."

"So you were aware then that the movie had a camp quality all the way through it."

"Oh yeah . . . it was a *slight* parody."

"It was, and it wasn't."

"Yeah, but you still do it serious; you don't wink. You see guys who do that, they're winking at the camera all the time they're up there, then the audience doesn't believe that. They sit back and say, 'Oh yeah, we're going to see Joe Slapstick here.' Even Chaplin and the Tramp—he played those scenes very serious. Or Gleason and Carney in *The Honeymooners*—they weren't sitting there talking to the audience, or the crew, or the backstage or anything. You gotta play the part and the camp will come out of it. And it took a lot . . . it *takes* a lot," he emphasizes. "You light cigars, you spit on the dog's head—it's easy to crack, to do takes on it. But I don't. It's played absolutely serious. You've got to believe it, and the audience wants you to believe it. It's not stand-up comedy."

Frankly, I'm happy to hear this. And yet I wonder, "Why do people think you're dumb?"

Eastwood sighs, shakes his head. "Because in an age of cynicism it's easier to believe he's just a big stupid guy standing there, doing these tricks and just accidentally pulling it off. I'm not the smartest guy in the world from a classic point of view, or an educational point of view—I don't pretend to be any Rhodes scholar—but I do have animal instincts about things and I rely on them."

"But your movies are incredibly violent," I say. "Do you worry about a carryover from screen violence to crime in the streets?"

"If that were the case," Eastwood says, "then every guy on Death Row would have reason to be released because Tom Mix or James Cagney or Hoot Gibson shot guys on the screen. Or go back before movies to literature—Shakespeare, Greek tragedy—everybody can find some fall guy for why they commit some act of violence. You can say 'My family insisted I learn about the Crucifixion of Jesus Christ.' That's a violent act where somebody is impaled on a cross."

"Besides," I agree, "there is a distinct difference between the violence in your movies and, say, *Taxi Driver* or *The Texas Chainsaw Massacre* where you literally want to throw up."

"Well, yeah," he says, "except I wasn't appalled by the violence in *Taxi Driver* because they went so overboard. Like, the guy holding his hand out so he could wait for his fingers to get shot off—I found myself laughing at that."

ASSHOLE IS TO A CLINT EASTWOOD FILM AS *ROSEBUD* IS TO *CITIZEN KANE.* A signature, a recurrent coda. He always mutters it with a distinct nasal vehemence. I mention it and Eastwood roars.

"That's my South Oakland background. I have college kids come up to me on the street and say, 'Hey man, say *asshole* the way you say it in the movies.' "

"Kind of a working-class talisman. . . ."

Clint is really laughing and nodding now. "Oh yeah. No matter how high you go, it's something you never lose. I use it, because it was from my background, a certain way I got pissed. If Laurence Olivier tried that, it wouldn't work at all."

"No," I laugh. "Perhaps 'Oss-hole,' high tea version."

Clint smiles again. "You don't leave your background behind," he says. "I'm the first in my family to ever make it. That's one more reason I don't play down to them; I came from that place. People know when you're talking down to them. They instinctively know what's going on. . . . All the good actors know this. Cagney, John Wayne, Gary Cooper. . . ."

"Were they your influences?"

"Cagney, especially. I loved that stuff."

"Yet he was outgoing. With you there's a kind of silence at the core of your characters. They're slightly removed."

"Well," says Eastwood, "I think if you analyze all the great actors of the past, it's not what they did so much as what they might do, what they were about to do. It wasn't what they said—a lot of guys can do dialogue better than those guys. Charles Laughton was a great character actor and he had all sorts of tricks, but if he was on the screen with Gable, your attention was on Gable, even if Laughton was doing the talking.

"There's a famous story. I can't remember the character actor's name, but he was talking about being on stage with Gary Cooper where he had this tremendous big monologue and Cooper didn't say a word. And the character actor said he went to see the thing and he thought he had really wrapped the scene up, and when he got into the theater he noticed that during his big monologue, everyone in the theater was staring at Cooper! And then he realized the worst part of all: *He* was staring at Cooper. That's what real acting is all about."

We both laugh and it's time to go. Eastwood sees me to the door.

"Where will you go from here?" he says.

"Baltimore," I say, grimacing a little.

"Yeah?" he says. "Do you get back to your old hometown often?"

"Not that often. And every time I do, my love-hate affair with the place surfaces and I end up kind of upset."

Eastwood smiles and pats me on the back. "I know what you mean," he says. "I feel that too. But you never want to lose contact with it altogether."

"I guess not," I say, not quite sure.

"Nah," says Eastwood. "You got to go back every now and then so you don't forget how to say it."

"Say what?" I ask.

With his best *Dirty Harry* smirk, Eastwood sneers: "*Asshole.*"

# Like a Frat Outta Hell

*by Jon Carroll*
*September 1978*

*On the set of* Animal House, *in unfortunate ways the quintessential late-'70s film. John Belushi was heading for the top, and over it. "I won't be corrupted," he'd told us a few months earlier. "I won't let it happen. Look how many people it's killed. Not me, pal."*

"You sit in New York all the time doing *Saturday Night,* and you think you're the only funny people in the whole country, the only funny people in show business. The SS officers of comedy, no, make that the Killer Elite of comedy." John Belushi is hunched and squat in the trailer where he dresses. His wife, Judy Jacklin, is squinched in a chair beside him. John Belushi is doing his famous imitation of himself. He is very sincere and hostile and charming and practically irresistible. I have heard much about this terrifying crazed-freak-early-burnout *madman,* and my basic reaction to him is that I want to take him home and give him to my daughter like a stuffed animal. Of course he would do unspeakable things from time to time, but he would always mean the very best by it.

So here we are in this tiny overheated trailer in Cottage Grove, Oregon, which is quite the hottest thing between Eugene and Medford on Interstate 5, the umbilicus of the Great Coast, and Belushi is talking about geography and comedy. "So I get out here with all these actors from commercials and Off-Broadway drama and nowhere at all, and these guys are funny. These guys intimidate me, they're so good. Really. Unless I don't know what I'm talking about, and that's always possible, this is going to be a very good movie. Everybody's so fucking *hot*, man."

Belushi is excited, and his sausage fingers dance like Disney pigs. "It's so loose here, and yet everybody knows what they're doing. Like Ivan Whatsisname Reitman. Most producers are the slimiest pigs, the lowest bastards, just useless. They take up your time and suck your blood. But Ivan, man, Ivan is actually doing something. That's what I got to say about Ivan: He's not scum. For a producer, that makes him Christ."

And the director?

"John Landis is great. I knew that the first time I met him. He knows everything about movies"—the door behind me opens, in walks Landis—"and he's a punk, just a punk director. Hi, John."

John Landis, director, bounces into the room and slumps into the remaining chair. "There's the boy prima donna, John Belushi. Little display of temper, yesterday, huh, John? Didn't want to run around so much."

Belushi looks at me. "Once a punk, always a punk."

"You should have seen this man yesterday. He's a dancer, this Belushi. We were filming this food fight at the cafeteria, and Belushi is doing pirouettes and running around on tiptoe and throwing hamburgers. The best chase sequence I ever saw, and I just filmed it yesterday. We have a saying in the movie business: 'When in doubt, go to Belushi.' "

"He's a punk, but a smart punk."

"Let me tell you about meeting Belushi. I'd already met Doug Kenney, who wrote this script with Chris Miller, and he was so hostile I couldn't believe it. I mean, I did want to cut a few things, but still. . . . Anyway, I fly back to New York to meet Belushi and I'm supposed to charm him and win him and seduce him, you know, and on the plane I read this article in *Crawdaddy* and John is like this fucking monster. And then I meet him and we go to dinner and he's like a folk hero, you know. Woody Guthrie. Very sweet. Later I find out what he's really like. He calls me collect from Mexico at three o'clock in the morning where he's doing this other movie, and he wants to tell me what he's done to these two producers. Their cars or something. What did you do to those poor guys?"

"I don't want to talk about it."

This was the Jack Nicholson movie?

"Yeah, well, Nicholson was no problem," Belushi confesses. "Nicholson was a pussycat. Listen, I *carried* Nicholson in that picture. Why should I get in any more trouble? I'm carrying Landis, too, and he knows it. This is all lies. This is Shangri-La. Really. It doesn't matter what I say; I'm getting out of the business. I'm running for senator."

Forget politics—there's a movie going on here. Doug Kenney and Chris Miller of the *National Lampoon* think it came from their college experiences—they went to different colleges—while they both give credit to the third writer, Harold Ramis, for actually making a movie out of their lengthy script. And some of it may have come out of the *Lampoon*'s very successful high school yearbook parody, which is what Matty Simmons, publisher of the *Lampoon,* thought when he put up some of the money for the movie. But at this point, *Animal House* is quite definitely John Landis's movie, and its writers, unusually present on the set, strongly and (for the most part) gratefully agree. Landis directed *Kentucky Fried Movie*—although he quickly points out that he wasn't responsible for the final edit—which is doing land-office business in the sticks and urbs alike. And when it finally gets into the theaters, *Animal House* will in all probability become John Belushi's movie—that's showbiz.

The door opens again and a tall, gangly youth is framed against the Oregon sky. Landis gestures. "Ladies and gentlemen, we have amongst us now Jamie Widdoes, whose career is about to take a sudden turn for the better with his role in *Animal House,* a hilarious new movie opening in August in a theater near you. Say a few words, Jamie."

"A few words," says Jamie.

Belushi leans to me. "Did I say he was funny? That was a lie. Widdoes is scum." Widdoes moves across the room and perches precariously on the tiny mirror-backed dressing table. Another head pokes in the door.

"John Landis?"

Landis has become the compleat ringmaster. "Entering the room now is Tim Matheson, who plays Otter, the make-out artist in *Animal House,* opening in August all over the country. Tim, this is a journalist whose name has escaped my memory."

"I'd like to explain about my TV series," Matheson says instantly. "Sure it was canceled. But it wasn't my fault. *The Quest*—is that any name for anything? I'm absolutely blameless. Go talk to Kurt Russell. He's somewhere in Aspen counting his money. I'm in Oregon with John Belushi."

"I've never seen this man before in my life," Belushi whispers. "Who are you?"

Matheson maneuvers to a corner between Widdoes and Landis. There are now seven people in a room that was crowded with three. The stateroom scene in *A Night at the Opera* is part of everyone's comic vocabulary, and several people seem ready to duplicate it here today. The noise level rises. The door opens again.

"Perfect," says Belushi.

This is real life, not a movie, so no one enters with an elephant or a catered breakfast for twenty-five, and eventually it is time for Landis to go direct some more movie. Everyone explodes out into the street, the main street of Cottage Grove, where a huge parade, entirely staged for the cameras (and therefore probably better attended than an actual homecoming parade would be) is in progress. This parade is the climax of *Animal House.*

Belushi, who is not in this scene, strolls down the sidewalk behind the citizens lined up on the curb to cheer the bogus parade. He is quickly surrounded. It is a remarkable thing that John Belushi should be a star, that he should be knee-deep in small, shy kids clutching scraps of paper and ragged ballpoints, some with mothers standing behind smiling proudly—look, Willie's meeting Santa now. Young women are making mild moues of submission and older men who are far too cool to ask for an autograph demand a manly exchange of words. And John Belushi, his face placid, is moving through the crowd like Queen Elizabeth at an orphanage, signing every autograph. "To Dennis: wise up. John Belushi."

That evening John Belushi is flying back to New York to lay a little TV on the nation, and John Landis is dining with the minority of mature actors in his college comedy, to wit: John Vernon, Cesare Danova, and Verna Bloom. Landis is talking about Belushi, waving his butter knife and squaring his shoulders with the confident set of a raconteur without a headache. "You don't direct John Belushi. Not really. You get his trust. You tell him what you want—not how you want it, but what you want—and he gives it to you. He's amazing. He needs more self-discipline, of course. He could party all night. But that'll come. He's a great physical comedian."

"Have you read this script?" This is John Vernon talking. Vernon looks sort of like Robert Shaw and sort of like Richard Burton. "Listen, I read a lot of scripts every year, and this is the first one that made me laugh out loud all the way through it. And what is amazing is that Universal, the great sausage maker of movies, should want to do this script. To think that these butchers of film would actually let someone do this good a movie, it's . . ." Words fail him. "I'm very happy to be here, that's all."

Landis looks uncomfortable. He points to my notebook. "Everyone at Universal has been very nice to me. Very, very nice. It's been a very pleasant relationship. They love this movie." He grins suddenly. "They're not scum."

PART V

*Wild and Crazy Culture*

# Marilyn Chambers:
# High School Confidential

*by Derek Pell*

*June 1974*

*Our writer was a former high school classmate of the Ivory Snow girl–turned–porno queen. Accompanying this article we ran a picture of Marilyn and black stud Johnny Keys, which got* Crawdaddy *pulled off newsstands all across the South.*

What can I say about a twenty-one-year-old porn princess I went to high school with? If Norman Mailer could reap a fortune by hacking off a coffee table fable about Marilyn Monroe, then I can make a few bucks writing about Marilyn Chambers, the girl behind the green door, the resurrection of Eve. Chambers has been called "the sex symbol of the '70s" and one respected critic has even gone so far as to bypass the Monroe doctrine and compare her instead to Grace Kelly. In reality though, the comparisons are perversely strained, especially the one about dear Grace. One was great on her feet, the other . . .

Chambers, the fresh-faced charmer on the Ivory Snow soap box, has become, for millions, *the* girl next door. For me, she literally was.

It seems like only yesterday that I was following the then-unknown Marilyn through the chambers of Staples High School. As far as I was concerned, Marilyn was the "untouchable virgin" and would no doubt remain so (to me, at least).

Biographies should contain "fresh revelations," so I'll begin by exposing Marilyn's real name (which is just a smidgen less waspish than Chambers). The town in Connecticut that we both called home, Westport, knew and loved her as Marilyn Briggs, a high school cheerleader who missed being "homecoming queen" by a hair. Not being crowned "queen" must have been a severe shock to the young blonde. Acting had not yet dawned on her. May we conclude that her first public defeat set her on the road to sindom?

It makes perfect sense that the innocent mother pictured on the Ivory Snow box should in reality be a seasoned sexoid from the suburbs. Marilyn made the American Dream come true in a way that would have made Horatio Alger blush. No longer do the members of the Class of 1971 wonder how far she "goes." She outdistanced all my schoolboy daydreams in the opening moments of *Behind the Green Door*.


AVID PORNOPHILES WILL RECALL THAT MARILYN'S FIRST BIG BREAK came in a film titled *The Owl and the Pussycat*. In one sequence she emerged from Robert Klein's bedroom scantily dressed. Though she spoke no lines and was seen for only a few seconds, she made a mark on the screen.

Following in the paw prints of *Pussy* came *Together*, which was billed as a film for couples—a wholesome peek at the liberated "love generation." But free love on the screen for five dollars seemed ludicrous, because it never lived up to its X rating. Few porn lusts were fulfilled, and it quickly vanished into the Los Angeles drive-in circuit.

Hardcore was just coming into its own with such flesh pleasers as *Deep Throat* and *The Devil in Miss Jones*. Judges were beating their gavels in disgust, while self-proclaimed censors foamed at the mouth. A smut storm was spreading across the country. Weird sex publications were traveling through the mails in record numbers. Irate parents locked their nubile daughters in attics and basements as chastity belts reemerged in catalogs from Sears & Roebuck. Not since the publication of Henry Miller's *Tropic of Cancer* had there been such a panic among puritans.

And yet, the forces of darkness seemed to be winning in the courts. Lewd liberals were flocking to celebrated trials in defense of necrophilia on film, and critics were praising the X-rated flicks as "profound" and "important." Spiro Agnew reportedly watched Linda Lovelace fellate in full color seven times. Everybody and their mothers seemed to be curious, as if the art of copulation had just been discovered by a sexless race. What indecent fantasies lurked in the loins of America?

Without warning, *Behind the Green Door* opened quietly, revealing young Marilyn in action. No Lovelacian gimmicks for our girl—no sir, just pure, unabashed groping and gobbling! She proved herself to be an expert—a vision of purity engaged in multiple sex acts on a trapeze, displaying a rare sense of freedom and a latent admiration for the circus profession. Never a brainchild in high school, Chambers had passed her exams with flying colors. Watching her was like seeing Shirley Temple high on Spanish Fly—absolute gangbusters! Her on-screen smirk of satisfaction was destined to be remembered—a Mona Lisa–like expression that beckons, panders, pulls at your prurient interests.

Though I never dated Marilyn Briggs, I often think of those who did. The ones who never even got to "second base" because they feared infringing upon a minor's morals. And what about the ones who made it "home"? They probably think she's laughing at them from up there on the silver screen . . .


"Exploit me," smirked Marilyn.

She raised her alba-white legs and leaned back on the couch. There she lay like a plastic vamp, right before my eyes, wearing only a tie-dyed T-shirt and a toothy grin.

Inches away from Marilyn in this womb-warm suite high atop a posh New York hotel, I caught a frog in my throat. "Please . . . don't photograph my *thing*," she pleaded.

My body froze erect as she pulled down her shirt. She had, sure enough, flashed her "thing." I rushed over to my camera, which sat on a tripod like Marilyn on the swings, and jammed in a roll of film. Next thing I knew I was on my knees, snapping off pictures like some depraved tourist—promising her anything. It was a scene out of an X-rated *Blow Up*.

How had this bizarre reunion come about?

By chance, I came across an item in the newspaper that announced that Marilyn, my Marilyn, was soon to appear onstage at The Riverboat supper club inside the Empire State Building. A live sex show? No, this was to be her musical debut, an orgy of song and dance . . .

The room was large and poorly lit. It was filled with tables and more waiters than clientele. I had expected to find the place packed with porn-ghouls, but the faces and fashions suggested pseudo-respectability. Gossip columnist Earl Wilson sat at a table up front, praying for an act in his lap. The band was no midnight special, sounding fresh from the Port Chester Hilton.

Suddenly, the drummer hit the skins. Marilyn's name was intoned, the audience hushed, and out she came in a torrent of spasms and sequins.

"Here I come," she sang, but her voice was difficult to hear over the blast of acid rock. What I could pick up made me yearn for the professionalism of some wide-screen filth. She followed with more of the same—limp rock (she sang "Satisfaction" but not "Come Together"), no nudity, a few costume changes, and a finale that featured two gay dancers who slinked along with Marilyn through a "Last Tango in Vegas," which ended abruptly when she stripped down to a bikini.

I dashed backstage and confronted her in the flesh, in a tiny, closet-sized dressing room.

"Oh, wow!" she cried, recognizing me instantly.

"You remember me from high school?" I chirped.

"Sure!" My ego pirouetted.

Standing behind me, two ladies from *The Washington Post* began laughing. I figured they were impressed, but I stood nervously eyeing Marilyn while she removed her mask of makeup. Chuck Traynor (her agent and ex-husband to Linda Lovelace) fixed her hair.

"Do you still have your cheerleader outfit?" I asked.

Her faced turned pink in the makeup mirror. She giggled, *embarrassed.*

"Not *with* me," she smiled, "but I have it at home."

We arranged an interview several days later at her hotel.

When I arrived, Marilyn greeted me in style (half naked). Chuck, the super porn-pusher, was there too and it promised to be a happy afternoon.

"Where is your act going?" I asked. "Will it involve sex on stage?"

"It depends on the audience," replied Traynor.

"Have you considered an audience-participation sex show?"

Marilyn smiled: "I think that would get a little *sticky.*"

Traynor mentioned plans for a "Super-X" film, which would involve gathering all the best technicians in the porno world and a lot of bread.

"Would it be a superstars' competition, featuring Tina Russell, Georgina Spelvin, Linda Lovelace?"

"No-no-no-no," cried Traynor. "Those people aren't *shit.* We wouldn't use any of them because they're porno people, and Marilyn isn't—there's a difference."

"How about getting Robert Redford and Marilyn together?" I joked.

"Well, we thought of that combination," he said quite seriously.

"We've talked to Ernest Borgnine, Lee Marvin, Sammy Davis Jr.—they all want to do a film with Marilyn. But the film we want to do is too . . . radical for them."

Marilyn laughed beside him. "They want to do a *light* X."

"Ernest Borgnine wants to do a light X?" Once you've had Ethel Merman, what else is there?

"Sure," said Marilyn.

"Has Westport had a 'Marilyn Chambers Day' yet?"

Traynor smiled. "Not yet, but they will in the future, I'm sure."

I asked Marilyn if her private fantasies had changed, since she had acted out so many on the screen. "The freakier the better," she smiled.

"They must be pretty complicated now," I noted.

"Yeah, kinkier and freakier. I have to keep thinking of new things to do."

Porn has always seemed less than enlightened. Did she think that porn exploited women? She shook her head. "The word *exploitation*," began Traynor, "is greatly misused. Marilyn has made over three hundred thousand dollars . . . she lives in a trilevel house in Beverly Hills and drives a new XKE Jaguar. If that's being exploitative—"

"Exploit me!" shouted Marilyn.

That was not the Staples High booster beaming from the couch, and I had to ask her.

"When did you lose your innocence, Marilyn?"

She giggled. "Just recently."

# Stop Those Evel Ways

*by Michael Jay Kaufman*
*December 1974*

*For unadulterated '70s hype, this even surpassed the Bobby Riggs–Billie Jean King tennis match.*

Evel Knievel's Snake River Canyon jump reminds me of a number we used to do when we were kids: "How much will you give me if I eat that dogshit over there?" Whether it was eating dogshit or whipping out your cock in front of the principal, the amount never seemed to be enough to justify carrying out the act. Knievel however, was reportedly paid something between $8 and $9 million for trying to jump the canyon, and for that kind of money a lot of people would eat dogshit or whip out their cocks in front of the pope.

Sure, there was a lot of con in what Knievel did, but on the other hand, it was risky as hell. He came awfully close to dying, and although cynics were talking about how he had "set up the rematch" by failing in his first attempt at the jump, at this writing he is saying he has no intention of trying it again.

We brought an expert with us for this telecast at Madison Square Garden. Desmond, who is nine years old, described himself as an Evel Knievel fan. On the subway ride downtown I asked him why. "I'm an Evel Knievel fan because he does a lot of daredevil stunts," he began. "He also seems like he's crazy about doing stunts . . . and he seems to be a nice guy."

Desmond could not have known that this "nice guy" was, in the words of promoter Robert Arum, "absolutely the most bigoted, rowdy person I've ever encountered." Arum, the lawyer who heads Top Rank, Inc., which guaranteed Knievel a minimum of $6 million for making the jump, explained, "When I first went to Montana to put together the deal with Evel, he refused to do business with me. He told me there were only three things in the world he hated: New Yorkers, lawyers, and Jews." Greed, however, can be a great equalizer, so Arum, who fits into all three of these categories, and Evel quickly developed a fast friendship in their pursuit of the fast buck.

Most of the seats at the Garden were empty, which was encouraging to those of us who found this Roman Circus repulsive. But the most likely explanation for the small size of the crowd is that the ducats were too high. The cheapest seats went for $7.50. The $10 and $12.50 seats were practically empty.

The crowd was mostly white, with few blacks and Latins. There were fathers and sons; guys with their girlfriends; teenagers; only a few of the well-dressed dandies, the middle-class types who patronize the basketball and hockey games. And only a handful of the shit-kickers and "beerhippies" who made up most of the live audience at the canyon itself, paying $25 a head for that privilege.

Both the sound and the picture were lousy, particularly in the upper reaches of the balcony where the "cheap" seats were. So the words of David Frost, James Lovell, Bud Furillo, and the other well-paid hucksters were mostly lost. Which was just as well, judging by what was audible.

"The great man is sitting right beside me," said Frost before a pre-jump interview with Knievel.

"Thank God I live in a country like this," said Evel. A fat middle-aged man with a mustache sitting near us clapped loudly.

The crowd waited patiently during the opening acts, none of which could be seen too clearly on the screen. Bobby Riggs was there, of course, and some French actress trying to make a name for herself, and even Jimmy the Greek was on hand. "When it comes to a man's life," he said somberly to an interviewer, "I wouldn't make any odds on it."

"Maybe the President is there," said Desmond. Then: "Nixon, he probably has a special TV to see this." They didn't mention it during the telecast, but it turned out that President Ford's two sons were there. If Nixon was watching anything on TV, it was his pardon, which was announced that day.

Someone introduced Father Sullivan, a Catholic priest described as "the cousin of Evel Knievel," and suddenly the screen was filled with a young Pat O'Brien face. "Let us pray," he began solemnly, and there were laughs and jeers. When he asked the Lord to guide Robert "Evel" Knievel to "a happy landing, wherever it might be," there was even more derisive laughter.

Knievel, looking like a Confederate Captain America in his white suit with blue stripes and white stars, was hoisted to the launchpad of his "Skycycle." He said goodbye to his staff as "The Ballad of Evel Knievel" was played in the background. Then they showed films of his great crack-ups of the past. "This is the one I was telling you about," said Desmond as the film showed Knievel falling off his bike and rolling on the ground. "He broke both his arms, his legs, his pelvis . . . and he just kept rolling and rolling and rolling."

As he prepared to take off, they played schmaltzy music and a tape made earlier of Knievel explaining his philosophy of life. He said he believed God put us on earth to do something with our lives, not to just stand around doing nothing. He said he had a dream and that everybody had a dream, and that it was better to die trying to fulfill your dreams than to live a dull and meaningless life. The crowd listened to all this in reverent silence, and applauded heartily at the end.

"Happy landings, Evel," said David Frost.

Nobody seemed to mind that the jump was a flop. Evel didn't make it but he narrowly escaped death, which is the kind of action the crowd had paid to see after all. When they saw he was okay, everyone cheered, including Desmond. "Maybe he didn't fulfill his dream," said an announcer, "maybe he didn't clear the canyon. But at least he's alive and he tried." More cheers. "Well," he continued superfluously, "this is a September 8th he'll remember, that's for sure."

# I Flunked Masturbation Class

*by Jane DeLynn*
*December 1975*

*Orgasm was her valedictory. The ultimate "Me Decade" story.*

Some women come easy, some come hard, and some don't come
at all. In my search for the Excalibur of sensation, I had tried everything from consciousness-raising to Jungian analysis to an improvised version of Musical People more suitable to the road company
of "Let My People Come" than a Jewish dropout from the Ivy
League. So it was with a feeling both of anticipation and déjà vu that
I looked forward to meeting Betty Dodson, who is to female eroti-
cism what Bobby Orr is to puck chasing. An artist friend of mine
had encountered her in Berkeley—where Betty lives when she's not
in New York—and had spoken about her in terms usually reserved
for descriptions of the Second Coming. I decided I would be content with the first.

Beauty is in the eye of the beholder. The forty-two-year-old sexual
guru of the Women's Movement sports a crewcut both above and below the waist. Ten years ago she was making erotic paintings by day
and going to A.A. meetings at night. She started doing yoga in 1969,
and in 1972 held her first workshops. In them, she teaches other
women how to get along better with their bodies—in particular, to
have better and bigger orgasms. Betty has sex with men, women,
and vibrators. But she always sleeps alone.

I took a taxi to Betty's apartment. A nude six-year-old girl—the daughter of Barbara, a neighbor who assists Betty in running the workshops—answered the door. She told me to leave my coat and shoes in the hall and go into the bedroom to undress. I felt odd as I walked through the living room, for on the deep brown wall-to-wall carpeting sat fourteen naked women, my classmates. They were mainly suburban housewives in their thirties and forties. At twenty-seven I was clearly the youngest. Most of them sat hunched over, arms around drawn-up knees, embarrassed at the nudity that revealed stretch marks, moles, sagging breasts, cesarean section scars. They were surrounded by the accoutrements of slick American sex—stereo speaker, large pillows, bowls of fruit, hand-crafted pottery mugs of herbal tea.

I slowly got undressed in the bedroom where a second set of speakers was softly playing Elton John. By the time I got myself some mint tea, the session was ready to begin and the little girl who had answered the door was sent—fully clothed and protesting—to her apartment down the hall.

It was not difficult to pick out Betty from this circle of overfed and underexercised women. Her muscular body, glistening with coconut oil, is a walking advertisement for her workshop. Which is lucky for her. Although she still sells prints and drawings, she now makes her living almost exclusively from workshops, lectures (at colleges, women's groups, and psychological associations), and writings (she has just finished a book on masturbation).

The first order of business was for us to introduce ourselves and explain why we had come to this sexual workshop.

Molly was the first to speak:

"I can't masturbate to climax in front of anybody but my husband," she said.

"You think *that's* bad," said Margaret. "I can only come by myself!"

"Did you ever try using a vibrator with another human being?" asked Betty.

"Yes," said Margaret, shrugging her shoulders. "But it doesn't help. I just get embarrassed."

"My husband and I have an open marriage," confided Elsa. "During this last year I got very involved with a woman. I was in love with her. Since then the relationship has broken up but I think I'm basically gay. I'd like to explore that aspect of myself a little more. Especially because I find it harder to get an orgasm with a woman than a man."

"That's probably because you're not as used to it," suggested Betty.

"I don't have trouble getting orgasms, either with other people or by myself," said Flossie. "But I'd like to get more of them—and whenever I want to!"

What these women were looking for—and finding—was an affirmation of their generally unconventional lifestyles. They had good lives they wanted to make better. Many of them were swingers. They got it on alone and in groups. With their husbands, friends, lovers, and vibrators. At swingers' clubs and parties and weekends. They had houses in the country and love pads in the city. There were women whose husbands took separate vacations, and women whose daily lives seemed *la dolce vita* in Isla Mujeres. Many of them had platonic but apparently happy marriages with men who over the years had turned into "best friends." They had children and money (a workshop of four sessions costs sixty dollars). None of them seemed to share my particular problem.

Oddly enough, I was the only woman from the city.

"I think that a lot of the so-called feminists—single women, professional women—don't feel they need help, or that they have other things to occupy themselves," explained Betty. "It's the suburban housewife who knows she wants to make changes."

One of the changes Betty suggested we make had to do with keeping ourselves in shape. "Women systematically mistreat their bodies," she said, flinging around a set of five-pound barbells. "We're conditioned not to develop our arm and leg muscles—because it's considered *masculine* to be strong. We wear bras and girdles that hinder our natural movements. We never exercise our pelvic muscles—even though they're essential to carrying a baby." Exercising the pelvic muscles is not one of Betty's problems. She can twist her genitalia with the agility of Gypsy Rose Lee.

We spent the rest of the first session doing maneuvers that were a combination of yoga and the Royal Canadian Air Force exercise book. As we squatted and stretched and breathed and lifted, Betty individually fixed our postures in front of the floor-to-ceiling mirror that covers one wall of her living room. According to her diagnosis, I would have been 4-F from the Girl Scouts.

Before we left we got our first homework assignment: to masturbate a minimum of one hour a day, preferably with a vibrator.

If the vibrator is to the women's movement as the Pill was to the sexual revolution, Betty deserves a sales commission for her tireless promotion of Japan's kinkiest nonhuman export . . . the Panasonic Panabrator: a large, heavy, disc-headed, variable-speed pleasure machine that is the Harley Chopper of technological turners-on. But the electric-powered Panabrator can only be used in relative proximity to a wall socket. So there is no danger that the handheld, penis-shaped cheapies will go the way of the Edsel or the pinhole camera.

"What I hate most about camping trips," complained Betty, "is that I'm stuck with my portable!"

"All those batteries . . ." commiserated Barbara.

"The very first thing I do when I get home," continued Betty, "even before opening my mail or checking the telephone service, is run to my Panabrator!"

The advantages of the Panabrator over a hand are these: (1) it never tires, and (2) you do not have to cut its fingernails.

The disadvantages, other than its lack of portability, are these: (1) a persistent drone (reminiscent of an electric razor); (2) an increased electrical bill; (3) its tendency to irritate the pubic region; and (4) a dehumanization that in extreme instances can result in one's inability to have orgasm with a human being.

The latter problem doesn't bother Betty much because she does not depend on her partner to climax. She says she's been able to do that herself since she was five. She does not strive for simultaneous orgasm. Her emphasis is on self-love, both sexually and physically.

"Look in the mirror and talk to yourself. Tell yourself you're beautiful, you're wonderful. Women are so involved with the romantic image of themselves that by themselves, they think they're nothing. Learn to be relaxed and loving with yourself first, *then* with someone else. Self-loathing is a long-standing habit that we can break!"

Betty joyously exhibited her favorite masturbation position: back on the floor, head on a pillow against the wall, knees up and apart.

We faithfully experimented with her various sized and shaped gizmos, careful to place a towel between our labia and the vibrating heads—lest our genitalia swell to the gigantic proportions of the penis-sized clitoris of the Kikuyus, a Kenyan tribe in which the females spend a large part of their adolescence yanking on their vulvae.

THE NEXT WEEK WE COMPARED NOTES.

Chris had bought a Panabrator and loved it.

"I laughed and laughed when I came," she said. "It was terrific!"

"Did you try using it with someone else?" asked Betty.

"Not yet, but I will!"

June did not have such a positive experience. "I prefer using my hand," she admitted. "I got off so quickly it wasn't any fun."

"Oh, that's no good!" exclaimed Betty. "I could come in two minutes if I wanted to. But now I won't even bother unless I have at least half an hour to play with myself. Did you fantasize?" she asked.

June shrugged: "It wasn't necessary."

"But it's important," said Betty. "Women have to start creating their own sexual imagery, instead of using the media images of Hollywood, or TV, or advertising. Caress yourself. Love yourself. The last thing you should do is concentrate on the orgasm."

Later in the session we tape-recorded our fantasies. The pillaging Russian army. Interspecies loving. Rows of men dangling in harnesses like hunks of slaughtered meat in a Chicago packing house. S&M. B&D. Water sports. Everyone had their special favorites that—like the U.S. post office—would make them come despite wind, rain, and flaccid dicks.

"I'm worried about this rape fantasy I have," questioned Roberta. "It seems so antifeminist. But it always gets me off!"

Betty turned to her. "Try something else," she suggested. "Like a loving C-R session that turns into an orgy. Stay with it a while. Then, if it doesn't work, you can always go back to your six brutal Irish cops!"

"Have you ever tried to live out a fantasy?" asked Margaret.

"Sure!" said Betty. "It can be liberating, but it can also destroy the fantasy. I used to masturbate pretending I was fucking a German shepherd. Finally I did it. It was exciting, but after that the fantasy just didn't get me off. So I switched to something else!"

Talking about fantasies made us revert to playing with the vibrators. But no amount of technological assistance had solved my problem. Out of pity for my lonesome plight, the group decided to masturbate precisely at midnight the following evening as psychic support.

The results of that night will remain a secret between me, the group, and the wonderful folks who brought us Pearl Harbor.

WE BEGAN THE THIRD SESSION BY GIVING EACH OTHER BODY MASSAGES à la Esalen—lots of coconut oil and continuous arm rotation. After becoming sufficiently relaxed, or excited, we then proceeded to look into our bodies the way gynecologists do. For many "students" this was the high point of the workshop experience.

"Mind-blowing!" said June.

"A whole new world!" said Molly.

Next we tried out the perineometer, a device doctors use to measure the strength of vaginal contractions. Survivors of multiple epi-siotomies use it to strengthen the walls of the uterus to prevent pro-lapses. My classmates and I tested our sexual prowess with it.

It was no surprise that I came in last. I peaked at 35, whereas the mean for our group was around 50. Huffing and puffing, Betty passed 100—clear off the charts—to our muted cheers. I vowed that next week I would devote more time to my homework.

THE LAST SESSION WAS THE ONE EVERYBODY HAD BEEN WAITING FOR. Classmates who had skipped the second or third session—all were there. For this was the week of the sexual demonstrations. (Due to legal considerations, Betty has since discontinued this aspect of the workshop.)

Betty's first partner was Doug Johns—a male artist who makes casts of vulvae. Often when he makes the casts he also makes his models. And, according to Melody, he is an excellent, thoughtful, tender lover.

But this night he was a washout. He had the chic male failing—impotence. Despite all that Betty—and later Molly and Brenda and Margot—could do, he couldn't keep it up. But it did not deter the determined women of the group, about a third of whom were soon working on Doug and/or each other. The rest of us sat around munching fruit, playing with the vibrators, and looking at our more active classmates pleasuring each other.

Finally Doug left—sans orgasm, but with our good vibes, for he had maintained grace under what could be considered most trying circumstances.

"It was *interesting* that he couldn't get it up," said June.

We all agreed he was a good sport, if not exactly the guy you'd choose to spend a furlough from the Women's House of Detention with.

We anxiously awaited the arrival of Eleanor—Betty's friend, our classmate, and the woman whom Betty had chosen to do her lesbian demonstration with.

"Sorry I'm late," she said, as she breezed in around 9:30, "but I spent all day at home practicing with a friend!" She got undressed in a flash and then climbed on top of Betty—after carefully placing a Panabrator between their genitalia. They lay, face-to-face, very businesslike, as the vibrator hummed. It was about as sexy as watch-ing Telly Savalas brush his teeth. After a while they came, or at least they stopped. I don't know. I was eating an apple and watching somebody else chew gum.

Sally said she thought it was a peculiar way to demonstrate homo-sexual loving—especially for those of us who had never experi-mented with bisexuality. "I mean," she exclaimed, "I still wouldn't know what to *do!*"

I went into the bedroom to put on my blue jeans. Most of the group was still sprawling casually, drinking mint tea, and discussing the implications of the evening. As I left, Betty was illustrating an-other of her favorite masturbation positions: heels pressed together, lotus-style, feet drawn up close to the body, head resting against a large pillow. Three women sat in a semicircle imitating her.

The sound of the vibrators was like the drone of a lawn mower on a hot summer evening. It's a pleasant sound, if you like lawn mowers.

# Star Trek:
# Oh Captain! My Captain!

*by Ed Naha*

*November 1976*

*To boldly sell where no one has sold before . . . We thought the Star Trek craze was cresting but it was only beginning. Ed Naha went on to write several screenplays himself, including* Honey, I Shrunk the Kids.

Gene Roddenberry, the man who created *Star Trek,* hardly ever gets upset. And when he does, it's difficult to notice. He doesn't raise his voice; he doesn't gesticulate wildly. When annoyed, he relaxes his massive frame and speaks his mind in a detached, almost monotonous calm. Sitting in his office on the Paramount lot in Hollywood, surrounded by *Star Trek* memorabilia, he slumps behind his desk and talks in hushed, awed tones.

Roddenberry has just returned from the unveiling of America's first space shuttlecraft, a science fiction writer's dream, named after Roddenberry's legendary television creation, the *USS Enterprise.* He is still in a state of shock. "Everyone from the cast was there," he recounts. "They rolled out the space shuttle *Enterprise.* The military band marched out and the leader raised his baton. I was waiting for 'Stars and Stripes Forever' or 'America the Beautiful' or something. Instead, they played the 'Star Trek Theme'! *Twice!* I had this funny feeling in my stomach, you know, like that was going just a little too far."

The phone buzzes and Roddenberry interrupts his train of thought for a quick chat with a studio executive about the forthcoming *Star Trek* film, a *2001*-ish epic planned as the ultimate *Enterprise* adventure. The conversation is brief, and Gene returns to the shuttlecraft incident. "I must admit that when it was first announced that the shuttle was going to be named after the *Enterprise*, I didn't completely approve. I was afraid that my friends at NASA and the space industry would think that it was a shrewd publicity ploy for the movie. You know, everyone has this stereotyped idea about producers who wear Hawaiian shirts, smoke big cigars, and do anything to see a few lines in print. And that's all untrue. It was the *Star Trek* fans that started all this. They began a letter-writing campaign to the President. I disassociated myself from it completely. I would have preferred the shuttle not bear a military name like the *Constitution* or the *Enterprise*. I would have named it after a famous rocket scientist.

"But a friend of mine told me later that I was just too close to the whole project to see it for what it was. The role of the arts, he said, was changing. The very function of art today is to give people goals, to inspire them." Gene Roddenberry, one of the few orthodox idealists left in the world, is now in familiar territory. "And apparently the *Enterprise* has inspired a lot of people," he chuckles.

*Inspiration* may not entirely do justice to what the *Enterprise* has wrought.

It has been ten years since the first *Star Trek* episode was televised by NBC. The series' initial run lasted only three seasons, seventy-nine episodes. In its six years of syndication, however, the show has touched the minds of millions of would-be space explorers of all ages. Today, the *Star Trek* movement resembles an organized religion.

Massive conventions are held across the globe on an almost biweekly basis, attracting hordes of ardent fans, dubbed "trekkies" by the media. These *Enterprise* boosters sometimes shell out as much as twenty-five dollars for a two-day smorgasbord of Trekobilia. The intense popularity of the show has also spawned an avalanche of *Star Trek* products.

And all this marketing madness can be traced back to Gene Roddenberry, an ex-cop, ex–airline pilot, and former head writer of *Have Gun—Will Travel* who decided to venture into the realm of speculative fiction over a decade ago in order to avoid television censorship. "I felt that I could say what I wanted to say and get away with it in science fiction," he laughs. "I didn't think anyone would catch on. And most of the time, the network didn't."

Roddenberry claims that he hasn't seen a cent of the money raked in on all the *Star Trek* paraphernalia. When the subject is brought up he just flashes a wistful "chalk it up to experience" smile.

POPULAR *STAR TREK* SERIES SPAWNS MULTIMILLION-DOLLAR PARAMOUNT FEATURE VERSION! screamed the headline of a recent issue of *Variety*. At long last, the trekkies' dream, the anxiously awaited film version of *Star Trek* was finally in the making. Talked about, dreamed about, written about for years, the reunion of the *Star Trek* crew was about to take place. The *Enterprise* would once again glide through the galaxies.

Some *Star Trek* fans, however, are worried that all the fuss may amount to nothing. And careful checking reveals that at present, the film has two scriptwriters—but no script.

Currently slated for filming next spring, and release during the '77 Christmas season, the full-length *Star Trek* project is quite a mystery to all concerned—a mystery that has been hovering around the Paramount offices for nearly two years. Its on-again, off-again fluctuation has become a sort of accepted routine at the studio, although this time, everyone insists it's definitely on.

Walter Koenig, the dashing young actor who portrayed Chekov on the show, says optimistically, "The movie is as close to being a reality as possible without actually being done."

Roddenberry, entrenched in his paper-strewn office, insists that the film will happen. It's to be the culmination of his *Star Trek* dream, a dream that, at one time, assumed nightmarish proportions. He freely admits that his own involvement with the studio on the project has involved an almost historic masochism.

"The film has been going on now for eighteen months. I moved into this office in May of 1975. The studio thought they'd like a *Star Trek* movie. We debated a long time whether it was to be a two-hour TV film or a movie for theatrical release. I didn't want to do it for television. When the original *Star Trek* ended, Paramount thought it had a real loser on its hands, a stinker. Oh, they'd make a couple of bucks on reruns but they knew the show would never amount to much. They destroyed all the sets. Everything. Even Spock's ears.

"I felt that for TV, the limited budget allowed just would not suffice for the rebuilding of the sets and of the *Enterprise*. [The original model is in the Smithsonian in Washington.] It would be the same quality as on the old show and, after all these years, I felt that that wouldn't be good enough. They said, 'Okay, we'll do a theatrical release. Go write a script.'

"I handed them a script and they turned it down. It was too controversial. It talked about concepts like 'Who is God?' The movie then sagged for quite some time. I didn't hear anything for over three months. Meanwhile, unknown to me, the executives then in charge were interviewing writers, accepting outlines. I found out about all this quite by accident. None of the outlines were accepted. I think the main reason for all the problems with those scripts rested in the fact that most of the people making the decisions concerning the film knew little or nothing about *Star Trek*. As it turned out later on, several of the principals had never even seen the show."

The struggle to get the *Enterprise* off the launching pad once more has even touched a nerve with William Shatner who, as the intrepid Captain Kirk, commander of the starship, was totally nerveless. Shatner is eagerly awaiting the beginnings of the film, and readily admits: "My reaction to Paramount's hesitation about making the movie is one of total bewilderment. Their logic escapes me. Forget art. From sheer economics, stalling the film makes no sense. *Star Trek* could have made money in theaters years ago. There's just no explaining studio thinking. Since the *Star Trek* phenomenon continues to grow, there's still a good reason to make the film today. I do understand why Paramount is rushing the film now. They want to catch on to the coattails of this entire *Star Trek* thing."

Whatever the studio's ulterior motives, Gene Roddenberry is now in the middle of legitimate story conferences and loving it. "I'm not bitter that it's taken so long for Paramount to understand the importance of the film," he says good-naturedly. "Look how long it took the Bank of America to realize the value of computerized checking."

ONE OF THE WRITERS INITIALLY INVOLVED WITH THE *STAR TREK* FILM was Harlan Ellison. As one of science fictiondom's '60s New Wave angry young men and the author of a host of controversial, award-winning works, Ellison has not mellowed over the years, retaining the feistiness that has characterized most of his writing. He is outspoken about the *Star Trek* film as well. "My mother died this morning," he says when reached at home, "what do you want to know?"

Ellison then recalls the rigors of Trekdom. "My involvement with the film amounted to bullshit," he philosophizes. "It was the kind of bullshit you get from amateurs and independents but you don't expect from a major studio like Paramount. They don't know what they're doing over there. Gene may know but the studio sure doesn't. They called me in on four separate occasions and they never paid me a nickel. I did one complete script that Gene liked. It was rejected.

"I'm not connected with the film now in any way, by mutual con-sent of myself and Paramount," Ellison announces. "I don't think the movie is going to happen. If it does, it will probably be lousy. They've been doing this now for ages. They've had a total of twenty-one writers working on this. Now they've signed those two guys [Chris Bryant and Allan Scott, two British writers responsible for *Don't Look Now*] and God knows what *they're* going to do. I mean, it's insanity to get two English writers who write very toney, European scripts to come in and do what is basically an action-adventure movie. I don't know what pompous aesthetics they're going to throw in. All *Star Trek* has ever been is an elaborate shoot 'em up, and con-fusing it with the *Bagahavad Gita* only muddies its waters. The thing that made some of the TV episodes so unbearable was the preten-tiousness."

In spite of the fact that no one really knows what the finished pic-ture will look like, some of science fiction's biggest guns are putting their faith in both Roddenberry and his entourage, trusting them to deliver to the general public nothing short of a milestone in science fiction filmdom.

Roddenberry is well aware of the *Star Trek* masterpiece expecta-tions. "I'll be glad to finally get started. The film is a very uncomfort-able burden. All the actors from the show get pestered about it wherever they go. 'When is it coming out? What's going on?' I get that too and I was never even on camera. The other day I was dri-ving home from work and a motorcycle cop pulled me over to the side of the road. I thought, 'Oh, Christ, here comes a ticket.' He must have recognized my license plates or something because he stuck his head inside my window and asked, 'When's the movie com-ing out?' Things like that happen all the time."

PARAMOUNT'S *STAR TREK* HEADQUARTERS CONSISTS LARGELY OF GENE Roddenberry's office, his reception area, and a smaller outer office across the hall. At one time, the entire building was used to house the *Star Trek* TV brass. Things are picking up in the tiny think tank, however, and a steady stream of collaborators files through the modest doors daily.

"I'm very pleased with the way the film is going," Roddenberry beams. "We've just signed Phil Kaufman—who's done many fine films—to direct."

One of the most publicized problems concerning the remaking of *Star Trek* has concerned the resigning of the original cast. Rumors abound concerning the rivalry between the show's two stars William

Shatner and Leonard Nimoy. Shatner quickly sweeps these stories aside, saying flatly, "There's no truth to that at all. I love Leonard. He's one of the most sensitive and committed human beings I've ever met. If we disagreed occasionally on the set, it was because we were so concerned about the show. If we squabbled, it was like two brothers squabbling."

The rugged actor is 100 percent behind the *Star Trek* film and wants the world to know it. "I'm anxious to play the role again. In the film, the character of Kirk will be a bit different than the character in the show, but there won't be any startling changes because Kirk was basically me. His reactions were essentially mine. No matter how an actor tries to do otherwise, his character gradually assumes his own characteristics. You say the words written for you, but respond as yourself.

"There are critics of the show who dismiss the characters as being superficial. I don't agree. Kirk was a challenging role. The question was how to portray a man responsible for four hundred thirty people on a battleship, facing battles every week, without looking like the weight of the world is dragging him under. He had to be played in a manner wherein he took the grave responsibilities with ease and rose above the somberness of the position, facing danger with a hint of humor. That truth that has just flowed easily from my tongue took me months to figure out."

Although William Shatner is more than ready to don the gear of the United Federation once more, some of his fellow crew members are not. Right now, Leonard Nimoy, the stoic Vulcan Spock, is counted among the missing-in-action on the Paramount lot. Nimoy, who has virtually no comment to make concerning *Star Trek* past, present, or future, was one of the original series' big drawing cards. Some observers feel that his absence from the film amounts to space mutiny.

Roddenberry, true to form, predicts the prodigal pair of pointed ears will return to the fold in the near future. "I think that Leonard wants to do this film, but he's in litigation with the studio concerning some monetary problems. I think he wants to do the film but wants to settle his legal problems before he makes a commitment. I don't blame him."

Shatner expresses some very Kirkian logic on the subject. "I don't mind talking about Leonard's problems at all," he says. "Leonard Nimoy has a beef and it's a legitimate one. It's about the merchandizing and it's something that irks me as well. Our faces appear on products all over the country, all over the world, and we've not really been compensated fairly for it. Right now Paramount wants

Leonard, and Leonard wants fair recompense. It's only reasonable that Paramount meet his demands. Something has happened here. Someone has made a lot of money from the show and the people who *were* the show have seen very little of it. I think Leonard is totally in the right."

With the entire cast tentatively reunited, Roddenberry takes time to deny the gossip that Nimoy is holding out because he HATES *Star Trek*, resents his pointed-ear stigma, and feels it is below him to do the motion picture. "I think the whole thing has been blown out of proportion. It happens to every actor who's in a popular TV series. When it ends, they're still identified with it. I think they've survived it. Actually, I think it's come full circle: I think the show's popularity and their involvement in it has done a lot for their careers. It's kept them in the public eye."

Even in light of Nimoy's calculated absence, Roddenberry is amazed at the smoothness of the casting. "I'm just plain thankful that the studio finally *wants* the original cast. We fought over that for quite a while. In the beginning they didn't want any part of the old crew. They said that *that* was television and *this* was the movies—you need big names to draw at the box office. I thought, my God, can you imagine that? Richard Burton as Kirk and Robert Redford as Spock? Geez. Somehow word of this potential disaster mysteriously leaked out to our fans and the studio was deluged with irate mail. Their Hollywood superstar period ended not too long after that."

IF THE *STAR TREK* FILM REALLY IS MADE THIS TIME AROUND, A LOT OF skeptics still see the movie missing the boat. The *Star Trek* phenomenon, they say, will be dead and gone before the wide-screen *Enterprise* has a chance to blast off. Among these doubters is Harlan Ellison, who glibly comments: "*Crawdaddy* doing a piece on *Star Trek* is like me doing a piece on Renaissance pottery: It's over. It's dead. The whole convention scene is falling apart. I've been to twelve conventions this year and all of them lost money . . . except for two. How many times can you listen to Jimmy Doohan talk in a phony Scottish accent?"

# Shoot-Out at the I'm OK/You're OK Corral

*by John Mankiewicz*

*January 1977*

*Gestalt, aikido, TM, primal scream, zen:* Crawdaddy *covered them all. Then came the Est Years of Our Lives. Here Werner Erhard presents Buckminster Fuller. John Mankiewicz, who hails from a famous Hollywood family, is now a screenwriter himself.*

My friends told me I was crazy. "Listen to Buckminster Fuller and Werner Erhard for twelve hours? All day? In New York?" My friend John, who loves the Big Apple, and whose idea of a good time is to spend five hours in CBGB's listening to punk rock and making his Coca-Cola last, suggested that my weekend might turn out better if I stayed in Los Angeles. "It's not worth it. Hang around here, maybe go to a movie instead."

Candace gave me the same advice. "Erhard's a fake," she said, exasperated, when I told her the plan. "Everyone knows that."

Werner received a lot of bad notices in the wake of the first wave of hosannas for *est.* The backlash hit right around the time pocket calculators were coming into vogue. Cynics started figuring out how much money *est* was making on $200 a head at mass trainings. To rub it in, Werner had freely admitted that he "wasn't selling anything that people didn't already know, or have." At best, *est* became dubious. Reporters talked more about Erhard's Lear jet and opulent home than how Werner's no-fault insurance was teaching the masses "to ride the horse in the direction it's going." Rumor had it

that *est* enrollment had hit its stride at eighty-five thousand graduates. People were still plunking down their money (the price was up
to $250) but interest was diminishing.

Bucky Fuller's stock, on the other hand, was at the same high
level it had been for more than forty years. Werner Erhard wasn't
even young Jack Rosenberg (his real name) when Fuller quit the rat
race to devote his energies to bettering the universe. No one could
argue with the spirit and substance of his contributions: the geodesic dome, World Game, maps, Dymaxion cars, and, perhaps most
important, an unflagging optimism about life on this planet. Cou-
pled with an appealingly poetic nature, this ultrapositive outlook
seems infectious. BUCKY FULLER, reads a still-popular bumper strip,
SAYS EVERYTHING'S GOING TO BE ALL RIGHT. What's more, Fuller, at
eighty-one, still goes all over the planet explaining his philosophy as
more than just a slogan. "There are enough resources in this world,"
he declares, "to provide every person's needs." With unconscious
enthusiasm, he mines those materials and encourages his audience
to "help make them work."

Why, then, were Erhard and the *est* Foundation "presenting"
Buckminster Fuller at New York's Town Hall? What stage could be
big enough for both of them? At first glance, it seemed about as appropriate as the Runaways announcing a jam session with Leonard
Bernstein and the Philharmonic. Maybe that's why the Event, as it
was called, was only advertised in the *est* newsletter. Admittance to
the twelve-hour presentation (with two meal breaks) cost twenty-five
dollars. The ticket came complete with vaguely authoritarian *est*ian
instructions: "Name tags will be worn at all times during the Event."
And, "Seats will not be reserved during the meal breaks. When you
return to the auditorium you will find new seats." I had not taken
the *est* training, and those "wills" gave me the willies.

Three weeks before the show, I got word that it was sold out. That
meant that there would be, roughly, 1,599 *est* graduates, and me. I
had nothing against these people as a group but obviously I'd be
somewhat out of touch with the common denominator of the day.
But when it turned out that I could make the trip with an old college friend, Jaime Snyder, the deal was clinched. Jaime was also going to the Event, but not just to watch. Jaime is Bucky Fuller's
grandson. He has spent considerable time working with Bucky and
accompanied his grandfather on at least one trip around the world.
Jaime is also an *est* graduate, and he'd offered his services to me as a
kind of guide.

Jaime was tired on the plane because he had worked all week finishing a short film about Bucky to be screened as part of the Town

Hall program. He was also a little nervous, because he would be on-stage with Erhard and Fuller for the whole twelve hours.

"It will be mostly Bucky speaking," Jaime explained. "Werner and I will be there to facilitate Bucky. The audience is too big, we decided, to ask individual questions, so we'll be trying to get a sense of where the audience is at. We can then help Bucky direct his talks so that the people will be able to share in his experience, not just the technical stuff, but Bucky as a person, too."

Jaime took the *est* training a couple of years ago, and enjoyed it immensely. His affinity for the *est* philosophy made him an important link between his grandfather and Erhard. A physics student at University of California, Santa Cruz, Jaime wrote a letter to Werner Erhard, expressing his interest in the upcoming *est* seminar with scientists. A young man in Erhard's office, Ron Landsman, responded to the letter. Jaime told Landsman that he was Bucky's grandson ("I don't know how it came up") and suggested that Fuller and Erhard might like to get together.

Eight months after the first letter, Erhard's schedule allowed him to invite Bucky and Jaime to dinner at Franklin House, which is *est*'s San Francisco headquarters and Erhard's home. Erhard says that "this was one of the greatest days of my life." A few more meetings took place. The possibility of a joint public appearance was broached; details were worked out between Fuller's office in Philadelphia and Erhard's staff, with their two young associates providing organizational input.

LIKE THE WEATHER FOR THE BIG GAME, THE DAY OF THE EVENT dawned crisp and clear. Jaime invited me to the Plaza Hotel to meet his grandfather. Fuller was dressed in a blue suit (his customary attire), and was fiddling with his watches (one digital on each wrist).

"You see," he explained, "this one's for my office time in Philadelphia, the other I set for wherever I am."

Having received a strong feeling that this man was interested in *everything*, I told him about a new kind of music that I'd heard just the night before, "country-disco." He knew what disco music was, so I explained that this new genre involved almost the same dance beat, but with the rhythm submerged under country melodies. His eyes brightened, and he motioned Jaime and me over to the edge of the lobby.

"I know what you mean," he said, immersed in the idea. And he started to dance a quick jig, creating a rhythmic rat-a-tat on the marble floor. He held his short, well-packed frame in a professional hoofer's pose—arms hanging loose, back fairly rigid, all the movement coming from his waist down.

"Like that?" he asked. "We used to do a lot of dancing, you know; that was the only social thing to do."

Ron Landsman did not witness this truly charming display; he was over at the other side of the lobby, worried about Werner's arrival. "It's 9:01," Landsman informed us. "Werner was supposed to be here at nine. He always keeps his appointment."

A minute was really nothing to quibble about, especially when you consider Erhard's splashy entrance at 9:02. He swept through the lobby and in one smooth swoop, put his blue blazer-clad arms around Jaime and Ron, one to a customer, and greeted them on the run, marching toward the street. "Jaime, Ron, Bucky," he said, and the four of them slipped into the waiting limousine. The scene was not without a touch of glamour.

Before the Event began, I walked around the hall, checking the crowd. (After all, the rules said that you were "allowed to visit with friends until 9:15.") There were about thirty ushers, volunteers whose main function was to find seats for people. Occasionally, they took their jobs too seriously. "*Sit down*," one hissed at me (*before* 9:15). "I'm trying to get a head count."

Exactly on time, Jaime, Fuller, and Erhard filed onstage and sat down in semimodern chairs. The audience erupted, handing out the first of countless standing ovations. Annie Fuller, Bucky's wife, was sitting next to me, clearly excited. How many times has she heard her husband speak? They had been married, I'd been told, since 1917.

Erhard began the program with some history—Jaime's first letter and the initial gathering at Franklin House. Apparently, for Erhard, this meeting ranked with his famous "Getting It" experience while driving down a California freeway. "I was exhilarated," he said, smiling, "by experiencing Bucky. I felt that many parts of our lives were parallel; I sensed that, while our experiences in life were different, we shared a sense of those experiences." Erhard thanked Jaime for bringing them together. "I got so much out of my sharing with Bucky that I wanted to introduce him to my friends," said Erhard, gesturing at the packed house.

The audience clapped, and the ball was handed to Jaime, who introduced the guest of honor.

"When I was traveling with my grandfather, I noticed that people would come up to him after lectures and not know what to say. They'd just heard a talk that was overflowing with information, but they had no idea of Bucky as Bucky." Jaime talked easily, with only a slight trace of nervousness. He described that morning's "country-disco" incident as an example of the way Bucky interacts with people beyond his technical expertise. "That's the experience of Bucky," he concluded, "that I wanted to share with Werner, and that Werner and I want to share with you."

Another standing ovation for Bucky. His appearance, while sitting in the chair waiting to speak, belied the fast wit and clarity of thought that was to come. Fuller's hearing is on the wane, and perhaps this is why he seemed out of it onstage. There was a certain vulnerability that could easily have been mistaken for senility.

Once he started talking, however, the confusion vanished. He was articulate and had facts at his complete disposal. In the morning session, Bucky talked about his early life, describing his ill-fated attempts to fit into the business world while at the same time supporting his wife and daughter (Jaime's mother). Bucky talked in elliptical terms, taking on many ideas at once, but by the time he came to a breathing space, each of the thoughts was coherently explained.

Erhard would step in, sometimes in these breathing spots, sometimes more abruptly. He seemed preoccupied with paraphrase and, since Werner never talked for more than ten or fifteen minutes, his accounting of Bucky's thoughts often rang superficial. Because he was presenting Bucky to these sixteen hundred friends, Erhard obviously felt his duties included that of translation—after all, when *he* first encountered Fuller, *he* couldn't keep up, but, with few exceptions, the interpretations he chose were extremely manipulative: "In other words, Bucky, what you're saying is that each person should take responsibility for his own life." After going from the specifics of Fuller's experience to the generalities inherent in the *est* training, Erhard would then give the audience a knowing smile, as if to say "Isn't this just what *we* do?" The graduates would usually respond with the laugh of the initiated, accompanied by scattered applause.

The afternoon session continued in much the same vein, although Fuller examined some more far-reaching topics (i.e., the Universe) and applied his principles to possible solutions. One must not be intimidated by technology, he cautioned; technology is a tool that should be used with respect and understanding. Often, he said, technology is mystified, shrouded by needless intrigue. He talked about his new system of mathematics, a book called *Synergetics*. "If a six-year-old child followed the steps in this book," Bucky advised, "he would be able to do advanced calculus."

Bucky performed some exciting demonstrations as well, using only sticks of wood with rubber joints. In forty-five minutes, he took

the audience through the thinking that led to discovery of the principle of the geodesic dome. At the end of this segment Werner
chimed in, "I'm able to follow you more and more, Bucky, each
time we meet. I fall behind sometimes, but don't consciously try to
catch up. I just get the flow of experiencing *you*, Bucky; I'm right
there."

The evening session was kind of anticlimactic, devoted, as it was,
almost exclusively to platitudes and more standing ovations. "I
wouldn't be up here," Bucky remarked, "if Werner wasn't a person of
integrity and doing things for enormous amounts of people." After
the applause died down, Erhard, not to be outdone, parried: "I can
feel the joy of Bucky's course." Again, the tired crowd rose to its feet.
Always, it seemed, praise was directed at the person who had *given*
the compliment.

Jaime posed a question: "It's clear to me that you two are totally
committed to the planet. I have a problem in sharing that commitment. How can you have the integrity?"

"It's because, Jaime," Bucky answered, "we're unwilling to let it
go."

"Your sense of yourself shifts," Erhard added. Facing Fuller, he
said, "You're not Bucky Fuller sitting in a chair, you're Bucky Fuller,
the universe."

"The commitment is a hard decision," Bucky concluded impas-
sively. "But it's the only choice each one of us has. For the last twenty
years I've made over two hundred thousand dollars each year, and
I've put everything back into the operation." Bucky emphasized his
faith in generations to come. "It's a young world," he said. "Computers can be run by ten-year-olds, and that's a good sign. I'm quite optimistic, because of three things: youth, truth, and love. My
grandson's a youth, Werner is truth and love. I can't tell you how
moved I am that we're all here together."

With that, the three kissed; Bucky even went into the first row to
kiss a man in the audience. The clapping became more furious,
peaked, and then died. The Event was over. Fuller had other speaking engagements, and had to spend some time at his office. Werner
was off to India, according to Landsman, "to be in India."

I CAUGHT UP WITH BUCKY FULLER A FEW WEEKS LATER IN LOS ANGELES,
where he was visiting with his family. "I first heard about Werner
through Jaime," Bucky said. "I was curious to know why he was so
taken, so I asked for an explanation." When pressed for details,
Fuller insisted, "I'm really bothered by judgment. The meetings

were extremely pleasing, and I enjoyed myself tremendously. New York was one of many, many meetings in my life and—like many others—it was very exciting."

Clearly, Fuller felt that he could not be much help in explaining the Town Hall Event. "I think you should write about how *you* were impressed, not me."

Indeed, onstage in New York, Fuller had said that he was "the custodian of an experiment." A storehouse of knowledge, he releases facts and fancy to anyone who wants to hear and Werner Erhard had said that he wanted to listen. Buckminster Fuller has never taken the *est* training (Erhard said, "He doesn't need it—Bucky's Got It"), but he has faith. Hopefully some of his spirit was absorbed by the "what's so is so" audience.

Ron Landsman, who had a big part in arranging the Event, has since left *est* and is working with Jaime and friend Roger Stoller in presenting future shows. These will be more intimate—Bucky Fuller, Superstar—and people can ask questions. At least one more, however, is planned with Werner Erhard.

When Landsman asked me what "the sense" of my article would be, I said, "Oh, just my experience of the Event," and he seemed glad, satisfied that I was not going to write another "negative" piece.

"You know," Landsman revealed conspiratorially, "Werner's not very good with media. He's getting better, though." And, although the ex-*est* employee had an earnest look about him, I started laughing.

Landsman started laughing, too, perhaps admitting that Erhard did know how to handle the press. Erhard's manipulative tactics have wide range, however, and run according to supply and demand. And if, as I suspect, Jaime Snyder was merely *est*'s conduit to his grandfather, his eyes were wide open, and he's ready to do it again. Like Bucky, Jaime does not like to judge things. He's just right there.

# Doctor J and Mr. Erving

*by Tony Kornheiser*

*March 1977*

*The original Michael Jordan. In typical* Crawdaddy *fashion we committed two '70s publishing sins with this article—we put a black man and an athlete on the cover. Of course, we had done that twice before with Muhammad Ali. Wouldn't sell a lick. We never learned. Kornheiser is presently a triple-threat star in Washington, DC, as a writer for the* Post, *host of his own radio show, and frequent co-conspirator with Mary Matalin on television's* Equal Time.

Dr. J is the best basketball player in the world. It's something you know the moment you see him with the ball. If you can remember the first time you heard Richard Burton speak or watched Nureyev leap, if you can remember that feeling in your chest, when your breath shivered and it whistled in the wind, you can remember knowing that something had happened, something had changed.

It's not so much that Dr. J does the basics better than everyone else. David Thompson skies; he can go up and turn left. Pete Maravich dribbles better; he makes the ball behave like a trained dog. Bob McAdoo shoots better; he sticks it with one guy on his back and another in his face.

It's something in the way he moves.

Style is what sets him apart. In basketball, style is every bit as important as sheer result, maybe more. You put a ball in Dr. J's hands and it's like putting a brush in Picasso's. Crowds get absolutely wired when he gets the ball. He did a thing in L.A. a couple of years ago that people haven't stopped talking about. At an all-star game, the pros against the UCLA players, the kids in the stands were slapping hands every time Dr. J touched the ball. Even the pros were standing around, watching him operate.

Julius has a broadcast tape of the game at home; the radio guy sent it to him. The last five minutes of the game, all you hear is the radio guy screaming, "The Doctor . . . The Doctor . . . The Doctor!" After a while, you've got no idea what's happening in the game. You figure he's making some humongous moves, but you've got no idea if the shots are dropping. Not that it matters. The moves are what counts. Dr. J going over, under, sideways on some guy, picking him clean. Making the shot is just icing, anyway. But the radio guy probably never saw Dr. J play before, because he gets progressively louder, until you think your ears are gonna bust. "The Doctor . . . The Doctor!"

Dr. J does this to people. Perhaps the only person he cannot do it to is Julius Erving.

They live in the same body, the Doc and Julius, but in different worlds. Fire and ice. Julius Erving knows that it must be that way; the delicate balance is critical. It is almost as if they are fighting for control of the one soul they share, and it is getting near the final battle, which will be private and terrifying.

Before the merger of the NBA and ABA, Erving was clearly in control. Dr. J was playing in places like Norfolk and Greensboro, datelines that rarely impress the major markets. He was virtually unknown where it counted, a legend without portfolio. In the city he was worshiped on altars of asphalt by guys with names like Helicopter and Sly, guys who live for today because they can't go to the bank tomorrow. Outside the city, in the anterooms of coaching conventions, only the bird dogs had a line on him, the smooth guys with perma-pressed hair and neon sport coats. He was in the ABA. The NBA guys spit on that league, and for some of them, even that was too much effort. Sure, they'd heard of Dr. J. But they hadn't seen him. Hearing's cheap. Show me, sucker.

Arrogance like that Julius Erving can deal with. It is simply a matter of letting Dr. J loose.

What no one saw coming was the single most traumatic event in Julius Erving's life. And as it is with almost all heroes, it was a tragedy. In the spring of his freshman year, Julius would be called home suddenly to attend the funeral of his younger brother Marvin. Marvin, who was surely going to be a lawyer, and perhaps someday a United States senator, died suddenly of a rare kidney disease. Julius was nineteen, not yet Dr. J. For the first, and probably the last time in his life, Julius felt weak, powerless.

Somewhere in his body one of the walls he had constructed cracked. Emotion poured out, drained from him in the tears he would weep—once gone, it was gone forever.

Years later, as he talked about it, sweat would collect in droplets on Julius Erving's nose. He would not wipe them away as he spoke. He would, in effect, deny they were even there at all.

"I cried all that day," Julius Erving said. "Cried and cried and cried. I went to the cemetery the first two days after he was buried, and I cried each day. Then I went the next day, and I did not cry. I told myself that I wasn't going to cry anymore."

That was 1969. He says he hasn't cried since, and he doesn't know what it would take to make him cry again. The walls are back, and they are stronger than ever.

After a tragedy, some people pick up religion and carry it like a shield. Julius Erving picked up a basketball and started doing things with it that had never been done before. He became almost possessed with motivation. He denounced his fears, denied his emotions. In a world of cool he became cold. Ice cold. Somewhere deep inside him, in the space normally reserved for tears, a void existed. Soon, sooner than anyone had a right to expect, that void was filled. By something that would later be exhibited, charted, and identified as "Dr. J." Something that Julius Erving would have no trouble recognizing, but some discomfort living with.

Probably the realization came to Julius in the manner it came to Mike, the chorus boy in *A Chorus Line,* who borrowed his sister's tap shoes one day, went down to her dance class and found, indeed, he *could do that.* Probably Julius was working on a move—because he never does anything in a game that he hasn't rehearsed—and noticed his teammates looking at him funny. Probably he understood they were looking that way because he'd done something they'd never seen before. Yet he'd done it easily. Probably he realized right then that if he'd only dare to let his imagination run wild, his body would carry him past everyone who'd played the game.

Probably he said to himself, "I can do that."

Julius Erving played basketball for UMass for two varsity seasons. During that time he learned one most valuable lesson, and he learned it one night in the campus coffee shop from Bill Russell, who had come to the school to lecture. Russ said the only reason a kid gets an athletic scholarship is because a school thinks it can use him. It's a business transaction, kid. "Make sure," Russ told him, "that you get out of something what you put into it."

Erving was young, but he was old enough to know he'd outgrown UMass. He was through letting Dr. J play ball for nothing. It was time to turn pro.

He would have to go to the ABA, because the NBA was not yet signing underclassmen. The older, more conservative league was standing on principle because no one had been smart enough to slap its face with an antitrust suit. The ABA was offering cash money to anyone with long legs. Julius Erving signed his name to a contract with the Virginia Squires that would pay him $125,000 a year for the next four years. The Squires had never seen him play—all they had heard was that there was this great player in Massachusetts. That his name was Dr. J.

THE MOST OVERUSED WORD IN SPORTS IS *SUPERSTAR*. IN FACT, THERE are only three superstars in professional team sports, three men whose abilities and personalities combine to set them apart from everyone else—O. J. Simpson, Reggie Jackson, and Dr. J.

They are news wherever they go, whatever they do. They are never far from a microphone or a notebook, and whatever they say is recorded for posterity.

Dr. J doesn't have to worry about that; all he has to do is play basketball. Julius Erving does his talking.

Many athletes, particularly those on professional teams, are spoiled and arrogant. They lust after pleasure savagely, and when they lose, they pout.

Julius Erving is entirely different. It is remarkable the way he deals with reporters, the way he plays them as chess pieces, giving them what they need and making them think he has given them what they want. His press voice is deep, somewhat aristocratic. It never carries the condescension of a Tom Seaver, or the studied, mirror-on-the-ceiling cool of a Walt Frazier. He never gives a reporter any reason to doubt his honesty, and he never ever makes a reporter feel stupid. In the locker room, Julius Erving is every bit as good as Dr. J is on the court.

Reporters have written so many testimonials to Erving, it's like when he dies, St. Peter will have to send a cab down for him.

A white NBA star once said that Erving would have wealth and glory beyond his dreams if he would only keep his nose clean and his voice soft. The message was: Just don't be another nigger. "I've never given anyone reason to criticize me," Erving said. "I've been very calculating in my affairs. That's the way I like to do things." Up yours, blondie.

But after one season at Virginia, Erving broke his contract. He decided that Dr. J was worth a lot more money than he was making, and he asked his agent-attorney, Bob Woolf, to renegotiate the deal, get some bigger numbers. When Woolf refused, Erving got a new agent, Irwin Weiner, and Weiner signed him to a contract with the Atlanta Hawks of the NBA. Not only was this in violation of Erving's contract with Virginia, it also violated the NBA draft laws; Milwaukee held the NBA rights to Dr. J. Unruffled, Erving flew to Atlanta and played some exhibition games with the Hawks. It took a court decision to send him back to Virginia. A federal judge said to Erving: Either play for Virginia, or don't play at all. That season, Dr. J played for Virginia.

The next season the Nets bought Dr. J from the Squires, and paid off Atlanta and Milwaukee to avoid any lawsuits. Erving signed an eight-year contract for something like $2 million. He said it gave him security, and he said he'd finish his career with the Nets, playing in the shadow of his hometown, Long Island, New York.

This is not an easy thing to define, this being an Island kid. It has something to do with a sense of rootlessness, an inability to feel completely comfortable outside suburbia. Island kids grow up longing for a driver's license; they see the car as their salvation, because in an hour's time it can take them to either the skyscrapers of New York or the potato fields of Bridgehampton. An Island kid spends his youth knowing that everything is an hour's drive away, that nothing is around the corner but more Island kids. This is a disturbing awareness. It causes you to expect far too much from where you're going.

After a while, you don't go anymore. Not unless you know exactly what you're going for.

Like city kids understand subways, and country kids understand the land, Island kids understand cars—what they promise, and what they can't deliver.

When Erving and I both worked on the Island, we'd take the Meadowbrook Parkway to and from work. I'd be in a Pinto, coaxing her up to 60 and hanging on through the shakes and the wheezes, down from Jones Beach Toll Plaza to the ocean, about three miles of straightaway. He'd come up from behind, in the Avanti or the Corvette, as close to me as butter on bread, and we'd start charging. I'd wrap my hands under the steering wheel, Jackie Stewart style, and get up to 70, then check him out in the mirror. With about a mile to go, he'd pull left and glide even, until I gave in and looked over. Then he'd smile, maybe wave, and blow by.

It was a game we'd play every so often. Nothing we ever spoke about. Something we understood. He was free in that car, free to be who he wanted, free to go where he wanted. Free to act like a kid. On the court, or in the locker room, he was always busy being someone else.

The day he signed with the Nets, I was assigned to do an extensive piece with him, to get inside his head. I tried hard to set up the only question I really cared about: Who is Dr. J, and what does Julius Erving think of him? I couldn't believe that he would be prepared for it. After all, he was twenty-three years old, and at twenty-three most people don't even know which end is up. I was surely going to stop him cold. I was going to take Dr. J to the hoop and put it in his face.

He took the question and wrapped it around my eye.

"I'm still Julius," he said, "but I realize that the Dr. J identity exists for many people. I know where my roots are, and I can relate to myself. But obviously some things have changed. Some acquaintances try to put me on the defensive by saying that I changed. It used to give me mental anguish until I realized that it was only my acquaintances who were judging me by Dr. J; my real friends let me be Julius. In my mind I feel I've kept the whole thing in check. I've never gone anywhere and introduced myself as Dr. J . . . [but] let's say I want to go down to the corner with a bottle of wine and hang out—I can't do that. It would affect too many people who look up to me. There are times when I've got to let being Julius Erving keep me in check. But that's the price you pay for being a commodity."

Dr. J was a Net—*the* Nets, actually—for three years. In that time he was so good, and so invisible—because the ABA couldn't get a television contract—that almost by himself he forced the merger. The public demanded to see him.

Between the announcement of the merger and the start of camp last summer, Erving's agent documented some twenty-five players who were making bigger numbers than Dr. J. What kind of way is that to treat The Doctor? Weiner wondered. Erving didn't want to appear greedy; he didn't want to give people reason to criticize him. But he wanted what he deserved from the merger, and surely twenty-five players weren't better than Dr. J. Erving refused to report to camp. He wanted to renegotiate his contract. He justified the move by telling people that Roy Boe, the Nets owner, had failed to deliver on some verbal promises.

Boe was supremely arrogant throughout *l'affaire Doc.* He lied about never having renegotiated a contract before. He probably also lied about fulfilling all personal promises to Erving. He preened like a warlord as he invented principles, then stood on them. In a hallmark show of stupidity, he even said that the Nets could get along without Dr. J. The only thing that saved him from a media lynching was the incontrovertible conclusion that here, again, was Julius Erving attempting to break a contract. Boe kept the contract in his office, and Erving's balls in his pocket.

Two days before the season opened Erving was sold, with his consent, to Philadelphia for $3 million. That night he signed a six-year contract with the 76ers for $600,000 a year.

When I heard the news, I recalled overhearing a conversation between Erving and Arthur Ashe during Erving's holdout. Ashe was praising Erving for his strength, the righteousness of his stand. Ashe had said something about "crossing the line." About, "there are so many lines out there."

I couldn't put it together until I read Erving's quote the next day in the paper, the one where he said, "John Q. Cash did it again." It was the bottom line they were talking about.

Erving didn't just cross it. He broke it.

In Philly, they treated the deal with a reverence reserved for a cure to Legionnaire's Disease. They stuffed the six and eleven o'-clock news with clips of Doc's most outrageous slam dunks, the kind that scream—*I'm Dr. J and you're not!* By noon the next day, eight hours before the San Antonio game, a game that figured to draw eighty-five hundred, the line was six deep at the Sixers ticket booth, and the twelve phone lines in the office were overheating.

The players, some of whom didn't know Erving, came to practice aghast at what they'd seen on TV. "They couldn't believe it," said George McGinnis, suddenly a number two forward at $500,000 a year. McGinnis then began his imitation of the Doc-Windmill-Slammer, rotating his arms in great, soaring circles. "They wanted to know—'Can he really do this shit in a game?' I told them, 'You ain't seen nothin' yet.' I saw him do it over Gilmore."

Artis Gilmore is seven-feet-two; the only things that go over him are planes.

Erving got to Philly in the late afternoon. Doc was dressed before most of the Sixers showed. He decided that his uniform needed tapering, but otherwise it was okay. Doc wasn't inclined to discuss cosmic significance. The bulk of the team arrived together as if they'd piled into a VW, ass-over-teakettle in the backseat, and driven over. Doc made light, graceful hellos. He listened as McGinnis and Darryl Dawkins traded jabs.

McGinnis (looking at Dawkins's twelve-piece black suit): "D, you goin' to a hay party?"

Dawkins: "No man. Be goin' to visit yo' mama."

Doc laughed, but he didn't say much, not even when the ubiquitous Dancing Harry pranced into the room, shouting, "Doc-Tah. Doc-Tah." Doc looked at him the way one looks at a penguin.

Meanwhile the reporters were waiting on the way Doc would greet McGinnis. Last year, McGinnis was the 76ers' savior. He's a thirty-shot-per-gamer, a player of enormous talent and ego. He'd been rhythm guitar to Doc's lead in the ABA, and now he stood a chance of being put back there again, on the team he'd rescued from mediocrity. The Philly writers were already suggesting that the Sixers would need two game balls and a traveling psychiatrist. And every reporter in the room tensed when McGinnis approached Doc.

But McGinnis is far too smart to get sucker punched. He did the scene straight out of James Dean—*later* on all that jealousy boolshit. After engaging Doc in a series of handshakes that looked like the initiation to the Mystic Knights of the Sea, Big George spoke.

"Man, you sure look funny in that uniform."

As soon as Doc laughed, the reporters did too.

THE SPECTRUM WENT DARK FOR PREGAME INTRODUCTIONS AS THE crowd of 17,200 waited for its cue. The scoreboard flashed, IS THE DOCTOR IN THE HOUSE! and Dr. J was introduced to a tidal wave of cheers. He jogged out to center court, bathed in a solitary spotlight, and stood there as the crowd went crazy. When he was handed a medical bag by a fan, and he waved it, the sound in the building was like an explosion in an amplifier. Had Erving remembered how, he might have cried.

Later, in his press voice, he would say, "Outstanding ovation. Probably the greatest I ever received. I almost didn't know what to do."

The Sixers have been setting attendance records in every city they play; Dr. J is the biggest draw since Wilt the Stilt. Having learned the lesson of celebrity, his teammates dress as far away from Doc as possible, to avoid being crushed by the press as Dr. J goes from gym to gym like a traveling salvation show.

"I can deal with it," Doc says, the words sounding like a mantra. "I can deal with it."

Erving is a logical positivist. Let all those around Dr. J worship at his feet, throw roses in the rain—Julius Erving will look straight at reality and stare it down. His wife says he sits for hours in his black leather recliner, thinking problems through in a trancelike state, coming up with a solution, then following it wherever it leads, never looking back.

"When he's in that chair," Turk says, "I don't bother talking to him; he wouldn't hear me anyway."

Erving says he doesn't even remember where he put the chair in his new house.

"If she says that's where I sit and think, maybe she's right," he says. "I don't know. I never sat and thought about it."

Dr. J is the hottest thing in basketball since bell-bottom warm-ups. People want to tug his coat. He lets Julius Erving deal with it; it's better that way. Dr. J does his thing on the court. There he can pull a move, give a feint, hit a shot and say: Eat that, sucker. The game is his thing. Julius Erving can take it to the press, if any of the questions require it. And they can both meet with the kids. The kids. Hanging around, smiling, always putting their slips of paper out, asking for autographs. Funny thing about autographs—you don't just sign your name, you make your pledge. You say more about yourself than you think. Now this kid wants a piece of you, he wants to know who you think you are.

He signs, "Julius—Dr. J—Erving."

# Club Fed

*by Eddie Ginetti*

*June 1977*

*Our man does time with E. Howard Hunt in a country club prison, as we tie together two of the major obsessions of the 1970s—Watergate and pot dealing.*

> *For nearly a thousand days and nights, I was a numbered creature among other subhumans stolidly serving prison time.*
>
> *—E. Howard Hunt*

FEDERAL PRISON CAMP, EGLIN AIR FORCE BASE, FLORIDA—"Reverly with Beverly. Reverly with Beverly. Ha! Ha! Ha! It's five-thirty, gentlemen. All lights on in all dormitories. Reverly with Beverly."

Where am I? My new home. Six short months ago a chicken-shit pilot lands a Lockheed Loadstar at the wrong airstrip deep in the heart of Florida and DEA agents find themselves richer by three-plus tons of Colombian Gold, three trucks, and five nefarious dope smugglers. And here I am in "da joint" with four months and eighteen days to serve on a six-month sentence. A hundred big ones is a lot to pay for lawyers, but they're worth it.

So it's five fucking thirty in the morning. Drag my ass to breakfast and then back to the dorm. Sit on my bunk tired and confused for a while, until: "Attention: All you men who got here yesterday, report to the Camp Hospital." Twenty-five of us waiting in a small hallway. A tetanus booster, blood pressure test, and a few questions: "Hear all right?" "Yeah." "See all right?" "Yeah." Then given a bound folder with several pages of personal medical history questions to answer.

Eglin is a nice campus. Open, airy, palm trees, Spanish moss, slight smell of the Gulf. No walls, fences, dogs, or guns. It is not an "honor camp"; it is a work camp. Minimum Security Federal. Sometimes called "the jewel of the Federal Prison System," or "the country club prison," it is widely acknowledged to have the best food in the entire system. Howard Hunt says it is far better than Allenwood, which is supposed to be pretty good. Hunt says if you have to do time, this is the place to do it. Two boccie ball courts, lighted tennis courts, lighted handball court, weight shack, recreation hall with pool and Ping-Pong tables, full-length basketball court, also lit; baseball diamond with backstop and stands, soccer field, even a putting course. And of course, that warm Florida sunshine.


*FEBRUARY 15:* IT IS SATURDAY. TODAY I GET UP FOR BREAKFAST, WHICH IS highly unusual for me. I have to have energy for this morning's big doubles game. Me and Burt Podell, former U.S. congressman from New York, versus Carl Hinton, former dope dealer, and E. Howard Hunt, former government employee. Podell is a junk player, Hunt is better but not as sneaky. He has a strong first serve, spin on his second; nice ground strokes but not much lateral movement. Hinton is a very strong player, skilled in all phases of the game. He could wipe any one of us off the court in singles but he has a serious weakness in doubles. He overcompensates for Hunt's lack of lateral movement by overrunning, abandoning his position with predictability. Podell is hot today and makes mincemeat out of him repeatedly. I stay where I'm supposed to. We win.


*FEBRUARY 17:* IT IS WARM AND SUNNY. I LEAVE MY JOB EARLY AND GET AN hour of sun before lunch. What the hell, I skip lunch and get another hour of sun. I get back to the camp hospital a little late, leave real early, and go back to the dorm and change into my tennis outfit. I go lie in the sun next to the tennis court and smoke a joint. The first person who shows up with a racquet, I will play. Until then, I will lie in the sun. I'm a short-timer now; I must have a nice Florida tan when I return home.

I am fortunate. I have a good gig in this camp. I am the camp hospital orderly. There are three inmate "employees" there, and we are not checked off. The HAO—hospital administrative officer—is rapidly approaching senility and just doesn't give a shit anyway. So I do my job well, sweeping my floors and emptying my wastebaskets, and generally taking advantage of the situation.

Howard Hunt comes in. "Hi Eddie. Got my medicine?"

"Fresh today, Howard. I'll join you."

The boss is at the administration building. The dentist and his assistant are busy down the hall. Sonny, the inmate who really runs this place, is taping someone's foot. Howard and I go into the back—the "hospital" section, where I have a little room where I sit and read or drink coffee or just hide out. It is also Sonny's sanctuary and one of the few decent places on campus where you can just sit and shoot the shit. I go into the refrigerator and grab the stainless steel pitcher of milk and pour some into a clean glass. I hand it to Howard. He sits down in the folding chair, and I make myself a cup of instant coffee and sit down in my funky office chair.

Howard works at the camp laundry where he hands out clean towels in exchange for dirty ones. He has an ulcer and usually drops by once a day for a glass or two of milk, which we have for him and one other inmate with ulcers. We go through a gallon of the stuff every other day. Sonny and Bunko, the third inmate "employee," and I like milk. It goes real good with the cereal we rip off from the mess hall.

"How goes the battle, Eddie?"

"Great, Howard, not a dirty wastebasket in sight. You?"

"Very well. Clean towels stacked to the ceiling. In fact . . ." he leans forward confidentially, "I've got a couple of nice white fluffy ones for you. Be cool about it. You know . . ." he looks furtively about. "Security."

Howard Hunt makes silly, self-mocking allusions to his illustrious past, but he never discusses it seriously with anyone here. He is an elitist, to be sure. He is not overly fond of the general inmate population. He complains about "the declining quality of the clientele." Too many blacks, too many Cubans, too many low-dollar criminals. High-dollar crimes are committed by white, middle-, and upper-income, well-educated people. He is a snob, I guess, but here he is just another inmate. He wears the same clothes (his are a little nicer, what with working at the laundry and all), eats the same food, and sleeps in the same crowded dormitories as everyone else. He gets more legal mail than anyone else, but he's still a prisoner like the rest of us. I like him because he is highly intelligent, interesting, and subdued. I don't ask him about Nixon and he doesn't ask me about the price of dope in New York. I have been told that he is a very dangerous man, but he has no fewer "friends," nor any more, than anyone else.

"Going home soon, Eddie?"

"Thirty-six days and a wake-up."

"Ah, the wake-up. Leave us not ever forget the wake-up." He hands me his glass and I go to the fridge and pour him some more cold milk. "What are your plans when you get home?"

"What are you—writing a book?"

He laughs. "Could be." He raises a dangerous eyebrow.

I laugh. "Howard, in a few days I turn thirty years old. Thirty years old in the joint, Howard. No wife, no kids, no house, no property. I don't know. It's depressing. I think I should start to think about my future."

"What do you want to do?"

"Write a book?"

"You're asking me?"

"No self-discipline. How do you do it?"

"Eddie, I *have* to do it. I love to write. I need to write. It's necessary for my mental well-being to write. I don't make myself write. It takes no self-discipline. It's not a labor of love; it *is* love."

"I'd like to write."

"That's not good enough. If you have nothing important to say, you won't write."

"Yeah. Yeah."

"Cheer up. In five weeks you'll be getting laid."

*March 9:* The "Good Time" Toastmasters Club held their weekly meeting with a variety of speakers speaking on a variety of topics. Two Toastmasters were leaving the next week and they gave their farewell speeches. Carl Hinton was one of them.

"Men, I learned a great deal here, I think. But one thing especially. Before I came here, I was a highly social person who, well, enjoyed the company of the ladies. Immodestly, I can say I did fairly well in that area. Occasionally it happened, as I am sure it has happened to each and every one of you gentlemen, that, whether too tired or too inebriated or just not in the mood I would not avail myself of the opportunity of enjoying the full fruits of a lady's charms. Well, gentlemen, as I stand here before you for the last time this evening, I can promise you this: Never, never, never in the future will I pass up that kind of opportunity again."

• • •

*MARCH 2, 1977 (TWO YEARS LATER):* I'M SITTING COMFORTABLY IN MY rented house in the country watching the news. There is Howard Hunt sitting before microphones at a big desk with newspeople all around him. "As we say in the can, 'I did my time and paid my debt.' I have suffered humiliation, indignity, and a gross loss of time."

Tell it like it is, Howard. I hope you get laid.

# Tom Robbins and His Sweethearts of the Rodeo

*by Greg Mitchell*
*August 1977*

*Even Cowgirls Get the Blues was the cult novel of the '70s and Robbins for a time was a Pynchon or Salinger character, bathed in mystery. This was his first interview. Cowgirls certainly didn't translate to the movie screen in the 1990s, but Robbins continues to spin metaphors like mad.*

It is not a bean: string, lima, pinto, or kidney; it is not a bean. It is not a carrot. It is neither artichoke nor avocado. It is not a tomato. It is not one of those garden vegetables favored for salad. It is not a cauliflower, for a cauliflower is round. It is something else.

It is an asparagus. One asparagus. It is a pencil-length asparagus stalk that he has lifted off a sidewalk stand in San Francisco's Chinatown and is now holding directly over his head like an emerald rocket trailing a grey hair exhaust. He is demonstrating to his companion Margy how, if technology can land a man on the moon, imagination can send an asparagus into space.

Margy nods appreciatively but passersby could be forgiven some measure of disapproval. They don't know that Tom Robbins is only playing.

"My whole life is devoted to playing near the edge," Robbins explains, peering into a novelty shop selling Japanese toys and kites shaped like butterflies. "And when I find that I get too far from the edge, Margy pushes me back, and I do the same for her." For twenty years, the great wet Northwest has dampened but not extinguished his soft Carolina accent. "She says, 'If you're afraid, then you've got to do it.' I don't think a person has to do everything he's afraid of doing, but we continue to do things that are risky. We're sort of a Tantric Bonnie and Clyde."

Holding hands, Tom and Margy enter a Cantonese luncheonette. A slim, attractive red-haired mother of two in her mid-twenties, Margy is quiet and composed in a neat brown jumpsuit. A generation older, Tom is funky-resplendent in black and purple embroidered satin cowboy shirt, light blue jeans, yellow socks, and shocking green Adidas. His movements, his manner—his mustache—are youthful, with only his salty hair, slight paunch, and crow's feet betraying middle age.

What you notice are the eyes, like blue dots on a flashbulb, the silent testimony of one psychedelic pilgrim who refused to become an acid casualty. Robbins orders bean curd and (as any reader of *Another Roadside Attraction* and *Even Cowgirls Get the Blues* would insist) mushrooms.

"I take my playfulness very seriously," he continues, stabbing a mushroom. "I spend a lot of time in the woods. I spend a lot of time in the company of women. Margy and I play together: intellectually, emotionally, spiritually, sexually. My five-year-old son lives with me three days a week and during that time I spend a great deal of time on the floor, playing with Spiderman dolls and toy cars. He inherited the one trait of mine that I would have chosen, and that's imagination."

At home, Robbins has a room full of cheap Hong Kong, Taiwanese, and Japanese toys nailed to the wall. "I like the element of popular culture when it gets pushed to the point where it becomes absurd and then gets pushed even further and becomes art. I hang out a lot at roadside zoos and circuses and carnivals and tattoo parlors, shooting galleries and penny arcades."

Robbins has climbed out of his woods' work this week in what is, for him, something of a media blitz. *Cowgirls* has just come out in paperback and his publisher, Bantam Books, is having a bash. Announcement of a movie based on the book is fluttering in the Bay Area breeze. Although he has been a recluse for a shorter period than Salinger or Pynchon, it is nevertheless unnerving to meet Robbins in the pale flesh; so much deliberate mystery has swirled around his existence. He is not as young as some of his admirers imagine; rather, he is precisely at that age of whimsical experience that Vonnegut, the last youth-culture literary hero, reached when he rose to campus infamy in the late '60s.

"I've tried in my work to pass along what bits of wisdom I seem to have accumulated on my quest," remarks Robbins. "One of those is: 'You've got to do it yourself. Be your own culture hero.' You wouldn't believe the people who tracked me down last summer. Evidently they haven't all caught on."

THOMAS EUGENE ROBBINS WAS BORN SOME FORTY YEARS AGO, A double-Cancer afflicted with a twin curse: He would be raised in a small town, and that town would be located in the rural tidewater fundamentalist South some time before lynchings ended and Jimmy Carter ascended.

His mother got Tommy interested in writing at a very early age. He was a sensitive child who read voraciously, and because of this, had to hide from his male peers. After graduation, he attended Hargrave Military Academy to polish skills that would take him to conservative Washington and Lee University, "the Princeton of the South," in September 1950. A social misfit, he would leave Washington and Lee two years later, *sans* degree.

Robbins thumbed around the country, ended up in Greenwich Village writing poetry. About to be drafted, he joined the Air Force, which sent him to Korea as a meteorologist. After his discharge, Robbins took a part-time job as copy editor on a Richmond newspaper, but was fired for (he says) slipping a picture of Sammy Davis Jr. and May Britt into the late edition. Computing the farthest point from Richmond on the American mainland, he fled to Seattle, where he became arts critic at *The Seattle Times*. His caustic commentary enraged readers, the Establishment arts scene, and his own editors almost equally.

In 1968, Doubleday editor Luther Nichols met with Tom at the Olympia Hotel in Seattle for a liquid lunch. Nichols had admired Robbins's criticism and wondered if he wrote fiction. "I've been toying with this idea," Tom replied, "about these people . . . who come upon the body of Christ and . . ." After *Another Roadside Attraction* was finished, Robbins would tell Nichols that he had improvised the plot on the spot. But the book sold poorly.

By this time Robbins had separated from his wife and married a woman named Tiny Terrie, who gave birth to a boy, Fleetwood Starr Robbins, in 1972. He desperately needed a chance to write full-time. Literary agent Phoebe Larmore hit on the novel solution of selling the book directly to paperback, where the young audience was. Phoebe put the new *Cowgirls* manuscript in a box with a blue star on it ("for good luck") and turned it over to Bantam editor Ted Solotaroff.

"That affectionate star stuck in my mind," Solotaroff recalls, "and by page three I was in love with it. I eliminated thirteen percent of the bad puns—stuff like astronauts getting poon-Tang on the moon—but Tom's a natural resource; you just have to let him go. Like Blake said, the road of excess leads to knowledge."

Bantam sold the hardcover rights to Houghton-Mifflin, which, in April 1976, published *Cowgirls* as an oversized trade paperback at $4.95, "the price," H-M executive editor Rob Cowley notes, "of a record album." Solotaroff had sent the *Cowgirls* galleys to Thomas Pynchon, who would write an ecstatic endorsement that, along with several key reviews, would help make *Cowgirls* a word-of-mouth success.

By this time, Robbins, confronted with the restrictions marriage places on freedom, had broken up with Tiny Terrie. Hitchhiking strangers and local energy vampires were hitting on him. Country stars were writing "Cowgirls" tunes; he had even collaborated on one with James Lee Stanley. "Sissy Hankshaw" graffiti was being scrawled across highway America and shops called Another Roadside Attraction's were springing up as bookstores, record stores, and fruit stands from Montana to Alabama. A movie of *Cowgirls* would be launched, coproduced by Phoebe Larmore and Robert J. Wunsch, and written by Stephen Geller (*Slaughterhouse Five*).

"We have directors, actors, musicians, calling all day," says Wunsch. "It'll be a commercial blockbuster like *Cuckoo's Nest*. We've really got a tiger by the tail."

CAFFE SPORT IS CLUTTERED WITH OLD WORLD ARTIFACTS IN A FANTASTIC display of ordered disarray. Lamps, wine bottles, and ornaments hover over wood-carved furniture inlaid with maps and drawings of Garibaldi. Profoundly tacky, it's a Tom Robbins paradise. "This place used to be even weirder," Robbins complains, spilling a quarter in the jukebox. "Photos of Rocky Marciano on the wall, midgets hanging up Christmas lights . . ."

Even in public Tom is playful and affectionate with Margy. Robbins inhabits a modest plant-bedecked abode, one of the oldest houses in LaConner, a fishing village that has, since the 1930s, become a sanctuary for artists and the inevitable hangers-on. The new book, *Woodpecker Rising*, is one-quarter finished. Much of its inspiration stems from *Lunaception*, a book by Louise Lacey detailing the influences of the moon on menstrual cycles and biorhythms.

*Woodpecker* demonstrates "the differences between being moonstruck and falling into lunacy," Robbins relates, sipping early-afternoon cappuccino. "It is also about metaphysical outlawism. The narrator is a fugitive. As an outlaw he was known as 'the Woodpecker' because of his red hair, which now, of course, he dyes. In this book I'm making the distinction between outlaws and criminals. Because of the way that I have been treated by the literary Establishment, I have come to regard *myself* as an outlaw novelist, which I feel comfortable with; in fact I kind of like it. I didn't seek it but it does give me a lot of freedom. Many critics don't think I'm a writer to begin with, so how can I go wrong?"

But with half a million *Cowgirls* sales, isn't that period over?

"No, I don't think so. Peter Prescott would not allow a review of *Cowgirls* to appear in *Newsweek* because he said he could not take it seriously as literature. I think among his peers that's very pretty much a shared view."

Robbins's rebuttal is more than a year away. In a process he compares to composing music, he can go a day without finishing a paragraph. "My only asset is my imagination," he says quietly. "I keep as much as possible submerged in my unconscious; I let it marinate, and when it's soaked real well, I try to squeeze it out. The third book is more conventional but that doesn't mean I'm going straight. I've still got a lot of surprises up my sleeve."


It's Tom Robbins Night at the Mission Rock Resort, a former bait and tackle shop transformed into two floors of rustic seaside ambience. Downstairs, pinball machines tilt against a lunch counter, pool tables, and a cowgirl bluegrass band; upstairs, West Coast literary heavies and oddly named Robbins cronies (such as Seattle artist Lead Pencil) hold up the bar, the walls, the porch railing. Rodney Crowell is talking excitedly about the on-the-road song he's just written for Emmylou Harris called "Even Cowgirls . . ." Women are buzzing around Robbins, as if drawn by a secret scent—females of all shapes and temperaments, from feisty blackleather Tiny Terrie to Joanna Cassidy, the murderous starlet from *The Late Show* who perhaps is auditioning to be a Cowgirl. In contrast, Robbins seems cut off from the men; sociable enough to cover obligations but anxious to meet more women or hide out in a hollow tree.

"About eighty percent of my mail comes from women," he explains, wearily accommodating autograph seekers. Despite his rainbow belt loops and hot dog–patterned T-shirt, he doesn't exactly stand out in a crowd. "My closest friends are mostly women. Quite young in life I found that I could not be my real self in the company of males. Women have societal license to be sensitive; males haven't.

Although it's changing, women will always be one step ahead of us on the road to the beyond, which is maybe one reason why child-bearing seems to be a recurring subtheme in my work."

Robbins's soft-core descriptions of lesbian lovemaking have emitted the bittersweet aroma of advocacy, but at the end of *Cowgirls* he comes out strongly for the yin-yang of heterosexuality. A lot of gay women have complained that this was a cop-out and could only have been put in at the publisher's insistence.

"No," Robbins admits, "it was done with complete consciousness. I had a girlfriend who was bisexual and I was there—I watched women make love; I've been in bed with women making love. So I did fieldwork. I was never threatened by it, but I suppose that, truthfully, I was titillated until I understood it on a deeper level. But after a great deal of introspection, I just came to the conclusion that while it's not wrong on any level, homosexuality is a diversion. For a lot of women, it may be at this point a necessary diversion, but mother consciousness means nothing without father consciousness. I think the women's movement is the most important thing to come along in four thousand years, but a lot of dumb women are pulling it down, confusing sexuality with sexism."

Robbins is working his way toward the exit sign, counting the hours until he escapes to Seattle, where he takes professors out for a beer and probes their brains for the poetics of science; and LaConner, where *Woodpecker* and volleyball await.

In his home there is no television; the last record he bought was a Billy Eckstine reissue, though he admits to being "a closet Neil Diamond freak." Around the house he does yoga, reads Neruda, and digs Howard the Duck. After *Woodpecker,* he'll visit the mystical woods of the British Isles to research paganism, "our true religious heritage." But basically he just wants to be cut off enough from the world to feed his fantasies and indulge his imagination, locked up in a room with sacrificial monsters nailed to the wall.

"It's important to me to be indigestible," Robbins relates. "To be permanently corruptive and subversive. The mail I get isn't 'Wow, your book was a good read,' but 'this book has affected my life, it has given me the courage to do what I want to do.' It's having a liberating effect. I think that most novelists are writing about problems and I'm writing about solutions."

Robbins is proud, flushed, impassioned for the first time. He's seen the light and thinks his word-magic, plugged into the secrets of the earth and the mysteries of the mind, is cutting through human befuddlement like a beacon through fog. "My characters suffer and die but I guess the single, simple thing that runs through all my books is: Joy in Spite of Everything. Playfulness can get corny and it can get dumb and it can get frivolous; it can also be a means of survival or the highest form of wisdom. It depends on how you play. Change reality through your attitude toward it; play near the edge."

# New Wave Music

*by P. J. O'Rourke*
*October 1977*

*Before he started harpooning liberals, P. J. O'Rourke wrote music parodies for* Crawdaddy.

One of the important trends in popular music of the 1970s has been the disappearance of any single dominant sound. In place of one current pop fashion we have, now, dozens of individual styles, each appreciated on its own terms. Some AM and FM radio stations mix these genres so freely that in an hour of air time you can hear country-western singers, heavy metal rock groups, folk artists, reggae bands, whales, dolphins, and porpoises.

Although toothed whales (fans call them the Order Cetacea) have never achieved the mass popularity of disco, they've certainly had a role in this aesthetic diversification. Toothed whales have been an important critical success. They've accompanied such well-known artists as Judy Collins. Their albums have sold steadily since the 1970 release of *Songs of the Humpback Whale*. And *Orca*, a movie that focuses on the whale subculture, is a box office smash. In fact, it's difficult to understand why these popular mammals haven't generated a real superstar. Perhaps it's because of uncompromising artistry: No whale group has even attempted to release a single, and the grass-roots concert tour has been neglected. John C. Lilly, who's written a number of pieces on the aquatic mammal sound, caught

some of this single-minded intensity in a recent interview with a bottle-nosed dolphin named Female, at her Florida home:

Lilly: How are you?

Female: Oow ahhhhh eeeee ooo eeh eee eee.

Lilly: How are you???

Female: Oow ahhhhh eoeee ooo eeh eee eee whistle whistle click.

But while whale groups haven't had large audiences or great
monetary rewards, they apparently have had musical influence. The
Punk Rock movement, in particular, would seem to owe a great deal
to ocean mammals—specifically in their arrangement of bass
chords and generally in their instrumental ability. Lyrics are also
similar. Compare the whale refrain:

> *hum . . .*
> *rumble . . .*
> *squeal*
> *long squeal*
> *squeal*
> *lots of little squeals.*

to the lyrics of "Pin Head" by the Ramones.

> *Gabba gobba hey*
> *Gabba gabba hey.*

The likeness would seem to be more than coincidental. But perhaps these are parallel developments stemming from similar intellectual interests. It's hard to say, in part because the origins of the
toothed whale sound are obscure.

If origins of the whale sound are obscure, its future is even more
so. Important as whales have been over the years, it's still hard to tell
whether they will continue to develop as an important genre or become merely an artistically rigid museum piece.

The two latest toothed whale recordings shed little light on the
problem. *Deep Voices* (Capitol ST-11598) is a sort of toothed whale
sampler including cuts by several Blue Whale and Humpback
groups and a solo by a large Right Whale. It's an interesting LP and
different from previous whale records—especially in such almost
atonal pieces as "Herd Noises" and "Whales Charging a Boat"—but
it's difficult to say whether any particular evolutionary direction is
being taken.

*Sounds and Ultra-Sounds of the Bottle-Nosed Dolphin* (Folkways FX
6132) includes human studio hacking but that doesn't really seem to

add anything new. Neither do the snapping shrimp who accompany the Dolphins on several cuts. There's a certain sameness to the toothed whale sound that's never seemed likely to capture the imagination.

Whales will certainly continue to be applauded by a hard core of fans. But after being so long on the scene it begins to seem unlikely that they're a major phenomenon with a large following waiting to surface.

# I, Claudine

*by Susan Braudy*

*February 1978*

*The Claudine Longet murder trial: another bit of tragic '70s trivia that made headlines for months. This was the cover story of a special issue we called "Getting Away with It"—a preview of the 1980s. Susan Braudy has since written two novels.*

Claudine Longet has always cast a spell over men. She was on trial in Aspen, Colorado, for killing her lover, ski pro Vladimir "Spider" Sabich, with a German Luger pistol when she cornered a young editor in the courthouse hallway. He stared at her pale, anguished face and felt something shift inside him. "It's not just those huge spaniel eyes and that petite, perfect body and that voice, that whispery soft, soft voice with the sexy French accent," he said later. "She's a siren, some classic beauty from a Greek play. That full, sad mouth, the deep-set mournful eyes, and the feeling of great passion she gives off. Like a siren, she assumes a beguiling shape and wins the hearts of men, turning them to her needs," he said. "She does not appear to be evil—maybe selfish or self-indulgent at times—but she always draws tragedy down on men who are drawn to her. Once, during a court recess, she spoke to me. I was overwhelmed. She has this dangerous power. I wanted to run away. Five more minutes and I would be bewitched."

• • •

ANDY WILLIAMS TELLS THIS STORY: AS A YOUNG MAN HE USED TO VISIT Paris often. "I would always go to the Louvre," Williams says. "I used to see this girl roller skating all the time on one skate. She was eight or nine years old and she lived by the Pont Neuf." Years later, Andy says, he discovered this little girl was Claudine Longet. In a coincidence much too good to be true, Andy found himself walking back to his hotel in Las Vegas, and there she was again—age nineteen—in a stalled car.

Neither Harold Robbins nor Sidney Sheldon could have invented a more exciting coincidence of two lives. The problem is that Robbins and Sheldon always know when they are *inventing* such stories. "I was walking back to the hotel," recalls Williams with the same wonder he must have displayed at the sight of his first rainbow, "and there she was."

Indeed Claudine was, at the time, a showgirl at the *Folies Bergère* in a Las Vegas casino. But Claudine's story of her life in Las Vegas is nothing if not virtuous. She did not stay up carousing until all hours. No, Claudine went to bed early, rising early to do healthy things like ski or enjoy the Nevada sunshine. In fact, she claims to have been very different from the other girls: She never danced barebreasted.

Claudine Longet's fast life began at her birth, in Paris, in 1941. Claudine was one of seven children of an upper-bourgeois family. Her mother was a medical doctor and her father manufactured X-ray equipment or he was an X-ray technician—depending on which version of her life story you are reading or hearing. As a child, she studied dancing and possibly appeared on French television. Everything beyond these early facts sounds like raw material for a pulp novel.

Claudine and her former husband, Andy Williams, appear to be knocking themselves out to retouch her life story into a blend of hyperbole, sentimentality, and romance. Yet one suspects that Claudine believes her tale.

ASPEN, COLORADO, NOVEMBER 20, 1977: A THICK BLANKET OF SNOW covers the sidewalks in front of the expensive boutiques and the craggy peaks and ski slopes of Ajax Mountain. Inside the Center Bar, tourists stand by the huge picture window and watch the white flakes falling. If there is any talk, it is about the snow, about the great skiing weather. Things are quiet in Aspen, very quiet; the weather and the townspeople join forces to create a peaceful silence. Nobody wants to talk about the godawful television mini-series about fast sex, dope, and cheap thrills that was called *Aspen*. Nobody wants to talk about the biggest event here of last winter, the killing of a local hero—ski champion Vladimir "Spider" Sabich.

"I'm not saying there was no shooting," says the editor of *The Aspen Times,* Bill Dunaway. "But Aspen is forgiving. This is not a typical American small town. We have a live-and-let-live morality. You have to understand Aspen: People figure your private life is your business, in terms of morality. We don't have preachers thumping Bibles and thundering about sin."

"People are close-mouthed about Claudine Longet," says *Rocky Mountain Observer* reporter James Files. "They figure the shooting and the trial made everybody here look bad. They're not just protecting Claudine, they're protecting themselves."

"Her life is her business," explains the wife of a famous journalist. "We have enough trouble making sense out of our own lives to cast stones at her. She keeps a low profile. People don't spit at her. They don't ostracize her. She lives here. She's one of us. That's it. Don't use my name."

EVERYBODY LOOKED TERRIFIC. THERE WAS THE CHRISTMAS EVE TV special that the glamorous couple and their brood of pretty children performed for years. Claudine had this mischievous smile, a slightly stiff, beribboned hair bob, and huge starlet eyes. She was a dark-haired, sexy Debbie Reynolds. Andy Williams was the clean-cut guy wearing pastel suits and crewneck sweaters in Easter egg colors. Their marriage lasted a substantial fourteen years and produced three children.

Each Christmas, the laughing wife and kids sat under a twinkling tree, tore wrapping paper off gifts, and looked into the cameras. There was a holiday goose steaming in the kitchen and there were Andy and Claudine, heads together, singing Christmas carols in blissful duets.

Meanwhile, there reigned the jock hero—the man who became her lover in 1972, perhaps the most glamorous of the skiers on the world professional circuit, Spider Sabich. "We were probably everything that a man and a woman should be to each other," Claudine sobbed to the jury in Aspen after she shot him. An Olympic skier and twice World Professional Champion, the blond, square-jawed Spider was as charismatic as Robert Redford (who played a character based on Sabich in the film *Downhill Racer*). Spider loved the ladies, and the ladies loved him back. He was a leading man in Aspen, an outgoing sport with a natural ease and confidence that never slipped into arrogance. "He was a great all-American type. No, no—not really," giggles one woman.

By 1974, Claudine said she had it made. "I have my husband, my children, and my man," she told a friend. Then she and the kids moved into Spider's $250,000 stone-and-glass A-frame home in Starwood, an exclusive subdivision of Aspen. The view was expansive, on the crest above a valley. Her glamorous celebrity neighbors included Jack Nicholson, Jill St. John, and John Denver. Claudine's version of her relationship with Sabich sounds just perfect. On the witness stand, wearing only a hint of mascara to accent her pale, strained face, she choked out an imploring whisper: "We loved each other so much. He was my best friend."

CLAUDINE SEES HERSELF AS A TRAGIC VICTIM OF CIRCUMSTANCES— grim circumstances. She says she saw the .22-caliber imitation Luger pistol for the first time on the morning of the shooting; she put a sweater next to it on a shelf. On the fatal afternoon, she headed out to ski with friends—including Spider's brother Steve (once convicted of marijuana possession—some 850 pounds worth) and Steve's girlfriend, Candy Block (of the H&R Block family). But it was too cold to spend the day on the slopes, so Claudine sat and drank white wine at the Center Bar. She watched the afternoon go by through the bar's huge picture window looking out on the bulk of Ajax Mountain. At 4:00 P.M., Claudine drove the ten miles back to Starwood. Spider returned home twenty minutes later and stripped down to his blue thermal underwear. He had been skiing despite the cold and needed a bath.

Claudine testified that while Spider was washing his face, she went and got the pistol. (There were two other guns—shotguns—in the corner of the bedroom.) She brought it into the bathroom, she later recalled, only to ask how it worked in case she was left alone and had to protect her children.

As she walked down the hall holding the weapon, Claudine later reported, she popped the clip out of it, saw that it was loaded with bullets, and reinserted the clip. Then she walked over to Spider. Somehow, while he was telling her how the weapon worked, her finger slipped around the trigger.

Claudine describes how she became a tragic victim of fate, guilty only of handling a gun with a broken safety catch in the presence of a loved one. She recalls that she raised the gun and said something like, "You are sure it won't fire?" And he answered, "You got it." That was all he had time to say; the gun went off, shooting a hole in his stomach. In ten minutes he was dead, still lying on his back in his bathroom, still wearing his blue thermal underwear. At Longet's trial, Andy Williams was not the only person who wiped his eyes as his ex-wife cried through her story.

THE PRECEDING SCENARIOS ARE NOT NECESSARILY TRUE, OR UNTRUE. For instance, a flustered Claudine had a different account of the shooting before she spoke to lawyers. She said she pointed the firearm at her lover as part of an ongoing joke between them. Two people swear they heard a distraught Ms. Longet at the hospital, one hour after the shooting, say that she had playfully pointed the gun at Spider and said jokingly, "Bang, bang. Boom, boom."

On the witness stand, however, she flatly denied having said anything of the kind. "I wouldn't joke with guns. I did not say 'Bang, bang. Boom, boom,' before the shooting. It just went off."

Williams also changed his stories without missing too many beats. Two locals swear they heard the crooner say, upon arriving at Aspen after the shooting, "She's always been a reckless chick who drives too fast, skis too fast, and takes too many risks." On the witness stand, however, Williams stalwartly denied ever making that remark. He spoke, instead, of his wife's gentle and careful attention to their children.

WHAT WAS SPIDER'S VERSION OF HIS RELATIONSHIP TO CLAUDINE? First of all, by the time he met her, his career had taken several downhill turns. He was doing badly in his chosen profession (he had been skiing for twenty years). He was recovering from a badly damaged knee he'd wrecked at a race in Sun Valley. He had broken "about seven legs," and had cracked many vertebrae. But he was making money pushing Dodge Aspen cars, K2 skis, and the Aspen Ski Corp. He had earned $150,000 one year posing as the Aspen outdoor hero, and he looked the part he played. Just as Claudine looked the part she'd played every Christmas on TV—the pert, young, snuggly housewife.

But one part of his life was not working. Spider confided to friends that Claudine and the children were too much for him. He still loved her, he told them, but he felt confined by Claudine's jealous tantrums and the constant presence of her kids. Other Aspenites report that Claudine and he had been going to parties and leaving separately, and that he was now going to races without her.

Spider's future plans clearly did not involve Claudine. His friends say Sabich had given her a deadline to move out of his house. He told a real estate agent, "It doesn't work, but I don't want to hurt her either. I want to do it gracefully." The real estate agent also remembered that two weeks before the shooting Claudine Longet came to see him "looking for a place to rent."

One bar owner summed up the town's view right after the incident: "He was a champ. His smile showed it. Everybody liked him. The whole thing pisses me off. A spoiled brat. Anyway, it just might not have been an accident in the way she said it was an accident."

WHAT WAS CLAUDINE'S APPEAL FOR SPIDER? THIS QUESTION QUICKLY occasions two more: What kind of teenager would run away from a prim family in France to a foreign city of sinful repute to kick in a chorus line? What sort of woman would point a gun she knew was loaded at her lover and "accidentally" squeeze the trigger? Claudine Longet was an angry, rebellious girl; she developed into a strong-minded woman who craves attention from men and who will go to the edge of danger to get it.

She often behaved wildly in public. Did Spider hit her? "No. Hell, no," said one neighbor. "She hit him! He was kind of mild mannered, laid back. She made things exciting." After one disagreement, Claudine was seen smashing Spider over the head with a ski. She was very jealous. At a local restaurant she pulled a chair out from under Sabich when she caught him talking to another woman.

Once, Sabich and a ski industrialist were talking business at a hangout called Steamboat Springs Bar. Claudine had gotten separated from them and was drinking down the counter, with a crowd of people wedged between. After enduring his lack of attention for a few minutes, she apparently shouted out "Spider!" and fired her half-empty shot glass at him. It hit him on the chest, then fell to the floor and broke into pieces. Sabich grinned; he was used to her flamboyant displays. It was a jittery sort of jest. He turned to his companion and said, "I guess she wants to talk to me."

Spider apparently indulged his desire for dangerous excitement physically on the ski slopes, and emotionally by keeping company with Claudine. Yet paradoxically, a large part of Claudine's appeal to men is the image she nurtures of herself as a childlike, helpless if untamed creature who simply must be bundled up and defended from harm. Once the trial was over, she raised no local eyebrows by running off to Mexico with her defense lawyer, Ron Austin. Austin, whose cases are usually in real estate and divorce law, left his wife to move into Claudine's newly purchased Victorian-style cottage, where he now lives with her and her three children.

CLAUDINE LONGET'S DIARY IS STILL THE HOTTEST MYSTERY OF THE trial. Its continuing saga is also testimony to the confusion of small-town and small-time law enforcement. On the night of the shooting, the ledgerbook was seized by a soon-to-be-fired sheriff's department official who was known for tippling on the job. The deputy claimed he had picked the book off the top of a bureau. But his own pictures of the bedroom show no diary in plain view—on the bureau or any-place else. (Claudine claims she kept it in a drawer.) The judge ruled the diary had been illegally seized and that it was therefore in-admissible as evidence. The book was returned to Longet, who later claimed she burned it.

But Frank Tucker, the outrageous and controversial district attor-ney who conducted her prosecution, claims he had made notes and Xeroxes of the diary when it was in his custody. Though he was not allowed to mention the diary in the courtroom, Tucker talked a lot about it outside the walls of justice. After the trial he told reporters that he planned to write a book based on his "notes on the diary," blowing the lid off the case and naming famous Hollywood heavy hitters who are mentioned in it.

IN THE PITKIN COUNTY JAIL, CLAUDINE WORE STANDARD COVERALLS and painted her cell several colors, including yellow and blue. She was serving a modest thirty-day sentence on a conviction of "crimi-nally negligent homicide." She shared her cell briefly with two women arrested for drunken driving. She ate standard institutional fare, but the sheriffs who were in charge of her admit to being charmed by Longet during her stay.

Tucker got bad notices for the handling of Longet's prosecution. He should have tried to prove that Claudine had some intent to kill Spider, but he made little effort to introduce evidence of their dete-riorating relationship, and he made no effort to prove the reckless-ness of character that would have undercut Longet's second version of the shooting. Tucker did get noticed for his courtroom attire—Levi's, boots, and a corduroy jacket. He also created a stir by telling reporters that the (inadmissible) blood tests taken on Claudine the night of the shooting showed traces of cocaine.

In the aftermath of the trial, one of the most puzzling questions is the reaction—or nonreaction—of Aspen locals to the public romance of Claudine Longet and Ron Austin. Austin is a big local favorite. "A sweet, decent man," he is the part-owner of a local restaurant and plays tennis with the town's leading citizens. One woman says, "Ron is a nice guy. What he has chosen to do with his private life is his business."

Claudine keeps a low profile. One woman saw her bathing at a local hot springs. A man saw her at a classical music concert. Her behavior is subdued. There is no bar-hopping; nothing like the wild, glass-throwing Claudine of a few years back. Folks say that Ron Austin's influence is a good one. "I change according to where I am and who I'm with," she once said. A true siren, she seems to sing her man's special song. And get away with it.

# The Cuchi-Cuchi Girl

*by Harry Shearer*

*February 1978*

*Waiting at the mall for Charo. Harry Shearer later became a cast member on* Saturday Night, *a bassist in* Spinal Tap, *and a key voice on* The Simpsons.

Three small red-white-and-blue "Grand Opening" banners fluttered meekly from the roof of the new Gemco store in Orange County, California. The store, a discount appliance and grocery operation, looked more like an artist's rendering than real wood and cinder block. Everything's new in Orange County, but this particular corner looked like the brave first roll of the dice for a developer. If Gemco makes a go of it, the developer will raise the money to finish the rest of the shopping center. But this afternoon, 150 people weren't waiting for the other stores to open. They were hanging around the parking lot waiting for Charo. Standing, quietly chatting, *waiting*. The waiting got so desperate at one point that when a man in a grey Oldsmobile drove into the parking lot, two Gemco employees—having been briefed to be on the lookout for a silver limo—rushed toward him, momentarily mistaking a middle-aged, bald gentleman for Xavier Cugat's newest ex-wife.

The confusion was only momentary. If there's one essential showbiz quality Charo does not lack, it's recognizability. Only Charo's lateness was forcing otherwise reasonable people to grasp at Oldsmobiles.

And only the ones in suits. Just the Gemco officials, a couple of Charo's representatives (more leisure than suit), and, most nervous of all, the men from Charo's record company, Salsoul. Charo was coming to the new Gemco to autograph copies of her new album. She had only a few royalty dollars to lose if the afternoon went down the Huntington Beach toilet. But the record guys were going to have to service this Gemco account long after Charo had become yesterday's news.

"You think she may have gone to the wrong store?" Leonard from the record company, a tall man in a plaid suit pacing the length of the store's patio like a referee marking off a thousand-yard penalty for lateness, asked one of Charo's people.

Why do 150 people wait an hour in an unfinished parking lot to see someone who shows up in their living rooms more often than Aunt Bluebell and Mr. Whipple combined? Maybe a little something called "star quality." A certain *je ne sais quoi*. An indescribable *yo no se que*. The obvious-minded would say "sex appeal." But most of the people waiting outside the Gemco for Charo were women and very young teenagers. People who probably see "*cuchi-cuchi*" for what it really is: a joyful affirmation of life, in which the tit-shaking is purely coincidental, caused only by the sparse, loose-fitting clothing worn during the performance.

There are some who persist in seeing Charo as a sex object. The writers of the *Chico and the Man* episode in which she appeared as "Charo, the great Flamenco guitarist," for example. In that show, taped the day after Charo filed for divorce and became an American citizen, Jack Albertson tells her she can't sleep on the floor: "If you roll over, you'll put a couple of dents in it."

"I can do anything with a car," she says a minute later in that show. One of those once-in-a-lifetime setups that people in sitcoms just can't help saying. "I'll tell you one thing you can't do with a car," Jack retorts, unable to resist. "You can't slide under it."

Latin sexpots always seem to be the butts of jokes like that, if jokes like that have butts. But trivial as Charo may seem now, five dollars of my smartest money says that the same cognoscenti who today flock to see Carmen Miranda revivals will in ten or twenty years collect Ronco videocassettes of Charo highlights from *Hollywood Squares*. And the woman does work for her fame. A nationwide tour opening discount stores is grueling for anyone, but doubly so for a person who after eleven years in this country still has trouble with the language.

So leave these people waiting for Charo alone. They know what they want. Charo did appear, after an hour, and with a flourish of cuchi-cuchi she led an excited parade into the record department where she autographed albums and side one played over and over again through a five-dollar stereo. Maybe it's not our idea of a good time, but at least this crowd wasn't lining up in a Waldenbooks waiting for a Watergate felon to autograph his novel.

# PART VI

*'70s into '80s*

# Stand Up and Be Comic

*by Mark Jacobson*
*September 1975*

*In the mid-'70s, comedy clubs were few and far between and stand-up on television consisted of that elite shot on Carson (later satirized by Scorsese in* The King of Comedy*). Yet a whole new generation of young comedians was emerging, including Richard Lewis, Freddie Prinze, and Elayne Boozler. It was a long way from Buddy Hackett.*

Brooklyn is famous for bums. The ballplayers said it all: "Hero one day, bum the next." And right now, a few blocks up from Pip's comedy club at Flatbush and Avenue U, people are watching a bonafide twentieth-century American hero. They're seeing the movie *Lenny,* in which Dustin Hoffman plays Lenny Bruce. It doesn't matter that twenty-five years ago Lenny himself was a bum at every low-life toilet club on Avenue N. And it doesn't really matter what Lenny was like in real life. People will argue about that for years. Some thought he was a schmuck. Others are noncommittal. George Schultz, who owns Pip's, says, "Let me tell you about Lenny. It didn't matter if he was a Bengal lancer or a glatt kosher caterer, he still would have been a junkie. That's just the kind of guy he was."

Lenny said, "People should be taught what is, not what should be. All my humor is based on destruction and despair. If the whole world were tranquil, without disease and violence, I'd be standing in the breadline—right back of J. Edgar Hoover." Lenny had a sense of his own importance, and it's clear from statements like this that he knew he was dying for America's sins. And people believed him. Lenny told them a comic can do much more than tell mother-in-law jokes; and people bought it. They believed that this "funny man," a sleazo stand-up from Sheepshead Bay, the asshole of Brooklyn, was telling the truth. An image like that is dynamite. And just as Christ got Jeffrey Hunter and Billie Holiday got a skinny and whiny Diana Ross, Lenny got Dustin Hoffman.

A twenty-seven-year-old guy named Richard Lewis has been doing damage at Pip's. A year ago Lewis was playing fourth bill to Freddie Prinze. At that time, Prinze hadn't been on *Chico and the Man* but already was the hottest young comic in creation. I didn't pay much attention to Lewis, except to pick up a couple of decent one-liners like, "My god, that IND subway—it's a bad neighborhood on wheels." Regulation New York horror material. A year later, though, Lewis's comic persona had grown enormously. He still did subway and high school stuff but now he wasn't afraid to let his fantasies run free. He talked about his dreams. Imaginary conversations. Very personal images. He wondered about the hair on his chest and what would happen if it all grew in one long strand; then he could put a piece of Bazooka at the end and use it for a vacuum cleaner, clean up the city that way. Crazy, but Richard Lewis was finding his own voice, much as Robert Klein, David Brenner, and Freddie Prinze had done before him.

George Schultz was helping, just as he helped the others. If George likes a comic, thinks he has promise, he'll listen, correct timing, and add encouragement. George is called a "comedy doctor": He can fix a sick routine. But besides using George's value as a "sounding board," Richard Lewis loves to hang around with him because he is "a link to the past, a link to Lenny." Lewis is a big Lenny fan. He saw the movie several times, thinks it's great. He doesn't try to emulate Lenny's way of working; that's silly—only Lenny worked that way. Richard Lewis only does Richard Lewis now. The one thing he learned from Lenny, the one thing he credits the growth of his comedy to, is to always tell the truth. "Yeah, that's what I try to do. Be myself. Talk about things from my own experience. Now I have a routine about Japanese monster movies. It's a good bit. Gets laughs. But I'm giving it up. I don't feel good about it anymore. Right now I'd rather do material about how I broke up with my girl-friend. Work in the first person. The truth about me."

Richard Lewis is responding to the Lenny legacy: Once given a forum, milk it, stroke it, suck it, fuck it, but most of all tell the truth, the truth from within. In most ways Richard Lewis isn't much different from most of the young comics making the rounds at Pip's,

Catch, and Budd Friedman's Improvisation on West 44 Street. He is male, less than thirty-five, Jewish, from the New York area, somewhat intellectual, neurotic, and moderately funny. Comics, from Woody Allen on back, have always fit this general mold, give or take a little on the intellectuality, neuroses, and laughs. Jerry Lewis was born Joseph Levitch in Newark. Joey Bishop was Joseph Gottlieb when he was born in the Bronx. Moe Berlinger is Milton Berle; he was born on 118th Street. George Burns used to be Nat Birnbaum.

Why Jews become comics and Italians are singers is bound up in the history of the pogrom and the romance of *Via Venete*. Suffice it to say it is still the same: At Catch, most of the singers pay tribute to the ultimate *paisano* by singing "My Way," and the comics still do bits about whitefish; it's a tribute to the enduring ethnocentricity of New York City. The young comics are still using the Apple as a backdrop to much of their best material. But these people—Lewis, Klein, Ed Bluestone, Elayne Boozler, and plenty more, operating with the Lenny legacy—are changing the face of what's funny.


A RECENT *VILLAGE VOICE* PIECE ON YOUNG COMICS POINTED OUT THAT these new comedians are not nearly as funny as the older ones, and besides, we all have friends who can tell stories and do bits that are just as funny as anything heard at the Improv. So why do we need these creeps? And why, of all things, pay money to hear them ramble on about their girlfriends or lunatic dreams, things we all know about from our own craziness? The answer is simple: In the Golden Age of Self-Awareness, it's a sign of our times.

When Lenny told his "truths" they were about things that really needed changing in the society. Who knew that most of those things couldn't be changed, not by our generation at least? Times have changed. Who would be dumb enough to do racial harmony material now? If Lenny had lived as long as Dylan, he would have learned too. Protesting was noble but useless. What are the issues now? Pollution? Aggggh. Try to get laughs out of beer cans in the river. No, man, that won't go. Let John Denver handle that crud. The world's just too crazy today, so dive inside yourself and bare everything. The new comics are following the same rules as the "new journalists" . . . express that persona, get out the emotion . . . everyone knows Mailer writes better about himself than anyone else. Make yourself naked. Confess. It's the truth of the '70s.

Maybe that's why we hate them so much. These new comics are the most vulnerable of entertainers. They don't appear to be doing anything, just talking. Bullshitting. Anyone can talk. When someone plays a guitar on stage it seems as though they must have some talent. Most people watching cannot play the guitar, so there's mystery, and we're more lenient. If, after a couple of numbers, we decide a musician is the pits, we say, "Wow, this cat can't play the guitar at all." Comics don't hide behind "talent"; when a comic bombs, the rejection is more personal—we say, "Wow, what a schmuck."

Lenny taught the young comics to open up, to do things comics never did before. If stand-up comedy is the logical extension of a twentieth-century neurotic need for attention, Lenny carried it to the logical conclusion. Say what you feel like as long as it's worth saying. Be funny—that's what the people are paying for—but mostly be honest because, today, reality is the best joke going. The young comics listened. When Robert Klein, one of the most successful of the younger comics, made up an ad for his new album, it said, "Robert Klein will make you laugh, sometimes think." That's not the copy Buddy Hackett would have chosen. It's clear. This is a different ball game.


ELAYNE BOOZLER IS TELLING JOKES AT THE IMPROV. NO ONE REALLY notices it or talks about it, but Elayne is a woman. . . . *tits and ass, ha, ha, ha, you bet your life she's a woman.* But she's not a dirty broad pushing her knockers up, or a droll lady writer on a panel show. Elayne is a woman comic. She kids about riding on "the 7th Avenue IUD" and wonders if she's not loved because last night a guy she was with "faked premature ejaculation." She's got a story about penises. Once her mother said, "Don't touch that thing, it's a monster." The only monster Elayne knew about was Dracula so she imagined penises looked like little men in black capes who always were going for your throat. Now she's wised up: She doesn't believe the part about the black cape, but it's still always going for her throat.

Still, no one at the Improv really notices anything is different about what's happening on stage. The Improv is one of the hippest comedy audiences in the country. "I go crazy here," Elayne says. "I can do whatever I want." But when Elayne plays Miami—which she's done—or ladies' luncheons—which she does more often—there's a nervous twitter in the room when she does the Dracula bit or talks about diaphragms.

Until recently, the only time women entered into comic routines was to be abused . . . *Take my wife.* Ugly jokes. Bad fuck jokes. Male self-hate pawned off on the likely party. Even the "dirty broads" like Rusty Warren and Belle Barth did little but appease male superiority. No surprise they made most of their money at stag parties. Phyllis Diller changed things a bit. With her stringy hair and saggy dress, she showed what a real drag it was to be a housewife. Now there is Joan Rivers, who quips with the best, and Lily Tomlin, whose comedy is so intense it wasn't hard to figure out she'd be fantastic in *Nashville.*

Elayne Boozler isn't as funny as Lily Tomlin. Not yet, anyhow. But she's only been doing stand-up a year and a half, so she's just a baby. Elayne's got a long way to go. She does mirthless singles bar routines and a lot of TV jokes, which is as low as a comic can sink. But Elayne is doing something special. She is saying things male comics would never say. Elayne just knows things they don't know. About TV and greeting cards, I can hear from anyone; but when Elayne does Tampax bits, or tells what it's like to be on the other end of a brusque pick-up scene, that's interesting. It's humor that could only come from a woman.

It's not exactly new, but Elayne is playing it honest. As she changes, her act changes. She's not stuck with an "attitude"; she's letting it flow. "If I show what I'm like on stage," Elayne says, "I've got to show what it's like to be a woman." And with lines like, "I guess I'm a masochist. Men shit on me all the time, but a fetish is a fetish," Elayne is breaking out. It's something we haven't heard before. And if, since Lenny, everyone's been asking who's the next "hip" comic—who'll be the next one to tell us something new—perhaps it's her.

ED BLUESTONE IS A DIFFERENT KIND OF HIP. MOST PEOPLE FEEL THAT of all the young comics currently making the rounds, Bluestone is the most inventive, most intelligent, and just might be weird enough to make it. You'd never guess that Bluestone is a bug-eyed Jew kid who looks like he'd be turned out at a minion. The kind of kid the tough guys in junior high school call a nerd and the chicks think looks like a concentration camp victim. Among the young comics Bluestone is the most Jewish. His accent is doggedly abrasive. He talks about old ladies who weave whitefish heads into necklaces and Hebrew School classes where all the letters look like crushed insects. Ethnic material has been around forever and is fading as fast as McDonald's can put up hamburger stands, but Bluestone's brain can make anything sound strange.

Bluestone is hot tonight. The people at Catch are gasping for breath. He's the only young comic (besides Freddie Prinze) I've seen completely kill an audience. He's got them begging for mercy and you can see by that maniacal look in Bluestone's fish eye he's not stopping until the last nail is in the coffin. He hits them with his funeral bit: Bluestone goes to the funeral of someone he doesn't like, so he shakes hands with the grieving wife with an electric hand buzzer; he congratulates the bereaved parents on outliving their son; and before he leaves he swears out loud that he thought he saw the body move.

More: Bluestone sends his dog to obedience school and now it wants to be whipped. He knows of a gynecologist who plays Gene Autry records as women put their feet in the stirrups. Bluestone's doctor has a sign in his office that says DEATH MAY NOT END YOUR FINANCIAL OBLIGATION. Then he goes into a wild fantasy about the effect of throwing turkey giblets at bus windows. A lunacy about a gum machine—each time you put money into it more of a dead baby inside becomes visible. After half an hour Bluestone's got them by the throat. Looking at the flushed faces he says triumphantly, "Aha, a good sick crowd."

Talking in public places wasn't always easy for Bluestone. When he first came to Catch's tryout night he was horrible. "Pitiful," Bluestone says. "I had material but no sense of being on stage, no method of dealing with an audience." Five years of knocking around, playing poetry readings and toilets in Queens, gave him style and courage. His way of thinking hadn't changed; during his years of getting ready, Bluestone worked for the *National Lampoon* where he did the infamous "Buy this magazine or we'll kill this dog" cover. He liked writing, but it wasn't enough. "At *Lampoon,* they let me do whatever I wanted. Out here I can't do that. Onstage I take chances. I really put my poor self on the line. I need that kind of danger."

Bluestone is fond of quoting Blake: "The roads that go nowhere often are those to greatness." Bluestone's road will probably go to the *Tonight Show.* You can kill them every night at Catch, but it doesn't mean very much without that five-and-a-half-minute spot on Carson. The *Tonight Show* is the new "big room." The ultimate auction. Take that five and a half minutes and sell the shit out of yourself. Hit it there and you're moving. Do it again and again. Get Carson to play straight for you. Then maybe you'll get a series. Forget the Copa and the big city rooms, they're all up for rent. Television and Vegas are the only way to make money being a comic. When Lenny was around he had Mr. Kelly's, the Hungry i, the Jazz Workshop, the Ash Grove—"hip" rooms to pay the bills. He could make bread and say what he wanted. Television might show couples in bed now, but "hipness" is still a rare commodity there.

So, for Bluestone and Elayne Boozler: a dilemma. Last year, Bluestone figures, he spent 150 nights telling jokes for less than $8,000. That's less than Shecky Greene makes in a good week. Less than a truck driver on half-time. A dilemma. Bluestone is close to signing for a TV special and probably some *Tonight* spots. But which Bluestone will emerge? Dead babies and soul singers who roast Jews may not play in Peoria. Bluestone says he's thinking about it. "I want to present a true reflection of my comic mind. I feel there's art to this and I don't want to compromise. If it's funny they should laugh . . . well, we'll see, I guess."

LAST YEAR, IN A TAXICAB, FREDDIE PRINZE SAID TO ME, "I LOVE LENNY. I want to work like him. Some people say I do. And that's the biggest compliment. Really. I really want that kind of respect." That's when Freddie was the hot comic at Improv and Catch. He was killing them with his hard-bitten ghetto kid number. He said, "Hey man, I don't dig drugs, no way, because I don't want a four-year-old kid coming over to me trying to sell a rattle." It was devastating. There was power in that truth.

Freddie was the genuine article. He'd grown up in bad-news Washington Heights: His father was a tool-and-die maker; his mother was a Puerto Rican. He'd been chased by the cops. He knew the other side of the New York horror stories. Here was a comic who would tell us something new, something hip.

Then Freddie made it. Carson. TV everywhere. And the series, *Chico and the Man.* He killed them there too; the show was top-rated (even if it did get cuter each week). His contract is already renewed. Freddie Prinze, ghetto kid with the truth, has become a national celebrity. At first there were pretenses. He said it was only an acting job; it wouldn't change him. There was a brief fling with Kitty Bruce, Lenny's daughter; Freddie was playing macabre tribute to the Muse. But Chico wasn't Freddie. The show called for an L.A. Chicano, not a New York Rican. Freddie said don't worry, he'd been hanging around with the brothers . . . *Viva La Raza!* . . . and knew about being a Mexican-American. He assured everyone he wouldn't forget his roots or his humility.

It didn't turn out that way. The *National Enquirer* had it first, a picture of Freddie with Raquel Welch. The caption said they were "in love." After that, you knew Freddie Prinze had bought it. Lock, stock, and barrel, The American Dream. That any red-blooded American boy, if he tried hard enough and didn't do bad things, could become a media personality and fuck Raquel Welch.

In Art Linkletter's "Game of Life," Freddie Prinze would probably pick up all the marbles. But in the Brooklyn and Manhattan show-cases, he's in the shithouse. People don't like him. Perhaps it's stone-cold jealousy, but stories of Freddie-as-prick abound. How he used people to get ahead, people who were only too willing to help be-cause they thought Freddie had the truth. About how now he craps on everyone. It's an old show-biz story, but karma takes hold after a while. Freddie Prinze has lost something too. Next time he gets up on stage and starts talking 'bout being a hard-bitten ghetto kid, everyone will know he's lying.

So what's happening here? All these young comics, all to one de-gree or another touched by the Lenny legacy, and the only ones who are certain to reach large audiences are bland-boys like Gabe Kaplan and opportunists like Prinze.

We need someone to wake us up. Someone to tell the truth. But if Dylan is too remote, Jean-Luc Godard dormant, Salinger a recluse, Ginsberg not producing, and rock 'n' roll dying, can a comic do it?

Until a savior comes, I'll take Rodney Dangerfield. HE KILLS ME.

Rodney's been around. First he was Jack Cohen, then Jack Roy. He messed around with Lenny in Sheepshead Bay. George Schultz too. In an apartment with six-packs they could be brutal. But on stage, Jack Roy blew it. Even on Avenue N, he lived in the shithouse. Later there were years of selling aluminum siding. Twelve years of selling produced bills, bills, bills. So he changed. It was crazy but he did it. At forty, he became Rodney Dangerfield and played the same dives as the rummies and the upstarts. It was like being the only adult in the fourth-grade class. But something happened during the layoff; he got funny.

One night, while talking with George at Pip's, Rodney hit upon the "hook," the best "hook" in all comedy: "I don't get no respect." It was Rodney's "attitude" but it was honest and real: the Jew schlep-per who gets beat by everyone but doesn't retire or feel defeated. He stands on stage with his silver hair, pointing his face like the front of a '55 Desoto, being outraged. He's mad he's getting the short end of the stick. He's mad his life "is a bowl of pits." He's mad that his wife's "so cold that last night her side of the waterbed froze." He's mad be-cause he bought a dog so he could start conversations with women and now he finds out "the dog is using me to get other dogs." He's mad that he "bought a parrot the other day and it called me a Jew bastard." There's no respect in the world for a guy like Rodney. He says, "It ain't easy being me." And what can you do about it? Except to stay pissed off, never accept total defeat, no matter what they throw at you. And to laugh. I'll tell you, man, I could use a good laugh.

# A One-Way Ticket from Palookaville

*by Peter Knobler*

*January 1977*

Crawdaddy *interviewed Sylvester Stallone before* Rocky *came out and caught him with his guard down. The first profile of the megastar in the making—a nano-second before he went Hollywood.*

Sylvester Stallone knows he's something special. He's getting the hot-property treatment from the prerelease hipsters whose business it is to spot the *real* comers among the coming attractions and Be There First. Sneak previews of his film have been advertised in the daily papers. "Come see an Academy Award–winning performance." Subtle stuff. The film is *Rocky.* Stallone wrote it and starred in it.

*Rocky* is a fight film. It made me cry.

Sylvester Stallone (he calls himself "Sly") wrote the script and plays Rocky. The movie lives through trials and chill and love and loss and the kind of final victory that is at once so big and so small that it forces you to live it too. It is tough and romantic and unashamedly sentimental.

Maybe it's because it's the first time you've seen his face up there, or because he's done such an inspired job, but having seen the film one gets the feeling Stallone isn't acting. His father is in it, his dog is in it—this has to be the thinly veiled autobiography of the classic first novel. But Stallone (rhymes with "alone") is a step ahead of you.

If it is a performance it's perhaps the best of the year, and, at thirty, Sly Stallone is preparing to deal with success. He hasn't been congratulated so often that he takes it for granted, nor so rarely that he still basks in the praise. He is developing a victor's grace in the still moment between the final bell and the referee's decision.

WE MEET IN THE NEW YORK MIDTOWN APARTMENT OF STALLONE'S publicist. The room is a showpiece of overstuffed velvet chairs, mirrors, and highly polished mahogany. The carpet is thick; you can't hear your own footsteps. Stallone seems relaxed in the environment but not of it.

Wearing double-knit slacks and a patterned black shirt of either silk or rayon (my guess is rayon), Stallone looks solid but not the brawny behemoth as he enters from a back room. On screen he is immense, but in real life he scales to a classy middleweight.

He is taping our conversation. ("In case the movie bombs," he says, "I'll have a record that it actually did go this far.") The only other interviewee I've ever seen do this was a private eye.

He carries himself with the ease of apprenticeship. It's as if he'd always known that he was important but all of a sudden many people are telling him he's better than even he thought and he's straining to catch up. As happens with any good massage, he is feeling tender and more strong. I tell Stallone that I was incredibly moved by his movie.

"I didn't, uh, think it was gonna have that kind of impact," he tells me. He has the street voice of a minor mafioso. In the movie he is close to monosyllabic; a grunt means a great deal in *Rocky*.

"Chuck Wepner inspired the story," he says. "I saw the Ali-Wepner fight—that was about two years ago—and here's a man who works in a liquor store, obviously is on an accelerated downward spiral . . ." I laugh. He plays to it. "His plane was in flames . . ." Aha. He likes an audience. " . . . no doubt about it. And he was offered as a trial horse, a warm-up, a brief little jaunt, nothing. Just to get the dust and the lactic acid out of Ali's muscle fiber." He turns to me. "What happened? Ali met this brawling . . . maniac who was fighting not for the money but fighting for his life, his dignity. He didn't want to go back to that store knowing he was knocked out in the first round. He knew he was thirty-three years old. This was the most money he ever made—but I think that the money meant nothing. Because now, at home, all he has is a picture of when he knocked Ali down in the ninth round."

"Of course," I remind him, "he was standing on Ali's foot at the time."

"They say that," Stallone says, "but then again, maybe . . . maybe . . ."

Here was the instant where the film made its first romantic leap, and he didn't want me fooling with it. ". . . Whatever it is, he hit the canvas. He doesn't care if he had rented a steamroller to knock him down! And yet, Wepner was knocked out nineteen seconds—nineteen seconds before the end of the fight. So I just took it and elaborated. I said, 'I wonder what this guy does when he goes home.' "

Even the story of how *Rocky* came to be is a romance. Stallone says he wrote it in three days. "But keep in mind," he cautions, "that it was in there for a year; it took me three days to transpose it onto paper, longhand." He took it to the studios and they loved it. The part was just perfect for Jimmy Caan, then Burt Reynolds, Ryan O'Neal, ". . . which is common sense. But the pioneer spirit prevailed; I think I might have had a mental lapse or something, 'cause the money they offered . . ." He shook his head. "It got up to three hundred grand—plus a percentage.

"But that was what the movie was about. I might've gone into such an inconsolable depressive state, knowing that I had actually become The Hack. I couldn't sell something that was written for me, tailored for me. It was as though I had gone out and bought a tuxedo and then I had to sell it to Mickey Rooney. 'No, it doesn't fit you, Mick. It belongs to me. It's mine, I'm gonna wear it. And if I don't . . .' I mean it, I was gonna take the script out in the backyard," he sighs deeply, "I don't know, and just cover it in, maybe, sauce and swallow it. Or sell it for fifteen cents a slice. This script wasn't going without me. No way."

United Artists finally agreed to give him a starring shot, with a tight budget of $1 million. Guided by producers Robert Chartoff and Irwin Winkler and director John Avildsen, the film came in nine dollars under.

I can't think of another unknown who has written and starred in his own major motion picture. Stallone has given it some thought, too. "I don't want to be so bold as to say that I was a first on this," he says. "I don't know." He restrains his pride, and shows pride in his restraint. He's also not unaware that it is unseemly to claim too much or too little.

*Rocky* is a street movie. It's got a stifled *Born to Run* exuberance, the same eye for detail off the curb. The people seem real.

"Did you show the script to your friends?" I ask.

"I could call all my friends with a dime," he says matter-of-factly.

I can't believe that.

"It's true." He turns in his seat. "That's one reason I'm sitting here with you. I took all that energy that would have been channeled into making a multitude of relationships and I have such a backlog of scripts, and when I'm not writing I paint, when I'm not painting I go to the gym, when I'm not at the gym I just go for hikes. It may sound ridiculous, but I turned my life into kind of like a factory process, an assembly line. And I enjoy it.

"I have friends, acquaintances," he says, "don't get me wrong. But as for being ultragregarious—nay. Plus, I'm about as demure as a whore at a christening when I get into crowds. I'm not," he says, "socially chic."

He's an unknown; there are details to be discovered: born in New York City, grade school in Maryland, "where I began to formulate all my philosophies, whatever they were. I wasn't interested in sports, I was just interested in heavy fantasizing. I . . .," he pauses. "This is a Scoop . . ." A scoop from a man who has given maybe a dozen interviews in his life. But it is said with such blithe assurance of my interest, even my gratefulness, that I find myself wanting to know. The combination of arrogance and innocence is marvelously affecting.

"I was really awestruck by the Superman persona at the time. I went downstairs in the basement and dyed a T-shirt blue, and with a crayon wrote an *S* on it. My father was a beautician and I took one of his barber capes and cut like jagged edges and tank pants, and I put it under my clothes. So I was at school and I had a friend there named Jimmy, and I said, 'Jimmy, come into the men's room, I want to show you something. It's been a well-kept secret for a long time.' He goes, 'What's the matter?' I say, 'Come on.' 'You have a rash?' Remember this, I was in fourth grade—ten years, nine years old— and I opened the shirt just slightly and said, 'I am not . . .,' " he pauses, and suddenly *I* am Jimmy, " '. . . who you think I am.'

"Well, I tell you, he went out right away, screaming that Superboy was in the bathroom. The teacher brought me into the lunchroom and they had a small stage there, and said, 'Children, your attention please. We have a celebrity among us. Sylvester Stallone is not really who he appears to be. He is Superboy. Show them, Sylvester.' " All the condescension of a school-marm tyrant is in his voice. "She made me take my clothes off, and there I was, standing there with ten-inch calves, right?! Rickety little legs, ribs sticking out, right, sunken chest. A neck that belonged on a cheap lamp. . . . And that was the end. That was when fantasy time was over. Boy, I got so mad I just flew right out of there."

Stallone jumped from school to school and began acting at the University of Miami. He started writing in 1971, "because I'd quit acting. I realized I'd rather be unemployed than be some flunky in the background knowing that I could do as well as the man up front.

They'd always say, 'Okay, would you mind taking off your pants, and would you stand over there, and would you lay in the gutter, and. . . .' And I began to write.

"I would sit at the edge of the bed and stare at the blank wall and say, 'All right. If you want this nice car, a bankbook that takes you two hands to carry; if you want a phone that's not in the hallway, a color TV, a dog that barks and is healthy, not something stuffed—if you want all these things you have to work. You have to plop your butt at that desk and push the pen. You have to push it till the ink runs out; when that ink runs out you pick up another pen and keep going.'

"I didn't want to be successful like, say, Alex Ginsberg [sic], in a small, what's the word, coterie? Not me. I wanted to have a film made the way I saw it. I covered every subject and I knew one subject had to click. I had westerns and space movies and horror movies and period pieces and fight stories and love stories and, oh Jesus, monster stories. . . ."

"But *Rocky* really touched me," I object. "It's hard to see you writing with such calculation, like, 'I'm gonna be a star. . . .' "

"I know it sounds odd," he says, "but even though I have a pattern of how I write, when I sit down there it is totally written with passion. You said you were emotionally moved by it, well so was I when I wrote it. When I write a good sentence I can't sit down. I jump up, run over, bother my wife. I get extremely excited. So it's not calculated."

Acting, working within limits imposed by size and physique, there is perhaps less room to maneuver. But Stallone has developed a concept around his position in this field as well.

"I believe, in films as in music," he says, "there are only a certain number of acts that can be at the top, because each of those acts covers a certain cross section of the country. For example, there was Glen Campbell. And when he faded, who came along? John Denver. Sonny and Cher kind of went on the wane, who's comin' in? Captain and Tennille.

"In acting you have the all-American, the devious type, the anti-hero type, the Brando type, the strongman type. And you can't have nine of the same category, it won't work. You have one John Wayne, one Gary Cooper. Then you had the loudmouth, then the speed demon. The professional slime, like Peter Lorre."

"Which actor are you?"

"I guess I fall into the, uh, Victor Mature category." We laugh. "I guess it's the, uh . . ." He fumbles for the concept a moment. ". . . The loner who refuses . . . it's almost like, I guess . . ." He's not stuck; he's trying at once to say what he feels and not look bad in print. "I shouldn't say a 'Charles Bronson with additional . . .' It's very hard for me to say without sounding kind of like, hey, a Brando type. I don't think I am a Brando type; Brando was uncommunicative, I'm not. He wasn't a talker, I am.

"I would like to be kind of like a Clark Gable type. I know that's weird-sounding, but what I mean is, he wasn't a brilliant actor but he had range, and he touched people because he had heart. You'd say, 'A guy like Clark Gable would never steal a car.' I know that's gonna sound terrible in print but if I could really say what kind of actor— the persona, not the talent—that would be the best appeal. Because there hasn't been another one like him."

"How close are you to Rocky?" I ask.

"I have real empathy for good-hearted people that are down and out," he says. "But I'm not too close to Rocky, other than in spirit, because I would never allow myself to get that far down. I would've known, say, at twenty-five or twenty-six years old that it was over as a fighter. I would've maybe become a manager or gone into construction. Rocky didn't have that—he's simple. He had a good heart.

"But it was a helluva challenge. Think about it. How're you gonna take this subject, which has like been done in *On the Waterfront* and in *Marty,* done a thousand times over . . . But it hasn't been interpreted this way. I looked at all the films and said, what are they lacking? Rocky was extremely vulnerable for a tough guy. And he was what he owned: a turtle. He had his shell, he was soft inside but scarred on the outside. And he moved slowly. Turtles don't talk, they don't bark, they don't cause confusion, they're just very simple. They eat and they grow and they crawl and they die. That's what Rocky was gonna have. But he got more.

"I am really sick of everybody's being anti-Christ, antisociety, antigovernment, antipeople, antilife, antihappiness. That everything has got this Hemingway fatalism about it. I think that we have to bolster our way through hard times by fabricating good times. If times are bad, all right they're bad, but do I have to see children being mangled by teeth? So I want to put emotion as the star; I don't want cars as the star, or bullets or javelins—I want people. Viscera.

"If I could summarize Rocky I would say he is an all-American cornball. His seduction scene where he says, 'Will you take off your glasses? You've got nice eyes.' Corny. Comes in the apartment, takes off his shirt, right? Corny. Walks into a gym and he's smoking a cigarette. Dumb. Corny! But corny is usually endearing; corny is usually honesty. I wanted to get down where it is real—a celebration of the human spirit. I plan on doing it in all my films. It's too easy to write a downer.

"The first draft it was kind of down. It ended with Creed as an old fighter, about thirty-nine, and Rocky as a vicious twenty-seven. And it was the thirteenth round and Rocky knew he had the old man. He had beaten him badly and then he purposely throws the fight, goes down for the count. And he walks out of the place and it's kind of lonely—all he has is his girlfriend—but he knows in his heart that he could have won.

"Oh, Jesus, if that doesn't chase them out of the fuckin' theater with a stick!"

Stallone's next script is based on the true story of the only police-man ever sent to the electric chair three times. "What's really the story is the entire Tammany Hall political structure," Stallone says. "In all my scripts now they have these incredible men that go against insurmountable odds. . . . It comes down to the basic desire of all men—which is to survive, to better themselves, and get their dignity."

"What about your third script," I wonder, "after the first two have been romantic struggles and your heroes have survived?" Well, he has certainly succeeded with me; already I am talking with concern about his future. "By the time even the first trial begins the audi-ence will recognize the trademark. . . ."

"If he dies heroically, or if he dies trying . . ." I get the feeling Stal-lone is auditioning a clip for me. "He doesn't yield, that's the point. In my next script the man dies, but he goes into that hole with a grin on his face. And the audience goes out with a grin that, hey, he ac-complished that one moment, that one slice of immortality he has put away. No," Stallone says surely, "I'm not always going to be play-ing Siddhartha."

# Steve Martin:
# The Fears of a Clown

*by Al Kooper*

*October 1977*

*He was just breaking big, via "wild and crazy" appearances on* Saturday Night, *but we found him to be rather wary about it all. In another bit of lunatic matchmaking, we hooked him up in a super session with rock and roll legend Al Kooper.*

Bille Jean Turner is sixteen and attends high school in Nashville, Tennessee. A gal needs some spendin' money nowadays, though, and she consequently has landed herself a job at the Krystal, a sleazeburger joint on one of Nashville's main drags. It's 10:55 P.M. and she's wiping the counter, getting ready to close on this her first night. She notices a commotion down the street, but pays it only peripheral attention. The commotion is getting real close, and when she finally looks up, some guy in a white suit with balloons on his head is leading a crowd of about three hundred people directly toward her window. Her finger is quivering on the panic button as the guy steps up and, in a consummate TV voice, booms:

"HI! WE'D LIKE 294 BURGERS; 74 WITH CHEESE, 76 WITH ONIONS, 144 WITH THE WORKS; 150 ORDERS OF ONION RINGS AND ONE DIET-RITE SODA, PLEASE . . . TO GO!!!"

PROFESSOR JOHN MCCORMACK HAS JUST FINISHED GRADING HIS ENGLISH papers for the night and is strolling across campus to his apartment for some well-deserved rest. McCormack is fifty-eight years old and is having difficulty dealing with the "new permissiveness." *Fucks* and *shits* are popping up routinely in his students' papers. He passes the auditorium and notices that the show is breaking, a student-sponsored affair featuring some comedian.

Rounding the corner, he passes the varsity pool, which has been drained for the winter, and suddenly he's frozen in his tracks: the pool is filled to capacity—with students! They are standing with arms uplifted, floating some character in a white suit over their heads. The guy is doing laps, swimming through the waves of arms from one end of the pool to the other. McCormack just shakes his head and continues home.

STEVE MARTIN, THE MAN IN THE WHITE SUIT, IS HOT. EVERYONE IS "doing" Steve Martin. Waiters, taxi drivers, rock stars, college kids, and well, yes, when I'm sure no one in the vicinity has seen his show, me too. One can just slip out of one's personality and become . . . the Perfect Fool. But Steve Martin has developed the Perfect Fool to utopian heights. He calls it "watching a guy make an asshole out of himself," and not only is he an ace at it, he has the uncanny power to shift instantly into reverse and embarrass his audience en masse ("How much did it cost to get in? Five bucks? You assholes!").

Turns out his natural habitat is Claudine Longet country, accessible mainly via Buddy Holly charters and Aspen Airways. I'm risking my life for this guy? Already I'm an asshole.

I'm in Aspen and *everybody's* blond. It's the *Village of the Damned*. I mean, the taxis at the airport are called Mellow Yellow Limos . . .

I check in at my motel and phone Steve Martin. I get an answering machine: "Hi! This is Steve Martin. I just went into town to get a sandwich. I'll be back in twenty minutes and . . . no, I gotta go to the bank, so . . . forty-five minutes. Anyway, when you hear the beep, hold on . . . Remember, hold on and whatever you do, don't hang up." I hang up. Twenty minutes later, I call again. This time a person answers. It's Steve and he agrees to pick me up in ten minutes.

WE'RE SITTING ON THE PORCH OF STEVE'S SOLAR-HEATED HOME JUST outside downtown Aspen, facing a breathtaking view of the mountains. It's 86 degrees and we're both in a good mood. He goes inside to get a cigar.

The house is furnished with a flair for neatness, and resembles a classy Manhattan duplex. The walls are adorned with originals by Thomas Cole and Frederick Church. Each painting is worth four or five figures and he takes tremendous pride in them. (He is, however, not above selling them for a profit. One man "offered me six thousand dollars for this one. I wish he'd come back.") He's got books and magazines dog-eared to the pages that contain reproductions of his originals.

His roommates are two likeable cats whose names, Dr. Forbes and Betty, sound like a great TV sitcom about a gynecologist and his gal. He's got various athletic gear hanging around: a brand-new Frisbee, badminton racquets, shuttlecocks, but no net ("I like to live dangerously").

We get to talking. Steve interrupts periodically, either to go inside and wash his hands or to try to lure his pussycats home. Between trips I ask him what his ultimate goal is.

"I want to finish my concert career in two or three years," he says seriously. "I'm headed for the movies. I want to write something once and it will always be great, instead of having to do it night after night."

A Woody Allen–type of gig—starring, writing, and directing at the same time?

"Nah," he says, "I really enjoy working with other people. It's real . . . cooperative. I don't really trust myself unless I'm writing for the act. I'd rather show the script to a director and check out his opinion on how the joke should be played."

A deal with Paramount Pictures has already yielded a short called *The Absent-Minded Waiter,* currently in release. "I wrote it with Carl Gottlieb, who also directed it. The two of us have also done a feature called *Easy Money* which Paramount is reading and considering now." The script involves Steve playing a guy named Garthwaite who is raised by a black family but can't seem to ever find his place—until one day he hears a Lawrence Welk record and runs away from home. He works in a gas station, where he accidentally invents an eyeglass nosepiece called Opti-Grab. He makes zillions of dollars off the brainstorm and then blows the mighty wad in short order.

*Easy Money* seems an ideal vehicle for Martin because all his best characterizations and worst fears are written directly into the script.

THE *TONIGHT SHOW* GUEST-HOST GIGS WERE INSTRUMENTAL IN BREAKING Steve nationally and filling up the concert halls. Many felt he was the logical successor to Carson.

"Yeah," he deadpans. "Every time someone hosts the show they always say, 'Oh, he's the logical replacement for Carson.' But there is none. I watch the show nights before and after I host it, and he's so great I get embarrassed for myself. But there's no way, in fact, they'd ask me to do it—or that I would do it. You see, I have a rather salacious interest in television. It's a demeaning medium, but I really like it. I don't see how I could ever do a weekly show, either. You know, by the twentieth week you're out of it, with lampshades on your head, doin' stuff you would never have thought of doing on a special. Like on the old Steve Allen shows. Those guys just went crazy every week. Plus, it's understood that you work until you fail. 'You're gonna fail and we know it's just a matter of time.' Now *that's* funny!"

If Martin's newfound success seems to have strengthened him, it has also made him reticent.

"I've always been kinda reserved in real life," he says. "Main thing is now I've become real disciplined. I quit drinking, staying up till four, and then catching an eight A.M. plane. Started exercising. I stopped picking up sleazy girls; quit standing around degrading myself for some chick. Did all these things, and the shows got ten times better!

"I wanna sign autographs after the gig but it's been getting dangerous. I don't mean dangerous in the strict sense . . . y'know, they start pushin' ya, try to steal things from the stage—that kinda shit. Some guy stole my hat. He swooped down, grabbed my hat, and ran off as I was coming out of a gig. I chased him down, though.

"It might be time to just do the escape thing and get outta there as soon as possible. I tell you, though, I've met a lot more people. Like, I can meet girls—I can start talkin' to 'em and it's not an immediate shutoff. But, God! What does Jack Nicholson do?"

So is the success worth all the new problems and changes? He ponders for a moment, "Well . . ." and breaks into a sly smile. "As my friend John Denver once said, 'It's a mixed blessing.' " He goes inside to wash his hands.


MARTIN HAS JUST RETURNED FROM PLAYING VEGAS, OPENING FOR HELEN Reddy. Ironic, because he has a devastating routine that peels the scaly skin away from the whole Vegas scene: "In Vegas it's twenty bucks to get in. But it's worth it. They've got costumes and sets and showgirls and it's all 'WOW! LOOK AT THE TITS!! THERE MUST BE FIFTY-SEVEN TITS UP THERE!!!' "

And then one night, suddenly for real, there he is onstage at the MGM Grand.

"Hey, I must have at least *three* hours of material," he says patiently. "But *there,* I had to scrape up every possible joke and *stretch* it to thirty minutes. They just don't give an *inch.* It's *nowhere.* There were a coupla good shows, but good in the sense that I *went over.* Not that it was a good *show.* At least they let me use profanity now; it always gets a laugh. I mean, they used to prohibit me from doin' that stuff in Tahoe and Reno. Like, I couldn't use the word Nixon. . . ."

I'm confused. If he thought it was going to be difficult, why bother playing Vegas at all, especially as an opening act?

"Well," he answers proudly, "I'm in show business. I could go two ways and say: 'Are you kidding? Work Vegas? Host *The Tonight Show*?? Are you kidding? *Talk* with Helen Reddy????' But on one hand I really like it. It's *show business* and I like to see what I can do with it. I like to feel like I'm ad-libbing, and that's about the only situation where you *have* to ad-lib.

"But the worst part of it is coming off a show like the Dorothy Chandler Pavillon [L.A.]. Three thousand people and it's sold out. You walk out and you get a standing ovation, and then you do your show and they're screaming the whole time and you finish and get five encores. WHEWW! So you come off of that and right to Vegas and that whole thing happens. And Vegas was the last gig on the tour. And so it ended up, I finished my tour feeling depressed. I mean, I was having nightmares about . . . dice! I'd really like to score there, but I guess it's not time yet. Maybe if I don't think about it, it'll just go away."


A LITTLE CREATIVE EAVESDROPPING. IT'S 8:30 IN THE ASPEN NIGHT AND the sun is still blazing away. Old friend Bill McEuen's wife, Alice, has joined us and we're just sitting outside bullshitting, the formal interview having ended fifteen minutes earlier. I have somehow forgotten to turn off the tape recorder.

*Al: You definitely need a girl, Steve.*

Steve: I got one, [sarcastically] an Aspen gal. But I'm not gonna see her anymore.

*Al: No, you need a girl you can . . . play badminton with.*

Steve: Yeah, well I'm not too interested in *her* any more. She's been seeing her old boyfriend . . . Her old boyfriend, like a year and a half ago, before I was successful, says, "What are you goin' out with these jerks for? I've already *made it!*" So this friend of mine took her out the other night and she asked him what I was making in Vegas, and her jaw just dropped . . .

*Alice (Quickly entering the conversation): What about Barbara?*

Steve: Barbara who? [*Thinking*] You introduced me to that other chick, didn't you? [*Mulling this over*] I should trust your judgment, Alice.

*Alice: Barbara's a friend of Mike and Karen's. She knows you but she says you don't really talk to her. She's playing baseball right now. Some people went out just to watch her play.*

Steve: Really? Just to watch her play? Is she real sexy, or good?

*Alice: She's probably good, she's a model. . . .*

Steve: A model person?

*Alice: I like her but I hated her for a while. [Turns to Al] One night we were waiting to see Steve on some TV show. So she comes over and Barbara says: "Ooooh . . . he's just like Bobby Watson!" Now Bobby is some local guy who's always imitating Steve!*

Steve: Yeah. Why *did* Steve Martin steal all that stuff from Bobby Watson?

*Alice: She says she likes you but she's sure you don't like her that much—"I know he doesn't know who I am. I know he doesn't notice me."*

Steve (Growing annoyed): That's what I hate about it, 'cause whereas it didn't matter before, now they all go and talk about it.

*Alice: But Steve, other people have always said stuff about you . . .*

Steve (Interrupting, getting a little hotter): I know! That's what I mean! Before, it didn't matter, but now they talk about it. You know what I'm saying [*almost in stage character*]—I've always been the same, but now it's a big deal. It's just that I know every time I go to bed with a girl . . .

*Alice: She's gonna tell everyone?*

Steve: Oh yeah. That's why I'm not going to bed with anyone anymore. [*He considers this, thinking out loud*] "Ah, he wasn't so hot!"

THE NEXT MORNING, STEVE PICKS ME UP AT THE MOTEL AND DRIVES ME to the airport. We arrive and he insists on carrying my gargantuan suitcase to the counter. Halfway there, he realizes he's made a big mistake, but grunts it the rest of the way nonetheless. We shake hands. As he turns to walk away, a kid with an Instamatic asks if he can take Steve's picture. Yeah, sure, Steve says, maybe a little sadly, as the kid leads him away to find a suitably absurd setting. The last time I look, Steve is trailing obediently.

# The Teen Aging of Jodie Foster

*by Louise Farr*

*April 1978*

*Oh you kid. At age fourteen she confides that she is "quite dependent. But maybe I'll grow out of it."*

On a cool Los Angeles night with just a tinge of brown smog wisping the air, Jodie Foster climbs into the little silver Mercedes 450 SL, fastens her seat belt, and with her Disney publicist in the passenger seat gripping the dashboard and hoping her car will survive, sets off to burn a little rubber on the side streets.

VRROOOM. VRROOOM. Actually, she is driving pretty slowly. Has to drive pretty slowly at not quite fifteen years old, and without a permit. If anything happens, it will be the publicist's head on the block while Jodie wings it across the polar route back to Paris. So slowly, carefully, her checkered tweed cap pulled over her eyes like a New York cabbie's, she drives past the mansions of Hancock Park with their Caddies and Rollses and Mark IVs parked in the garages underneath the servants' quarters. Slowly, carefully, just going "Vrrooom, vrrooom" in her head as she turns onto Wilshire Boulevard, glides past the Scottish Rite Auditorium . . . then . . . yipes! . . . a cop parked up ahead astride his motorcycle examining his fingernails and waiting.

"Take it easy," says the publicist. "Just be cool. Act natural." So through the intersection, being cool, acting natural. Then—*whap*—over to the curb to unfasten the seat belt, climb out, knees turned to porridge, then back into the passenger seat. But . . . oh . . . she looked so neat in that little silver car, fully automatic, with leather seats and stereo tape decks. *So neat. . . .*

JODIE FOSTER STANDS UNDER AN UMBRELLA STROBE LIGHT WEARING A chic black velvet Ted Lapidus pantsuit. On one side of her stands a Disney Studios representative wearing a knit suit and a Mickey Mouse watch. On the other hovers a frizzy-haired makeup woman. Dancing agitatedly around the edges are a photographer and his assistant. These four grownups are engaged in the tricky business of deciding whether Jodie's bow tie should be tied or untied. Whether the shine should be removed from her forehead. Whether the blush-on adds enough cheekbone to the soft baby face. Whether the shadow on the sensuously drooping little eyelids is adequate . . . or perhaps . . . just a *touch* more?

"All these funny people," says Jodie Foster, gazing into the distance. "All these funny people looking after *me.*"

Jodie Foster and a handful of other little girl actresses have emerged recently to make "nymphet" a key word of the late '70s. Child-women with knowing eyes, seemingly wise beyond their years, hinting at or displaying on the screen—to the mingled glee and hushed shock of critics—a mixture of innocence and sexual precocity. When Jodie Foster was thirteen, she received an Academy Award nomination for playing a twelve-year-old hooker in *Taxi Driver.* The same year, she bleached and spit-curled her hair and glopped on makeup so that she could say to her gap-toothed *Bugsy Malone* costar, "How about smearin' my lipstick?" Since then, she has appeared in two Disney movies. "It was," she says, "time for a little light relief."

But the image sticks. A *Playboy* review recently congratulated Jodie for, as usual, "undoing dirty old men—in the audience as well as on the screen." "I have reached the stage in my nymphet-mania," said a *Village Voice* critic, "when I will trudge anywhere to see anything with Jodie Foster in it." Said *People:* "Shirley Temple and Margaret O'Brien were never like this."

"WHAT'S A *NYMPHET?*" JODIE FOSTER ASKS, THE WEEK BEFORE HER fifteenth birthday, as she sits in a Disney Studios conference room irritably destroying a Styrofoam cup. "You're *kidding.* I'm not attractive to *anyone.* I have a big nose and zits. Huh . . . *nymphet* . . . I never even *heard* the word before." She has sat through about—oh—fif-

teen hundred interviews by now, she says. This must be her sixth
this week. And all the interviewers want something from her, which
she thinks is pretty weird. She's just this little *kid*. What they most
probably want is the secret of life. Maybe one of the consolations for
growing old is remembering a tortured adolescence and thanking
God that it doesn't have to be suffered through again. Then, in
walks this kid who blows the whole thing. This fourteen-year-old
who travels the world with her Louis Vuitton luggage, makes about
$100,000 a film, and seemingly has it all together—while the jour-
nalists at twenty-five, thirty, forty are still like most people, schlep-
ping and sweating and hoping that life will work out.

It's not even that her films have been that good. Critic John Simon mentioned that she goes "from strength to strength in bad
movie after bad movie." And he was right. The only one of her films
worth mentioning is *Taxi Driver*. But in the midst of mediocrity,
Jodie's presence is always felt. Her particular kind of quiet screen
authority makes it seem as if she'll manage the transition from cute
kid to adult after that stock-in-trade of child actors—childhood itself—is gone. Not that she ever was just a cute kid. Even when she
was eight, hauling a lion around in Disney's *Napoleon and Samantha*,
with her stringy hair, skinny legs, and husky voice, there seemed an
intelligence in her eyes that went beyond the usual parrotlike diction and poise of other Hollywood moppets.

Jodie Foster gives a polite little yawn behind slightly chewed fingernails. She didn't sleep well last night. Eventually had to bury the
phone underneath a pile of pillows. These kids kept calling. "Hi,
I'm a fan of yours." "Hi, you don't know me, but I'd like to be your
pen pal." She thinks it's crazy. "Look," she says patiently, sitting
there in her preferred uniform of jeans, tweed jacket, and white cotton blouse, "I'm just a normal American kid."

A normal American kid who's stayed away from Los Angeles' Ly-
cée Français school for six months so that she could go to France to
star in *Moi, Fleur Bleue* as a tough-talking French teenager in love
with a poet. A normal American kid who's in town for six days of interviews at the Polo Lounge, photo sessions, then more interviews
to promote her latest Disney release, *Candleshoe*, in which she plays
a tough-talking American teenager who, presumably because it's a
Disney movie, isn't in love with anyone. A normal American kid
whose fifteenth birthday bash will be thrown at a chic Paris club to
promote her first record, "When I Look at Your Face"—a talking-
over-the-music disco number.

Healthy, maybe. But normal? And one wonders why Jodie Foster
feels compelled to defend her normality. As if being normal is some

kind of virtue. As if anyone even knows any more just what normal is. She's defensive, of course, partly because of this "nymphet" business. "Lolita . . . *Lolita* . . . why does everyone say that? I get so sick of it." But mostly it's because everyone assumes the kid's got to be neurotic. All that attention. All that money. All those Most Promising Newcomer Awards, and the dancing with famous people at awards dinners, and the Cannes Film Festival press conferences where she wowed them with perfect French . . . and, for God's sake, putting on satin hot pants and wedgies to play a hooker at the age of thirteen. Getting under the covers for a bedroom scene with a teenage costar in *The Little Girl Who Lives Down the Lane.* Somebody must be exploiting her, say the people who don't know it was her big sister unzipping De Niro's fly in *Taxi Driver.* Her big sister doubling for her in *Little Girl* in what *Variety* described as a "medium shot of Foster in the buff." It must be the mother, they say. As if all this were somehow on a par with those four-year-olds whose mothers sell them for a day's groceries to *Lollitots* or *Nude Baby Frolics.* "That mother," people say. "She must be really something."

BRANDY FOSTER IS BUSY PACKING UP THE HOLLYWOOD HOUSEHOLD FOR the return to Paris. Brandy Foster doesn't want to talk. Brandy Foster is leery of the press. Anyway, says Jodie, who started acting when she was three, "She says it's my career, not hers. Everyone thinks my mother's so mean. But she's really nice. She's behind everything. I guess she's done it for me because she didn't have the time and couldn't do it for herself. She's guided everything. And she's always right. Always."

If a normal, American fourteen-year-old kid thinks her mother's always right, the mother can't be that bad.

Brandy Foster and Lucius Foster IV split up when Brandy was four months pregnant with Jodie who, everyone says, was different from the beginning. She spoke when she was nine months old. Her brother and her two sisters used to pluck her out of her crib and trundle her up and down the street, making her say dirty words to the neighbors. Pronounced perfectly, of course, so that one might even think she understood what she was saying.

Jodie's brother, Buddy, was a child actor. He supported the family—someone had to, as Lucius Foster didn't. The two older girls were beautiful, but shy. If their mother had put them in the movies, they'd have turned out neurotic, Jodie thinks. "You have to know what your own kid's like." Jodie was strong. "I think it's something you're born with. I'm pretty sure it's not environment. I just am very strong."

By the time she was three, she'd taught herself to read. That's when she decided—or so the tale goes—that she wanted to do what her big brother did. And so Brandy Foster signed her daughter with an agent. The only way they could get her into a dress was to tell her she had to wear one to work. "She always looked like a ragamuffin," says her sister, Connie. "She wore my brother's jeans all the time. When she was a baby, for her first bicycle, she wanted a motorcycle. And she never liked dolls, except for G.I. Joe. She was a real tough little kid."

Jodie doesn't think she was so tough. She says she just tried to be. "Actually, I feel kind of bad because I was the goody-goody in the family. The one who got the best grades. The one who always called home—I've never even had to have a curfew. Actually, I'm quite dependent. But maybe I'll grow out of it."

The *National Enquirer* loves Jodie now that she's growing up. So do the European papers. They say that she's a champagne alcoholic who smokes cigars. They say she's in love with David Soul. She can't stand David Soul. Her taste runs more to Jackson Browne—and Peter Frampton, because he's so cute. An Italian paper—she's suing—said they interviewed her on her deathbed after she tried to commit suicide because she hates show business and hates her mother for pushing her into a career.

"Look," says Julia Cameron Scorsese, who watched Jodie and her mother on the *Taxi Driver* set, "of course Brandy's a stage mother. But she obviously really loves her daughter and really wants what's best for her." Jodie's mother is always with her when she works, because Jodie likes the encouragement. "You need someone to tell you that you're pretty and that you're good, and all the things that aren't true." Says Jodie's sister, Connie, "I think Jodie was so bright that she'd have been bored if she hadn't gone into the business. She'd have been skipped in school all the time, and that would have been worse for her."


JODIE FOSTER SITS IN THE SUN ON A PHOTOGRAPHER'S BALCONY. HER fourth photo session of the week is over. The lip gloss and blush-on have been wiped off, and she has half an hour before she takes off for the Polo Lounge to talk to a gossip columnist. Actually, she'd rather spend her time in front of the Polo Lounge opening car doors and directing traffic the way she does sometimes for her brother-in-law who runs the parking concession.

No, she says, she doesn't worry about getting old. "I guess I'm halfway grown-up, but I'll always be a kid, even when I'm forty. I don't think anyone really grows up. Maybe you grow up a little and get more intelligent, but I think your character's finally set by the time you're about . . . oh . . . twelve. You can't change drastically after that unless there's something wrong with you. Being a kid's the best thing in your life. Children are so liberated. They have everything. You know, if they say something stupid, you can just pass it off as being a kid."

But what about the responsibilities that go along with being a kid in the '70s? What about drugs? What about sex? "That's no responsibility. You just have to make a decision, just so long as you've made one. Some people are strong and some people are weak.

"You'll notice," says Jodie, "that whenever anyone asks me if I date, I say 'no.' That way, there aren't any more questions."

"*Do* you date?"

"No."

If childhood's that great, doesn't she think she's missed out on a lot of it by working? Sure, there were a couple of times it made her unhappy. Like when her *Paper Moon* TV series was canceled. But it all worked out for the best. If it had been a success and run for years, she couldn't have done *Taxi Driver* or *Bugsy Malone.*

Oh, yeah . . . there was this other time last year when she hosted *Saturday Night Live.* "I was so scared I dropped a whole Orange Julius down my jeans just before I went on."

She seemed out of place on the show. As if the writers didn't quite know what to expect, what to do with her when they got her. As if they'd been expecting a sophisticate and had to work things around this ordinary kid who'd shown up out of nowhere to stand there looking tomboyish and self-conscious.

"My show wasn't good at all. And I think from the time I hosted it, it went down in its standards. Maybe it went down because of me. I don't know . . . I'm not sure. I was real unhappy—but it didn't really *hurt* me any."


JODIE SAYS SHE HAD ONLY ABOUT SIX MONTHS OUT OF HER LIFE WHEN she wished she came from a family with a father as well as a mother.

She changes the subject when her father's mentioned. Yawns. Points to something on the wall. Fiddles with the tape recorder. Pulls at the hank of pale hair that always falls over her left eye. She only met him twice in her whole life, she says. She didn't like him.

Anyway. There's this kid who's a beautiful kid when she has her makeup on, and a sweet-faced kid when her skin is bare. She has answers and opinions on just about anything. About Jimmy Carter: "I like him. He's done a lot of good things. They tried for six years to get amnesty for war resisters and he managed it his first day in office." About punk rock: "It'll be out of fashion in six months. It's awful, but I'm glad someone's doing something instead of just sitting back watching TV and drinking beer." About religion: "It's important for some people, because it gives you a strength you don't have yourself. But for me it isn't important, because I've got the strength inside." She clams up a bit about personal things.

And if anyone's exploited her, they've certainly left her in pretty good shape for the future. She wants to major in political science and journalism in college, just in case show business doesn't work out. Eventually she'd like to direct. Dark, pessimistic films like Martin Scorsese's. "I've always loved things that were sick or weird." Or love stories. With unhappy endings, because she thinks unhappy endings are more interesting.

Until she gets to direct, she wants to act. And not just as a hobby any more. The turning point came for her with *Taxi Driver*. She'd always been this kid who was proud because she could read her script and go on the set and do it cold. But working with Scorsese was the first time she could go home at night and feel as if she'd accomplished something.

"It was the first time I'd felt anything. I forgot myself completely." But she looks embarrassed after she says that. As if, somehow, feeling something is wrong for someone who's supposed to be as strong as Jodie Foster. "I'm not a Method actor or anything. I've always hated the idea of the Method. But I find myself falling more and more into that trap. And I'm really very sad about that. You know, I think I'm going to end up one of those women who feel the part. Isn't that terrible?"

Oh, yeah. As soon as she's sixteen, she's going to get this really neat little Panther car. Two-tone brown convertible two-seater automatic with a tape deck, a spare wheel in the back, and all this grillwork on the side. She could get it now, she says, "But it would just sit there—I wouldn't be old enough to drive it. Oh . . . I'm gonna look so neat in that little car."

# Susan Sarandon:
# Barefoot in Babylon

*by Peter Knobler*

*May 1978*

*After* Pretty Baby *(but way before* Bull Durham *and Tim Robbins and politics), we found her to be that rare down-to-earth film star. Yet she posed for our "Wild Dreams and Wicked Desires" concept cover wrapped in mink, with a tattoo on her breast and wielding a large knife.*

A vagabond mink hair brushed against her tattooed left breast. She tried not to notice. The soft fur jacket was positioned professionally so its line revealed significantly more than was bargained for, then was retucked to satisfaction. Lying on the floor, a swatch of material folded beneath her right side for a boost, her right heel propped against a two-by-four, Susan Sarandon did not seem uncomfortable. Finding the offending mink fluff, with one puff she blew it away. Sarandon grasped the switchblade, cold pro, and looked to the lens for direction. With the barest hint of amusement, she wondered: "What do I do with this?"

ON NEW YORK'S BEEKMAN PLACE, FOR YOUR $1,000 A MONTH YOU GET three rooms with a bath and a Fiorucci ice bucket. Having completed her role as Brooke Shields's prostitute mother in the film *Pretty Baby,* and facing three months in New York shooting *King of the Gypsies,* Susan Sarandon (pronounced Sa-*ran*-don) needed a place to stay. "I thought, 'Who would be away for three months?

Who would run from the winter? What jet-setters do I know?' " The one she found was Spanish and is gouging her for the rent. Despite the chic decor and remarkable view of the city, when you punch in on the Princess phone in the bedroom it is likely to get not one digit right. Between waiting for the repairman and piling up photography books to prop open an expansive picture window, Sarandon is positively playful.

She is also no conventional glamour queen. In a collarless cotton pinstripe shirt and square-hipped, thirteen-button Navy pants, she looks like a pretty girl in grad school; though she has large, phenomenally captivating eyes—sleepy, in films; alive up close—she is hardly a starlet. She carries herself with a disarmingly casual candor. Incredibly sexy before a camera, off-screen she looks . . . approachable. The cupboard is bare, we're drinking instant coffee, the milk is the only thing in the refridge.

"Oscar Levant once said, 'Hollywood: underneath all that tinsel is the real tinsel,' " she laughs. "At least in our business, in the show-business business, there is no pretense about its being bullshit. You're not pretending, like in politics, that you're going to do some good in a very serious, sincere way. The emphasis is totally where it belongs, on the absurdity, on the duality between making a buck and pouring your guts into something."

Sarandon, thirty, was raised in Edison, New Jersey, the oldest of nine children. The first thing she really wanted to be was a wave in the ocean. "Being brought up a Catholic, with everything turning from water to blood, it didn't seem a strange ambition." At Catholic University she majored in drama and got onstage once: "In *Peer Gynt*, I was a Scrimmette; I stood behind the scrim and chanted these little songs." She also met Chris Sarandon, a graduate drama student when she was a freshman. "Back then you couldn't live together, so we got married." (They are now separated.) Her first film role was in 1970 in *Joe*, "a terrible little soap opera that made about $45 million.

"I've never been 'smart' in my career. If I had been smart—thank God I was stupid—I would've gone to Hollywood right then and become Kim Darby." Instead, she played the soaps. "It was like doing all the B movies that everybody else got to do that weren't being done anymore. I was the girl everything happened to. I was on every day, either having a miscarriage or a suicide attempt. . . . Everyone I loved went to jail or was killed or poisoned. The minute I fell in love you knew they were doomed."

Several years later she was in Hollywood, an eastern college girl among the statuesque strutters. "I thought it was Sodom and Gomorrah. I'd never seen such a thing! All this couch casting—I kept thinking, 'If they're talking about it so much it couldn't possibly be true,' but it was." She worked in *The Great Waldo Pepper,* and *The Rocky Horror Show,* and on TV in *The Last of the Belles.* "I never had a chance to go to acting school. I kept thinking, 'Well, when this calms down then maybe I'll learn something.'" She did the Johnny Carson show ("They asked me to come in, and asked me not to wear a bra and come back") and was well on her way. Last year she was featured in *The Other Side of Midnight.* Yet somehow the Hollywood life seems not to have taken its toll.

"I do it as a job," she says, "so it's not really that much of my identity. The problem is that it involves soul suicide, constantly. You're like a kamikaze in terms of your ego and fragility of your spirit and your self-esteem. Before they were shooting *Pretty Baby,* for example, I kept having these incredible fears that they thought I was Susan Blakely, that I would get off the plane and they would take one look at me and say, 'Oh . . . there's been a terrible mistake. . . .'"

"IF YOU HAVE A DIRECTOR YOU CAN REALLY TRUST," SUSAN IS SAYING, "it's like . . . falling in love." Her current companion is the French director of *Pretty Baby,* Louis Malle.

It's springtime, people are unbundling, taking their clothes off for the fun of it, pirouetting down the avenues. Falling in love in the spring is a snap.

"I don't fall in love easily," Susan says, "but I fall in love well. I love to be in love. I haven't had a lot of men in my life at all, considering the business I'm in. But each time I think maybe this will be it, and each time it *is* it, in whatever way. I've never regretted any of the drastic mistakes I've made," she laughs, "and usually whenever I make a fool of myself it's really in a big way.

"I think I'm always available, by nature—that's the problem. But I have certain things that I respect; I draw the line. I'm fairly loyal. I tend to be monogamous, just because the logistics get me confused. But love is probably the most important thing in my life. In my work, the feeling when you're really working well is exactly the same. And when you're working with people, you have to find something about them you love on some level, for me; be it their foot, their hand, the way that they're incredibly aggravating. . . .

"Most of my fantasies have to do with having total freedom and having some kind of family unit. I have great fantasies of living naked with about seven offspring, somehow that working just perfectly without Pampers and any of these horrible things that go on.

I'd like to have children, preferably with a man," she laughs. "I've had several offers to have them by myself, but I'm still holding to the hope that perhaps the man will at least stick by me for the first few years. I've given birth all those times in the movies but never got to take one home.

"My fantasies, huh?" she says. "I guess this wonderful, idyllic kind of life, almost this gypsy kind of life, and having no ties, being able to take off and go anywhere . . . a romance with someone you don't even speak to . . . a magic carpet, and at the same time having a child and all the things that family means. It's a very difficult fantasy to execute, try as I may. Not too many people have succeeded in the spirit of that kind of thing."

Her Catholic background has not prevented her from appearing nude in several movies. In fact, her first moments on the screen were naked. "In *Joe*, when I first saw it, I was convinced that nothing showed. My hair was long, there were things in front of the camera. Then I saw it recently and, of course, *everything* showed and I had just totally blocked it.

"I've never really done any erotic scenes. It's very difficult to take your clothes off, no matter how many times you've done it. It has nothing to do with modesty, it has nothing to do with values; it has to do with the fact that you are the only one with your clothes off. If you were standing in the room with the whole crew naked I'm sure you would find it much different.

"You choose clothing to enhance your personality and hide your faults, and suddenly there you are. If you're naked, it's necessary to have something to play, so that you're not thinking about the fact that you're naked. In *The Other Side of Midnight*, for instance, I thought that the seduction scene, which unfortunately is so badly mixed that you can't hear anything, was very funny. The idea of someone losing their virginity where they talk through the entire scene, and there's fumbling. . . . In movies' love scenes, first encounters always go so smoothly. I don't know about you but I don't know one that's ever gone smoothly!

"In *Pretty Baby*, I take my top off because she's a whore. It would be kind of coy to go around tricking with your clothes on. Yet there is nothing in the way it's filmed that I feel was exploitative. As I said to Brooke [Shields, the twelve-year-old who plays her daughter] when she was going to be naked: Ultimately, if you're going to do it, and you've said you'll do it, and you think it's necessary for it to be done, and you trust the cameraman and the director, the only thing you can do wrong is make the audience uptight by you seeming to be uptight, so you might as well find some way to seem relaxed, because it'll draw more attention to it if you seem very uncomfortable. Though I have never found a way to really be comfortable, the goal is to forget it; it's just not that big a deal."

Stills from *Pretty Baby* have appeared in *Playboy*, one of which showed her topless. *Playboy* has approached Susan about doing a centerfold. "Heartbreak and neurosis keep me thin," she says. "In my old age it would be very reassuring to have pictures of myself very flatteringly, before everything fell. You know that you're going to look incredible. If they had asked me in the '50s when it would have been shocking, I probably would have done it. But actually, what always bothered me was that everyone always looks alike. They never have any personality. And so I very pretentiously started to discuss that and found that it was true. In fact, Hugh Hefner was always complaining, 'Why do all these women look alike?' And as a woman looking at these women, I was always seeing tits and ass. What is wrong? Is it the photographer? Is it the fact that the minute you take your clothes off you are reduced to an object? Is there no way to shoot a naked or seminaked picture, erotic even—let's say you don't mind being shown erotically—without reducing her to a nonentity? They offered me any photographer, any place. I could have gotten a world cruise out of this. A ridiculous amount of money. I would never think of spending forty grand to have naked pictures taken of me by a great photographer, going around the world.

"The deal was that I would have total control over the pictures, whether they printed them or not. Come up with a theme. Anything I liked. I started talking to women, to men. What would you find erotic? I've never seen a picture of a joyful nude woman. What could we do that was different? Everyone could say what it shouldn't be, but no one could come up with a way to start. I was offered everything from swimming naked with dolphins to my fantasies for the months of the year. You know, you could totally revolutionize the idea of a sexy picture if you could present one where there was some vitality to it."

SARANDON LAY ON A LINT-STREWN SETTEE IN A CORNER OF THE STUDIO, having a snake and a heart emblazoned on her left breast by a woman she did not know. The tattooist, *Crawdaddy*'s art director, had cold hands. Two editors and various other bedside participants all acted natural. "What shall we put in the heart?" someone wondered aloud. "Lou," she said. "Lou?" She tried it out on the air to see how it sounded. "Lou," she said. "Fuck 'im if he can't take a joke."

# Meryl's Choice

*by Tony Scherman*
*February 1979*

*An early look at the actress of the '80s. "Passersby don't give her a second, or even a first, glance."*

A young woman in a raincoat and blue jeans, long blonde hair tucked away in a bun, steps out of the subway at 57th Street. She walks through the drizzle, looking in shop windows, rummaging in her pocketbook for coffee change. Peering in a window, she checks to see if a small sty in her right eye has gone down. Passersby don't give her a second, or even a first, glance. That's just the way Meryl Streep likes it.

"I'd be really upset if my life changed, if everyone stopped me on the street," says Streep, a wisecracking Nordic-Dutch beauty. Keeping her anonymity will be a problem; one of New York's reigning stage actresses after only three years in the city, Streep is now on a formidable movie streak. She's already appeared in *Julia;* with Robert De Niro in *The Deer Hunter;* with Alan Alda in *The Senator;* in the new Woody Allen project, *Manhattan;* and as Dustin Hoffman's estranged wife Joanna in *Kramer vs. Kramer,* currently shooting. A TV stint led to an Emmy for her starring role in *Holocaust,* which led in turn to one of Streep's not-very-conclusive brushes with the public. "The day after the Emmys," she says, "someone came up to me in Bloomingdale's and said 'Did anyone ever tell you that you look exactly like Meryl what's-her-name?' I said, 'No, nobody ever did, but thanks anyway.' "

Until the jaws of movie publicity close on her, Streep won't sit around worrying about it. "Films are nice, but I don't live in this world," she says, looking at the shooting schedule tacked to the wall, the publicity shots and other movieland detritus in the *Kramer vs. Kramer* offices at Columbia. "Movies aren't going to be my life. I come in, do my job, and don't hang around."

Her major passion, discovered during high-school days in Bernardsville, New Jersey, is the theater. "I can put more energy into plays, I can involve my whole body, I can open my mouth and scream. In films, everything has to be about this big"—she minces a Styrofoam cup around the table—"and it puts you right to sleep."

Poised between plays and films, Streep is always comparing: "Doing a play is like being a little kid playing in the basement. You've got an hour, so you throw a blanket over your head and you're a princess in a castle. You get in some concentrated playtime. In movies, you're down there with the blanket over your head and your mother shouts 'Get upstairs and brush your teeth!' After that, you go back down, and just as soon as you're the princess again, it's 'Get upstairs and clean your room!' The only way to get through it is to go upstairs as the princess. That's why movie people stay in character all day, and sometimes even after the movie's over. After a play, you can just go to a bar with your buddies and forget it."

Streep found work in plays as soon as she came to New York from Vassar College and Yale Drama School. Soon the work was pouring in: Roles in Brecht's *Happy End* and in the experimental Andrei Serban production of *The Cherry Orchard,* and Shakespearean roles including Catherine in *Henry V* and Kate in the *Taming of the Shrew.*

"It was the weirdest thing. I started getting all the jobs coming up in New York. Suddenly I was the one they wanted—except now the work came through my agent instead of through the dean's office." Her self-confidence is disquieting: "It didn't seem unusual; there was nothing extraordinarily heady about it. At Yale, I was sort of the class hotshot, which was hard psychologically. People resented my always getting the best roles—*they* were paying tuition, too. It was a *relief* to come to New York and compete with 200,000 people instead of eight."

Her greatest theatrical dream, aside from playing Hamlet—"all the best Shakespeare roles are for men"—is to put together "an American all-star traveling show. We'd take maybe three different Shakespeare plays to cities in America that don't have repertory

companies, places less glamorous than Gary. It sounds so pretentious, but I feel that this amazing writing is just slipping away from
generations of people." Streep is seriously discussing her idea with
New York Shakespeare Festival head Joseph Papp, as well as with
Dustin Hoffman and Al Pacino.

For now, aside from recently marrying Don Gummer, a New York
sculptor, and shooting *Kramer vs. Kramer,* Streep is rehearsing the title role in Elizabeth Swados's musical version of *Alice in Wonderland.*
"It's going to be realistic fantasy, a tangible Wonderland." She gives
one of her sidelong glances around the Columbia offices: "It was a
real job, convincing these people that I could do two things at once.
It's theater that sustains me."

# ACKNOWLEDGMENTS

We would like to thank all the former editors and art directors and others who helped to make Crawdaddy (and the excerpts in this book) possible. We would especially like to acknowledge the following long-time editors: Patrick Snyder, John Swenson, Gina Lobaco, Denis Boyles, Mitchell Glazer, Timothy White, and Jon Pareles.

# About the Editors

**PETER KNOBLER,** former Editor of *Crawdaddy,* is the coauthor with Mary Matalin and James Carville of the bestselling political memoir, *All's Fair: Love, War, and Running for the President.* He has collaborated on the autobiographies for former Governor Ann Richards, Kareem Abdul-Jabbar, Thomas "Hollywood" Henderson, and Peggy Say. A songwriter, his songs have been recorded by Chris Hillman, the Desert Rose Band, and the Oak Ridge Boys. He lives in New York City.

**GREG MITCHELL,** former Senior Editor of *Crawdaddy,* is the author of *The Campaign of the Century: Upton Sinclair's Race for Governor of California,* winner of the Goldsmith Book Prize. His other books include *Acceptable Risks* and *Truth and Consequences.* He is presently completing books on the Richard Nixon-Helen Gahagan Douglas campaign and (with Robert Jay Lifton) the impact of Hiroshima on America. He lives in Nyack, New York.